CANADA
AS A SELECTIVE POWER

SOCIETAS

seria pod redakcją
BOGDANA SZLACHTY

100

CANADA
AS A SELECTIVE POWER

Canada's Role
and International
Position after 1989

Marcin Gabryś
Tomasz Soroka

Kraków

REVIEWER:
prof. Patrick Vaughan

PROOFREADING:
Michelle Atallah
Artur Zwolski

COVER DESIGN:
Paweł Sepielak

The project was funded by the National Science Centre
on the basis of the decision no. DEC-2011/03/D/HS5/01123

ISBN 978-83-7638-792-5

KSIĘGARNIA AKADEMICKA
ul. św. Anny 6, 31-008 Kraków
tel./faks: +48 12 431 27 43, +48 12 421 13 87
e-mail: akademicka@akademicka.pl

Online bookstore:
www.akademicka.pl

Table of contents

Introduction 7

1. Canada's power in international relations: major
   theories 19

   Canada as a satellite 19

   Canada as a major/foremost/principal power 28

   Canada as a middle power 39

2. Canada as a selective power 59

3. Canada as a selective power under Stephen Harper 77

   Economy and the environment 88

       Trade 92

       Energy resources 102

       Keystone XL 113

       Environment 115

   Arctic sovereignty 123

   China 136

   A value-based approach 144

       Freedom of religion 149

       Respecting the territorial integrity of others 154

Middle East 158

     Arms sale 166

Official development assistance 170

International organizations 179

     The United Nations 184

     Institutions of global governance 188

The military, security and peacekeeping 193

4. CANADA IN INTERNATIONAL RELATIONS UNDER
   JUSTIN TRUDEAU 207

Foreign policy in the 2015 Liberal campaign platform 208

"Responsible conviction": Trudeau's foreign policy doctrine 215

Return to multilateralism 219

Peacekeeping and military missions 221

Immigration policies and refugees 228

Environmental and energy policies 244

The economy 257

CONCLUSION 275

BIBLIOGRAPHY 281

ABBREVIATIONS 319

INDEX OF NAMES 323

Introduction

Canada's role in world affairs, its international position – but also the perception of the country by other states and international organizations – have long been matters of political and academic discourse. Such debates, however, have mostly been Canadian discussions, which, strictly speaking, have rarely gone beyond Canadian borders and never really managed to involve large numbers of non-Canadian scholars or discussants. The point here is not that Canada's international position is immaterial or irrelevant. In fact, it is important, not only because of the role Canada played historically as a co-creator of the institutional and legal framework upon which the postwar world order was built, but also because Canada matters today when it, for instance, vocally supports and promotes worldwide such progressive social values as: gender equality, LGBTQ rights, inclusiveness, an open society, tolerance, etc. Canada, thus, and its external policies should be interesting and inspiring topics of research for outsiders. However, one can find relatively few academics from outside Canada (except the ones from the U.S. and perhaps Britain) who would make Canadian foreign relations, not to say Canadian international identity, the main object of their scholarly explorations.

One explanation for this can be Canada's limited international influence. In general, countries with a lower global "impact factor" would typically attract less attention of analysts and researchers than those which have military and political power. Constraints on Canadian global influence constitute a familiar and in some cases a self-evident phenomenon: Canada's population is relatively low, its military potential is limited, and the economy has long been ailing from the lack of diversification of trade partners. Sharing the border with the United States

– Canada's only neighbour by land, ten times larger demographically and economically – with all its advantages (for security and trade), also restricts Canada's international impact. In fact, being a neighbour of the only remaining post-Cold War global superpower puts Canada in a paradoxical position, where the country with the second largest area in the world cannot even play the role of a regional power, remaining incessantly in the shadow of the military, economic and political might of its much stronger next-door partner. As Michael Hart puts it, Canadians cannot deny – even if they so desired – "the incontrovertible fact that geography makes Canada an American nation" (83). All these constraining factors – demography, economy, geography (United States) – affect the ways non-Canadians tend to perceive Canada's global role and position. This perception is far different from what is viewed by the Canadian international relations experts. The approach of the latter, as Maureen Molot observes, would rather reflect "a fixation with either [Canada's] power or the lack thereof which needs some rethinking" (qtd. in Haglund and Onea 61). While Canadians have a tendency to make "a cult out of a perpetual national crisis, seeking to be a European nation, an Atlantic nation, a Pacific nation, and even an Arctic nation" (Hart 83), non-Canadians, according to Nik Hynek and David Bosold, are stereotypically inclined to either perceive Canada through the prism of its dependence on the United States for most of its decisions in foreign policy or associate Canada, despite its oil sands in Alberta, with the "splendid nature of untouched forests and lakes, especially in Canada's North" (xv).

Another explanation is that Canada's role and position in contemporary world affairs is particularly difficult to define for outsiders unacquainted with the intricacies and subtleties of the Canadian debates over Canada's international identity. For an outsider, the position of Canada on the global forum, at first glance, appears to be profoundly puzzling and ambiguous. On the one hand, Canada with its vast territory, abundant natural resources, economic importance is too big a player to be ignored or disregarded. Its membership in the G7/G8 and G20 clubs, in the Organisation for Economic Co-operation and Development (OECD), the Organization of American States (OAS), the North Atlantic Treaty Organization (NATO), the North American Aerospace Defense Command (NORAD), the Arctic Council, the Asia-Pacific Economic Cooperation (APEC), the Commonwealth or La Francophonie puts it in a unique position of a state involved in a multitude of international forums, which, in consequence, extends the potential influence of Canadian diplomacy to almost every corner of the world. On the other hand, the U.S. demographic, military and economic dominance makes it virtually impossible for Canadian politicians either to discount or overlook "the American factor" in the process of the formulation and implementation of a foreign policy.

When we started to examine the position Canada occupies in the complex global system and the perception of this northern country in international politics, it was 2010. Although the Conservative Party under Stephen Harper won the federal election for the second time in 2008, it was still too early to predict whether the so-called "neoconservative revolution" in Canadian politics would be a long-lasting one. Even though it was impossible to foresee how the international situation would evolve in the following five years and that Prime Minister Harper would finally form a majority government, we realized that the evolution of Canada's foreign policy, which obviously started with the end of the Cold War, accelerated with Stephen Harper's rise to power. Many of his decisions seemed for us to be at odds with the common wisdom both in Canada and abroad that perceived Canada's role in international affairs through the prism of soft power, peacekeeping and human security. Canada, naturally, still retains its capabilities to influence and inspire, and by this it fulfills Joseph Samuel Nye's definition of a country that possesses "cultural and ideological attraction" through such elements as the openness of its culture and society (especially towards minorities and immigration), sticking to the values of democracy and human rights, the power of persuasion based on moral authority and a positive global reputation. Canada – "a Peaceful Kingdom" – has had a long history of using "soft power" elements in its foreign policy. Its positive image and fine international repute have been built by promoting and conforming to the rules of international law, by membership in international organizations and commitment to international development agendas. Ottawa has a strong record of peacekeeping, promotion of human rights, multilateralism and dispute resolution. Canada has also been the foremost promoter of minority rights and gender equality and the first country in the world to proclaim multiculturalism as the state's official policy. Still leading in multiculturalism policy indexes, Canada attracts a large number of immigrants every year.

On the other hand, it required a closer examination of the Canadian military mission in Afghanistan, its engagement in multi-power competition over the Arctic or the recent decisive stand against Russia over the conflict in Ukraine to observe a significant change in Canadian foreign policy behaviour, evidenced, among others, in the fact that Canada dropped its traditional foreign priorities, such as peacekeeping and foreign aid. Although Canada has emphasized both these elements as its foreign policy identifiers after the Suez Crisis of 1956, since the end of Cold War, this emphasis seems to be of only rhetorical value. When one adds to this the criticism Canada has faced from the United Nations (U.N.) (for example for Quebec's language laws and mistreatment of its Indigenous population) or from influential international organizations, such as Greenpeace and other NGOs, for its withdrawal from the Kyoto Protocol (Canada was the first country to do so), large-scale and controversial seal hunting or massive extraction of the "dirty" oil and gas from Alberta's oil sands, Canada's traditional reputation seems to have been questioned.

Back in 2010, we also focused our attention on the business aspects of Canada's foreign policy, concentrating mostly on enhancing trade opportunities in various regions. Taking Canada's diplomatic representation in Africa as an example, we realized not only that the Canadian presence there had been radically cut (Ottawa had only 15 Canadian diplomatic missions in the 54 African countries), but also limited to those African countries that were seen as the ones which could provide Canada economic opportunities and potential profits, such as South Africa. As far as the foreign aid is concerned, Ottawa has focused on a list of "priority countries," most of which are also targets for Canadian business investments. However, at the same time, Harper's role during G8 and G20 summits, where the most severe economic crisis since the Great Recession of the late 2000s was handled, and his later idea of an "enlightened sovereignty," were not only a voice of leadership – an appeal to foreign governments to prioritize the needs of foreign populations over the needs of the electorate – but also connected him to the best traditions of Canada's civility and soft power arsenal.

As two political scientists deeply engaged in Canadian studies from the international relations perspective, we decided that the question of the discrepancy between the perceived and the factual role of Canada in international relations deserves a deeper analysis. We are convinced that Canadian role and position on the world stage has changed not as a result of a short-term policy preference of any of the governments since 1989. Moreover, we think that Canada's international position and role is, to a large extent, delinked from a government of any particular party colour. Building on that assumption, we decided that the examination of the transformation of Canadian foreign policy behaviour from a typical middle-power attitude to a more robust and unilateral approach requires a new treatment. To that end, we propose a new perspective which argues that Canada's foreign policy priorities after the end of the Cold War have undergone such a deep conversion that they go far beyond the traditional perception of the country as a "middle power." A "selective power" category that we introduce in this book and apply in our research is thought to deal with what we see as two major flaws of the debates on Canadian foreign affairs, that is the exaggeration of Canada's international influence on the one hand, or the unjustified downplaying of Canadian accomplishments on the other.

In our new framework, the basic assumption is that a selective power ranks as an issue-structured major power. The countries that fall into this category, in our opinion, are able to play a leading role in a limited number of areas, but due to reasons of a political and economic nature cannot aspire to the role of a superpower. In Canada's case, the selective power status is supported by a number of factors. First of all, Canada runs an open and free-market economy with exceptional economic ties with the U.S. – the largest economy in the world and a huge market for Canadian products, which guarantees the stability of Canada's exports. Secondly, Canada has abundant reserves of natural resources (minerals or forests, fairly clean air) including energy sources (non-renewable sources such as natural gas or oil – primarily as oil sands located in the Prairie Provinces or deposits located in the Arctic, which might be potentially extracted in the coming decades – but also renewable sources such as fresh water deposits). Thirdly, Canadian democratic political and legal systems provide predictability and stability. Fourthly, during the recent financial crisis of 2008, Canada successfully managed to counter the negative effects of the global economic slump, thanks to the stability and openness of its economy. Fifthly, ethnic diversity and the growing proportion of immigrants arriving from the rapidly developing, most populous countries in the world, such as China or India, is a factor that helps Canada establish bilateral economic relations with emerging economic powers. Sixthly, the Canadian society has reached a high level of education. Overall, in our selective power concept, we try not to underestimate the political, economic and social stabilization achieved by Canada, which helps to avoid internal conflicts, prevents the influences of populist parties and creates a positive image of Canada in the world. On the other hand, selective prioritization of Canada's international activity fields reinforces important aspects of domestic politics (immigration policy strengthens social cohesion, alleviates racial conflicts, and ensures relatively peaceful coexistence).

In our research, we have learnt not only that Canada concentrates its international activities on several consciously selected fields in which it plays significant roles, but also that Canada deliberately limits the number of spheres of its international activity. The highly selective choices primarily take Canada's own interests, frequently narrowly defined, into account. Clear assertiveness in the pursuit of foreign policy goals clashes with a stereotype or a label of a middle power, which is usually attached to Canada when its international role and position are defined. This may not be so easily observable as Ottawa is skilled at using "soft power" mechanisms that strengthen Canada's international standing in the economic, political and reputational senses. But, on the other hand, also under the guise of a good image, Canada avoids certain international obligations or delays the implementation of previously declared policies and initiatives (in immigration, development aid, peacekeeping, environment, NATO).

We think that the highly selective hierarchization of Canada's international activity fields, which since 1989 has been relatively constant, is based on simple profit and loss calculations. This pragmatic aspect of Canadian foreign policy decisions has often been overlooked by analysts. The general rule of Canada's foreign policy conduct, in our opinion, is that when potential costs exceed potential profits, Canadian politicians tend to abstain from international commitments or delay their implementation, and do not hesitate to give up even traditionally rooted roles (withdrawal from the Kyoto Protocol due to implementation costs and its potentially negative influence on Canada's economy; the limitation of Canadian participation in peacekeeping missions; cuts in development assistance).

Pragmatism as a feature of policy making of a selective power is also noticeable in Canada's strategic culture – initiated by Harper, but also forced by changes in the international environment – from Ukraine, through Syria, to the Arctic. Since the end of the Cold War, subsequent governments have maintained relatively low military spending levels due to alliances with much stronger partners, mainly the USA. For pragmatic, internal and geostrategic reasons, Canada does not raise defence-related investments, which would be a logical consequence of responding to the loosening of the international system. At the same time Canada has kept its involvement in key military missions (Afghanistan, Libya) and a strong military presence in strategic regions (special forces in Iraq operating against the Islamic State, presence in Central and Eastern Europe in NATO missions, training of the Ukrainian Army, etc.). Such a selective engagement allows for the limited involvement in other military spheres. Similar pragmatism may be observed in selective immigration and refugee policies.

We also argue that the traditional roles played by Canada, which are firmly rooted in social perception, often obscure or make it difficult for politicians to make rational decisions. On many occasions, various rhetorical elements have been implemented to hide the fact of making (or not) certain decisions, especially when it involves significant political costs. Our research reveals that the verbal declarations of Canadian politicians are often inconsistent with political practice (for example Canada's participation in peacekeeping missions).

While, in general, we contend that a highly selective approach to the participation in international relations strengthens Canada's global standing, the negative side effect of the result-oriented foreign policy, based on the primacy of effectiveness, is that the quality of the foreign policy decision-making process suffers. Another element, particularly evident under Harper, was the departure from traditional multilateral mechanisms, a greater emphasis on unilateralism in relations with particular states and regions, and taking autonomous actions. We treat this element as a derivative of another feature of a selective power, which is taking an uncompromising position while promoting selectively chosen priorities and values, and being more focused on goal achievements than on the international (but also domestic) reputation. However, comparing the Harper and Trudeau governments, a correlation can be observed between the strength of Canada's international position and the skilful use of "soft power" tools or specific rhetoric that put humanitarian issues, not material or economic values, to the fore. This effect, we think, is a consequence of the power of the liberal consensus that predominates among international actors and focuses on the humanitarian issues, traditionally attributed to Canada.

In fact, however, Canada's selective prioritization of foreign policy goals is based on the primacy of economic interests over intangible values, such as the protection of human rights or ecology. As a selective power, Canada puts a particular emphasis on free trade and open economy and criticizes all forms of economic protectionism, especially when it becomes an element of Canada's key economic trade partners' policies; the U.S. in particular. Various Canadian governments have for years negotiated and signed numerous bilateral, regional or intercontinental free trade agreements. Since the Cold War, Canada has also considerably developed the oil and gas industry, which stands in contradiction to Canadian pledges to increase environmental protection and is vehemently opposed by environmental organizations and Indigenous communities. As was mentioned before, the Canadian immigration policy is also highly selective, largely subordinated to the interests of the economy and labour market needs. Last but not least, Ottawa channels its foreign development aid in close association with the interests of Canadian investors. Generally speaking, the effectiveness of trade and other elements of economic program set the tone in Canada's foreign policy and largely define its objectives.

For Canada, an important determinant in the process of selection of international activity fields is the dominance of the U.S. in Canadian trade, which has both positive and negative effects – the latter are partly compensated by the U.S. guarantees of military security within NATO and NORAD. Additionally, Canada aspires to be a stabilizer of the global geopolitical situation by acting as a predictable and secure supplier of energy and natural resources. This, however, should be treated as a plan for the future, as currently the U.S. is almost an exclusive recipient of Canada's oil and gas.

We think that the selective power concept enables better comprehension of Canadian foreign policy, as it shows it in a broader context and reveals nuances that have heretofore remained unnoticed. It seems important, since many observers still have problems with grasping what the driving idea was behind the shifts in Canadian foreign policy under Stephen Harper, whose intentions were, among others, to position Canada as a "rising power" in the global economy and as an "emerging energy superpower." We argue that Canada's global role can only relate to narrowly defined spheres of international relations (immigration policy, banking sector policy, energy sector, education, linguistic policy, minority rights). In these areas Canada can play a far more significant role than before.

No country, however, is able to successfully conduct its foreign policy or shape its international role without an understanding of the strategic environment of international affairs. Canada has been no exception here. The seven years that separated the beginning and the completion of this project have been marked by unique evolution of the international order and significant changes in both regional and global security architecture. For Canada, the ability to respond to these developments – whether in the traditional security realm (Russian-Ukrainian conflict, NATO's transformation, competition in the Arctic), emerging threats (lone-wolf terrorism), international trade or environmental security – helped to create its image as a selective power in contemporary international relations.

We completed our research project at the beginning of 2017, several months after Justin Trudeau's sweeping victory over the Harper Conservatives. Trudeau's campaign promises accounted for what could be seen as a bid to restore Canada's reputation by returning to its traditional middle-power role. Canada was to be again involved in solving global problems (refugee crisis, climate change) and – as an "honest broker" – in promoting peace, openness, multilateralism, compassion, empathy and compromise. Its policies were to be based rather on values, responsibility and convictions, less on cold selectiveness and calculations of costs and profits. In other words, the new prime minister declared to run a foreign policy that would be the exact opposite to Harper's. Obviously, we realize that too little time has passed since Trudeau assumed the prime ministerial office to be able to present a comprehensive evaluation of the current government's foreign policy. However, as we thoroughly analyzed Trudeau's foreign policy doctrine and his existing political actions and practice, we argue that his policies are not as distant and different from his predecessor's as they appear or are presented. Naturally, we acknowledge the rhetorical change and also Trudeau's personal impact on boosting and promoting Canada's positive image abroad. We recognize his good intentions and sincere efforts to combat climate change, Canada's generosity and openness to refugees and immigrants, and the return of Canada to the role of a constructive interlocutor in multilateral international fora, such as the United Nations and climate summits. On the other hand, we see no significant change in the Canadian approach to, for instance, the extension of pipelines, or no meaningful contribution of Canada to U.N. peacekeeping, except in words only, or no increase in military spending despite NATO's requirements and appeals (though this might change under the pressure of the Trump presidency). Even economic priorities are roughly the same as under Harper – based on free trade and tackling protectionism, mainly the American one. Trudeau's immigration and refugee policies might be rhetorically completely different but, on a practical level, are only slightly less selective than Harper's. In general, Trudeau's foreign policy seems to be as selective as Harper's. Where this entails huge costs and risk and provides little profits, Trudeau's Canada is reluctant to act (peacekeeping) or resign from its initial plans (such as the extension of the Keystone XL pipeline or withdrawal from the sale of arms to Saudi Arabia).

With this book, we would like to fill a gap in the debates over Canadian foreign policy. Our research tool – a selective power framework – in our judgment allows to observe, on the one hand, that Stephen Harper's almost ten-year term as prime minister of Canada climaxes the transformation of Canada's position and role in the world that started with the end of the Cold War. But on the other hand, comparing the Harper decade with the Justin Trudeau government, we may argue that the change has not been as significant as suggested by many critics. Expanding the above thesis, we see that Canadian foreign policies in the post-Cold War period show considerable similarity, regardless of the differences resulting from the ideology and party colours of a particular government. Furthermore, the selective power framework helps to differentiate between rhetoric, the actual behaviour and its results.

The structure of this monograph is as follows. The first chapter surveys three dominant conceptions that have evolved in the course of academic debates over Canada's position in global affairs, namely: 1) Canada as a satellite, 2) Canada as a foremost power, 3) Canada as a middle power. Chapter 2 discusses the notion of a "selective power," a key category through the prism of which we perceive Canada's international role and position; it also presents the methodology used in this study. Chapters 3 and 4 examine foreign policies of the Harper and Trudeau governments in broad historical contexts, exposing their selective approaches to Canada's external activities.

In the process of working on this project, we benefitted from the assistance of numerous people to whom we owe a debt of gratitude. For institutional support, therefore, we wish to thank McGill Institute for the Study of Canada in Montreal, Center for Canadian-American Studies and Border Policy Research Institute, Western Washington University in Bellingham, WA, Robarts Centre for Canadian Studies, York University in Toronto, and the OECD Library and Archives in Paris. The completion of our research would not have been possible without their help.

Our research in this particular project, but also on Canada in general, would have probably never started had it not been for the continuous and kind support we have been receiving from our colleagues and students from the Institute of American Studies and Polish Diaspora, Jagiellonian University. Their comments, suggestions and advice have been absolutely invaluable. We would like to direct our warmest thanks to Prof. Anna Reczyńska, Head of the Institute's Department of Canadian Studies, and Prof. Radosław Rybkowski, Director of the Institute of American Studies and Polish Diaspora.

Among other individuals, we owe special thanks to the Ambassadors of Canada to Poland, Alexandra Bugailiskis and Stephen de Boer, for their continuous and strong support of the development of Canadian studies in Poland as well as their assistance in the realization of this particular project.

The core hypotheses of our project were presented and debated during several international academic conferences, including two International Studies Association conventions in Toronto and New Orleans, the Congress of the Polish Association for Canadian Studies in Toruń, where a special session was held, devoted specifically to discuss the premises of this project, and the conference of the Polish Society of International Studies in Łódź, where Canada's foreign policy was examined during a separate conference panel. We are also very grateful to Polish Canadianists for inspiring recurrent exchanges we have had for many years.

During our research, we interviewed several Canadian and European diplomats, who generously offered us their knowledge, experience and viewpoints on Canada's international position. In this regard, we are particularly grateful to Canadian diplomats in Poland, but also the diplomats working for the Mission of Canada to the European Union as well as for the European External Action Service. Moreover, we found it inspirational and motivating that our project raised interest among non-academic people, including the Canadian media. We would like to thank the CBC London team for providing us a possibility to share our thoughts with the Canadian audience.

Last but not least, we are grateful to our life partners, who kept us motivated and helped us navigate through this project.

The research project and the publication of this monograph was entirely funded by the grant of the Polish National Science Centre.

1. Canada's power in international relations: major theories

As indicated in the introduction to this book, scholars and foreign policy analysts do not agree on how to define Canada's status in international relations. This issue has over the years been debated by Canadian politicians and political scientists. In the course of these debates, according to Kim Richard Nossal, three major contending conceptions characterizing Canada's position in world affairs have emerged: 1) Canada as a dependency/satellite, 2) Canada as a major or foremost power, 3) Canada as a middle power (*The Politics* 52-64). John Kirton presents a similar classification, also stating that three major perceptions of Canada's international role have functioned in the studies of Canadian foreign policy: 1) the peripheral dependence perspective, treating Canada as a small power; 2) the neo-realist perspective, perceiving Canada as a country that matters; 3) the liberal internationalist perspective based on the assertion that Canada functions as a model middle power (*Canadian* 12-14).

Canada as a satellite

The oldest and the most pessimistic of the three theories assumes that Canada has always been subordinate to the will and policies of much larger superpowers and as such it has never really acted in a completely autonomous way in international relations. The proponents of such an approach find arguments both in the Canadian colonial past as well as in its present position in international affairs. The theory offers both a historical and a contemporary perspective. As for the historical context, the centuries of Canadian subordination to the colonial powers of France and Britain have often been presented as major obstacles that prevented Canada from constructing its own political identity, nationhood or statehood, and, as a result, made it impossible for Canada to gain expertise in diplomacy and international policy. Lacking such expertise, Canada could not serve as an influential or independent actor on the world scene.

It is crucial to point out that theories which present Canada as an entity permanently subjugated to the influences of dominant powers have a long tradition in Canada. Their roots can be traced back to the early colonial period. Moreover, such conceptions frequently gained popularity among the ranks of foremost Canadian political philosophers and prominent politicians, who not only perceived Canada as dependency, but also denied Canadians the right to establish their own country and even treated the very concept of a distinctively Canadian identity as an irrelevant idea, something non-existent in fact. History provides more than just few examples of such an approach.

In 1849, for instance, over 300 Montreal businessmen, opponents of Britain's free market policies and supporters of the U.S.-style republican system of government, signed an annexation manifesto. In this political document they advocated for "a friendly and peaceful separation from British connection and a union upon equitable terms with the Great North American Confederacy of the Sovereign States" ("Annexation"), which was, in fact, a euphemistic call for the annexation of Canada (British North America at the time) to the United States, had other proposed solutions failed to work. Among the signatories of the manifesto one could find, paradoxically, John Abbott, future prime minister of Canada, and Alexander Galt, future federal minister of finance and the first high commissioner of Canada to the United Kingdom (MacLaren 34).

In 1891, Goldwin Smith, a British-Canadian journalist and historian, published his major book *Canada and the Canadian Question*, which – according to one Canadian historian – was "perhaps the most thorough and devastating attack on Confederation that has ever been penned" (R.C. Brown 140). In his book, Smith drew the image of Canada as an artificial, unnatural and ill-governed country, so resembling its southern neighbour that there was no reason for Canada to exist independently of the U.S. What Smith proposed instead was the creation of a great Anglo-Saxon North American nation by the immediate union of Canada and the United States. The author had no doubts "[t]hat a Union of Canada with the American Commonwealth [...] would in itself be attended with great advantages." In Smith's opinion, it would give the whole continent a "complete security for peace" and "a great increase of prosperity" (268). Smith's book gave rise to the annexationist movement in Canada at the turn of 19th and 20th centuries. It also inspired some modern authors to repeat Smith's theses (see Brimelow).

Many authors in the postwar Canada echoed Smith's arguments. Nossal, in his publication on Canadian foreign policy, quotes some of these authors. Amongst them one can find Arthur R.M. Lower, who in 1946 dubbed Canada a "subordinate state [and] complete satellite of the United States." James M. Minifie, in 1960, described Canada as "the glacis for the defence of the continental United States" and "the choreboy of the Western world." Other authors would go even further with their predictions, claiming that "Canada's disappearance as a nation is a matter of necessity" (George Grant in 1965) or concluding pessimistically, as George Martell did in 1970, that "[a]s a country, I believe, we have had it. Our culture, our politics, our economy are almost entirely packaged in the U.S. [...]. We're Americans now, and I think we have to begin dealing with that fact" (qtd. in Nossal, *The Politics* 61-62).

There were also authors, like Hugh Aitken or Andrew H. Malcolm, who believed that Canada was not a fully independent state at any point of its history. The former in 1959 argued that:

> Canada from the beginning of its history, has been a vulnerable economy, exposed to pressures and stimuli from more advanced nations. [...] Canada has never been master of its own destiny; as a satellite staple-producing economy, it reflected, and still reflects, in its rate of development the imperatives of more advanced areas (qtd. in Laxer 143).

Malcolm's view, in turn, was based on the assumption that Canada never practically managed to become a nation on its own in world affairs. The country, he claimed instead, just went through a process of transformation, which was finalized after the Second World War, by which the British colonial dominance over Canada was replaced by the U.S. hegemony. Thus, rather than achieving international independence after Britain lost its empire and global power, Canada – after the World War Two – found itself under the military, economic, political, and even cultural dominance of another global superpower – the United States. Canada, as Nossal observes – quoting the arguments of authors believing in Canada's continuous dependence -"was pulled into an emerging, even if informal, American empire," or – in other words – "went from colony to nation to colony by the end of the Second World War" (*The Politics* 60). A peculiar political transition it was for Canada, claims Malcolm: "It was, in effect, replacing a colonial mother with a colonial big brother" (282). Even Lester B. Pearson, Canadian prime minister whose political actions could by no means be associated with the vision of Canada as a dependent state, declared nonetheless in one of his interviews: "We moved from British influence to American influence without much feeling of purely national identity in between" (qtd. in Walz and Walz 111).

For those who viewed Canada as a subordinate state, even separate Canadian membership in the League of Nations or the passage by the British parliament of the Statute of Westminster in 1931, which granted Canada and five other British dominions full legislative and diplomatic independence from Britain, did not immediately elevate Canada to the status of a full and legitimate member of international structures. In actuality, until the outbreak of the Second World War, other nations, the U.S. included, did not take the competence of Ottawa to manage its own foreign policy seriously and continued to look at Ottawa through the prism of its colonial past, treating Canada rather as a British satellite, not as an "international person" or "a power independently capable of making treaties" (Stacey 56). As a matter of fact, as late as the Suez Crisis of 1956, Canada still faced difficulties with eliminating the external image of itself as a British periphery. The problem became evident in November 1956 when Egypt objected to the dispatch of Canadian peacekeeping soldiers, whom Egyptians perceived as not impartial enough because of their excessively British appearance – the soldiers wore very British-looking uniforms, they served under the Red Ensign, a Canadian flag of the time which had the British Union Jack in the left upper corner, and their battalion bore a profoundly monarchical name – the Queen's Own Rifles of Canada (Hilliker and Barry 128; Granatstein 345). It was no sooner than after the Suez Crisis that the Canadian government seriously started to consider the creation of new, less-confusing and distinctively Canadian visual identifiers to be used by Canada abroad. The process led to the adoption of, among others, the Maple Leaf flag, which replaced the Canadian Red Ensign in 1965.

Nowadays, the view of Canada as a country dependent on stronger partners focuses mostly on Canada's linkage to the United States. The arguments justifying the Canadian status of subordination revolve around the fact that Canada remains under the profound demographic, economic and military dominance of the U.S. As of July 2015, the official estimate of the Canadian population was slightly over 35.8 million (Statistics Canada, "Population"), which was almost ten times less than the population of the United States at the same time – estimated at 321.4 million (United States Census of Bureau). A similar disparity can be seen in the economy. The American gross domestic product (GDP) (nominal) in 2015 was almost USD 18 trillion, while Canada's exceeded only USD 1.5 trillion (International Monetary Fund).

Such an imbalance had to affect bilateral Canadian-U.S. relations. American influences on Canada's economy have grown larger and larger since the end of the Second World War until they expanded to their present scale after Canada's accession to the Canada-United States Free Trade Agreement (CUSFTA) in 1989, and later the North American Free Trade Agreement (NAFTA) in 1994. They are now best reflected in a peculiar structure of Canadian foreign trade – Canada is in fact the only highly developed and industrialized country whose economy is so dependent on trading with just one international partner. The statistical data is alarming: as of April 2016, the U.S. received as much as 74.8 per cent of all Canadian exported goods and was the source of 66.4 per cent of all Canada's imports (Statistics Canada, "Table"). As for Canadian exports of crude oil and natural gas, the dependence on the U.S. is overwhelming – in March 2016, 98.8 per cent of Canada's oil sold abroad and nearly 100 per cent of exported natural gas in 2014 went to the United States (National Energy Board, "2014"; National Energy Board, "Crude").

Canadian economic dependence on the U.S. has raised international controversies, too. For instance, the inclusion of Canada in 1976 to the Group of Seven (G7) forum, the elite club of the most industrialized countries, was repeatedly questioned by the critics, who argued, not without reason, that Canada found its place in the group only thanks to the pressure from the Americans who wanted to add to the forum a North American country to provide a counterweight for European states and Japan, which had already been a part of the group (Keating, *Canada* 196).

French President Valery Giscard d'Estaing most fervently opposed the admission of Canada to G7, "notably on the grounds that Canada was an economic appendage of the United States and that, consequently, a separate representation was unnecessary" (Massie, "A Special" 235). What currently is emphasized most, however, is the fact that Canada, statistically, does not deserve to be a member of G7 – it has the smallest population of all G7 states, its economy is disproportionately dependent on trade with one partner and is not the world's seventh largest (Marshall). In terms of nominal GDP, China, Brazil, Russia and India – i.e. most of the so-called BRICS countries – are now ahead of Canada in the rankings of the largest economies in the world.

Militarily, Canada also relies largely on the U.S. In actuality, the core element of Canada's security policy is its membership in military alliances such as NATO and NORAD or in such intelligence alliances and surveillance programs as Echelon, where the U.S. plays a key role, being in fact the major guarantor of security to its allies. Some political analysts are of the opinion that Canadian participation in these alliances, because of the overwhelming dominance of the United States, limits the independence of Canadian military policies and subordinates Canada to the military interests of its southern neighbour (Massie, "Canada's" 502-506). They cite a number of historical and contemporary examples of Canada's military submissions resulting from the American political pressure. They mention, for example, that Ottawa often yielded in the past to American expectations and agreed to have U.S. cruise missiles tested on Canadian territory (Chambers 214). It is also stressed that – due to the opposition of the U.S. – in 1959, Ottawa had to abandon the development of its own Avro Canada Arrow fighter aircraft, which, according to critics, "meant the continued reliance on foreign-produced aircraft for Canadian air defence" (Dyck 182). Some analysts, such as Kim R. Nossal or Justin Massie, even claim that true Canadian sovereignty in military affairs is a thing long gone. The former argues that once Canada joined NORAD, it lost "a great deal of room to manoeuvre" and subsequently, in practice, it could never make a decision to withdraw from the agreement as "the costs of doing so would have been high" and such a move would have been treated in Washington as "a distinctly unfriendly act with negative strategic implications." "As long as the United States government wanted some form of northern air defence," Nossal contends, "Canadians had the choice of participating – or facing unpalatable consequences" (*The Politics* 27). Massie, in turn, believes that Ottawa's attitude towards American military initiatives was not changed remarkably when the Cold War ended – Ottawa is still driven by fear of "the likelihood and potential impact of American unilateral gestures" ("Canada's" 504).

At the same time, there are also opinions which recognize the positive aspect of Canada's dependence on the U.S. regarding its security. According to the NORAD principles, the amount of expenditures of a country depends on its population. Canada, therefore, covers approximately only 10 per cent of the entire costs of NORAD systems, with the remaining part being covered by the U.S. (Nossal, *The Politics* 27). Such an arrangement means that Canada is "protected by the U.S. military arsenal and [...] pay[s] relatively little for its defence" (Dyck 183). Indeed, feeling relatively secure under the American protective umbrella, Canada lags behind most of the other NATO member states in military expenditures (World Bank, "Military"), and – like most of the NATO countries – falls short of meeting NATO's guidelines of spending at least 2 per cent of GDP on defence (Bendavid). A couple of reasons can be presented to explain Canadian sluggishness in investing in its armed forces.

First and foremost, Canadians realize that it is neither the number of troops nor even the amount of funds allotted to the military that play key roles in ensuring the safety of Canada. Canadian security is instead guaranteed, on the one hand, by the principle of collective defence, binding all NATO members through Article 5 of the NATO treaty, and, on the other hand, by the U.S. defence doctrine. According to the latter, any possible threat to the territorial integrity of Canada would have to be treated in Washington as a potential attack on the United States. A strong belief that the U.S. could not refuse to react in case Canada was attacked has been held for dozens of years in Canada. Its beginning can be traced back to 1938, when President Franklin D. Roosevelt assured Canadians during his Canadian visit that "the people of the United States will not stand idly by if domination of Canadian soil is threatened by any other Empire" (qtd. in Thompson and Randall 139). During the Second World War a system of a close military cooperation between Canada and the United States was established by the Ogdensburg Declaration and the Hyde Park Agreement (Elliot-Meisel 148). The collaboration continued after the war and in the late 1950s it evolved into NORAD, a joint U.S.-Canadian air defence system, whose primary task was to protect North America against a Soviet bomber attack. This way Canadians received what Joseph Jockel and Joel Sokolsky call a "U.S. 'involuntary guarantee' of Canadian security," which provided an excuse or a substantial incentive for Ottawa to cut its military spending (318). As a matter of fact, Canada did not need NATO or NORAD to be certain of American guarantees. It was enough to use common-sense Cold War logic to know the Americans would have had no choice but to defend Canada, had its territory been attacked. Since "it would have been impossible to tell if Soviet bombers approaching North America from over the pole were heading towards Canadian or U.S. targets," Washington simply had to treat every possible attack of the USSR on Canada as an attack on itself (Jockel and Sokolsky 318).

Paradoxically, the proximity of the United States meant that Canadians did not feel so directly threatened by a Soviet attack as the Europeans. Obviously, what played a role was the fact that, compared to Europe, Canada had a different historical experience – it had never been the arena of bloody world wars. Not only, therefore, was it much easier for Ottawa to cut its military expenditures, but also to oppose the expansion of nuclear weapons. Despite the fact that the guarantees of Canadian security arose from the NATO, particularly American, arsenal of nuclear weapons, a so-called "nuclear deterrent" aroused much less enthusiasm in Ottawa than in Washington or in Western Europe. While for Western Europe a possibility of the U.S. using nuclear weapons against the countries of the Eastern Bloc was an important element of defence strategies, Ottawa observed the process of nuclear armaments in Europe with anxiety. It was believed that such a policy would lead to the intensification of the arms race, increasing the likelihood of a nuclear war, which Canada wanted to avoid at all costs. What Ottawa officials feared most was that the U.S. "would be too assertive in a crisis, and that war would result before all political and diplomatic options had been explored" (Buteux 161). The real danger of war, posted one Canadian diplomat from Moscow, "comes from a trigger-happy U.S. military who argue that the best way to prevent the next war is to drop a bomb on a Kremlin" (qtd. in Keating, *Canada* 88).

Among other things, these were the reasons why Canada, mainly due to the initiative of Howard Green, head of Canadian diplomacy from 1959 to 1963, became one of the most important advocates of arms control and denuclearization (Legault 168-172). Under the prime ministership of Pierre E. Trudeau (1968-1984), Canada signed the Treaty on the Non-Proliferation of Nuclear Weapons, pledging not to produce or purchase nuclear weapons. Also, at that time, previously deployed American nuclear warheads were removed from the Canadian territory (Holloway 87). Prime Minister Trudeau was widely regarded as an outspoken opponent of military issues and among his advisors one could even find people who called for Canada to withdraw from NATO (Keating, *Canada* 162). Although it was never very close to taking such a radical step, the Trudeau administration implemented drastic cuts in military spending. The number of troops was limited, the military personnel stationed in Europe was cut, the defence budget was reduced to less than 2 per cent of GDP (Sartry 135-136) and the Canadian expenditures on armed forces have never again returned to the level before Pierre Trudeau. As a result, Ottawa has often been criticized for too modest of an involvement in the NATO military affairs in relation to Canada's economic potential. Some analysts would go so far in their accusations as to label Canada, rather unfairly, an "Atlantic free-rider" or the "slacker of transatlantica" – a country that benefits from NATO's collective defence system but contributes very little to it itself (Zyla "NATO").

Obviously, the long-lasting period of underinvestment in armed forces and the dependence of Canada's security on the U.S. military arsenal have negative consequences for Canada, which can be best seen in the Arctic, which is discussed in more detail in Chapter 3. Many also argue that Canada's internal problems of 1990s, including the separatist tendencies in Quebec, "bred introspection and the subordination of foreign policy to domestic politics" and reduced Canada's role in the world. Moreover, there are also opinions that the end of the Cold War marked the beginning of the decline of Canada's global influence. Canada stopped being a crucial Cold-War ally for the United States because there was no longer any Cold War (Kirton, *Canadian* 13).

***

Although the vision of Canada as a small or dependent power rightly points out to the limitations of Canadian economic and military potentials, the view of Canada as merely a satellite or a subordinate state with diminutive powers is of little relevance if applied to the evaluation of Canadian contemporary position in international affairs. While the followers of this concept rightly expose in their argumentations that

Canada, to a large extent, remains under the military and economic dependence on the U.S., they at the same time ignore the crucial role Canada has played in various fields of international relations, such as in:

- establishing key international political, economic, and military organizations (incl. the U.N., NATO, G7/G8 and G20);
- creating the peacekeeping forces (United Nations Emergency Force) and as the most involved participant of peacekeeping missions during the Cold War;
- opposing some of the U.S. postwar policies, including the Canadian-U.S. tensions over the Bomarc Missile Crisis of 1958, the Cuban Missile Crisis of 1962, the Vietnam War or the invasion on Iraq in 2003;
- protection of human rights and gender equality, and in promoting democracy;
- foreign aid and humanitarian assistance;
- wildlife conservation and protection of environment;
- initiating the denuclearization process.

In light of all those contributions, discussed in detail below, which by no means constitute a complete list, Canada cannot and should not be downgraded to the position of a mere dependency. The obvious achievements of Canadian postwar policies and diplomacy rank that country much above that status.

Canada as a major/foremost/principal power

Out of the three concepts presented in this chapter, the view of Canada as one of the major powers offers the most optimistic and the most assertive approach to Canada's position in international affairs. The proponents of such a concept justify their stance citing numerous international economic rankings, which locate Canada amongst world superpowers in terms of natural resource abundance, its energy potential and technological advancement. Also, Canada's key contribution to the process of building a postwar world order is put forward as proof of Canada's position of the foremost global power. Being a principal power, naturally, means no subordination to another country, so the logical consequence of the adoption of the concept of Canada as the world's key player was the rejection of theories recognizing the U.S. political or cultural dominance over Canada. The roots of such a perspective can be found in the pamphlets and considerations of 19th-century Canadian political thinkers.

One of the first groups to propagate Canadian greatness was Canada First, a nationalist movement established in the 1870s, which grouped young Anglophone Protestant intellectuals, politicians and journalists. They promoted a vision of a self-sufficient Canada and opted for economic autonomy both from Britain and the U.S. What they considered as particularly important in building a distinctively Canadian identity was implanting a purely Canadian sense of national belonging and a faith and pride in their own country in Canadians. The future of Canada – as declared Edward Blake, premier of Ontario from 1871 to 1872 and one of the main leaders and founders of the movement – "depends very largely upon the cultivation of a national spirit" (qtd. in Waite 35). Canadians, claimed Canada First activists, "must acquire an understanding of their historic origins, a proud realization of the many sources of their strength, an awareness of their national identity, and a confident belief in the unlimited possibilities of their future" (Creighton 24). Canadian patriotism was to be developed hand in hand with the territorial expansion and the economic growth of Canada as well as with the exploitation of natural resources. Therefore, Canada Firsters supported the settlements in the Canadian Prairies and the construction of the Canadian Pacific Railway. They also approved the creation of political institutions that could contribute to the development of Canada's statehood and identity. They advocated, for instance, for the establishment of the Supreme Court of Canada, which happened in 1875, and also proposed, without success, that appeals to the Privy Council of Britain, which until 1949 served, as the final court of appeal for Canada, be abolished (Waite 38-40).

Canada First was a short-term movement. Its activities ended in 1880s, a decade after it was established, due to a total lack of recognition among Quebeckers and rather dim popularity among English Canadians. The former were discouraged by the strong anti-Francophone rhetoric of Canada Firsters. The latter, in turn, were not attracted to Canada First's visions mainly because the movement's political message was built on false and naïve assumptions about the self-sufficiency of the newly formed Dominion of Canada and its ability to conduct economic policies independently from London and Washington. The Canada First movement, however, initiated a debate about the path that Canada should take building its own statehood and national identity.

Nevertheless, two decades had passed before a prominent politician believed in a prospect of Canada as a major power and was ready to announce his ambitious vision publicly. This politician was Wilfrid Laurier, Canadian prime minister from 1896 to 1911. In 1904, he proclaimed: "The nineteenth century was the century of the United States, the twentieth will be the century of Canada" (qtd. in Riendeau 218). Looking at Laurier's prediction today, it appears to have been overoptimistic or even naïve. However, at the threshold of the twentieth century his vision was not entirely devoid of rationale. Canada at that time seemed to have carved a path of success for itself and had – at least from the Canadian point of view – achievements comparable to those of its southern neighbour. The country was experiencing a rapid economic development, already enjoying the relative economic independence from Britain. Autonomy in the economy was accompanied by progressing political emancipation and the democratization of government structures. The second half of the 19th century was also a period of an unprecedented rapid industrial and demographic growth and territorial development of Canada. In just four years since the Dominion of Canada was created in 1867, Canada, like the United States several decades earlier, had become a country from sea to sea – *A Mari usque ad Mare*, as the Canadian motto says – occupying a huge area between the Atlantic and the Pacific oceans. Canada's population grew mainly due to an open-door policy for newcomers from Central and Eastern Europe, introduced by the Laurier administration. Every year, from 200,000 up to even 400,000 immigrants were admitted to Canada, who largely settled in the Canadian Prairies, transforming these previously sparsely populated areas (Brooks 520; Lunn and Moore 88). In addition, political, economic and demographic development of Canada appeared to have been smoother and calmer than similar processes in the U.S. The changes were phased in, political and economic goals were achieved evolutionarily – Canada's history was not marked with bloody revolutions, civil wars or prolonged armed uprisings. Canadians were paying a lower price in the process of attaining statehood than the Americans.

All these facts combined allowed Wilfrid Laurier to draw scenarios of a bright future for his country. Canada, at the end of the 20th century, according to his vision, was to become a country with an economy equal to the American economy and a population reaching 60 million people (Lunn and Moore 89). In fact, Laurier's vision was similar to the conviction of one of his predecessors – Alexander Mackenzie, prime minister of Canada from 1873 to 1878, who once had promised that Canada "would one day surpass England, not only in territory and population but in political grandeur too" (qtd. in Donaldson 45). Inaccurate as both Laurier's and Mackenzie's visions were – over 100 years after Laurier's predictions, Canada's population, as mentioned above, is slightly over 35 million – Laurier was one of the first and foremost true believers in Canada's superpower potential.

His belief in a strong, wealthy and great Canada was shared by a number of his contemporaries, including politicians and journalists. Although they never formed a coherent group or movement, some of them – because of the ideas they promoted – could be called anti-imperialists. They saw the first step in the process of building Canada's greatness in making Canada a fully independent state. They stressed the urgent need for the political emancipation of Canada. They questioned the very idea of Canada being a part of the British Empire and opted for a gradual reorientation of Canadian policy towards the independence from British influences. They claimed that the imperial connection was a main obstacle to complete Canadian sovereignty and that within the Empire, Canadian national interests were too often subdued to the interests of Britain and its colonies. Imperialism imposed cultural, economic and political inferiority – argued John Skirving Ewart (1849-1933), a legal scholar and a writer, but also one of the leading anti-imperialists. He accused the supporters of the Empire of betraying the interests of Canada by consolidating resources only "for the power, profit and prestige of England" (*Imperial Relations* viii). As early as in 1911, he believed that Canada was already "independent fiscally, legislatively, executively, and judicially" (Ewart 5). All that Canadians needed was to have this fact officially acknowledged by the British Parliament and at international councils (16). Therefore, he wrote, "we do not like the word *colony*. It connotes subordination, and subjection, and humiliation. [...] We feel that we are big enough to manage our own affairs" (1). He called for Canada to be given a status of an independent partner at international forums. "I am not satisfied," he lectured, "that Canada should occupy a place in the world inferior to that held by dozens of nations who cannot compare her in wealth, strength, or intelligence" (16-17).

Anti-imperialists rose to prominence in the interwar years under the premiership of William Lyon Mackenzie King. Some of them even served as influential government officials or, like John Ewart, as prime minister's legal advisors (Hilliker 90-91). Their expertise gave rise to independent Canadian foreign policy. In this context, the most important figure was Oskar Douglas Skelton (1878-1941). In 1925, he was appointed undersecretary of state in Canada's Department of External Affairs (DEA) and left a distinctive mark on the politics of Canadian external policies. It was under his leadership that the DEA became a real centre for shaping the foreign policy of Canada. O.D. Skelton, just like Mackenzie King, was a strong believer in Canadian diplomatic sovereignty. Before taking his position in the DEA, he had authored an extensive book titled *General Economic History of the Dominion, 1867-1912*, the first detailed economic history of Canada, "in which he examined anti-imperial ideas [and] the development of Canadian representation abroad" (Hilliker 93). Making Canadian foreign policy independent from the British influence was, according to him, a natural and integral part of the historical and political development of Canada. As early as in 1902, in a letter to his friend he referred to Canadian independence as "the ideal I've always cherished" and questioned the existence of common interests within the British Empire. According to Skelton, there was not "any real or lasting community of interest between Canada and Australia or Timbuctoo, or whatever other part of the map a Jingoistic spree may chance to paint red" (qtd. in Hillmer 65).

In Skelton's opinion Canada had the right to take its rightful place in the international arena, not as merely a supplement to the British foreign policy, but as an independent actor, who in its external actions should be guided not by the interests of London, but by its own *raison d'état* (Hillmer 72-77). Skelton's skeptical attitude to all matters related to the British Empire led to a change in the way Canadian foreign policy was practiced and managed. External relations under his supervision of the DEA ceased to be perceived as international activities that were only to be conducted via the British Empire and the Foreign Office in London. Making Canadian foreign policy independent had become a major challenge and an objective of the DEA. In fact, under Skelton's direction, the DEA rose to the status of the real centre where the foreign policy of Canada was shaped. However, due to the lack of diplomatic tradition in Canada and the shortage of personnel, the DEA's operations for some time continued to be, as John Hilliker noticed, "based on limited research and a non-Canadian perspective, since much of the department's information came from the British" (105).

Skelton, however, initiated changes that in the long run contributed to the creation of a truly independent Canadian diplomacy. He developed a system of training for new diplomats, which was treated as another element which made Ottawa more independent from London, and led to the recruitment of young and well-educated candidates to work for the DEA, many of whom supported the idea of the autonomy of Canada in international relations. Prime Minister Mackenzie King supported Skelton and was greatly satisfied with the direction and pace of the development of independent Canadian diplomacy in the interwar years, believing that Canada "had the beginning of a diplomatic service which has not been surpassed by any country in the world" (qtd. in Hilliker 117). As a matter of fact, both Mackenzie King and Skelton, in the longer run, contributed significantly to the emergence of the idea of the British Empire as a commonwealth of fully independent dominions, equal in status with the UK, and played important roles in the process that preceded the adoption of the Statute of Westminster in 1931, which granted Canada and five other British dominions complete diplomatic independence from Britain.

Gaining independence did not mean, however, that Canada desired to forget or completely remove the ties that bound Canadians to Britain and Europe. On the contrary, what the politicians in Ottawa wanted was to elevate Canada's global position by skillfully using the British and European links. As Paul Buteux wrote, Canadian war and postwar security policy was largely "determined by the perception that Europe was an integral part of Canada's definition of its role in the world [...] and that Canada was not simply a North American country locked into a continental embrace" (156). Such a perception gave way to the idea that one of Canada's roles in world affairs was to serve as a bridge-builder or interpreter between the U.S. and Europe, and such an idea was then transformed into a theoretical concept of the so-called "North Atlantic triangle" or "Triangle ABC," because it referred to relations between Americans, the British and Canadians (Roussel 132).

The term "North Atlantic triangle" was first formulated in 1949 by John Bartlet Brebner in his book *North Atlantic Triangle: The Interplay of Canada, the United States and Great Britain*. What stood behind it was a broader vision of Canada as one of the key powers in the global security system. The whole concept was based on two assumptions. The first one was that very close and amicable relations with both Britain and the U.S. were of key importance for Canada's political and economic development and played a crucial role as guarantees of the country's military security. According to the second assumption, Canada, as the closest British and American ally, was predestined to become the major decision maker in the postwar world order. Naturally, the latter vision has never come true and, from today's perspective, the whole concept sounds more like an expression of Canadian hopes, dreams and perhaps over-ambitious aspirations than reality.

Nonetheless, at the time of its formulation the theory was not entirely irrational. In the 1940s, Canada had already directly participated in key events determining the fate of the world. Owing to the initiative of Canadian Prime Minister Mackenzie King, for instance, two war conferences attended by Franklin D. Roosevelt and Winston Churchill were held in Quebec in 1943 and 1944, where war plans were discussed and crucial decisions on war cooperation between the U.S. and Britain were made. Canadian scientists were also involved as junior partners to the Americans and the British in the Manhattan Project, whose result was the production and dropping of atomic bombs on Hiroshima and Nagasaki in 1945 – the radioactive material used to produce the bombs was supplied by Canada (Bratt, *The Politics* 8-11). Moreover, Canadian diplomats were among the main drafters of the charters and statutes of such international organizations as the U.N., NATO, the Commonwealth and a few other (discussed below).

Despite those contributions, however, Ottawa never gained the position of an equal partner to the Americans and the British within the triangle. In this tripartite scheme, Canadians rather served as a trusted intermediary between London and Washington – they would suggest solutions or initiate talks, but almost never make decisions or have a final say. Even at the Quebec conferences, Mackenzie King only played host to the meetings but took no active part in discussions. Once Churchill proposed to include the Canadian prime minister in discussions, "Roosevelt vetoed this suggestion instantly, using the argument that […] if Canada were admitted, Brazil, China, Mexico, and the other Dominions would clamour to be admitted too" (Stacey 334). Roosevelt's reaction clearly showed that if Canadians wanted to be on an equal footing, it was not going to be at the table with the Americans and the British. Such an outcome was, as the minutes of the Canadian War Cabinet of 1943 suggest, approved by Mackenzie King, who announced the following:

> The Canadian government had accepted the position that the higher strategic direction of the war was exercised by the British Prime Minister and the President of the United States, with the Combined Chiefs of Staff. It was recognized that the participation of the Canadian military heads, in meetings of the Combined Chiefs of Staff, might give rise to difficulties with the United Nations (qtd. in Stacey 337).

How minor Canada's role in the North Atlantic Triangle was, even for Canadians, is best illustrated by this entry in the Canadian Encyclopedia:

> In 1998 the debate over [Mackenzie] King's – and Canada's – role in the [Quebec] conferences erupted again with the unveiling of a statue commemorating the conferences in Québec City. The Québec government under Lucien Bouchard justified the omission of King from the statue by arguing that he played no role in the meetings. Thus King was denied by his own countrymen at least the role of host that even Churchill and Roosevelt had afforded him (Marsh).

Therefore, even if the North Atlantic triangle ever existed, it was only a concept of a handful of Canadian thinkers and politicians. Obviously, with the progressing decline of Britain's postwar international position, the theory was also losing its relevance; nonetheless, until this day it has been discussed from various perspectives in the number of scholarly publications (see Haglund).

Paradoxically, however, in the years following the Second World War, Canada's major-power position was not merely a futuristic vision or a theoretical concept, but, at least in some aspects, had become a fact. As Adam Chapnick wrote, "Canada could have claimed great-power status for itself in 1945: it had one of the most powerful armed forces in the world and one of the world's strongest economies" ("The Canadian" 193). In fact, when the war ended, Canada had the world's third largest navy and fourth largest air force (Pratt 67). Despite those facts, until 1970s, very few, even in Canada, seriously considered Canada's international role as a foremost power. Canadians after the war, as Chapnick noticed, "did not aspire to great-power status; they simply wanted to be recognized as having a distinct role in the international community" ("The Canadian" 193) and were satisfied with the role of a middle power (discussed below).

The principal-powerhood arguments, however, returned in 1975, when James Eayrs presented a theory according to which Canada had all the sources of power (including the manpower, natural resources, technology) typical of leading global powers and thus should pursue such a status and be considered as a principal power by international partners (Nossal, *The Politics* 62). His arguments were later shared by a number of political scholars, whose perspectives on the Canadian international role are outlined by both Nossal and Chapnick in their publications. These authors included: Norman Hillmer and Garth Stevenson, who in 1977 edited a collection of essays on Canadian foreign policy, giving it a symbolic title: *Foremost Nation*; Peyton Lyon and Brian Tomlin, who asserted in their book *Canada as an International Actor* that Canada's international position was far above the rank of such middle powers as Australia or Sweden and rather equalled the position of principal powers such as Germany, China, France, or Britain; David Dewitt and John Kirton, who promoted a vision of Canada as a major power – *Canada as a Principal Power* was the title of the book they authored in 1983; Allan Gotlieb, a former diplomat, who in 1987 penned a newspaper article, in which he attempted to prove that classifying Canada as a middle power underestimated Canada's actual capabilities and status and opted for categorizing Canada as a major power (Nossal, *The Politics* 63-64; Chapnick, "The Canadian" 198). In 2007, John Kirton wrote a book entitled *Canadian Foreign Policy in a Changing World*, in which he asserts that Canadian foreign policy should be studied carefully because "Canada counts. It is a major power whose international behaviour matters to the world" (14). One of the factors that, in Kirton's opinion, pulls Canada into a major-power position is "the emergence of a more diffuse international system" and "the sustained, significant and probably irreversible decline of a once predominant and now vulnerable America" (1-2). This empowers Canada's international status because it extends Canada's freedom to choose its foreign policy strategies. Such freedom, according to Kirton, can paradoxically be less constrained than the freedom enjoyed in international relations by such unquestionable global powers as the United States. He argues that:

[A] major power can conduct a foreign policy driven more by its own
governmental and societal choice and less by classic external, relative
capability-grounded constraints. Thus a Canada confronting a pervasively
vulnerable America in an intensely interconnected world can more freely
choose its foreign policy path. In practice, capable Canada has chosen to
compensate for declining America, for the sake of the two countries and the
world as a whole (Kirton, "Vulnerable" 134).

Thus, in other words, Canada in the post-Cold War world, according
to the proponents of the vision of Canada as a foremost power, became a
power able to pursue its policies and interests with relative independence
from external influences. This allowed the country to play an increasingly
meaningful role internationally until it achieved the status of a principal
power ("a big league player," a power "to be heard," a "serious" power)
(Kirton, *Canadian* 14).

As a matter of fact, the concept of Canada as a principal power seems
to be well justified by various rankings and economic data. First and
foremost, Canada serves as one of the world's largest repositories of crucial
mineral and energy resources, by its own government being dubbed "a
world leader of mining," fully deserving such a label (Natural Resources
Canada 6). It is, among others, the global leader in nonferrous mineral
exploration budgets and attracts 14 per cent of the world's investments
in this sector. Over 60 minerals and metals are extracted or produced
in Canada, including potash, of which Canada is the world's largest
producer. Canada is also the second largest producer of uranium, nickel
and niobium; the third largest producer of primary aluminum, cobalt,
platinum group metals, and diamonds; it also ranks at the top of the
largest global producers of salt, sulphur and gold. Moreover, the Toronto
Stock Exchange is the world's largest centre of mining financing, listing
over half of the global publicly traded mining companies (Natural
Resources Canada 2-6). According to the U.S. Energy Information
Administration, Canada also ranks the third globally in terms of proven
crude oil reserves and the fifth in terms of petroleum production; it
is also the world's third largest producer of natural gas and the sixth
largest producer of electricity (United States Energy Information
Administration). Canada also has the world's largest freshwater reserves
and, after China and Brazil, is the most important global generator of
hydropower (International Hydropower Association). The country is also

ranked by the Food and Agriculture Organization of the United Nations among the world's top five producers of such agricultural commodities as wheat, barley, and oats (Food and Agriculture Organization).

What also puts Canada in the global leadership, positively distinguishing the country internationally, is its relatively predictable economy and the stability of political and social relations. Canada for years has occupied leading positions in various rankings assessing economic development and the quality of life. In the annual reports on human development, published by the United Nations since 1990, Canada has been declared the global leader eight times and is generally found among the ten highest classified countries. In the 2015 Human Development Index, Canada was ranked ninth (United Nations, "Human" 208). Also, Canadian cities dominate the rankings of the world's most livable cities. In the 2015 ranking of the best cities to live in published by the Economist, three out of top five world's cities were Canadian – Vancouver, Toronto, Calgary ("The World's Most").

In addition, in 2013, the Organisation for Economic Cooperation and Development ranked Canada as one of the best-educated OECD member states (Organisation for Economic Cooperation and Development, Education at a Glance 2013 35-40). Educational and economic opportunities are a magnet for immigrants and overseas students. Canada currently has one of the highest rates of immigration per capita in the world, approximately a quarter of a million per year. The influx of new residents translates directly to the constant population growth of the country, the highest among the G7 countries (Statistics Canada, "Canada's population estimates: Age and sex, July 1, 2015").

At the same time Canadians remain famous for their tolerance and openness to immigrants. According to public opinion polls, nine out of ten Canadians consider immigrants to be as good citizens as those born in Canada (Stastna) and reject the opinions that immigration to Canada is too high, or that it has a negative impact on the country's economy, or that immigrants are responsible for taking jobs away from Canadians. However, there is a concern that too many immigrants fail to adopt Canadian values. At the same time, the vast majority of immigrants, eight in ten respondents, feel more strongly attached to Canada than to their country of origin, which is the best result among all G8 countries (Environics Institute 19, 44-46).

***

The strongest point in the concept of Canada as a principal power is that it notices the fact that Canada occupies a prominent position of one of the world's largest reservoirs of natural, mineral and energy resources. The proponents of this perspective also rightly indicate the fact that Canada has played an outstanding role – much above its demographic or economic potential – in creating international institutions and organizations (discussed in detail below).

However, the theory seems to ignore Canada's low population and low nominal GDP. In both elements Canada ranks the lowest among the G7 countries, despite stable economic growth and one of the highest immigration rates per capita. Also, while the abundance of natural resources in Canada is an undeniable fact, almost all of Canada's exported crucial resources, such as oil and gas, are – as it was already mentioned – purchased by the United States. Therefore, as Gordon Laxer argues, Canada's position cannot be equalled with the impact of such energy superpowers as the U.S., Saudi Arabia or Russia. Because of its economic and military dependence on the U.S., Canada does not have a capability, unlike the aforementioned states, to use its energy resources to "influence other countries' behaviour," boost its military strength, strengthen its own "soft-power positions," or effectively use it as "foreign policy instruments." Neither can Canada regulate global prices of fuels by increasing or decreasing their production. In fact, the country does not even have a sufficient infrastructure (i.e. pipelines) to satisfy domestic needs (Laxer 141-152). All these issues are widely discussed in Chapter 3.

The fact is that economic dependence on trading (not only energy resources) with one partner, combined with a relatively small population and economy, which is not even ranked among the world's ten largest economies, does not make Canada a natural candidate for a major or principal power. The concept of Canada as a foremost power cannot therefore be applied uncritically to describe the current position of Canada in international relations.

Canada as a middle power

The middle power theory refers to the terminology introduced in the late 16th century by an Italian philosopher and diplomat Giovanni

Botero, who in his famous philosophical work entitled *Della ragion di Stato* (*The Reason of State*, 1589) divided the states of his times into three categories: *gli stati grandissimi* (significant states/superpowers), *gli stati mediocri* (medium states/middle powers) and *gli stati piccoli* (small states) (Wight 299). Since the end of the Second World War, the term "middle power" has been used to refer to the countries that cannot be regarded as global superpowers, but which on the other hand have a far greater impact on international affairs than their economic or demographic potential suggests, and which generally enjoy a good international reputation. The middle power theory has become the most popular approach, used by both practitioners and a wide range of theorists, to assess Canada's postwar international position.

The end of the Second World War and the beginning of the Cold War triggered a radical change in the geopolitical position of Canada. Previously remaining far from the global conflicts, Canada – because of its specific geographical location, i.e. between two major belligerents: the U.S. and the Soviet Union – suddenly found itself in the centre of the Cold War rivalry. While it had always been obvious for Canadian political leaders that their country was a part of the Western world, that did not mean that Canada was going to be an uncritical supporter of the United States. Participating actively in the creation of the postwar world order, Canadian politicians sought to build Canada's unique brand in international affairs. What became Canadian identifiers in world politics was devotion to multilateralism, internationalism and the middlepowership.

This new direction in the Canadian foreign policy was most accurately outlined in January 1947 by Louis St-Laurent, at that time Secretary of State for External Affairs and later prime minister of Canada. In a lecture he delivered at the University of Toronto, St-Laurent pointed to the fundamental principles of Canadian postwar foreign policy. They included the following: a) respect for international laws, because "the freedom of nations depends upon the rule of law among states," b) the protection and promotion of human rights and values based on the "emphasis on the importance of the individual, on the place of moral principles in the conduct of human relations [and] on standards of judgment which transcend mere material well-being," c) the adoption by Canada of the attitude of "willingness to accept our international responsibilities" for the fate of the world (internationalism), and therefore the rejection of isolationism in favour of the policies that promote compromise and multilateral solutions to build global peace and order (qtd. in Pratt 65).

In such circumstances Canadians revived Botero's concept of middle power and adapted it to the postwar realities. In fact, middlepowership had been a point of reference for some even earlier. For instance, in an article in the *Economist*, published in 1943, it was recognized that due to Canada's outstanding war effort, "the distance which separates Canada from the Great Powers is less than that between her own achievements and that of any other of the small powers" (qtd. in Chapnick, "The Canadian" 192). A similar argumentation was used by Canada's Prime Minister William Lyon Mackenzie King, who in May 1944 defined Canada as "a power of a middle size" and warned his British counterpart, Winston Churchill, "how difficult it would be for Canada, after enlisting nearly one million persons in her armed forces and trebling her national debt in order to assist in restoring peace, to accept a position of parity [...] with the Dominican Republic or El Salvador" (qtd. in Nossal, *The Politics* 54-55). Mackenzie King's arguments were, in turn, echoed by Lionel Gelber, a Canadian diplomat, who in 1944 justified Canada's aspirations to become a middle power:

> Under the impact of war, Canada has moved up from her old status to a new stature. With her smaller population and lack of colonial possessions, she is not a major or world power like Britain, the United States or Russia. But with her natural wealth and human capacity she is not a minor power like Mexico or Sweden. She stands in between as a Britannic Power of medium rank. Henceforth in world politics, Canada must figure as a Middle Power (qtd. in Nossal, *The Politics* 54).

Adam Chapnick suggests that the middle-power concept was invented to "confer permanent recognition to the smaller states that contributed the most to the war effort" and to grant these states "access to what had been an exclusive great-power privilege," that is to give them more influence in the postwar international organizations. For Canada, Chapnick argues, campaigning for the middle-power status meant "promoting its own disproportionate influence in international affairs" ("The Canadian" 191).

Middlepowership was understood in at least three ways. In a so-called positional (or hierarchical/statistical) model, which took a country's rank and capabilities in international structures into consideration

(Gecelovsky 77-78), such countries as Canada, Brazil or Australia could be referred to as "middle powers" as they had a demographic, military or economic potentials significant enough to enable them to have a remarkable impact on shaping the postwar international relations. These potentials, however, were too modest to locate these countries in the positions of global superpowers. As for Canada, as Robert W. Murray and John McCoy observed, the country "simply did not have sufficient material capabilities to wield a heavy hand" and had no choice but to resign itself to the role of a middle power (175). The positional approach, apart from assessing the countries "on the basis of quantifiable attributes such as area, population, size, complexity and strength of the economy, military capability and other comparable factors" (Hynek 35), also analyzed the country's ideological location. In this context, middle powers were defined as "those who occupied positions between the extremes of the two competing power blocs during the Cold War [and] regarded themselves as "mediators" or "linchpins" who worked to ease tensions between the two superpowers" (Gecelovsky 78).

Apart from the positional perspective, middle powers were also defined using a behavioural approach, which examined the style of the country's foreign policy. Typical international behaviour of a middle power, according to these criteria, was "maintaining a peaceful and stable international system through participation in efforts to manage and resolve conflicts when problems arise" (Gecelovsky 78). Hynek adds that "the behaviour of middle power is driven by role conception resting on the notion of a distinctive mode of statecraft, i.e. good international citizenship, multilateralism, coalition building and mediation" (36). In the Cold War era, that meant that middle powers needed to adopt a role of – as Nossal calls it – "an interlocutor between East and West" or a country that would "mitigate political tensions" (*The Politics* 57). This, however, required from middle powers skills in diplomacy and expertise in negotiations and compromise-building. With such capabilities, middle powers tried to mark their presence and provide a good example, or even leadership, in those niches or issue areas of international relations that could not be dominated by superpowers, e.g. in mediating in international conflicts or in peacekeeping initiatives etc. "Middle power," thus, was not only a term defining the state's place in an international hierarchy, but "became descriptive, connoting a particular state role in the international community" (Chapnick, "The Canadian" 195). A middle power thus meant being a functional and effective power – being a player in global affairs that was "capable of exerting influence in the international community based on its ability and capacity to contribute to an international issue that had relevance to contemporary affairs" (Chapnick, "The Canadian" 205).

Middlepowership, though defined by a specific style in foreign policy, as outlined above, should not, however, be confused with political neutrality. Canada, for instance, though often regarded as a typical example of a middle power, in fact never acted as an impartial mediator between the two hostile blocs during the Cold War. The country was an integral part of the Western bloc and directed its diplomatic efforts to promote the so-called Western values: free market economy, liberal democracy, human rights, civil liberties, and opposed the expansion of communism. Nonetheless, Canadian policies towards the Eastern bloc countries seemed to be less emotional and more conciliatory than those pursued by the Americans or the British. On many occasions, including the Korean War, the Suez Crisis, and in Vietnam, Canadian diplomats tried to impede Washington's or London's radical political moves and "to restrain both American fits of nuclear imprudence and conventionally armed zeal" (Ross 350-354; Nossal, *The Politics* 58). Often to no avail, though.

Apart from positional and behavioural classifications, geographical criteria were also used to define middle powers. A middle power, in this case, was a state "in the middle – geographically located between adversarial powers" (Nossal, *The Politics* 57).

The concept of middlepowership was, however, much more complex than the above characteristics suggest. For decades, it was widely discussed in Canada by political experts; many politicians, scholars and media embraced "middle power" as a label with which they described Canada's international position and its foreign policy. "Middle power" became the identifier of the Canadian approach to international affairs. Obviously, with new political issues and problems arising, the very concept of the middlepowership evolved throughout the Cold War. In their respective articles, Adam Chapnick and Nikola Hynek present an overview of how the definition of "middle power" developed and changed in Canada and beyond. They quote numerous academic experts and political activists participating in the discourse over the middle-power concept. The table below presents only a simplified and outlined version of the ideas that Chapnick ("The Canadian" 193-205) and Hynek (34-38) refer to in their respective publications.

NAME	DEFINITION OF A "MIDDLE POWER"	YEAR
David Mittany	In general, there are only small and great powers, but some small powers can be greater than other small powers.	1933
Hume Wrong, William Lyon Mackenzie King	Contribution to international affairs and active involvement in global issues (in this case, war sacrifice) should elevate a country's position in international structures.	1942-1944
Lionel Gelber	Middle powers have greater functions to play internationally than small powers (though cannot be equal to great powers), and thus should have a stronger voice in international organizations.	1945
G.P. de T. Glazebrook	A middle power is a country that claims to be greater than a small power, but not as great as a great power.	1947
Louis St-Laurent	Middle-power status in Canada's case meant that Canada was not going to be British or American or anyone's satellite, but a country that would make its choices and decisions objectively, in the interest of its own citizens and for the betterment of the international community.	1948
R.G. Riddell	A middle power is a state with a sufficient size, stability and material resources, willing to accept international responsibilities.	1948
Edgar McInnis	Unlike a small power, a middle power is able to act independently – in cooperation with other middle powers – to pursue its international interests and obligations and have its ideas accepted by other states.	1960
Lester Pearson	A middle power is a country with limited influence, but is able to have international impact through peacekeeping, promoting multilateralism, mediations.	1965
John Holmes	A middle power is a state with a position which allows it to initiate and lead international actions, such as peacekeeping. Because of its weaknesses, Canada will never be recognized as a global power. Middle-power status is, however, more practical from the Canadian perspective – paradoxically, it gives Canada more freedom in such areas of international affairs as peacekeeping or conflict-resolving than is enjoyed by major powers, which are perceived as more biased than middle powers.	1966, 1984
David Vital	There are only small and great powers. A middle power is, in fact, a small power with specific international roles.	1967
R.A. Mackay	A middle power is a state which is able to promote its vision against the visions of others.	1969

NAME	DEFINITION OF A "MIDDLE POWER"	YEAR
Robert Keohane	Unlike great or secondary powers, middle powers can influence international affairs only through international organizations.	1969
Carsten Holbraad	Middle powers promote international balance, mediation, cultural understanding, and have sufficient economies and populations. There are, however, upper, middle, and lower middle powers. On the basis of economic, military, and demographic strength, Holbraad identified eighteen middle powers.	1971, 1984
Annette Baker Fox	The position of the U.S., a global superpower, should be a point of reference in the assessment of the international position of a country. From this perspective, Canada (a middle power) weighs less than Britain or Japan (secondary powers).	1977
Martin Wight	A middle power is a state that has insufficient military strength and resources to hope to win a war against a great power, but is strong enough to prevent superpowers from attacking it as the costs of such a war would be too high for a great power.	1978
Bernard Wood	Middle powers are states that are regional and functional leaders, and moral and conflict-stabilizing powers.	1988
Robert T. Cox	Middle powers abstain from being involved in major conflicts, promote stability and involvement in world affairs.	1989
Laura Neack	Middle powers are secondary powers of a specific sort – their major goal is to maintain and promote world order. Still, they choose to follow great powers with which they share values and interests.	1993, 2003
Andrew F. Cooper, Richard A. Higgott, Kim R. Nossal	Not ignoring the economic position of a country, middle-power status is most of all reflected in the effectiveness of diplomacy and the behaviour of a state, which works for the promotion of multilateral solutions, compromises, and world order and peace. Middle powers are concentrated only on and, in fact, can be influential and successful only in certain areas at a specific time. They cease to serve as middle powers when their influence diminishes. Middle-power status – unlike great-power and secondary-power status – cannot be taken for granted. Some middle powers, Canada included, tend to perceive themselves as more important internationally than they really are.	1993, 1997

NAME	DEFINITION OF A "MIDDLE POWER"	YEAR
Louis Bélanger, Gordon Mace	Middle powers are not only moral guides, constraining radical moves of others, but they are also ready to act (not merely speak) for the improvement of global relations.	1997
Denis Stairs	Canada means more globally than small powers and less than great powers, but "middle power" is a vague term when it relates to international behaviour. Any country can promote peace and multilateralism, even a small power. Therefore, if the country is not one of the great powers, it can only have a temporary influence only on some spheres of international relations.	1998
Lloyd Axworthy, Sarah Taylor	Middle power is a country that is not a permanent member of the U.N. Security Council, but takes a particular interest in conflict management and in being a leader in promoting human standards and security, peace, order, rule of law. Middle power – using its hard and soft power – is ready to act whenever and wherever human lives and rights are at risk.	1999

No matter which theoretical model was applied to describe what a middle power was, Canada – like no other country – seemed to fulfil the criteria of middlepowership. On the one hand, with the abundance of its natural resources, it was much more than a small power, but on the other, the size of its population and economy left it short of a major-power status. The values Canada spoke for internationally during the Cold War – multilateralism, compromise-making, peacekeeping, human rights, democracy, foreign aid spending – also seemed to justify Canada's claim to be recognized as a middle power. Last but not least, being "sandwiched between the Soviet Union and the United States," Canada was geographically located in the middle of the antagonistic powers (Nossal, *The Politics* 57).

Most of all, however, for almost the entire second half of the 20th century, Canada tried to construct its middle-power identity on the conduct of its foreign policy and justify its middle-power status by its behaviour and the roles performed in the international system. Canadian diplomacy had successes as a stabilizer and legitimizer of the global order. Typical of middle powers, Canada also proved its capabilities to find niches in international relations where it was a very skillful, sometimes even a dominant actor. In actuality, there are a number of areas that can be easily singled out as the ones in which Canada prevailed, or at least played high, after the Second World War.

First and foremost, Ottawa was very actively involved in the creation of the postwar international organizations. Canadians, for instance, played an important role in the establishment of the postwar Commonwealth of Nations. A crucial document that laid the foundations for the modern structure of the Commonwealth, the *London Declaration* of 1949, was adopted as a result of Canadian mediations. It contained a compromise formula, which has survived to this day. It created a mechanism of moving away from the colonial status and monarchical government to independence without breaking ties with the Commonwealth (Welsh 158). Using that mechanism, a great majority of British colonies, after being granted independence, adopted the republican system of government and abolished monarchical connections to Britain, but remained the members of the Commonwealth (Doxey 35-36). On the forum of the Commonwealth, Canada also proved to be a vocal opponent of the racist and undemocratic policies of some of the Commonwealth member states, South Africa in particular. In 1961, for instance, Canadian Prime Minister John Diefenbaker, declaring racial equality as a core principle of the Commonwealth, was in fact the only white leader who opposed the re-admission of South Africa to the Commonwealth because of South Africa's apartheid policies. The result was that South Africa withdrew its membership bid ("Peace and Security" 15). Under the Brian Mulroney government, Canada became an international leader of the anti-apartheid movement, pressing the case for Nelson Mandela's liberation (Mulroney, "Canada"). Mulroney's personal "crusade," which included battles with Western leaders, putting Mandela's case on the G7 and U.N. General Assembly's agendas succeeded in freeing the South African leader from jail in 1990. Mandela paid a tribute to the people of Canada during his speech in the Parliament in Ottawa, and singled out Brian Mulroney "for his willingness to break with his allies, U.S. president Ronald Reagan and British prime minister Margaret Thatcher, over the question of South Africa" (Freeman). In 1985, at the insistence of the Mulroney government, the Commonwealth adopted economic sanctions against South Africa and threatened to cease diplomatic relations with Pretoria. Canada lifted its sanctions on South Africa only in 1993, after the apartheid had been abolished ("Canada and the United Nations" 18).

Canadian diplomats also played an important and constructive role in the establishment of the United Nations. Canada's enormous contribution to the Allied victory in the Second World War made Canadian politicians very assertive in their demands that Canada be a recognized member of the international community. As a result, Ottawa consistently opposed the marginalization of middle powers in post-war international organizations, protested against the domination of the superpowers in world politics, thus becoming one of the most audible spokesmen for multilateralism and middle powers' role in international affairs (Riddell-Dixon, "Canada at the United" 147).

For a country with a relatively small population and long colonial past, the list of Canada's achievements at the U.N. is robust and impressive. Canadian influences can be seen, among others, in the provisions of the Charter of the United Nations, a treaty upon which the U.N. was founded. Thanks to Canada, Articles 23 and 44 were included in the Charter. The former regulates the election of the ten non-permanent members to the U.N. Security Council, while the latter gives the right to all member states which are not represented in the Security Council and whose armed forces take part in the U.N. military missions "to participate in the decisions of the Security Council concerning the employment of contingents of that Member's armed forces" (United Nations, "Charter"). Both articles provide multilateral arrangements based on the principles of collective decision-making.

Arguably, Canada gained the reputation of a global player during the so-called "golden age of Canadian diplomacy," that is under the prime ministerships of Louis St-Laurent (1948-1957) and Lester B. Pearson (1963-1968). Undoubtedly, at that time Canadians could boast a number of international achievements. The constitution of the International Labour Organization was adopted in 1946 in Montreal (Schabas 145). Montreal was also chosen, in 1947, as the headquarters for another U.N. specialized agency – the International Civil Aviation Organization (Jackson and Jackson 540).

In 1948, the U.N. General Assembly adopted the Universal Declaration of Human Rights (UDHR), whose principal author was John P. Humphrey, a Canadian law professor. Today, the Edmonton-based John Humphrey Centre for Peace and Human Rights, established in 1998 to promote the principles enshrined in the UDHR, celebrates the UDHR as "quite possibly the most cited legal document ever drafted by a Canadian [which] has contributed to growing human rights paradigm since the end of the Second World War" (John Humphrey Centre for Peace and Human Rights).

In 1955, owing to the initiative of Paul Martin Sr., who chaired the Canadian U.N. delegation, the U.N. Security Council approved a package deal thanks to which membership in the U.N. greatly expanded. As a result, over the following decade the number of countries belonging to the organization more than doubled, making the U.N. a more credible and viable organization of a truly universal nature (Riddell-Dixon "Canada at the United" 148).

Canada has been elected six times to sit on the U.N. Security Council (Jackson and Jackson 540) and many prominent Canadians occupied important positions in the U.N. system. Lester B. Pearson served as President of the U.N. General Assembly in 1952-1953; Maurice Strong chaired the U.N. conferences on the human development and environment in 1972 and 1992; Louise Fréchette was appointed U.N. Deputy Secretary-General in 1998; Philippe Kirsch, from 2003 to 2009, held the post of the first President of the International Criminal Court, whose creation was largely a result of Canadian diplomatic efforts; Louise Arbour became the U.N. High Commissioner for Human Rights in 2004. In addition, Canadian diplomats were among the major drafters of the *Convention on the Rights of the Child*, adopted by the U.N. General Assembly in 1989. On the U.N. forum, as one Canadian author summarizes,

> [w]e were relentless in our pursuit of exceptional Canadian-driven initiatives: the international landmine treaty (or the Ottawa treaty), the International Criminal Court, the Kimberley Process (regulating the sale of blood diamonds) and the human security paradigm, to name some of the more dramatic examples (Berzins 7).

However, it was peacekeeping that became a major Canadian identifier internationally. After the Second World War it did not take long for Canada to be able to mobilize its army again and send troops to observation missions in Kashmir and the Middle East and to intervene in the Korean War. In actuality, Lester B. Pearson, alongside Sir B.N. Rau of India and Iran's Nasrollah Entezam, was one of the so-called "Three Wise Men" who proposed solutions to settle the conflict on the

Korean Peninsula (Gecelovsky 87). This increased the trust in Canadian diplomatic skills and enabled Canada to sit for almost two decades (1954-1973) in the International Commissions for Supervision and Control in Vietnam, Laos and Cambodia (Rhéaume 224).

What gave Pearson greatest international repute and eventually won him the Nobel Peace Prize in 1957 was his idea of the formation of a U.N.-led international peacekeeping force to prevent the escalation of the Suez Crisis. Consequently, the first United Nations Emergency Force (UNEF) was created, commanded by a Canadian General E.L.M. "Tommy" Burns (United Nations Association in Canada 3-5). The success of that mission (the conflict was resolved in November 1957) led to the institutionalization of the U.N. peacekeeping operations and "forever identified Canada with U.N. peacekeeping activities" ("Peace and Security" 13). The Suez Crisis, thus, created a myth of Lester B. Pearson as a founding father of modern peacekeeping and gave Canada the status of a peacekeeping nation, even if the solution to the crisis was in fact not reached singlehandedly by Canadian diplomats but rather was a result of a multinational diplomatic effort (Berzins 7).

Nonetheless, Canadians seemed to like the image of themselves as peacekeepers. Large parts of Canadian political elites, but also the public opinion, truly believed that – as Hugh Segal puts it – "international brokerage politics, with professional Canadian diplomats punching above our weight as a middle power in the world, is the most important instrument by which global peace might be sustained and secured" (331). Canadians thus readily embraced peacekeeping as a part of their national mythology and proud tradition, but also as their international responsibility. The Canadian involvement in peace operations after the Suez Crisis was outstanding. As a matter of fact, during the Cold War era, Canada was the only country to participate in all U.N. peacekeeping missions. From 1957 to 2006, the country deployed over 125,000 troops and personnel to over 50 missions, which constituted one tenth of the U.N. total (Dorn 7; United Nations Association in Canada 15-20). Some Canadian political leaders and military commanders gained international fame, becoming symbols of peacekeeping. The list includes, among others: Harry Angle, chief of the United Nations Military Observer Group in India and Pakistan in 1950 (Dorn 9); Prime Minister Pierre E. Trudeau, who in October 1983 launched his own initiative aiming to reduce nuclear weapons and tensions between the Eastern and Western bloc, for which he was awarded the Albert Einstein Peace Prize in 1984 ("Peace and Security" 15); Major General Lewis MacKenzie, commander in the United Nations Protection Force in Bosnia in 1992; or Roméo Dallaire, Force Commander of the U.N. peacekeeping force in Rwanda in 1993-1994 (Dorn 8).

Not only did Canada send their military, but also promoted certain values in peacekeeping forces, gender equality being one of them. In 1973, Canada was the first country to deploy women to the second United Nations Emergency Force in Egypt (Rudderham 373). Moreover, after the NATO intervention in Kosovo and genocide in Rwanda, the Canadian government created the International Commission on Intervention and State Sovereignty. In 2001, it released a special report "Responsibility to Protect" (R2P), which was later adopted as an official U.N. strategy, which is widely discussed in Chapter 3 (Schabas 152).

Last but not least, Canadians eagerly embraced peacekeeping on a national level, honouring and celebrating peacekeepers at home on a scale unknown in other countries. Peacekeeping symbols were included on the national currency; the National Peacekeepers' Day is observed annually on the 9th of August to commemorate the veterans of peacekeeping missions; special medals (including the Canadian Peacekeeping Service Medal) are awarded by the Canadian government to acknowledge the sacrifices of the peacekeeping services; the National Peacekeeping Monument was erected in Ottawa as a tribute to Canadian peacekeepers; one of the towers of the parliament buildings in Ottawa is named "the Peace Tower," and numerous other memorials, monuments, parks and streets named after peacekeepers have been created across Canada (Dorn 7-8). Moreover, in 1994, the Pearson Peacekeeping Centre was established – initially in Cornwallis, Nova Scotia, but later moved to Ottawa – to train military and civilian personnel in peace operations. Before it was closed in 2013, it had trained over 18,000 people from more than 150 countries (Rudderham 378-379; Peace Operations Training Institute).

In the area of peacekeeping, Canada seemed to behave like a typical middle power. It found a niche in international relations that could not be dominated by great powers and marked that niche with its own initiatives, ideas and policies, which, in effect, gained Canada better global recognition. Canada's motives for active engagement in peacekeeping during the Cold War are best summarized by A. Walter Dorn:

Whether the motive is idealistic or pragmatic (probably both), Canada seeks a place and some recognition in the wider world. Canada seeks to find a special role that great powers like the U.S. have difficulty filling. These powers did not participate in peacekeeping during the Cold War because they were deemed unable to act impartially, given their global involvement, ideological struggles, and intelligence activities. A middle power like Canada was seen as a better choice for the peacekeeper role, perhaps the ideal candidate, even though Canada was part of the NATO alliance (20).

Apart from the efforts to keep and build peace, Canada has also been identified internationally as a generous donor of foreign aid to poorer and less developed states. Initially, in the years directly following the Second World War, Canada's assistance went mainly to the European allies, supporting their postwar economic reconstruction and the liquidation of war damage. However, after the Chinese Communist Revolution of 1949, Canada's foreign aid started to be used as a tool in "the western alliance's crusade to contain communism" in Asia, Africa and Latin America (Riddell-Dixon, "Canada at the United" 153). Therefore, from that moment onwards, the main beneficiaries of Canadian aid programs were the Third World countries. Until late 1960s, Canadian assistance went primarily to Southeast Asian and Middle East countries allied with the West. To address the needs of those states, Canada, along with other Western countries, initiated the Colombo Plan in 1950, under which most of the subsidies were conveyed. A breakthrough came in 1968 with the establishment of the Canadian International Development Agency (CIDA), a government department with a large scope of autonomy and huge resources available, completely devoted to managing Canadian foreign aid. As a matter of fact, after the establishment of CIDA, Canadian spending on aid programs increased considerably; from 75 per cent up to 80 per cent of all Canada's foreign aid went through CIDA (Smillie 184).

Aid programs were designed to contribute to the economic and social advancement of the developing countries, to promote human rights, democratic development and gender equality, and to strengthen bilateral economic and political ties between Canada and the recipient countries. Owing to Canadian foreign aid, numerous programs for the relief of famine, poverty reduction, infrastructure upgrades, rural development, or improvement of health, agriculture, education were launched. As a matter of fact, few countries distributed their foreign aid on a scale comparable to that of Canada – in total, 155 countries benefitted from Canadian aid programs (Smillie 185-198). This proves that, on the one hand, Canada was financially and institutionally well prepared to serve as a donor country, and on the other hand, that Ottawa showed remarkable openness in its development assistance policies, helping countries that were ruled by both right-wing and left-wing governments. That was a feature that made Canada's foreign aid significantly different from the assistance programs offered by great powers, which – like the U.S. or Soviet aid programs, for instance – were much more ideologically and politically motivated.

Giving foreign aid was and until now remains an important foreign policy tool which enables Canada to build its international prestige, status, and exert its influence over global affairs. Even today, despite the fact that the structure of Canadian foreign aid programs has recently changed, Canada still remains one of the most active participants and biggest contributors to the budgets of organizations that group and/or help developing countries, including, among others: the Commonwealth, La Francophonie, the Organization of American States, the International Monetary Fund, the World Bank, the Inter-American Development Bank, the Food and Agriculture Organization. As Ian Smillie argues:

> The quality and size of the aid program determines Canada's place at the table in a variety of fora, not least within United Nations agencies, at the Organisation for Economic Co-operation and Development [...] and among international financial institutions. [...] And foreign aid has much to do with the prestige Canada seeks in its posture as a middle power and trusted broker at difficult times, and in difficult parts of the world (187).

Gaining recognition and prestige in international affairs had its costs for Canada, also the material ones, with foreign aid being one of these costs. As John Manley, Canadian foreign minister, told media in 2001, referring to Canada's involvement in the G8 forum: "You can't just sit at the G8 table and then, when the bill comes, go to the washroom. If you want to play a role in the world, even a small member of the G8, there's cost to doing that" (qtd. in Hart 320). In other words, being a part of the elite G8 club – now G7 – required Ottawa to adopt and present certain attitudes and values in international relations, including international responsibility, generosity and philanthropy. Therefore, according to some international relations observers, one of the factors that mobilized Canadian governments to provide such an extensive development assistance to so many developing countries was Canada's membership in the G7 or G8:

> Ministers tell themselves, and Canadians, [argues columnist Jeffrey Simpson] that we are a G8 country and thus must have a profile worthy of one. Scattering aid around the world is apparently what ministers think helps to fulfill that role. [...] [W]hen ministers travel abroad they like being able to point to Canadian aid projects just about everywhere they land (qtd. in Cohen 92).

Whether such were Ottawa's major motivations for launching aid programs or not, Canadian diplomats served as the main advocates lobbying to increase the financial support for the poor regions of the world, especially during the G7/G8 Summits (discussed in Chapter 3).

Analyzing Canadian involvement in the creation of the postwar international organizations, one cannot omit Canada's role in the establishment of the North Atlantic Treaty Organization. According to some historians, the very idea of the North Atlantic alliance was first proposed in September 1947 by Louis St-Laurent, Canada's foreign minister and soon-to-become prime minister. During his speech at the U.N. General Assembly he warned that had the international community failed to halt the Soviet expansion in Europe, Canada and some other U.N. members "may seek greater safety in an association of democratic and peace-loving states willing to accept more specific international obligations in return for greater measure of national security" (qtd. in Chapin 19). In fact, it was the United States, not Canada, that played a major role in the establishment of NATO, although the actual process was initiated by Canada and Britain, whose politicians and civil servants had been urging Washington diplomats "privately and confidentially, informally and tentatively" to form a military alliance of Western countries that could serve as a counterforce to the Soviet military and ideological threat (Reid 56). During the negotiations leading to the creation of NATO, Canadian diplomats – seeking a middle-power role for their country – advocated for an alliance operating within the most multilateral possible framework. An alliance based on multilateral security guarantees, as it was believed in Ottawa, could be an effective counterweight to the dominance of great powers, in particular it would put some restraints on the U.S. military domination over Canada. Canadian concerns from that period are best illustrated in the opinion expressed by Lester B. Pearson:

> [I]t would be far more difficult for Canada to collaborate in planning against Soviet aggression on the basis of a unilateral U.S. assurance than it would be if both countries were parties to an Atlantic agreement. Furthermore, under such an agreement the joint planning of the defence of North America fell into place as part of a larger whole and would diminish difficulties arising from fears of invasion on Canadian sovereignty by the U.S. (qtd. in Keating, *Canada* 86).

Therefore, Ottawa proposed a formula of wide cooperation that would go far beyond military matters and include also economic, social and cultural issues. As Jockel and Sokolsky wrote, "it was the Canadians more than anyone else who sought to transform the alliance at its inception into something more than just a defence pact" (321). These efforts were, at least partially, successful.

At the Canadian insistence, the Article 2, hence dubbed the "Canadian article," was incorporated in the final version of the *North Atlantic Treaty*; it summons the NATO member countries not only to cooperate militarily, but also to "eliminate conflict in their international economic policies and [...] encourage economic collaboration between any or all of them" and to work for the "strengthening [of] their free institutions" and "promoting conditions of stability and well-being" (North Atlantic Treaty Organization). However, during the Cold War, NATO operated most of all as a military alliance, which meant that the provisions of Article 2 were of little importance for NATO's practical functioning. Neither European members nor the United States were particularly interested in a non-military cooperation within NATO. After the fall of the Iron Curtain, NATO took a more active role as an organization promoting democracy and began taking more responsibility for peacekeeping; it was only then when Article 2 gained more significance (Gheciu 253). Canada, naturally, actively supported such new NATO engagements, sending one of the largest contingents on NATO "peace enforcement" missions to the Balkans, the Persian Gulf and Afghanistan (Zyla, "NATO" 31-34; Jockel and Sokolsky 329-331). Ottawa was also a vocal supporter of the aspirations of Central and Eastern European countries to join NATO, being in the 1990s NATO's fourth largest donor of foreign aid given by the Alliance to candidate countries (Zyla, "NATO" 357). While Canada has frequently been selective and fussy in its involvement in NATO's military actions and plans, and there have definitely been more gains than losses for Canada in NATO, some observers claim that "Canada did more for NATO than NATO did for Canada" (Zyla, "Years" 34).

***

The above characteristics are only an excerpt of Canadian involvement in the postwar international organizations. Canada's participation in a multitude of international fora – in actuality, one can find few other states engaged in a higher number of international organizations, agreements, and alliances – definitely helps Canada to further its multilateral agenda and goals, which is, naturally, a strong argument supporting Canada's middle-power status.

Moreover, Canadian international contributions and achievements, as presented above, might serve as proof that the status of a middle power can enhance a country's effectiveness in international relations. Today, Canada operates very effectively within the structures of international organizations. As a country that is abundant in energy and natural resources and is also a member of the G7, G20, NATO and NORAD, Canada has a significant influence on global affairs, far above its demographic or economic potential. On the other hand, Canada does not exercise hegemony in any field. It may inspire discussions, but rarely plays the role of the main actor or key participant. As one Canadian journalist wrote: "In the United Nations, we are Iceland with trees. In APEC, we are a panda among tigers. In the OECD, NATO, the World Trade Organization (WTO), OAS: Whatever the organization's acronym, Canada gets five minutes at the podium, polite applause and not much more" (qtd. in Potter 359). And at the same time it is unable to function as an equal partner in bilateral relations with Washington. Canada's dependence on trade with the United States rather excludes it from the club of major powers.

Out of the three theories characterizing Canada's position in world affairs, presented in this chapter, the middle-power concept provides the most complex description of Canada's international position. The table

Theory/ concept	Dependency/ satellite	Major/ foremost/ principal power	Middle power
Theoretical assumptions	Canada is permanently dependent on stronger partners: colonial subordination (France, UK) U.S. dominance	Canada is one of key world's powers (natural resources, energy potential, technology, builder of international system, quality of life, openness) excludes any idea of subordination	• medium size and potential (material capabilities) • "in the middle" (geography) • "middle ground" (diplomacy) • Finds a niche in international relations and dominates it
Historical background/ representatives	annexationist movement (Goldwin Smith) A.H. Malcolm	• the 1870s – Canada First • PM Wilfrid Laurier • the interwar period - O.D. Skelton • J.B. Brebner • J. Eayrs	• Giovanni Botero (1589) • L. Gelber, W.L. Mackenzie King • Louis St-Laurent • J. Granatstein, N. Hillmer, R. Bothwell
Political practice	dependence on trading with U.S., oil & gas, population, nominal GDP, U.S. military and cultural dominance	• international rankings • membership in G7/G8, G20 • outstanding role in creating postwar international organizations	Multilateralism; stabilizer and legitimizer of world order; progressive foreign policy agenda; soft power (prestige); niche diplomacy

Theory/ concept	Dependency/ satellite	Major/ foremost/ principal power	Middle power
Strong points	rightly exposes the dominating role of the U.S. in Canadian economy	emphasis on natural resource abundance, Canada as an active intl. player, open society, attractive to immigrants	exposes successes of Canadian postwar policies (international organizations, peacekeeping, mediation, democracy promotion, foreign aid, denuclearization)
Weak points	ignores Canada's international contribu-tion (U.N., NATO, G20, peacekeeping, human rights, denuclear-ization, foreign aid)	ignores limited potential (low population and nominal GDP; dependence on trade with U.S.)	Canada no longer "in the middle" of antagonizing powers; Canada no longer pursues middle power policies (peacekeeping, Israel, Kyoto)

below outlines the provisions of each of the theories, indicating both their strong and weak points.

As one may see in the table above, the middle-power theory does not provide an ideal model for defining Canada's role in world affairs. In fact, our opinion is that this model has lost its validity as a useful summary of Canadian present status in global politics in the light of the recent dynamic global changes. We feel that there is a need to redefine the position of Canada. The most suitable category that in these new geopolitical circumstances, in our opinion, Canada falls into is a selective power.

2. Canada as a selective power

While all the theories presented in the previous chapter are important as they seek answers to crucial and now particularly relevant questions about how to describe and evaluate international roles Canada has played and can play in the future global politics, all of these conceptions were created or gained popularity during or even before the Cold War. As such they seem to be rather outdated, because they do not take the new determinants of the place and the status of states in the modern system of global relations into full account. The current international position of countries is less determined by military factors (strong, technologically advanced army, level of military expenditures etc.) and more by economic and material determinants (economic stability, balance of trade, raw material and energy security, economic growth, technological advancement) as well as by immaterial factors (power of persuasion and soft power, cultural diplomacy, reputation in the international arena, respect for human rights, intellectual contribution to shaping the legal framework of international institutions).

Also, new players emerged in global politics after the fall of the bipolar model. The role of the states that aspire to the position of global powers, such as China, or regional powers, such as Germany, is increasing. The influence of international and non-governmental organizations on world politics is also growing. Furthermore, as a result of global warming new challenges and problems must be faced – the rivalry in the Arctic, the development of renewable energy sources and environmentally sustainable exploitation of fossil fuels. Most of these problems involve Canada directly. Moreover, Canadian foreign policy makers must carefully consider the dynamics of the activities of other international actors before drafting guidelines and strategies of Canadian foreign policy.

Given those new determinants, even the theory that appears to be most relevant and adequate – i.e. the middle-power concept – seems to be obsolete and, in our opinion, has lost its relevancy as a useful tool for defining and explaining Canada's international position. We have two arguments to support our claim.

Firstly, the term "middle power," as already mentioned, was interpreted not only as a country of a medium-rank power or potential, whose foreign policy had a specific style, based on mediation, negotiations, and seeking compromise. It also referred to countries with specific geographical locations, physically situated "in the middle" of potential conflicts, between two antagonistic superpowers. Canada was one of the few countries that represented all of the above features, including the location in the geographical middle between the United States and the Soviet Union. That feature has now obviously been lost after the fall of the Iron Curtain. Naturally, Canada is engaged in the rivalry in the Arctic, but this has little in common with the past Cold War conflicts which were far tenser and more global. Thus, in this regard, Canada – in our opinion – has ceased to serve as a middle power.

Secondly, there are doubts if Canada still pursues – or ever pursued – middle-power policies. Such doubts and debates over Canada's middle-power status were given rise to by Stephen Harper's prime ministership (2006-2015) and his foreign policy doctrine. The critics of Harper's conduct of external affairs stressed that under his government Canada departed from what had previously defined its international identity and middle-power status – that the country significantly limited its involvement in the U.N. peacekeeping missions and in tackling climate change (Canada withdrew from the Kyoto Protocol), and that the image of Canada as an impartial observer and balanced mediator suffered, among other things, due to Ottawa's unequivocal support for Israel in the Middle East conflict. All those shifts in Canada's foreign policy strategy resulted in Canada's losing its uniqueness and impact on world affairs and because of that for Canada, as Christopher Berzins suggests, the term "middle power" simply means being average, mediocre, unexceptional, unoriginal (7). While we agree that under Harper Canada moved away from what is considered a typical middle-power behaviour, we also think that it is not only Harper's legacy, or fault, that Canada has drifted away from the ideals of middlepowership. In actuality, long before Harper, Canada had conducted policies compromising its lasting reputation as a middle power. Also, the policies of Justin Trudeau's current government in many aspects are very distant from an ideal of a middle power; they are highly selective and calculated, though this fact is often veiled by the smart rhetoric (Harper's and Trudeau's policies are discussed in detail in the following chapters). Therefore, in our opinion, a middle power theory cannot uncritically serve as a precise description of Canada's global position and role.

In fact, a problem with all the three theories presented in the previous chapter is that all of them seem to present only a fragmented image of Canada's international activity. Obviously, many scholars have dealt with the deficiencies of the above three theories and proposed their own approaches. Among them, Patrick Lennox's observations are particularly close to our perception. We tend to agree with his opinion that the hierarchy of power in North America – i.e. the dependence of Canada on the United States – puts pressure on Ottawa to "pursue an array of specialized roles abroad" (Lennox 1). Therefore, Lennox categorizes Canada as a "specialized power" – a country best inclined to act in areas or niches which are "unsuited to great powers" but necessary to keep the smoothness of the "status quo international system." He accurately observes in his theory that for a country like Canada "dependency on another sovereign [the U.S.] for its physical and economic security" is a virtue as it gives Ottawa the economic and military stability and thus the opportunity to consolidate its soft power and channel its resources to the non-hard-power spheres, such as "education, or health care, or infrastructure" (Lennox 8). These spheres can serve as the areas of the country's international specialization, which includes the performance of soft-power roles that lead to the construction of the country's "recognizable and distinct international identity." In Canada's case, as Lennox rightly suggests, these can be "mediation/supervision, interlocution, problem solving, advocacy, and intelligence gathering" (Lennox 9).

Lennox also correctly notices that there are important domestic constraints that restrict the country's freedom of international behaviour. There are societal limitations among them, which include, for example, dominant ideas about a country's place in the world as seen by its society. In Canada's case these would be, for instance, openness to immigrants and refugees, peacekeeping, development assistance, protection of human rights and freedoms, promotion of free and fair trade. As Lennox argues, these societal expectations, "on the one hand, […] limit what the state can and cannot do in the external sphere with the broad-based support of its population. On the other hand, they suggest what the state ought to do when presented with certain opportunities of perceived obligations to engage in world affairs" (Lennox 9-10).

Still, we regard Lennox's understanding of a "specialized power" as only a slightly modified version of a middle power concept. His theory seems to revolve around the same premises as the middle-power approach. Canada continues to be seen mostly as an unbiased interlocutor or an honest broker and compromise builder. His concept appears to ignore the fact that Canada in its international conduct, apart from presenting altruistic behaviour, may also act purely egoistically and highly selectively. Also, there are certain roles that Canada can never fulfil because of its limited potential and geopolitical location – not only will it never be a global superpower, but – being a neighbour of the U.S. – even a regional power. Nonetheless, some roles typically assigned to superpowers are within Canada's capacity. These are not only soft-power roles. For instance, in the case of natural resources and energy security Ottawa can be a first league global player.

Moreover, unlike Lennox, we do not see Canada's roles and positions taken by its leaders after the Cold War as imposed decisions resulting only from an inferior position to the United States. We rather see them as conscious moves, taken under specific conditions, which policymakers have taken into Canada's best interests. Naturally, friendly and stable bilateral relations with the U.S. constitute the key determinant of Canada's foreign policy goals. However, what Lennox seems to overemphasize is that Canada's role in the world "is structurally conditioned and impelled by its place at home in North America" (Lennox 14). While, obviously, Canada's international performance is largely dependent on how it is seen in Washington, there are other crucial factors that define Canada's foreign policy.

From a historical perspective, the U.S. impact on global affairs, including on Canada's international actions, has decreased. But Canada's role in American global leadership has become more important. For example, Canada's participation in the numerous U.S.-led military interventions – in the Gulf War, the Balkans, Afghanistan, Libya – apart from providing crucial assistance, to some extent also legitimized American policies. As neo-realists, such as John Kirton, rightly suggest, Canada's decision to contribute was interest-based, made voluntarily ("The Harper"), and was neither imposed on Canadians by their subordinate position to the U.S. nor had anything to do with Canada's seemingly mediatory roles "unsuited to great powers" as Lennox would suggest (Lennox 1).

Lennox's model appears to be based on excessively deterministic assumptions. In his theory, he implies that Canada in its specialized behaviour on the international stage must exploit niches and assume roles that cannot be assumed by the U.S. Otherwise, he suggests, Canada would be reduced to a "northern extension" of the U.S., concentrated on trade, border, and security issues, but lacking a distinct identity both internally and abroad. While having its own specialized capacity in international relations, distinct from the U.S., can be very helpful in building Canada's identity abroad, the past and present political practices have shown that Canada may as well act in the same areas as Americans, such as international trade, energy policies, military interventions, without losing its own status. Furthermore, the Canadian identity is not as fragile as it was a few decades ago. Canadians are more self-confident participants of world affairs, aware – and often proud – of their country's position, achievements and contributions to the international community. Canada's international identity is thus less and less founded on being distinct from America, but rather on providing global leadership in certain areas, which may or may not be in line with the current American agenda. We argue that Ottawa selects the fields and the scope of its international involvements mostly on the basis of its economic interests, cost-effectiveness and efficiency.

In light of the recent dynamic global changes, we feel that there is a need to redefine the position of Canada. The most suitable category that, in our opinion, Canada falls into in these new geopolitical circumstances, is a selective power. In our understanding, a selective power is a country that is capable of global actions in selected and limited areas of its external relations and this capability is acknowledged and recognized by other international actors. A selective power, as we define it, unlike universal, principal or "top tier" powers, does not possess sufficient potential to impact global issues in all areas. Thus, a state that fits our concept cannot aspire to the highest rank of powers due to the limitations of its political, economic, military or other capabilities. However, in a particular field or area, a selective power plays a leadership role and stands out from other countries.

In this sense, our selective power theory is inspired by neo-realist ideas of a foremost or prominent power, as presented, among others, by John Kirton. According to these concepts, a state that ranks as a foremost power is less limited by classic external and "relative capability-grounded constraints." It is able to achieve goals that correspond more with governmental and societal choices (Kirton, "Vulnerable" 134). This is due to the fact that major powers "have the surplus capability to choose to do in their foreign policy what their government and society determine back home, rather than what the system requires abroad" (Kirton, "Vulnerable" 135). Our selective power concept is also connected with the way a state uses its leadership. Selective powers, in our view, are able to choose the fields of their international involvement, they choose them consciously and their premeditated choice is conditioned by a particular geopolitical situation and by the possible profits – economic, social, or of other types, such as improving the country's image and international posture – the country can make by certain actions or inactions. In other words, a selective power can be characterized as a state which has a globally recognized power status in at least one or more areas, for example in the production of energy, that are relatively important for a large part of the international system at a given time period.

In some aspects of their international behaviours, selective powers can be confused with middle powers. The latter would also concentrate their "resources in specific areas" (Cooper 1-24) or focus their international engagement on a "single issue or theme" (Blencowe). A difference between the two categories of power, however, lies firstly in the fact that a selective power is already leading or is on the verge of becoming a leader in the particular area of global relations. A selective power not only constantly emphasizes where its policies are headed in that area and tries to remain a leading player within the field, but also chooses its role much more precisely and from a narrower selection of issues. Selective powers would thus make their particular external policies conditional on the sphere in which they are leading. On the other hand, they would deliberately limit the number of areas of their activities to save their resources. Decisions would be primarily based on the calculations of profits and losses. Policy makers would thus constantly check which poles of activity are beneficial and which "generate" an excessive burden. Those which would be assessed, at a given time, as too costly, would be immediately and unscrupulously given up, even if the international community would not sympathize with such moves. In other words, selective powers use their leadership much more pragmatically and realistically than middle powers. The key elements of their international policies are high efficiency and selectiveness.

Therefore, the key difference between a selective power and a middle power using niche diplomacy or "functional specialization," as Denis Stairs puts it, lies in the attitude. Middle powers favour a mission-oriented style of diplomacy, while selective powers affirm a self-centred, objective-oriented approach, which runs contrary to the traditional mindset of foreign policy observers who assume that foreign policies of middle powers are supposed to be guided by less selfish motives. By contrast, under the selective power framework, the very nature of the "selection" process leads to more selfish choices. This attitude, combined with a more self-orientated vision, makes politicians very flexible in terms of engagements, adjustments, or even withdrawals from foreign policy projects and traditional roles after negative cost assessments. In general, a pragmatic profit-based approach prevails over grand idealistic visions. To that end, a selective power would narrow down its active involvement to a small number of spheres where positive and expected outcomes could be reached relatively quickly. This does not mean that selective powers do not defend universal human values. They do that, but without overusing their resources. This means that they would be reluctant to engage in issues that entail a combination of high risks, high costs and low probability of a promptly achievable success.

In Canada's context, our selective power concept attempts to bring a sharper focus on the fact that Canadian foreign policy is primarily based on interests, less on untainted altruism or promotion of certain "Canadian values." We agree with Paul Chapin's and George Petrolekas' comment that many Canadian observers experience a difficulty in getting out of the rut of two traditional myths concerning Canadian foreign policy. The first one can be described, using Chapin's and Petrolekas' words, as a "pervasive mythology." According to it, Canada, "not being a former colonial power [...] had no interests, and its role in the world was exclusively to promote 'Canadian Values,' which were somehow to be preferred over the values of the other liberal democracies" (Chapin and Petrolekas 11).

This illusion, contributed to good feelings among Canadians and led to the belief that "Canada was an important, selfless, unique beacon of civilized understanding, and beloved by all." On the other end of the scale, although far less popular, was the second myth or "the pessimist/ pseudo-realist colonial view" that treated Canada as "a semi-autonomous bit player that had to slavishly follow in every respect the lead of the great power or powers with which it was allied" (Chapin and Petrolekas 11). Both these myths have affected negatively a thoughtful discourse about Canada's interplay between interest, goals and values and obstructed "even a modest consensus on a cohesive vision of its contemporary interests, let alone a grand strategy to further them" (Chapin and Petrolekas 11).

In our selective power framework, we wish to emphasize the fact which is often omitted in analyses, that Canadian foreign policy is mostly oriented on economic results. More generally speaking, a selective, economy-oriented approach is a constant element of Canadian foreign policy goal formulation, although the areas of interests and intensified activities changed over time. Since the end of the Second World War, Canada has been a primary promoter of neoliberal economy in international trade. An important part of Canadian international identity is built on the conviction, repeatedly expressed, for instance, by former Prime Minister Stephen Harper, that Canada is a trading nation (Conservative Party of Canada, "Harper Announces"). Canada's incumbent Prime Minister Justin Trudeau tends to use similar wording when he claims that "Canada's prosperity has always depended on trade with the world" ("The Last").

Canadian economic well-being is indeed substantially reliant on international trade. Hence Ottawa has long advocated, on both bilateral and multilateral levels, such as in the WTO and the General Agreement on Tariffs and Trade (GATT), for lifting economic barriers to trade. Few other countries are parts of as many bilateral and multilateral free trade agreements as Canada. The most evident example is the Canada-U.S. Free Trade Agreement of 1988, which was expanded to the North American Free Trade Agreement in 1994. Having secured the access to the most important American market, Canadian governments started to look elsewhere to promote trade and Canadian businesses. The result was signing a few dozen of free trade agreements (FTAs) and foreign investment promotion and protection agreements (FIPAs) with partners from around the world (Global Affairs Canada, "Trade"). This includes the Comprehensive Economy and Trade Agreement (CETA) between Canada and the European Union, which was signed in October 2016 and which is very likely to be provisionally applied by mid-2017. Should that happen, Canada will have free trade access to two world's largest economies – the United States and the EU.

Canada's focus on economic efficiency can also be noticed in the fact that Canada advances its economic interests in all possible spheres of its international activity. This, for example, includes development assistance. There is a growing link between Canada's trade interests and the foreign aid it offers. Such a business-like approach started under the Jean Chrétien government, was continued by Paul Martin, then mastered by Stephen Harper, and has not been changed by Justin Trudeau. Similar observations can be made about Canada's participation in the U.N. peacekeeping missions, its climate or immigration policies. In other words, concentration on the business side of foreign policy restricts Canada's engagement in what seems to be traditional Canadian foreign policy areas.

An economy-oriented foreign policy does not mean that Ottawa abstains from the promotion of what is called "Canadian values," which, among others, are – using Harper's words – "freedom, democracy, human rights and the rule of law" (Harper, "Text"). Ottawa constantly advocates for these values. However, their impact as variables in defining Canadian foreign policy seems to be lower than it is officially pronounced by Canadian policy makers. On the contrary, in the political rhetoric, economic issues are usually downplayed as factors shaping the nature of Canada's involvement with the world. We find Canadian foreign policy principled and values-based, nevertheless, those values are always promoted pragmatically and selectively, that is in a way that does not endanger Canadian economic interests or does not drain available resources. In fact, Canada's economic successes and well-being, in our opinion, provide background for the promotion of certain Canadian values internationally.

We are aware that such a perception of Canadian foreign policy can be seen by idealistically oriented observers of international relations as contravening Canada's Pearsonian tradition of the foreign policy, based primarily on values, while in fact, in our opinion, the effective conduct of external affairs is always a balance between egoistically defined economic or political interests and the advancement of universal values (Kissinger).

Admittedly, however, when economic resources allow it and Canada finds it beneficial, values promoted by Ottawa abroad are usually of a progressive nature and are relevant for the world. In other words, by performing calculations of gains and losses, Canada aims primarily to secure its own interests. But what Canada advocates internationally is usually in the best interest of the wider world as it touches important social issues, such as human rights, global health or the promotion of democratic standards and freedoms.

By presenting the selective power concept, we aim to avoid the flaws present in the debate on the Canadian position in global affairs. We neither intend to exaggerate Canada's international influence and accomplishments nor downplay Canada's global role. Our theory accepts the obvious fact that Canada has limited resources, that it is bordered by a superpower, and is not capable of doing all it desires on the world stage, as no country is. But at the same time, in Canada's case, the abundance of natural resources and their importance for the world economy or Canada's contribution to the creation of international organizations and the promotion of an open market economy, render Canada's role and position in the world much higher than that of a typical middle power.

For us, Canada rises to an emblematic example of a selective, issue-structured power. Its external policies have long been marked by a self-centered, highly selective and pragmatic approach. We do not see it as a phenomenon that started only with the Conservative Party's rise to power in 2006. It has existed since the 1990s, but on a rhetorical level it has often been covered by liberal internationalism and altruistic elements of foreign policy. Under Harper, however, this veil was removed and economic interests, profits and stability ranked openly as the top elements in the minds of the policy makers instead of more idealistically presented goals. The Harper government decided that Canada's image should be most of all that of a sound, stable and leading economy. Harper's deeply held philosophy of governing, based on limited government and low taxes, in foreign policy meant that only when a country was economically sound and stable it could make a difference in the international system. Additional functions, roles or positions Canada assumed could only be built on that basis. The Harper government praised the value of a balanced budget – actually treated it as a legitimate goal in foreign policy – and built Canada's international reputation, among the G8 countries and beyond, on the fact that Canada was one of the few highly developed countries whose economy went smoothly through the 2007-2008 financial crisis. Canada dropped its traditional soft power strategies and replaced them with a more selfish or self-centered approach, where profits, effectiveness and economic efficiency constituted the main driving force of foreign policy formulation. Different ingredients of Canada's new soft power proved to be effective, as only through its "power to attract" did Ottawa manage to draw other countries to start a stimulus program and put the deficit under control (Kliff). Canada also became more selective in many foreign policy areas – Ottawa, for instance, reduced the official list of the countries eligible for Canadian official development assistance and limited diplomatic representation abroad. Also, without much sentiment, in 2012, the funds for public diplomacy programs, such as support for Canadian Studies abroad, called "Understanding Canada," were cut entirely (Blanchfield, "Canada").

Additionally, the roles of an "honest broker," "consensus builder" and "peace maker," traditionally assigned to Canada – a country that generally tries to keep friendly relations with as many entities as possible – seemed to be treated by Harper as an obstacle or, at least, were no longer considered an asset. For the Conservative prime minister, they were perhaps excessively middle-powerly while a preferred image of Canada was that of a major power, at least in some areas, or a key country capable of making decisions that matter globally and are followed by international actors. Canada, which repositioned itself as a global player, was on the one hand more aggressive in the assertion of its strength and distinctiveness and, on the other hand, far less interested in unity or consensus for the sake of being seen as "a friendly country." When it was convinced about a goal, however, a selective and assertive Canada was capable of building international consensuses, as evident in the Maternal and Newborn Health Initiative. In asserting global leadership Harper was able to attract the G8 members, private foundations and even the U.N. as supporters of the idea of the reduction of infant mortality and the improvement of maternal health. As it occurred after the 2015 election, the Trudeau government promised to continue the program.

But, as was mentioned before, we see Harper as no big exception when it comes to Canada's highly selective, very pragmatic and economy-oriented approach to foreign affairs. His policies, harsh and blunt rhetoric excluded, were in many spheres not much different from the way Ottawa had pursued foreign policy since the end of the Cold

War. Canada's military expenditures, for instance, continued to be low under Harper, especially after the government withdrew from the most expensive promises in 2009, but were comparable with previous periods; participation in the U.N. peacekeeping missions was reduced, but it was a continuation of the trend that had started over a decade before Harper; also, Canada's spending on foreign aid during the Harper era was only slightly higher than before, under the Liberals. Overall, Canada's global engagement has decreased since the 1990s to the point when Canada has come to be dubbed "international free rider" due to budgetary cuts or shifts undertaken by both the Liberals and Conservatives.

The same can be said about Canada's climate change policies. Although Harper abandoned the Kyoto Protocol, his government adopted emissions targets, which were later kept by the Liberal government of Justin Trudeau. More importantly, Harper's conviction that a global climate change agreement must involve all major emitters (including China and the U.S.) was shared by Trudeau when he was negotiating the 2015 Paris Agreement. As a matter of fact, in many regards, the present government, led by Justin Trudeau, shows the same – one could call it Harper-style or hard-power – attitude when prioritizing its foreign policy goals and exercising political decisions and actions. Such a selective attitude, discussed in detail in Chapter 4, is evident in Trudeau's policies towards, among other things, peacekeeping, immigration and refugees, climate change, energy resources or economic relations in general (and free trade promotion, in particular). The major differences between Harper and Trudeau relate not to the overall foreign policy directions or decisions, but mostly to the tone or the narrative, usually much tougher and harsher under Harper, which accompanied Harper's particular decisions or actions and was mistakenly taken as the sign of completely new policies or even a revolution or a new era in Canadian foreign affairs.

Also, when analyzing Canada's attitude to international institutions and, broadly speaking, towards multilateralism, a very selective approach and, in fact, a gradual departure from Canada's traditional middle-power roles can be observed. In the middle power framework, internationalism and multilateralism were treated as instruments that leveraged the power of smaller states on the world stage. In Canada, during the Cold War, it was a commonly accepted axiom, beyond political divisions, that Canadian interests were buttressed by being a member of as many multilateral institutions as possible for a Western country. The situation has changed since then. In the international context, the role of multilateralism has waned. In the 21st century, we have observed that nations have increasingly focused on domestic and fiscal issues, and – to put it in more general terms – on "narrower solutions based wholly on national interests." The effect has led to the weakening of "the collegiality of leadership of earlier days which looked for broad common solutions to issues" (Petrolekas and de Kerckchove 18). The power, potency and, as a result, reputation of many global multilateral organizations have decreased, as seems to be the case with the United Nations. More resilience is shown by less multilateral and more elitist organizations, such as the G7, G20, NATO or OECD. This obviously impacts the conduct of Canada's its foreign policy.

In Ottawa, despite verbal declarations, some multilateral organizations are treated as not serving Canada's interests and image well, even harming them. Stephen Harper, for instance, indicated the fact that such organizations as the Commonwealth of Nations, La Francophonie, even the United Nations, in some aspects of their activities may be the antitheses of Canadian values – by elevating authoritarian regimes to equal standing with democratic states and by relativizing moral values. Another type of argumentation against multilateral fora is that they are usually institutions missing real power, composed of "talking heads," for whom discussing is more important than acting. Therefore, in general, a restraint towards some of the multilateral institutions in Canada is growing. Canada treats such institutions very selectively, channeling its resources and increasing its involvement in those fora that are perceived as effective, efficient and profitable at a particular period of time. In other words, Ottawa seems to go away from the conviction that it needs to be highly active at every possible multilateral institution and rather tends to concentrate on a limited number of international venues by making a deliberate, selective choice. For us, this strengthens Canada's features of a selective power.

An illustrative example can be Canada's decreasing interest in the International Criminal Court (ICC), which started long before the Harper's Conservatives took power. Although established with crucial Canadian support, Ottawa has limited its level of engagement in the ICC since the 2000s, preferring to leave leadership to others and "settling for a followership role, assisting the ICC with as little effort as possible and cashing in on the reputation it built up in earlier years" (Bernard Jr.).

On the other hand, selectiveness of engagement in multilateral fora can be observed in Canada's support for the elite clubs of global governance – the G8 (now the G7, as Putin's Russia was excluded in March 2014) and the G20. They serve as vehicles for direct dealings and, using Stephen Harper's words, for "the close co-operation of friends and like-minded allies" (qtd. in Campbell, "Stephen"), not for a quiet diplomacy tactic which had been preferred earlier. Canada has been heavily involved in diplomacy of both elite circles, frequently being at the forefront of international economic debates, especially after the 2008 financial crisis. The fact that Canada is a member of the G7 is, on the one hand, a matter of prestige for the country (and personally for Canadian prime ministers), but, on the other hand, helps to build personal relations with world leaders, offers a chance to have insider knowledge of the planned political moves of major international players. It also leverages Canada's influence in debates on the most important global economic and political issues. As Harper argued, Canada should be "at the table and drive discussion" only in the "real" assemblies (qtd. in Whyte).

We also think that it is important to examine the changing role of the U.S. in the shift of Canada's attitude towards multilateralism. In the Liberal tradition, multilateralism was seen as a strategy of counterbalancing U.S. power and augmenting Canada's influence as an active member of international institutions, but also as a tool of promotion of the global free market. However, even in the Liberal mindset, as Tom Keating observed in the early 1990s, there were also elements of a "selective" engagement with multilateral fora. Keating argued that Canadian foreign policy-makers had begun "to move in more elite circles," which led to a "difficult choice in the future between their desire to be part of the [global] elite and the need to protect the institutions and norms that the vast majority of nations must rely on" (Keating, *Canada* 248). Keating assigned this situation to the fact that after the end of the Cold War, Canada's priorities have been increasingly aligned with the U.S. ones. In the Harper strategy, multilateralism was a tool to advance primarily, if not only, Canada's own interest.

Another factor that enables Canada to adopt new global roles is the decreasing position of the U.S. in the world, which in effect diminishes the relative influence of the U.S. on Canada. Research conducted by complex neo-realists – John Kirton, among others – suggests that the relative power of the United States has declined, especially after 2001.

Although the U.S. still occupies the first place in various capabilities that are "critical to how world order unfolds," the combined impact of the terrorist attacks of 2001 and the financial crisis of 2007-2008 have reduced "self-confidence of America at home and reduced soft power abroad." Those elements, along with the system diffusion and growing connectivity, have made Washington more vulnerable than it was in the 1990s. Kirton argues that in this situation Canada has decided to fulfil the space left by "declining America" and "has chosen to compensate for the sake of the two countries and the world as a whole" ("Vulnerable" 134-37). What is important is that this decision has come as a result of understanding in Ottawa that Canada and the United States "share an increasingly common fate." In the first decade of the 21st century, for the first time, Canadian policymakers did not follow the old way of "anticipated reaction and adjustment in advance" to gain U.S. recognition and diplomatic capital "by supporting America abroad so that it can cash in the continental benefits at home." Instead, Canada started global leadership "ahead of, without or instead of America, in a wide array of cases led by the United Nations Convention on the Law of the Sea (UNCLOS), biodiversity, the International Criminal Court, Kosovo and the responsibility to protect." As Kirton argues, "Canada pursues a global order that is both constructed in its own image and takes care of a more vulnerable America as well" (Kirton, "Vulnerable" 134). Neo-realists see the proof of Canada's leadership in the fact that defining issues in Canadian foreign policy are less and less of North American, continental, and U.S.-oriented dimension, but are more often matters of a global nature, such as political and financial stability, free trade, sustainable development, tackling terrorism, promoting global peace and security, constructing a new order in the Arctic.

We agree that Canadian foreign policy is shaped by global issues to a greater extent, which allows Canada to play an increasingly important role in global affairs and gives Ottawa more options to choose from when it comes to the selection of the activity areas in international relations. In other words, it boosts Canada's position as a selective power. On the other hand, the neighbourhood with the United States has always been and will remain the single most important element restricting Canada's role and position on the world stage. Any international role Canada will ever adopt will have to take into account the need of maintaining friendly and stable bilateral relations with the U.S. Nonetheless, Canada independently defines its foreign policy objectives, not only taking into account the significance of the U.S., but, first and foremost, calculating its own global interests. Hence, Ottawa very selectively decides about the scope and nature of its involvement in U.S.-initiated military projects. When it is deemed to bring insufficient returns, Canada may refuse to participate or contribute, as was the case in Iraq in 2003. However, as the recent history proves, Ottawa, supporting the U.S.-led military missions, can also play a powerful role in shaping the world order by, for instance, serving as a key actor in the global war on terrorism, as it was in Afghanistan (2001-2014), and in interventions against human rights breakers (Libya in 2011) or international law violators (Iraq in 1991, the Balkans 1992-2004).

As scholars who specialize in Canada-related political matters, we discuss the concept of a selective power through the prism of Canadian foreign policy. The motivating factor that made us consider a new approach to define Canada's global position was Stephen Harper's ascension to power in 2006. In too many regards, the policies he adopted seemed to cut with the traditional ways Canada had behaved internationally. Looking closer and analyzing deeper, however, we have come to a conclusion that the Harper era was not as revolutionary in the history of Canadian external relations as it tends to be seen. For us this conclusion became more and more evident with the passage of time. Contrary to the common belief that under Trudeau Canada has returned to its traditional global roles, perceived as so much un-Harper-like, we see many similarities and continuing trends between the Harper and Trudeau governments when it comes to how certain elements of foreign policy are defined and exercised in practice, even if Trudeau's rhetoric is completely different. The two subsequent chapters present the practical conduct of Canadian foreign affairs under Stephen Harper and Justin Trudeau.

In actuality, we constructed the theory of a selective power because of Canada and for Canada (we think it describes better Canada's international roles than the concepts that were formulated heretofore, the middle power included). Yet, under certain circumstances and conditions, we see a potential for the application of the selective power concept in reference to other countries, namely those which do not hold positions of foremost global powers in a universal sense but still have capabilities of having a global impact or playing leadership roles in certain areas of international relations. They choose these areas consciously and with premeditation, on the basis of their own geopolitical, economic, social or otherwise-defined interests and profits. The leadership of selective powers can be manifested in various fields, relating either to hard or soft power areas. It can be observable in a country's specialization in research and development and technological innovations or in its crucial role for international security (because of its geopolitical location, intelligence expertise, or know-how), stability of natural resource supplies or for certain sectors of the international economy or trade. But the international position of a country can also be boosted by the effective promotion of its soft power, although it is difficult to imagine that soft power tools alone would suffice to elevate the country to a full-fledged selective power status. Nonetheless, such soft power elements as, for instance, a country's diplomatic traditions and achievements, its efficiency in managing human resources, the stability of its political, social and legal systems, international attractiveness of the values it promotes worldwide, popularity and positive reception and the impact of its culture may be important factors which improve the global status of this country. Our goal, however, as was mentioned above, is focused less on "universalizing" the concept of the selective power but more on analyzing it from the Canadian perspective. Still, there is ample room, we believe, for the expansion of the theory beyond Canada.

3. Canada as a selective power under Stephen Harper

There is little doubt that between 2006 – when Stephen Harper as the leader of the Conservative Party won the federal election for the first time – and 2015 – when he lost to Justin Trudeau's Liberal Party – Canadian foreign policy, and in consequence Canada's international image, experienced a period of transformation. The resulting shift is illustrated by how Canada has been depicted in the international press before and after the Harper era. In 2003, the *Economist* labeled Canada as "rather cool" ("Peace"). Such positive adjectives were used again by this influential British weekly no sooner than in 2016, when Canadians were proclaimed as "the last liberals" ("The Last"). In between, under Harper, Canada was rather described as "a free-rider" ("Strong") while her prime minister used to be called "a political predator" ("The Political").

Such opinions were compatible with a legion of voices coming from former prime ministers, ministers of foreign affairs, senior civil servants, defence and foreign policy specialists, and journalists from main Canadian media, published both in print and online. As an example, let us quote what Mark MacKinnon observed in a 2015 article for the *Globe and Mail*:

> Many abroad say that the very ring of the word "Canada" is different after nine years of Conservative governments that have chosen to fight hard for a handful of select causes – Israel, Ukraine, maternal health – while downsizing the country's engagement with the rest of the world. Embassies in places such as Iran, Cambodia, Bosnia-Herzegovina, and Zambia were closed, aid funding was slashed, foreign governments were deliberately offended ("Harper's").

Also, the majority of Canadians, as indicated by surveys conducted in 2012 and 2015, thought that under the Conservative government Canada's global reputation declined (Hannay) and generally one in two Canadians held an unfavourable opinion of the prime minister (Grenier).

It would be an oversimplification, however, to analyze Harper's foreign policy decisions either only through the prism of public opinion polls or merely from the perspective of differences with the previous governments. We think that it is rather useful to look for the elements of continuity. Obviously, Canadian foreign policy under Harper lacked many elements of bipartisanship, but the same can be said about all governments before Harper. The truth is that although Harper approached external affairs from a perspective that was fairly new in Canadian politics, at the same, in our view, he kept the foundations that had been introduced after the end of the Cold War to Canadian foreign policy by the previous prime ministers.

To analyze this duality, we propose to look at Harper's Canada beyond the traditional middle power perception and examine Canada's external activity through the prism of a selective power concept that was explained in the previous chapter. This perspective, in our opinion, may help demythologise some aspects of the Harper era. Two points are worth noting in this context. Firstly, the attitudes of Canadians to their country's international role and position have changed considerably in the recent decades. This assumption is supported by various polls, suggesting, for example, that Canadians are substantially (15 per cent) less likely to identify peacekeeping with Canada's "most positive contribution to the world" (Paris 289). A more inward-looking attitude of Canadians is also evident in the preference for trade over foreign aid or "military presence on the world stage" as foreign policy priorities (Hannay). Secondly, foreign policy was an area where Canadians seemed relatively comfortable with the positions the Harper government was taking. According to a 2014 Abacus Data poll, the prime minister enjoyed solid approval among Canadians for most of his main foreign policy positions. For example, 45 per cent of Canadians agreed with Harper's position on helping Ukraine or on the use of Canadian forces to fight terrorism in Iraq and Syria, against 27 and 32 per cent, respectively, who disagreed. Even in a controversial issue of the conflict between Israel and the Palestinians, 36 per cent of Canadians approved the government's policy while 33 per cent disapproved (Anderson and Coletto). In a 2015 poll, Stephen Harper was seen as the most trustworthy of the three leaders of main Canadian political parties – the Conservatives, the Liberals and the New Democratic Party (NDP) – on questions of international leadership (Hannay).

We are aware that our argument runs contrary to the most popular views of Harper's legacies, but we think that there is a need to reach beyond those traditional perceptions. Obviously, it is not our intention to claim that Stephen Harper's foreign policy did not diverge from Paul Martin's or Jean Chrétien's – it undoubtedly did. But we also want to pursue the undercurrents of Harper's policies, which often turn out to be more similar to the previous governments' actions than one had expected before. In our research, we also try to establish whether it was precisely under the Harper government that Canada radically changed its global policies or rather that the Conservatives embarked on a prepared ground and continued the trends that had started after the end of the Cold War. Examining the roots of Canada's current role and its position in international relations can be helpful in bringing a clearer picture of those issues.

Since the beginning of the 1990s, the goals and methods of Canadian foreign policy have shifted in essential ways. Canada no longer fits into the middle power concept, designed for the Cold War period. This is a result of changes in the international milieu that intensified after 1989. We identify four main shifts that influenced the transformation of Canada's role and position. The first one, and the most important, was the collapse of the Soviet Union and the subsequent end of the two-block world and the rise of the United States to the status of the sole superpower. The second element was the victory of the liberal market ideology and intensified globalization. The third component, which aggressively entered the foreign policy equation on September 11, 2001, was terrorism, which resulted in the rapid securitization of the U.S. policies and the fundamental change in military engagements of all Western countries. The fourth shift related to the financial crisis that started with the Lehman Brothers bankruptcy in 2008. The economic downturn forced Western countries to implement austerity policies, to reduce international commitments and to focus on domestic problems. In reaction to and, in some cases, in anticipation of those trends, Canada modified not only its foreign policy but also its "grand strategy." In the economy, it meant the embrace of the neoliberal market-oriented approach of easing the access to the U.S. and broadening other trade markets. In the security area, it resulted in the deepening of the cooperation with the U.S. and in the decisions to use military force in unstable regions of the world. In terms of the methods, the shifts in the international milieu led to the adoption of a "selective" attitude towards many multilateral fora, e.g. strengthening cooperation in the G7/G8, G20 and NATO at the expense of Canada's involvement in the U.N. Other visible diversions in Canadian foreign policy included, for example, the near depletion of peacekeeping forces or tying development assistance to possible benefits for business and the reduction of foreign aid spending. Some scholars, Jerome Klassen among them, argued that such an approach was in accordance "with the class interest of the new power bloc" and was "a logical expression of the internationalization of capital and recomposition of the power bloc around dominant class interests" (*Joining* 221). We disagree with a social-class element of Klassen's viewpoint. Nevertheless, we agree that Canada's international position and role is, to a large extent, delinked from a particular government or a particular political party. The core level of the Canadian foreign policy strategy is not much different, regardless of whether the Conservatives or the Liberals are in power – with safety and economic well-being of Canadians in a stable global system being at the forefront for all governments. However, at the same time, we argue that Harper's almost ten-year term as prime minister was a turning point in the transformation of Canada's position and role in the world. The Harper government, for various reasons, willingly dropped the last elements of a middle power-style foreign policy.

Many observers of Canadian foreign policy still have a problem grasping the driving idea that stood behind Harper's intention of positioning Canada as a "rising power" or an "emerging energy superpower" in the global economy, and the resulting shifts in Canadian foreign policy. For example, Ferry de Kerckhove, even though he accepts the sense of those shifts from an economic standpoint, argues that what was missing in Harper's strategy was "a correlation between these legitimate pursuits and an overarching foreign policy concept which would define Canada's role on the international stage and ensure consistency in terms of values and interests and in upholding international law" (de Kerckchove 43).

The Harper doctrine was sometimes summarized as "simpler, less nuanced, seen in black and white, good and evil terms, result-oriented, ruthlessly guided by Canada's self-interest, and reflective of core Conservative perceptions and values [...]" (Ibbitson, *Stephen* 340). There is a grain of truth in this statement, especially in the element of good versus evil that is perhaps the most discussed one, but there are also oversimplifications that, in our opinion, put the Harper doctrine in an artificial and untrue opposition to his predecessors and even the successor – Justin Trudeau.

The Harper government, as any other Canadian government, wanted to project Canadian values and interests in foreign policy as best as it could. Among them were the most basic fundamentals, such as sovereignty and independence, justice and democracy, peace, security and economic prosperity, but also a desire "to make a difference in the lives of people who are struggling to achieve what [...] Canadians have worked hard at and been fortunate in achieving" (Petrolekas and de Kerckchove 61). These fundamental objectives have not changed since the end of the Second World War. The Conservatives seemed assured, however, that in the first decade of the 21st century Canada's position and international roles had to be changed in order to sustain the country's prosperity, security and influence in the world. To reach this end, the country's global status could no longer be projected and summarized by the middle power theory. Thus, the previous liberal internationalist reservoir of methods used in foreign policy, according to the Conservative government, had to be altered. In some areas this included breaking with the past ways of international behaviour – through, for example, a more active but at the same time selfish international attitude – while in other parts only minor adjustments of priorities were introduced.

Firstly, the redefinition of Canada's international position and roles led to the concentration on a limited number of selected priorities, based on a cost-efficiency analysis. Such an approach, which was sometimes labelled as a "3-E approach" ("economy, efficiency, effectiveness"), was in accord with Harper's philosophy of governing, based on cutting taxes and on the concept of a limited government (Clark, "Canada"). According to this idea, foreign policy should be a sphere of economy- and outcome-oriented approach. Policy makers ought to always think whether their plans are cost-efficient and, at the same time, socially sustainable. Only economically sound and stable countries can make a difference in the international system.

The stability of Canada's economy was the basic element on which the Harper government wanted to build Canada's international position.

By exposing some other advantages of Canada, such as, for example, an open character of the economy, the abundance of natural resources – especially energy – a predictable, stable democratic political system and an educated, open and multicultural society, the Conservatives wanted to improve Canada's global image. As a predictable and democratic foremost provider of energy – an "emerging energy superpower" – Canada would contribute to global security. To pursue this strategy Ottawa needed to secure the freedom of trade and stand against protectionist sentiments. For Harper, economic protectionism was one of the most pressing dangers the world faced in the 21st century (Harper, "Prime Minister Harper"). Under Harper, Canada focused on the economy and, as a result, adopted a more self-centred and selective attitude that led to altruistic-motivated international endeavours. Those domains of Canada's external activity that had before been traditionally identified with liberal internationalism, such as active involvement in international fora, official development assistance, climate policy or peacekeeping operations, were now subjected to cold and rational calculations and economic gains.

According to the critics, this type of logic was equal to compromising Canada's reputation as a conciliator, a generous donor and an eco-friendly country, which in effect had a devastating impact on Canada's diplomacy and foreign aid policies. Stephen Harper was accused by former Prime Minister Joe Clark of being personally responsible for starving Canada's "diplomatic and development capacity" (Clark, "Canada"). Such a judgement is, however, doubtful. Firstly, because Canada's performance in terms of global engagement, defined by its foreign aid and military expenditures, had started to decrease long before Harper – in the mid-1990s. According to the research by Robert Greenhill and Megan McQuillan, it was under the Liberal governments of Jean Chrétien and Paul Martin that Canada significantly lowered its contribution towards defence and international aid and was even dubbed in 2000 an "international free rider" – a country that does not pay its share towards collective defence. Other figures also do not support Joe Clark's accusations. For example, under the Harper government the budget of the Department of Foreign Affairs and International Trade (DFAIT) grew by almost one third and Canada's support for multilateral institutions, such as the United Nations, increased by 73 per cent (Gilmore, "Has Harper"). Also, steering away from the middlepowermanship ideal had started long before the Harper government took power. Simple calculations seemed to stand behind that change – although global peace and prosperity had always been declared important goals, but when confronted with the objective of balancing a budget or increasing spending on spheres that were directly related to a domestic electorate, they were moved to further positions with slashed funding.

The second argument concerns Canada's reputation on the world stage. On the one hand, academics, the members of the opposition parties and civil servants warned that Canada's relative influence in the world either declined or was under threat and we started our research with a skeptical attitude to this assumption (Chase and McCarthy). Obviously, the withdrawal from the Kyoto Protocol or losing a bid for a seat in the United Nations Security Council in 2010 had an impact on how many Canadians perceived their own country and how Canada was seen internationally (Paris). On the other hand, many Canadians agreed with the line of reasoning presented by the Harper government which stipulated that the election process of non-permanent members to the U.N. Security Council (UNSC) was a "rotten lying bastards" phenomenon, as it was referred to by the Australian ambassador to the U.N. (Ibbitson and Slater), or that without China and the U.S. the Kyoto Protocol placed Canada at an economic disadvantage. Thus, neither the lost bid for the UNSC seat nor the withdrawal from Kyoto can be easily interpreted as Harper's total disregard for the entire liberal internationalist tradition.

We argue that the negative effect of Harper's policies on Canada's reputation was temporary. International rankings did not support the view that Canada's image substantially suffered in the period of 2005-2015 (Schönwälder; Gilmore,"Has Harper"). According to organizations that publish annual indexes of the reputations of countries, the Canadian position was solid. These included: the Anholt-GfK Nation Brands Index, the BBC GlobeScan Country Rankings Poll or the FutureBrand's Country Brand Index. Canada occupied a position of one of top three or top five most positively perceived countries in all of them (see more in Gilmore, "Has Harper"). Moreover, the 2007-2008 financial crisis can be seen as a soft-diplomacy success for Canada, as Canadian debt-to-GDP ratio and low unemployment made Harper an exemplary leader, who could "stand before the world as a paragon of sound political and economic management" (Ibbitson, *Stephen* 341). Ottawa pressured other countries to closely observe their banking systems, to start globally coordinated stimulus programs and to put deficits under control (S. Gordon). As a result, in the 2015 global ranking of soft power, Canada occupied a strong fifth position ("The Soft" 30). One should also not forget that, although Stephen Harper was never as popular around the world as Justin Trudeau is now, the Conservative government had also its moments of triumph in social media. For example, during the Russian invasion on Ukraine, Canada's NATO delegation posted a tweet with a map that was designed to help "confused" Russian soldiers refrain from wandering into Ukrainian territory (Tran).

It is also worth noting that, eventually, the Harper doctrine was effective in many aspects. The opposition parties usually agreed with the government's directions in foreign policy. The extension of the bombing of Libya was opposed by only one vote in the House of Commons. Some commentators saw it as an unusual achievement for Harper, "hard to imagine in any other western legislative body when deciding of involvement to war" (Stewart; see also "Staying"). For Prime Minister Harper, the ability to achieve results was not only one of the most important features of a leader, but also of a country. In 2011, during an interview with Peter Mansbridge, a CBC anchor, Harper praised his government strategy, saying "[…] in 2004 we were in the middle of the pack of advanced countries, today if you look at most economic indicators we are on the top" (Mansbridge). Defence Minister Jason Kenney added in the *Globe and Mail*: "I think Canada is more relevant, broadly speaking. I think we're on the right side of history" (Chase and McCarthy). The Conservative government had important arguments to support these claims, which included the stability of Canadian social relations as well as relative political predictability. Not only did Canada place second in terms of the largest number of cities in both the 2016 Economist Intelligence Unit's Global Liveability Ranking and the 2016 Mercer Quality of Living Survey, which rank cities according to the quality of life. Vancouver ranked as the only North American city in the top ten (Brinded; "The World's Most"). Canada also ranked first among the G8 countries in terms of demographic development (Statistics Canada, "Figure 1"). OECD reports indicated that Canadians topped the ranking with the highest percentage of the population with a higher education and were one of the world leaders in terms of expenditures on higher education (Organisation for Economic Cooperation and Development, *Education at a Glance 2016*; Table A1.4, Table B2.3). Also, Canada has so far been declared the world's leader in human development eight times and since the 2000s has rarely fallen out of the top ten (United Nations Development Programme; Woolley; Campbell, "Canada Falls"). Economic and educational opportunities offered by Canada, combined with an open and tolerant society, have been magnets attracting masses of new immigrants (Stastna).

This is of course not to defend every policy choice that Harper made as prime minister, but we argue that there is a need for a perspective that will set aside individual preference for a particular decision or attitude. Obviously, it is easier to assess Harper's legacy now that he lost power. We think, for example, that the fact that Stephen Harper managed to stabilize Canada's economy and diversify its trade relations has helped the country to stay away from the waves of populism that have been sweeping across the western part of the world. In our opinion, this element is underappreciated by many observers of Canadian foreign policy, as bitterly observed by David Frum: "[t]o dismiss [Harper's] record as creeping authoritarianism [...] is to reveal an appetite for grievance so ravenous that it will swallow anything and pronounce it a meal." Thus, it should be emphasised that only *some* of the Harper government's choices can be explained by Harper's ideological background or his personal dislike for liberal internationalism. The most important decisions, in areas such as trade, energy, security or even, to some extent, the engagement in international organizations, were conditioned on the hard reality of the first decade of the 21st century, when Canada had to limit its spheres of engagement and concentrate on those fields that deemed to be essential and encompassed the major probabilities of success.

At the same time, it cannot be said that the Harper government always pursued a simple mercantilist policy. Canada generally uses trade – "the lifeblood of the Canadian economy" – as one of the key tools in its foreign policy. As Derek Burney suggested, trade is "the one on which [Canada's] scope for influence is actually commensurate with [its] strengths, hence our relevance and our leverage" (qtd. in "Six Diplomats"). Under Harper, Canada tried to use this leverage to make a difference in the "lives of others," promoting widely Canadian values. Obviously, these values can be defined and accentuated in many ways, depending on the government or time period.

Liberal Minister of Foreign Affairs Lloyd Axworthy (1996-2000) had defined Canada as a "valued-added nation in the international system" – a country that could serve as a model for the world's less fortunate peoples. His vision of Canada was based on the new understanding of the notion of principle in world affairs. The new meaning emphasized collaborative leadership in the defence of the weak to forge "a broad consensus to break great-power-inspired diplomatic logjams" (Chapnick, "A Diplomatic" 151). On the other hand, Harper's vision also emphasized values and principles, except that Harper was far less interested in achieving unity or consensus. Canada, repositioned as a global player, was more aggressive in the assertion of its strength and distinctiveness.

But it is important to notice that despite replacing Canada's traditional honest-broker role with a more assertive stand that played down traditional multilateralism, the Conservative government still managed to successfully promote the Maternal and Newborn Health Initiative (so-called the Muskoka Initiative). And it was not treated by Harper as an altruistic exception, but rather as a key initiative in his global leadership project. This project emerged during the 2010 G8 meeting held in Huntsville, Ontario, where the Canadian prime minister advocated for the reduction of child mortality and the improvement of maternal health ("Muskoka"). Harper's lobbying did not stop after the 2010 summit. Ottawa pushed the ideas at every possible venue, including the U.N. – Stephen Harper, for that matter, co-chaired with Tanzanian President Jakaya Kikwete the U.N. Commission on Information and Accountability for Women's and Children's Health. In 2014, he also hosted the *Saving Every Woman, Every Child* global health summit in Toronto, and constantly argued for stronger public accountability and greater transparency at other various multilateral meetings (Robertson 108). It proved successful – the Muskoka Initiative attracted significant financial contributions (CAD 7.3 billion) from other governments, the private sector and foundations (Do; Payton, "Baird"). The OECD praised the commission as a model for "effective international cooperation" and a "concrete example of [...] putting people and results at the core, addressing accountability and transparency, bringing coherence to country-led priorities" (Organisation for Economic Cooperation and Development, "Canada" 17). As a result, since 2010, according to Aniket Bhushan's research, Canada has served as one of the leaders in transparency (Do).

The most controversial part of the Muskoka Initiative was lack of funds for abortion services. In fact, only 1.4 per cent of Canada's money went to birth control (Payton, "Canada's"). This trend was reversed by the Trudeau government in 2016, when Canada pledged CAD 5 million specifically to the United Nations Population Fund for contraceptive supplies ("Liberals Commit"). Apart from that, the Trudeau government kept its promise to continue the program along the lines that had been adopted when Harper was in power (Connolly, "Liberals").

As already mentioned, since the end of the Cold War, Canada's foreign relations have increasingly turned toward economic aspects. This was best manifested by Jean Chrétien's preoccupation with tackling Canada's growing deficits and improving the country's stagnated economy. During his term of office, budgetary restraints, benefits from the free-trade agreement with the United States and the booming prices of energy and commodities helped to put consistent surpluses both in Canada's federal budgets and in its trade and current accounts. Rising energy prices accelerated Canadian vast energy investments, including the Hibernia development off Newfoundland's coast, or massive developments of oil sands in northern Alberta. In 2005, Canada was already the biggest supplier of oil and natural gas to the United States. The unconventional sources in Alberta made Canada a country with the world's second-biggest oil reserves after Saudi Arabia ("Peace, Order"). In 2005, Prime Minister Paul Martin wrote in the *International Policy Statement* that "[f]oreign policy is how a nation best expresses itself to the world," economy had already been Canadian government's priority (Government of Canada, "A Role").

In Stephen Harper's vision, Canada was as a specialized open economy, pursuing its economic opportunities, in particular in the energy sector, with an open, tolerant, diversified society, ready to defend values in the most troublesome places in the world. Although the image in many elements was strikingly different from the one presented under Martin's Liberals, the foundations were not so much at odds with each other. The continuity was expressed, for example, in the support for free trade agreements, e.g. with Colombia, the foreign investment protection treaty with China, support for the extraction and export of oil sands bitumen, or the global expansion of Canadian mining capital.

Generally speaking, a large degree of continuity between the Liberals and the Conservatives can be observed not only in economic matters, but also in national security, continental integration, or, as noted by Jerome Klassen, in "war and militarism" (*Joining* 252). Contrary to many commentators, including the authors of the book *Warrior Nation* (McKay and Swift), Klassen argues that both major Canadian parties have presented similar attitudes toward defending of the "globalizing capital" as visible in constant support for various military missions and defence spending projects (*Joining* 253). Although Klassen's arguments excessively concentrate on the economic aspects of foreign policy, many of them support the findings we have reached in our research. Generally speaking, the reason why the continuity exists lies in the fact that the concept of traditional multilateralism and internationalism in the Canadian context has lost much of its uniqueness and creativity and that the term "middle power" has in fact begun to mean average. Critics of Harper's foreign policy emphasize that under his government Canada moved away from what had defined its international identity. We, however, argue that it was a gradual adaptation to the changes in the global world, to the problems that countries had to face and, more importantly, to the shift in Canada's position on the international stage.

Economy and the environment

In the Harper doctrine, Canada's international place was among the world's major powers. The Conservative prime minister did not aspire to be a leader of a country of a middle rank. Quite the opposite, Harper deliberately decided to concentrate on selectively chosen goals and areas where he could play a role of a leader. As rightly suggested by Duane Bratt, the Harper government narrowed down a conception of Canada's national interest along realist foreign policy lines. In such a view, the guiding motives in foreign policy have a limited connection with "sacred" liberal internationalist qualities such as "multilateralism, peacekeeping, model global citizenship, multicultural harmony, and generosity in foreign aid" (Bratt, "Stephen" 494). Bratt identifies Steven Kendall Holloway's 2006 book *Canadian Foreign Policy: Defining the National Interest* as a manual for the international behaviour of the Conservative government. Holloway highlights security and trade, but in general identifies five of Canada's national interests that every foreign policy needs to pursue. Among them are the most important themes – some of them we already acknowledged – of Harper's approach to international affairs: national security combined with territorial sovereignty, political autonomy, national unity, economic prosperity and principled self-image (identity) (Holloway 5-19). Moreover, Harper, as a trained economist, introduced the principles of efficiency and effectiveness in various fields of external activity.

Along Harper's chief policy objective – to strengthen the Canadian economy – other supportive objectives were introduced. "Economic diplomacy" became the central element of foreign policy conduct, whose purpose was to help enable free access to markets all over the world. Bilateral and multilateral relations were centred on those fora where economic gains could be achieved. Immigration policies were transformed to better serve Canadian interests, as well as development aid, which was not only incorporated to the structures of the Department of Foreign Affairs and International Trade – which was reflected in a new name: Department of Foreign Affairs, Trade and Development (DFATD) – but also modified to better reinforce commercial interests (Trent 34).

It is a matter of dispute to what degree Harper succeeded in the transformation of Canada into a major power. But without much doubt Canada's international image, in some respects, changed for the better, as confirmed by a survey among citizens of the G20 countries. This 2010 poll showed that nearly 80 per cent of people questioned in Brazil, Russia and China saw Canada as a global economic power and a recognizable leader (Friesen). However, the G7 members were much more skeptical, or in other words, more reluctant to see the change in the established balance of powers. Nevertheless, we think, that the British government's decision, made in November 2012, to nominate the first foreigner – Mark Carney, as the head of Canada's central bank – to take the position of the president of the Bank of England should be treated as a symbol of a changing attitude and appreciation of the knowledge of Canadian economists, Canada's economic policy in general, but also Canada as a country on the world scene (L. MacKinnon).

At the same time we tend to agree with John Kirton's observations that the change of Canada's position was achievable only because of the continued relative decrease of U.S. power ("The Harper" 3). Canada under Harper engaged to help its neighbour in niches that were left by the U.S. This was possible due to the lowering level of continental irritants or disputes, although, contrary to what Kirton argues, leader-level complaints continued to appear, e.g. between Harper and President Obama ("Vulnerable" 134). Definitely – and we agree here with Kirton's opinion – during the Harper era defining issues in Canadian foreign policy were not located in North America, with the exception of trade, energy relations and pipelines. Ottawa concentrated on fighting wars in Afghanistan and Libya, and since 2014 also in Iraq against ISIS, but also on the global "campaign for financial stability, strong, sustained and balanced growth, and sustainable development in an integrally interconnected, increasingly single world" (Kirton, "Vulnerable" 134).

In Harper's foreign policy, among the important roles Canada should play, was the one of an economic power. On the one hand, the claim was based on the possession of vast amounts of diverse natural resources, technologically advanced mining and processing industry. On the other hand, it was supported by developed trade relations, first of all with the United States – the most important trade partner for Canada in terms of scope and scale – but also with a variety of other countries, with whom Ottawa had already signed or was planning to sign free trade agreements or foreign investment protection arrangements. Apart from resources and technologies, Canada also possessed a diversified, educated and growing population, whose level of social cohesion was among the world's highest.

Since the 1970s, Canada has participated in G7 summits and even though, initially, its role in the global elite club was perceived as a U.S. counterbalance to European countries, in the post-Cold War era Ottawa has become an increasingly active participant in these meetings and an important part of all arrangements. Harper was troubled by the financial situation of Canada in the 1990s – in 1995 Canada's net government debt, 72 per cent of GDP, was the second highest among G7 countries. It was then that Canada's political leaders focused their energies inward on a difficult task of cutting fiscal deficits and balancing the budget without alienating key constituencies and regions across the country (World Bank, "Canada – Central"). Canada's economic performance improved only after ten years. Economic growth in the mid-1990s and early 2000s – especially the growth of export, fuelled by new trade agreements, and industrial production, backed by low inflation, strict monetary policy, relatively low unemployment and the stability of the banking sector – strengthened Canada's position. The Conservative government wanted to keep Canada on the position of a G7 leader in economic performance by providing consecutive fiscal surpluses, a strong currency, a sustained current account surplus and "a pension plan able to provide for its expanding population for the next 70 years" (Kirton, "Canada Shows").

Those elements became especially visible when, in the autumn 2008, the Lehman Brothers investment bank collapsed, the United States plunged into a financial crisis and the global recession started. In this situation sound management of the economy became a virtue and Canada aspired to the status of one of the most financially stable countries. Canada's major banks emerged from the financial crisis as one of the strongest in the world, owing this success to the early intervention by the Bank of Canada and the financial sector's tradition of conservative lending practices and strong capitalization. With a smooth transition through the economic crisis of 2008-2011, Harper projected Canada as an economic symbol for other countries. As it was mentioned before, Harper's realist foreign policy attitude implied that all other international roles started with a sound economy and a stable political system.

Additionally, in Harper's vision, the size of Canada's economy was its asset, as Canada was "big enough to make a difference, but not big enough to threaten anybody" (Ljunggren). In the 2009 G20 summit in Pittsburgh, Harper presented Canada not only as the only major developed country that had no responsibility for the depression, but also as a provider of solutions – a country whose economic policies could be followed. This very special place Canada occupied allowed Ottawa to influence the global world.

An important part of Harper's economic agenda during the economic crisis was the policy of austerity. The idea of a balanced budget and at the same time continued economic growth overshadowed other elements of the policies of Harper's government. The cuts to federal spending programs were deep, reaching those fields of the external activity of Canada which did not support commercial purposes. The economic objectives were considered the most important and cuts were introduced to reduce costs as much as possible. For example, the Department of Foreign Affairs, Trade and Development budget was slashed by some CAD 400 million by 2014-15. This included the elimination of the Canadian Studies Program as well as the Commonwealth Secretariat (Trent 33). Money was also withdrawn from other public policies and academic or diplomatic programs. The government also closed all of Canada's consulates general in Japan, Italy and Russia (Kirton, "The Harper" 11-12). Moreover, Harper decided to freeze military spending and money for the official development aid.

Harper clearly succeeded in his economic policies. The prime minister was able to balance the budget in 2015 and government's net debt was only 37 per cent of GDP (Blatchford, "Canada's Books"). Canada recovered from the financial crisis faster than other G7 members, with a solid economic growth at an annual average rate of 2.6 per cent since the recession in 2008 ("Energy" 19). This growth was possible mostly thanks to a boom in commodities, especially oil. However, Canada was able to keep marginal growth in the years 2010-2016, despite the drop in oil prices ("A Rough").

Canada's foreign policy, re-oriented towards achieving business goals, was set upon on natural resources, in particular energy resources, and supported by trade diversification. Harper outlined his government's economic agenda in 2012 at the World Economic Forum in Davos, where he spoke of Canada pursuing new trade opportunities – "we will continue to advance our trade linkages. We will pass agreements signed, particularly in our own hemisphere, and we will work to conclude major deals beyond it" – and selling oil to the world markets – "we will make it a national priority to ensure we have the capacity to export our energy products beyond the United States and specifically to Asia" (Harper, "Statement Made"; see also Kennedy). Both elements became the two pillars of Canada's selective power approach to foreign affairs.

Trade

Canada, as a trading nation, has prioritized international trade and investment since the Second World War, joining the General Agreement on Tariffs and Trade and the World Trade Organization, signing in 1988 the Canada-U.S. Free Trade Agreement and four years later its successor – NAFTA. After the Cold War, regardless of their political affiliation, Canadian governments have supported a neoliberal idea that openness and economic progress go hand in hand. Given the abundance of natural resources and the need to export them to the world markets, a strong consensus has been reached, based on a belief that the international push toward reduced barriers would greatly benefit Canada.

Obviously, the most important market for Ottawa is its southern neighbour, with NAFTA treated as a core deal. Nevertheless, subsequent Canadian governments have tried to establish as many additional trade agreements as possible, seeking to reduce trade barriers through the GATT framework, but also through bilateral trade agreements. The Liberal governments of Jean Chrétien and Paul Martin actively promoted Canadian business abroad, pursuing outward-oriented trade agenda to achieve diversification and depoliticization of its trade with various international partners.

In general, the trade policy of the Harper government followed the predecessors' course. The prime minister, as an economist by training and an enthusiast of liberal economy, deeply favoured trade liberalization. In his political message, he continuously repeated how important trade was for all Canadians (Robertson 98). For example, in the 2013 Speech from the Throne, he underlined that "with one in five Canadian jobs dependent on exports, our prosperity hinges on opening new markets for Canadian goods, services and investment" (Harper, "The 2013"). Harper also strongly supported an open-market approach and the establishment of viable mechanisms for dealing with trade disputes. As summarized by Laura Dawson, "export orientation [was] necessary for prosperity – relying on domestic sales [was] not sufficient to sustain domestic standards of living and rules are needed to mitigate against maltreatment by more powerful economies" (163).

Thus, since the 2006 election campaign, the trade policy of the Harper government was split between two elements: refining relations with traditional trading partners, with whom Canada shared solid economic interests, and intensified searching for new partners ("Harper Signs"). At the same time Ottawa continued negotiations aimed at the tariff and non-tariff barrier elimination through the GATT framework (Dawson 162). The latter component became Harper's trademark, as he strongly advocated that Canada should catch up with other countries that were rapidly enlarging their pools of bilateral free trade agreements. Harper was confident that, in order to strengthen Canada's economic position, the enhancement of a free trade component was needed. While the main foundations of Canadian trade policy had been established by his predecessors, Harper's policies were exceptional in terms of the pace and direction of the activities – what new markets to look for and what sectors to promote or protect. The Harper government made a substantial progress in trade, providing Canada with more trade agreements than all his predecessors combined (Dawson 162).

Harper initially was convinced of the importance of deep and sound trading relations with the United States. This was in line with the conservative ideals that for Canada the relations with the U.S. – a "bedrock partner" – should be as highly beneficial, stable and irritant-free as possible. Harper promptly did away with anti-American overtones visible in the Jean Chrétien's and Paul Martin's attitudes to George W. Bush, which, in Harper's eyes, negatively affected trade across the common border.

Despite a post-9/11 atmosphere, which brought border security restrictions, and the effects of the 2007-2008 financial crisis, the Harper government was successful in improving the bilateral trade relations. One of the most important achievements in this field was the adoption of the U.S.-Canada joint declaration entitled *Beyond the Border: A Shared Vision for Perimeter Security and Economic Competitiveness*, announced by Obama and Harper on February 4, 2011. In the declaration, both countries committed themselves "to pursue a perimeter approach to security." To that end, in order to counter threats and increase safety, Canada and the U.S. made a declaration to improve and enhance intelligence and information sharing, set up an integrated system of travelers' identification and screening, as well as "cooperate to identify, prevent, and counter violent extremism" by working together "on research, sharing best practices, and emphasizing community-based and community-driven efforts." More important for Canada, however, was the economic dimension of the perimeter agreement, in which it was declared that both governments would work together "within, at, and away from the borders of our two countries" in order to "accelerate the legitimate flow of people, goods, and services." To achieve this, Obama and Harper promised, among other things, to "focus investment in modern infrastructure and technology" at the border and to "support the volume of commercial and passenger traffic inherent to economic growth and job creation" by "expanding trusted traveler and trader programs, harmonizing existing programs, and automating processes at the land border," introducing common customs procedures and "developing an integrated cargo security." In December 2011, both countries presented an action plan setting out details, specific solutions and timeline for achieving the above goals ("United States – Canada" i-iv). The plan is being gradually implemented and many of the promised initiatives are already delayed. Nevertheless, the perimeter security agreement helped smooth the flow of people and Canadian goods through the border by, *inter alia*, opening ways to the enhancement of preclearance facilities (discussed below). The critics, however, argue that Canada, for the very sake of removing trade barriers where possible and achieving a relative economic stability, is simply "acquiescing to U.S. security requests" and "mimicking U.S. security measures," despite the fact that it has so far brought "few available accounts of progress on the Beyond the Border Action Plan" (Sinclair and Trew 116).

Also, the Harper government opposed so-called "Buy American" policies, i.e. stridently protective procurement included in the *American Reinvestment and Recovery Act*, passed in the U.S. Congress in 2009. The main goal of the legislation was to protect American production and manufacturing jobs by committing the U.S. authorities of various levels to buy manufactured goods to be used in publicly funded infrastructure and building projects from U.S. producers. If extended to Canada, as initially planned, the "Buy American" provisions would have damaged many Canadian suppliers economically. The Canadian government launched an anti-protectionist campaign against the legislation. Thanks to Prime Minister Harper's insistence, "Buy American" became a major topic of bilateral debates on numerous occasions, including the NAFTA summit and Harper's visit to Washington in 2009. As a result, President Obama agreed to start negotiations with Ottawa which resulted in the signing of the bilateral procurement deal in February 2010. It exempted Canadian firms from the "Buy American" regulations (Hale 296-298). The "Buy American" issue clearly reveals how challenging the U.S. economic protectionism is for Canadian governments, but also how it can mobilize Ottawa's governmental ranks to use the best of Canada's diplomacy and negotiating skills to achieve success. The Harper government, though rarely demonstrating efficiency in the use and promotion of Canada's soft power, when pressed by the risk of economic damage, proved – as Geoffrey Hale rightly pointed out – its "ability to secure an agreement after only five months of negotiations on terms fairly close to Canada's original offer" (298). That only demonstrates the crucial importance of the trade with the U.S. to Canadian economic well-being. As Barrie McKenna of the *Globe and Mail* notices, "[l]ike it or not, the Canadian economy is more dependent on the United States than vice versa. Scratches can cost Canada dearly in lost trade and economic opportunities, even when there is minimal collateral damage to that big U.S. Chevy." Therefore, he argues, consecutive Canadian governments have for years clinged to what he calls "the notion of a 'special relationship' with the United States," which for Ottawa means, among others, a "privileged access to the U.S. market" (McKenna, "The U.S.").

The Harper government, for that matter, was actively engaged in ending the so-called softwood lumber dispute which had negatively affected bilateral relations since the 1980s. The Americans had for years accused Canada of dishonest practices, i.e. subsiding its softwood lumber industry unfairly, which from Washington's perspective contradicted the rules of a free market competition and seemingly harmed American timber producers, causing unemployment. In response, the U.S. had imposed countervailing tariffs on Canada's softwood lumber products against which Canada had been fighting – with varying degrees of success – in the NAFTA tribunals. The dispute was finally settled in 2006 by the softwood lumber deal, which was reached largely thanks to the personal involvement and support of Prime Minister Stephen Harper (Hale 288-293).

After the agreement expired in October 2015, the Liberals followed the footsteps of their Conservative predecessors and after taking power announced their will to start negotiations over the renewal of the deal. The Trudeau government is aware that failure to extend the agreement may result in the adoption by the U.S. of anti-dumping duties or strict quotas on softwood lumber products. This would have severe consequences for Canada's timber industry in general, and in particular for British Columbia, the largest softwood producer and exporter, where around 40 per cent of rural population is estimated to be reliant on forestry and over 65,000 jobs are directly linked to the lumber sector (Meissner). Initially, there were signs the Liberals would succeed in talks with the Obama administration. During Trudeau's visit to Washington in March 2016, Obama assured Canadians they had no reason to fear about the future of softwood lumber trade. Both leaders declared their intention to work together to avoid a dispute on the issue and committed themselves to find ways for a new deal (Hunter). However, when the presidential election progressed, a more protectionist mood emerged in Washington. In June 2016, at the bilateral talks during the Obama visit to Ottawa, CBC noted that "the tone abruptly changed from convivial to tense" when the softwood lumber issue was raised (Hall, "Behind"). Obama and Trudeau confirmed in the joint statement that "significant differences remain regarding the parameters of the key features" of the future deal ("Joint Statement"). In August 2016, Canada's chief negotiator Michael Moen admitted before the parliamentary committee that Canada and the U.S. were "far apart" on the new agreement (Wherry, "On softwood"). That in fact meant that the negotiations came to a standstill.

With the Trump administration now in office, the Liberals' chances for a positive negotiated breakthrough look even bleaker. The new president's rhetoric and policies seem to be driven by highly protectionist sentiments; the conditions are unfavourable for expanding freer trade with the U.S. Washington is determined to assess and review its international economic relations with the ultimate goal of guaranteeing a trade surplus with other countries, including Canada, by imposing anti-dumping tariffs on imports from trading partners that use anti-competitive, unfair, abusive practices, such as public subsidies, to boost their exports to the U.S. In such circumstances, Canadian softwood lumber may be one of the first victims of the new policies, especially because in January 2017, the U.S. International Trade Commission already ruled in its preliminary finding that "there is a reasonable indication that a U.S. industry is materially injured by reason of imports of softwood lumber products from Canada that are allegedly subsidized and sold in the United States at less than fair value" and declared to propose a "preliminary antidumping duty determination due on or about May 4, 2017" (U.S. International). Even if the Liberals fail to reach a favourable and beneficial softwood lumber deal with the U.S. – a goal which, strictly speaking, would be equally difficult to achieve if the Conservatives were in power – the softwood lumber issue shows one important feature of Canada's foreign policy, which has not changed since Harper lost the election: free trade with the U.S. and guarantees of open access to the U.S. market for Canadian producers remain Ottawa's key foreign policy priorities.

But there were also areas where Harper's economic policies bore no fruit. Canada, for instance, did not receive a special treatment from the Obama administration when the U.S. imposed the *Foreign Account Tax Compliance Act* (FATCA) in 2010 to pursue wealthy Americans who avoid taxes by hiding their cash on foreign bank accounts. While the legislation was not passed directly against Canada or any other specific country, the Harper government feared it would hurt Canada particularly badly as 1 out of 7 million Americans that the U.S. government wanted to track lived in Canada. The protests, however, produced no results and some

Canadian banks, fearing high penalties in the U.S., started cooperating with the American authorities, for which the Canadian government has occasionally been sued to courts for violating constitutional protections against discrimination ("The Foreign").

The Harper government also failed to convince Americans to co-finance the construction of a new border crossing parallel to the Ambassador Bridge, an almost 90-year old link spanning the Detroit River and joining Detroit and Windsor. The bridge is the busiest land crossing in all North America, through which up to 10,000 trucks daily and a quarter of all bilateral Canada-U.S. trade flow. Starting in the early 2000s, successive Canadian governments had for years been negotiating an agreement that would initiate a joint investment in a new bridge with the U.S. federal government and the state of Michigan's authorities. But all to no avail. The Americans never considered the proposal seriously. Firstly, because the U.S. part of the crossing had been built by a private business and is privately owned by the Moroun family, who successfully lobbied against the new bridge in the Michigan legislature. Secondly, because of the economic recession, which particularly affected the auto industry in Michigan, thinning the state's budget. Having lost hope in the American participation in the investment, but at the same time considering the new crossing crucial for Canadian economic interests – Harper called it "Canada's No. 1 infrastructure priority" – and thus being desperate to have it constructed in due time, the Harper government announced in February 2015 that Canada would fully cover the CAD 4-billion construction of the new bridge, plus that a Canadian Crown corporation would build customs facilities and road infrastructure on the Michigan side. All these investments would be paid from Canadian taxpayer money alone with a hope of having the work completed by 2020. As one author accurately commented on this decision, Harper simply "promised the United States a free bridge" (Savage, "Land"). Again, the whole issue proves that stable, unimpeded trade relations with the U.S. are crucial for Ottawa and Canadian provinces, and are of much lesser importance for Americans. And that Canada, in its highly selective and economy-oriented approach to foreign relations, is ready to go to great lengths to keep the U.S.-Canada border open for trade, not only by fighting against American protective tariffs and duties, but also by being active in removing physical barriers.

Facing increasingly longer border waits and a slowdown in the American economy that struggled to recover from the recession, the Harper government was forced to start a diversification strategy aimed at reducing risks contained in trade strategy concentrated too much on the U.S. Instead of tightening traditional north-south links, Canada's trade had to re-orient into east-west. Although not without "missteps and missed opportunities," as was the case of trade relations with China (discussed in the following parts of the book), the government, as was referred to by Laura Dawson, led Canada with "the right policies at the right time" (160-161, 165). This was the case with the 2009 *Global Commerce Strategy* – expanding trade with non-U.S. markets – as well as the 2011 *Economic Action Plan* or the *Global Markets Action Plan* – aimed at fighting against the recession by, among others, lessening trade tensions with the U.S. – and the 2013 *Global Markets Action Plan* – re-establishing the strategy of expanding trade relations with selected markets (Dawson 165).

Since 2009, in Harper's speeches Asian markets started to appear more and more frequently (Poy and Cao 70; Evans 117-119). For example, the prime minister told the audience in South Korea that "[t]he markets in the United States and in Europe that have been our more traditional market will probably experience slower growth for some time to come. So the greater opportunity is obviously in the Asia-Pacific region" (qtd. in Ibbitson, "A New"). Canada could offer raw materials and resources that only "very few developed countries" possessed and in new and expanding Asian markets Canadians could use its personal ties, as millions of immigrants in Canada came from this region. From this perspective, Canada had a competitive advantage over other Western nations (Ibbitson, *Stephen* 388-389).

This new trade strategy also resulted in the rejection of protectionism in trade agreements. Initially, the Conservatives made relatively ineffective attempts to shield Canadian textile, agricultural, shipbuilding or auto-sector interests in trade talks with other countries, for example with Brazil ("Harper Signs"). But having gained more experience in trade negotiations, the Harper government was able to establish trade agreements with a record number of countries. When his government was in the process of assuming power, Canada had free-trade deals with only five countries. At the end of Harper's term, as the Conservatives boasted in the election campaign, "Canada had concluded free-trade agreements with 39 additional countries" (Conservative Party of Canada, "Harper Announces"). Ottawa added to Canada's portfolio bilateral free trade agreements with, among others, Peru, Colombia, Panama, Honduras, and the European Free Trade Association (EFTA). Ottawa also started negotiating several other bilateral trade agreements, including the ones with: the Canada-Caribbean Community, Dominican Republic, El Salvador, Guatemala, Nicaragua, India, Singapore, Morocco, and Japan. In October 2012, Canada officially joined negotiations over the Trans-Pacific Partnership (TPP) with eleven Asia-Pacific countries (including the U.S. and Japan), which were concluded in October 2015 (Global Affairs Canada, "Trade").

Not all trade talks ended in successful agreements, as for example Ottawa was not able to finish negotiations with India (Goold and Palit; MacCharles). But some of the trade agreements were symbolic, as was the case of the free trade agreement with the European Union, signed in September 2014. The Comprehensive Economic and Trade Agreement fulfilled Harper's expectations for a bold win while Brussels could present it as a sign of the ability of the European Commission to look forward and face modern economic challenges. The agreement with South Korea, signed in March 2014 – the first free trade deal that Canada had signed with an Asian nation – was of a similar magnitude.

The Harper government was also able to sign a trade agreement with Jordan. This deal was presented by the government as a major achievement, an example that ran contrary to the critics accusing the Conservatives of alienating Canada's interests in the Middle East with its excessively pro-Israel attitude (Nicky). In 2013, when Canada also promised to grant Jordan, which was dealing with the influx of refugees from Syria, CAD 100 million for the development of the education system, the Harper government emphasized that Jordan was "a bulwark of moderate stability and a country that has been willing to engage in some co-operation with Israel" (Campbell, "Harper").

The Harper record of new trade agreements was impressive, but in addition to free trade agreements, until the end of his term in office, Canada had the Foreign Investment Promotion and Protection Agreements in force with 30 different countries. The Trudeau government, as of January 2017, added six more ("Trade and Investment").

An additional element of Harper's trade policy was the concept of "economic diplomacy." It was introduced by the 2013 *Global*

Markets Action Plan. As this concept became a key driver of Canadian international policies, the Trade Commissioner Service was enhanced to focus on marketing Canada's business and actively seeking international investors. The Trade Commissioners also served as advisors providing potential investors with the necessary knowledge about Canada's economy (Foreign Affairs, Trade and Development Canada, "Global Markets"). Economic diplomacy was oriented towards helping to strike new business deals with new partners that would result in diversifying Canada's export, for example by developing markets for non-traditional exports. This required the improvement of the influence and credibility of Canada in those markets. To reach this end, Ottawa for example, opened four new trade offices in China, bringing the total number of offices in this country to 15, having more than 100 trade commissioners there. It also expanded its presence in India, with 8 offices and almost 50 trade commissioners (Macdonald and Paltiel 2-3).

The *Global Markets Action Plan* was an element of a larger shift of Harper's foreign policy, which resulted in putting the economic dimension to the forefront of Canada's international activities. The effect was the strategy of pursuing political relationships together with economic ones. However, the economic interest would and should predominate even when it was in conflict with values. This tendency was clearly seen in the Harper government's approach towards the selling of arms or in tying trade to development and foreign aid (Burney and Hampson, "No More").

To some degree, we see Harper as a continuator of the previous Canadian governments' tactic of mixing business and diplomacy. However, the Conservatives linked it with an intelligent and aggressive trade strategy. Laura Dawson summarized it as "expanding in the right directions when times were good, and providing pragmatic alternatives when times were not" (165). What is also important, the trade strategy of the Harper government is now largely followed by Justin Trudeau. Apart from the personality-related and rhetorical contrast between Trudeau and Harper, when it comes to the commitment to trade and investment liberalization, the Trudeau government appears to match his predecessor. From that perspective, Harper's approach to free trade may be among his most lasting policy accomplishments or it may even constitute his legacy.

Energy resources

As observed at the beginning of this chapter, the Harper doctrine was largely based on the self-centred and outcome-oriented approach when it came to the selection of foreign policy priorities or areas of concentration. The Harper government was particularly focused on two fields, both located on the economy-related side of international relations: the expansion of trade relations and the export of natural resources, particularly energy resources, especially oil and natural gas. Both these elements served as main pillars of Canada's new international stature.

Under Harper, natural resources have become a crucial part of Ottawa's foreign policy thanks to the rich deposits of the resources that are located on Canada's landmass and are on high demand globally. Canada has grown into a self-sufficient and a major exporter of energy resources. In 2014, the conventional oil production was 1.58 million barrels per day (Marceau and Bowman 13). Apart from the conventional oil reserves, Canada also has heavy bitumen deposits, known as oil sands or tar sands. Since 1980, the unconventional oil has been responsible for the tenfold growth of Canada's oil exports, which ultimately made Ottawa the largest exporter of oil to the United States (United States Energy Information Administration, "U.S.").

A modern petroleum boom in Canada started, but only with the price surge of world commodities after 2000, resulting in the reclassification of 170 billion barrels of oil sands bitumen as official oil reserves. With a barrel of crude oil well above a minimum CAD 50, the costly mining of oil sands and the conversion of crude oil into liquid finally became economically profitable (National Energy Board, "Canada's"). As a result, Canada had, until 2015, experienced a continuous expansion of the new or existing projects of oil sands production (National Energy Board, "Canada's"). The growing contribution of the energy sector to the Canadian economy, combined with a stable growth of demand in Asia, made Canada's natural resource development a strong priority. Canada was promoted to the role of a serious global petroleum player, or – as it was suggested in a 2003 *New York Times* article, written by a geophysicist Manik Talwani – to the status of an energy superpower.

The growth of oil production was impressive: in 2000, Canada produced 1.97 million barrels per day, six years later – 2.52 million, and after 10 years it was more than 3.67 million barrels per day ("Canada

Crude"). Canada became the sixth largest producer of oil in the world, with about 4 per cent of world's total daily production (National Energy Board, "2012"). Canada's oil exports between 2006 and 2015 grew by almost 70 per cent from 1.8 to 3.0 million barrels per day. At the same time, imports decreased by about one-third (National Energy Board, "2015").

The United States has historically been Canada's largest customer for crude oil and energy products. This trend has strengthened since 1980 – American imports of oil and products from Canada grew from 450,000 to 3.76 million barrels per day in 2013. In that period the U.S. domestic production and imports from other countries declined and Canada sent between 98 and 99 per cent of its exported oil to the U.S (United States Energy Information Administration, "U.S."; National Energy Board, "Canada's").

What was more important, Canada's 2035 oil production was forecasted to reach 5.8 million barrels per day, i.e. nearly 75 per cent more than in 2012. Oil from oil sands was projected to constitute nearly 86 per cent of all oil production in Canada in 2035, compared with 57 per cent in 2012 (National Energy Board, "Canada's"). There is also a gigantic potential of shale oil resources, estimated between 9 and even 420 billion barrels. If developed, shale exploitation would give Canada the largest crude oil potential in the world (National Energy Board, "Canada's"; Alberta Energy Regulator 2-9). Due to the enormous size of Canada's known oil deposits, economic, labour, and environmental policy considerations are major constraints on production rather than finding new oilfields. The International Energy Agency forecasts that Canada would be among the three largest global suppliers of oil by 2040 (Kirby, "The Perils"). Similar developments are observed when it comes to Canada's natural gas production. In 2014, it reached 4.7 trillion cubic feet per year, i.e. 2.22 million barrels per day (Marceau and Bowman).

Other statistics also seem to prove Canada's enormous potential to become a major energy power. In 2006, Canada was the fifth largest energy producer in the world – first in uranium and third and seventh in global gas and oil production respectively. It was also one of the few developed nations that was a net exporter of energy, with the production largely exceeding domestic demand, and a country with the highest energy supply per capita among the International Energy Agency (IEA) members (Taber, "PM Brands"; Kirton, "Harper's"). In 2014, the energy sector contributed to about 10 per cent of Canada's GDP, employed approximately 280,000 people and was responsible for about 30 per cent of Canada's total exports. Each year, the energy sector brings an average of CAD 20 to 25 billion in taxes, royalties and other payments to federal and provincial governments (International Energy Agency 12).

The idea of Canada as an energy powerhouse was consistent with Harper's guiding principle according to which foreign policy should support economic growth and increase Canada's international position. The abundance of natural resources is, without doubt, Canada's most vital comparative advantage. The development of the extraction industry and the export of natural resources fuel other parts of the economy. For Harper, who linked his professional life with Alberta, where the largest concentration of the oil industry is located, the concept that the oil sands should be treated as a path to Canada's riches and elevated status was something natural. But this view was also supported by many Canadians, as they thought that Ottawa should take advantage of the favourable circumstances and reap the economic benefits from the abundance of natural resources even when it harmed the environment (Lyle 42). This was also in line with Harper's point of view. On the one hand, he believed that, in Canada's situation, renewables such as solar and wind represented an attractive and viable source of energy and an industry in which Canadians could and should be the world's leader. But, on the other, this in no way should impede the continuing capitalization on the enormous wealth in oil and gas assets. The traditional energy resources would remain relevant for decades to come. In the Harper doctrine, Canada, an important producer of oil and natural gas, was destined to become an "energy superpower."

Canada differed from other major energy exporters as it was a reliable, democratic Western country – a trustworthy "energy storehouse" and a global geopolitical stabilizer, which was particularly important in a situation of growing instability in key regions of the world and the decreasing production. Ultimately the new energy superpower status would open new fields to develop its influence for Canada, including in political and security matters, such as nuclear proliferation, human rights issues and "counterterrorism and peace in the Middle East" (Kirton, "Canada Shows"). By the time Harper was sworn in as prime minister, the idea of Canada as an energy superpower had become a cornerstone of his politics (Greenspon et al., "How").

This idea was initially presented in the prime minister's first international speech. In the Canada-United Kingdom Chamber of Commerce in London in 2006, Harper unfolded a vision of Canada as "an emerging energy superpower" – the only non-OPEC country with "growing oil deliverability," but first of all "a stable, reliable producer in a volatile unpredictable world." According to the prime minister, Canada stood out from other oil-rich countries by the fact that it supported "the free exchange of energy products based on competitive market principles, not self-serving monopolistic political strategies." This made Canada a secure and dependable partner for the U.S. – bigger than Saudi Arabia. In London's speech, Harper also began to promote Canada's oil sands as a great place to invest – "the most attractive place in the world offering access to the large U.S. market" (Harper, "Address by the Prime Minister at the Canada-UK").

Harper declared that although the extraction and refining of the unconventional petroleum represented a "monumental challenge" – as "an enterprise of epic proportions, akin to the building of the pyramids or China's Great Wall. Only bigger" – Canada was prepared to take it (qtd. in Gattinger, "Is Canada"). This statement was reinforced when prime minister visited Canada's northern territories and promised that if the Canadian North opened itself to investments it could achieve "the potential to transform into what some call 'the next Alberta'" (Harper, "The Call").

The invitation of the Harper government to invest in Canada's energy resources was met with a warm response on the part of the investors, particularly from Asian countries. Only in 2007, private and state-owned producers invested CAD 18 billion (Gattinger, "Is Canada"). More than CAD 180 billion worth investments from the U.S., Asia and Europe came to Canada until 2016, although the investments declined in late 2014, when the U.S. shale production brought prices down from USD 100 to USD 26 (Williams; Statistics Canada, "International").

The idea of Canada's rise to the status of an energy superpower was spelt out on numerous other occasions by the prime minister and other members of the Conservative Party after the London speech. It was also subsequently repeated by various governmental agencies. Environment Canada, for example, emphasized that Canada played:

[…] a major role in the long term energy security of North American and
world energy supplies [as] one of the few secure places in the world to invest
in energy development, and one of a very few energy exporting nations that
has reserves sufficiently large to provide a secure long term supply of fossil-
fuels ("A Climate").

However, the idea of Canada's energy superpower status raised doubts
among energy pundits (Hester; Schofield; Cleland). They argued that
the energy superpower status entailed more elements than only having an
abundant quantity of energy resources. First of all, Canada's production
was relatively small – not even 4 million barrels per day, which was
more than twice less than Saudi Arabia or Russia. Secondly, Canada's
production was exported to virtually one destination – the United States.
Thirdly, Ottawa, with mostly private-owned oil companies, did not
have the ability to impose its will on others to control prices. And lastly,
Canada lacked the most important element of an energy superpower,
i.e. "ability to leverage energy resources to extend its sphere of political
influence beyond its regional markets" (Hester 6).

Using the above-mentioned definition, as most experts agree, Canada
was not on the path to become an energy superpower and would likely
remain an important but secondary producer at most (Gattinger, "Is
Canada"). However, even Russia hardly meets such defined criteria, as
Moscow has not always been able to leverage energy resources outside
of one region – Europe (Way 78-79). In our opinion, such a realist and
narrow classification misses Harper's point. The prime minister not only
expressly scorned the idea to impose Canada's will on others to gain
political benefits, but he also particularly criticized Russia's attempts to
use its energy wealth to manipulate other countries (Schofield). Instead,
Harper saw Canada not simply as a supplier of energy, but wanted to
use Canada's advantage in natural resources to serve as a stabilizer of the
world markets. Ottawa, according to the Conservatives, would address
the problem of global security of energy resources. And in the North
American context specifically, with rising oil prices, Canada hoped to
reduce the U.S. energy vulnerability (Kirton, "The Harper" 3). In his
speeches, Harper frequently stressed the value of political stability and
transparency of Canada's regulations, as well as Canada's commitment to
remain a reliable contributor to global energy security (Harper, "Notes";
Harper, "'Enlightened"). Such a point of view was confirmed by the IEA,

which in 2015 described Canada's policies as "contribution to global energy security by ensuring diversified, competitive, secure and reliable energy supplies" (9).

One of the key objectives for the Harper government, in his pursuit of energy power status for Canada, was to expand the capacity to export energy resources abroad. To achieve this goal, Ottawa first of all tried to sell more energy resources to the American market. But after 2008 this was becoming more and more problematic, due to the growth of U.S. own production from tight and shale sources, but even more because of the Keystone XL debacle (discussed in the next subchapter).

The uncertainty that persisted throughout that period seriously undermined the trust of the Harper government in the U.S. as the most important and reliable partner for Canada's oil, a country that could be counted on to buy as much oil as Canada could produce (Greenspon et al., "How"). This was even more shocking for Canadians as the energy relationship between Canada and the United States since the creation of NAFTA had been market-based and run rather smoothly (de Kerckhove and Petrolekas 3). The situation created the growing need to eliminate the Achilles' heel of Canada's oil industry – the total dependency on exports to the United States – through the diversification of its export markets – particularly to Asian and European countries.

The strategy of diversifying markets was expected to bring at least two results. From the political perspective, as suggested, for example, by Brian Mulroney, former Canadian prime minister, had Canada started selling energy resources outside of North America, it would have been able to "'walk the talk' of a resource super power." Ottawa would have obtained a leverage to "engage the Americans from the position of strength and relevance [to make] energy independence in North America a near term reality." This would have generated "significant capacity for influence in world affairs [...]" (Mulroney).

Secondly, from the economic perspective, opening for other markets would have reduced a discount on Canada's oil price when selling oil to the U.S. Such a discount can be regularly observed when comparing the prices of Canadian oil with U.S. products. It results from the costs of the transportation and additional costs of refining heavier crude. The International Energy Agency suggested that diversifying export markets "would enable Canadian producers to access global markets and apply global prices for Canadian natural gas, crude oil and petroleum products" (29-30).

To achieve those both objectives, the Harper government started to pursue several pipeline projects, which would allow Canada to sell its oil to other countries. Among the projects, apart from the already mentioned Keystone XL, were: Kinder Morgan's Trans Mountain Expansion Project, Enbridge's Northern Gateway and Line 9, and TransCanada's Energy East. They have not been completed until today and have encountered significant delays in approval processes and serious public contestation. Under Harper, the Northern Gateway case was the most visible illustration of the problems associated with the idea of expanding Canada's export capacity. Although the pipeline, after a lengthy and controversial procedure, was approved by the National Energy Board (NEB) in June 2014, the decision was appealed and eventually overruled by the Federal Court of Appeal two years later (Gattinger, "Is Canada"; Proctor). A similar situation stalled Ottawa hopes to export liquified natural gas (LNG) to Asia. Terminal construction issues and political protests were responsible for serious holdups (de Kerckhove and Petrolekas 2).

From the government's perspective, without the necessary infrastructure, Canada risked missing out the opportunity for wealth and job creation. Thus, the Conservatives decided to aggressively facilitate lengthy infrastructure approval processes. The way the government chose to defend its vision caused them enemies not only among environmental organizations, but also among ordinary Canadians. For example, in 2012, Joe Oliver, the then minister of natural resources, published an open letter in which he accused foreign-sponsored "radical groups," plotting with "jet-setting celebrities" of "hijacking" approval processes with their "radical ideological agenda." The "ultimate goal" was to "delay a project to the point it becomes economically unviable" (Oliver). Stephen Harper repeated similar accusations, saying that foreign environmental activists were trying to subvert the public comment in pipeline approval processes (Goldenberg, "Oil").

Joe Oliver's unusually strong language attracted widespread criticism, but the remarkable international interest in Canadian energy resource development projects, especially connected with oil sands, started in a December 2011 decision to formally withdraw from the Kyoto Protocol. We address this issue in a subsequent subchapter, but at this point it is sufficient to note that from a public relations perspective, Canada had earned a reputation of a country that did not keep promises and had no intention of living up to its pledge to reduce greenhouse emissions, whether below 1990 levels – as was enacted in Kyoto – or below 2005 levels – as Ottawa pledged in Copenhagen (Sorensen).

The fiasco associated with pursuing the pipeline projects was accompanied by the significant drop in oil prices that started in 2014. This was followed not only by a recession in Alberta and a federal budgetary crisis in the early 2015, but also significantly slowed down the development of Canada's energy resource industry. As a result, after almost ten years of being in power, Harper's vision of Canada's energy superpower status remained unfulfilled, as Canada continued to be an energy warehouse at best. The most persistent problem – the fact that Canada's energy resources were land-locked and connected with only one export market – the United States – continued. In fact, the dependence on the U.S. intensified under Harper. Between 2009 and 2015, according to Canada's NEB, oil exports to the U.S. had grown by 70 per cent, while Canadian oil exports to the rest of the world had gone up by just seven per cent (Kirby, "The Perils"). This situation became problematic with the upsurge in U.S. tight oil and shale gas production. This rise not only reduced U.S. energy imports and resulted in the lowering of oil and gas prices, but it also called into question the size and viability of the American market for Canadian energy in the future (Gattinger, "Canada Is").

Given the fact that Canada's energy resources are abundant and underutilized, the decision to pursue the export strategy outside of North America seemed still viable after Harper's Conservatives lost power to Trudeau's Liberals. Given Asia's insatiable demand for energy and hopes in some parts of Europe for more energy security, meaning less imports from Russia, Ottawa has chances to become an exporting energy power (Zaretskaya; Canada-Asia Energy Futures Task Force 3; see also de Kerckhove and Petrolekas 5-6). For example, Canada as a significant producer of LNG – in 2013, it was 165 billion cubic meters annually – may, in a situation of tensions between Russia and Europe, reduce threats of supply shortages and this way contribute towards the Europe's energy security. In 2013, Canada's production of LNG equalled the amount of natural gas sold by Russia to the European Union and Turkey (de Kerckhove and Petrolekas 1). Memoranda of understanding and even the first biding agreements have already been signed. However, the amounts are not impressive. For example, in 2013, the German company E.ON struck a deal with Canada's Pieridae Energy to import around 7 billion cubic meters of LNG for 20 years, beginning in 2020. The deal represented an important diversification of supply for the German company, which relied mainly upon imports from Russia and Norway (Cutler). The Conservative government acknowledged the fact that Canada should move ahead with the export of not just oil but also natural gas and, to mention Foreign Affairs Minister John Baird's words, "that opportunities are not all exclusively south of the border or to the Asia-Pacific region but also to our traditional allies in Europe" (Krugel, "Canada"). However, Canada's opportunities will be realized only if supporting policies, infrastructure, and public support can be put into place. Apart from problems with building the oil pipelines, the export of liquefied natural gas from Canadian East and West coasts will take at least a few more years. Of about 20 LNG terminals planned, not a single one has been built so far. Nevertheless, the Trudeau government did not shelve the idea of exporting LNG. If only "several strategic terminals" are built, Canada will have a chance to become a "cost-competitive, secure and stable supplier" of gas globally, according to a 2016 internal government memo (Lou).

Yet, there have been dangers inherent in pursuing natural resources export dependent strategy and concentrating on one industry. On the one hand, the commodity prices surge shielded Canada from the worst effects of the global financial crisis. On the other hand, Canada, as a net exporter of energy, was hurt by the drop in oil prices. Prices peaked in summer 2008 at more than USD 140 a barrel for West Texas Intermediate crude (WTI), stayed above USD 100 a barrel until the summer of 2014, then dropped to the minimum around USD 27 a barrel in January 2016. Since June 2016, oil prices have stayed at around USD 50 a barrel ("WTI"). The fluctuations were the effect of the cyclical nature of the resource-based economy – i.e. recurring downturns following cyclical growths. Another problem is the rising share of oil in Canada's total exports. By the mid-2014, it reached 19 per cent – an increase from about six per cent a decade earlier. At the same time auto industry export fell to 14 per cent from 22 per cent. Also, research and development (R&D) in other sectors of Canada's economy decreased. Some economists thought that the Canadian dollar had effectively joined the ranks of petro-currencies. A five-time stronger correlation between movements in the price of oil and the Canadian dollar was observed between 2000 and 2015 (Bloomberg).

Reliance on unprocessed and semi-processed resources in export grew during the first decade of the 21st century, reaching in July 2011 two-thirds of Canada's total exports. In 1999, higher-value finished products had accounted for almost 60 per cent of Canada's exports. For Jim Stanford, this change towards staple products symbolized a reversal of diversifying strategy of Canadian exports (3).

One of the reasons why the Harper energy strategy failed to achieve the set goals was the style of pursuing it. The Conservatives were unsuccessful in establishing trust in their capability to develop a carbon-intensive resource in a sustainable fashion. When in 2007, a year after the initial declaration of Canada as an energy superpower, Prime Minister Harper added a narrowing element, stating that Canada would meet a "real challenge" and a "real responsibility" to become "a clean energy superpower," the critics took his words as a "smokescreen" to "buffer international disapproval of Canada's failure to meet its Kyoto targets" (Way 76-77). As Chris Sorensen noted, Ottawa painted "a target on the industry's back" as the Keystone XL became "a poster child for climate change" at the same time when President Barack Obama wanted "to create an environmental legacy for himself in his last two years" (see also Goldenberg, "Canada"). Even though in 2013 Harper redoubled his lobbying efforts and proposed the Obama administration a "joint action to reduce greenhouse gas emissions in the oil and gas sector" to gain the approval for the Keystone XL pipeline, he lost the battle for the presidential permit (Mas, "Harper"; Hall).

The lack of sensitivity and creativity when approaching energy politics overshadowed the reasonable goals of the Harper government. Had Canada followed a Norwegian path, creating a carbon tax framework simultaneously to developing an offshore oil industry, the chances of becoming an energy superpower would have been higher. Some provinces, such as British Columbia, Quebec, even Alberta, introduced some forms of climate change regulations during Harper's tenure. Even Canada's oil industry started to demand greenhouse gas regulations and urged Ottawa to invest in carbon capture and storage technology. But discussions with the provinces and the oil industry failed to bring any fruit as several deadlines to bring in regulations for the energy sector promised by the government were missed, to the point that Environment Minister Peter Kent lost his job (Sorensen; Hall). Some pundits, Chris McDermott for example, suggested that, in order to keep the oil sands out of the international spotlight, the Harper government needed only some regulations for oil and gas (Sorensen). The result of Harper's approach was that Canada's oil industry, and the country in general, got a loathsome reputation (Goldenberg, "Canada").

The Justin Trudeau government seems to have learned Harper's lesson. The way the Liberals have tried to approach Canada's energy sector connects two big issues: the need to build pipelines and address environmental concerns firstly by setting a price on carbon that in effect would lead to the reduction of greenhouse gas emissions. The energy strategy includes these two opposing elements. Moreover, this strategy has elements of selectivity and, in its specifics, it does not differ much from Harper's plan, which is more elaborately discussed in the next chapter.

As we mentioned above, Prime Minister Harper's foreign policy selectively emphasized Canada's energy resources as a way to influence international politics. Although Canada has not yet become an energy superpower, due to the failure to establish sufficient export infrastructure and the inability to address climate change issues, we think that Canada can be referred to by a term coined by the Bloomberg agency – an "energy superpower in waiting" (Greenspon et al. "Harper's"). With an energy demand that, according to the U.S. Energy Information Administration, in the longer term will continue to grow, Canada has no choice but to develop its oil and gas industry and look for alternative markets ("International Energy" 7). At the same time, in our opinion, Canada's status as an energy power should not be understood in the hard-power sense, i.e. as a country that aggressively imposes its will on other countries, but rather in the soft-power sense of persuasion, influence and energy diplomacy. As suggested by Monica Gattinger, Canada has developed wide-ranging expertise not only in extracting and transporting energy resources, but also in creating policy and regulatory systems to produce and transport energy safely, efficiently and sustainably. Such qualities "make Canada a highly sought-after advisor by developed and developing countries alike" (Gattinger, "Is Canada"). Ottawa can also use diplomacy to encourage potential importers of its LNG to retire from coal power and reduce emissions this way (Coleman and Jordaan). Canadian governments could also commit to ratchet up the stringency of their own regulations in response to emission-reduction regulations elsewhere. For example, British Columbia could commit to increases in its carbon tax once China has implemented a stringent carbon price. Canadian LNG can play a positive role in addressing one of the world's economic and environmental problems if Canadian regulators maintain a focus on controlling emissions within their authority and rely on diplomacy to encourage emission reductions overseas.

Keystone XL

The Keystone XL pipeline was a flagship project for the Harper government's vision of making Canada an energy super power. The pipeline would have made this vision closer to reality. It was planned to carry over 800,000 barrels of oil from Alberta to the U.S. refineries along the coast of the Gulf of Mexico, bringing economic benefits of a great scale. On the other hand, it became a contentious issue, as critics of the Keystone XL warned of its environmental impact. Because the pipeline crossed the Canada-United States border, it required that the U.S. president granted a permit for the construction. Due to intensified lobbying from environmentalists, American celebrities and Hollywood actors, and even the Republican governor of Nebraska opposing "Canada's dirty oil," the process of issuing the permit was constantly being delayed (Savage; "Republicans"; Hall). Such a situation created tensions and a major rift between Canada and the U.S., and especially between Prime Minister Harper and President Barack Obama (Ibbitson, *Stephen* 336).

In response to the delays, the Harper government started a public relations campaign in the United States, aimed at convincing Americans to approve the construction of the pipeline. Not only did the campaign, which used the methods that Canadian scholars called "megaphone diplomacy," fail to bring the U.S. presidential permit, it also deepened the differences of opinion between the leaders of both countries (Bratt, "Stephen" 488-489). An important element of the megaphone diplomacy was the "ethical oil" rhetoric, whose author was Ezra Levant, a far-right Canadian political commentator. The purpose of such argumentation was to oppose the criticism of Canadian oil sands, by, for example, repeating that environmental degradation due to the extraction of oil sands was overstated by environmentalists, or by reminding the American public that the alternative to the imports from Canadian oil sands was oil from unstable and undemocratic petro-states, with poor human rights records and low standards of environmental responsibility. Canada, in Levant's view, stood practically alone as an ethical oil producer (Levant). This type of argumentation was picked up and used in numerous speeches by the prime minister or his cabinet members, such as Joe Oliver or Peter Kent, to defend the need to build the Keystone XL and to confront depictions of Canada as a "dirty oil" nation. Oliver, in 2013, said in Washington that the U.S. energy security could be enhanced by Canada if the U.S. chose "Canada – a friend, neighbour and ally – as its source." Otherwise, the alternative was "to import oil from less friendly, less stable countries with weaker – or perhaps no – environmental standards (qtd. in Koring, "Resources"). In New York, Prime Minister Harper added that Canada would "not take no for an answer" from the U.S. on the Keystone XL project and would "keep pushing forward [...] until it's approved" (qtd. in Slater, "Harper won't"). Yet, Prime Minister Harper did not anticipate the U.S. resistance ("Kyoto").

Such a conjuration of reality did not help the Keystone case, as it antagonized the American president even more ("Keystone"; Robertson 110). The delays continued as Obama refused to reach a final decision until finally, in February 2015, he vetoed an attempt by the Republican-dominated Congress to push through the approval of the pipeline. The veto was in large part a result of the bad publicity Canada had had since it left the Kyoto Protocol in 2011 (discussed in the subsequent part of this chapter). Canada's withdrawal from Kyoto infuriated U.S. environmentalists, who efficiently lobbied the Democratic administration against the pipeline. The Harper government was unwilling to change its skeptical view on the climate change policies and refused to help president Obama with some regulations of emissions from the oil and gas industry. The Canadian Embassy in Washington informed Ottawa that Canada was presented in the U.S. as "lax, almost indifferent on the environment" ("How"). Nevertheless, the only response diplomats got from the Canadian government was that regulations were "in the making." Canada never went beyond the promises, as Harper and his closest advisers concluded that Obama would not change his mind anyway and "Canada would be digging itself into a competitive hole" (Gattinger, "Is Canada"). The rift between Harper and Obama started to grow. Obama presented the Keystone XL as "providing the ability of Canada to pump their oil, send it through our land, down to the Gulf, where it will be sold everywhere else. It doesn't have an impact on U.S. gas prices" (Koring, "Keystone"). To make the matter worse, at the 2014 summit in Toluca, Mexico, Obama publicly demanded that Canadian prime minister should start seriously working for the reduction of greenhouse gases (GHG) emissions (Nossal, "Primat" 8-9).

Summarizing, the Harper government failed at including the Keystone XL in his vision of making Canada an energy power. Not only did the tactic aimed at receiving the presidential permit not produce the anticipated results, the process of constructing alternative pipelines was also halted. Moreover, the Conservative government also neglected the importance of the growing shale gas and oil production in the U.S. for the U.S. energy security. Ottawa still insisted on being the most secure supplier of fossil fuels to Americans when import pressure in the U.S. was dropping. Prime Minister Harper also lacked understanding of the climate change, not only at the domestic level but also at international summits, which resulted, as John Kirton puts it, in "failing to build bridges and leaving Obama little to work with" (qtd. in Gattinger, "Is Canada"). However, as some suggested, not only Harper was to blame for the failure of negotiations over Keystone XL. Colin Robertson, for example, partly blamed Barack Obama, who "appeared to exhibit the least appreciation of the strategic importance of Canada to the U.S." (Robertson 110). Allan Gotlieb, former Canadian Ambassador to the United States and respected commentator of Canada-U.S. relations, went even further, arguing that Canada was at "at an historic turning point in this special relationship," as it could no longer rely on the United States for its economic well-being (qtd. in Gattinger, "Is Canada"). The above opinions were, however, largely overstated, although the dispute over Keystone was definitely an important lesson for Canada, which influenced both Stephen Harper's and Justin Trudeau's trade policies.

Environment

One of the most frequently debated elements of Harper's foreign policy were environmental policies. For the opponents, between 2006 and 2015 Canada was transformed from an environmental leader into an international laggard. The positive image Canada had earned since ecology started to influence the international agenda at the end of the 1980s was ruined. Initially, Canada promptly engaged in "green" initiatives, mostly through Canadian scientists who were leaders in research that brought the climate change issue to the attention of governments. But there were also many Canadians who worked for international organizations directly involved in climate change discussions, such as the United Nations Environment Programme, the World Meteorological Organization and the World Climate Research Program (Bernstein and Gore 30). In modern times, Canada has undertaken various important environmental initiatives, starting with the 1987 Montreal Protocol – an international agreement aimed at phasing out substances that damage the Earth's ozone layer – or the 1991 Air Quality Agreement – a bilateral transboundary treaty with the U.S., which resulted in tackling the so-called acid rains. The Montreal Protocol was praised by Secretary-General of the United Nations, Kofi Annan, as "perhaps the single most successful international agreement to date" (United Nations, "Background"). In 1988, Canada also hosted the Conference on the Changing Atmosphere in Toronto. The main recommendations of the conference led directly to the negotiation process which resulted in the adoption of the United Nations Framework Convention on Climate Change (UNFCCC) in 1992 ("The Changing"). Thanks to those initiatives, Ottawa became a pioneer among world's governments in adopting basic climate change regulations. The government of Brian Mulroney committed Canada to lower greenhouse gases emissions to 1990 levels by 2000. In 1992, Jean Chrétien's Liberals declared to go 20 per cent below the 1988 GHG levels by 2005. Nevertheless, both governments did not introduce mandatory policies and promoted only voluntary actions. As a result, Canada never met any of these commitments.

Regardless of that, Canada was actively engaged in the subsequent phase of deliberations over the climate change, which was the Kyoto Protocol. In 1997, Jean Chrétien negotiated an obligation to reduce Canada's annual GHG emissions by 6 per cent, i.e. below the 1990 levels, by 2012. The commitment was similar to the declarations of other developed countries, especially the U.S., although Australia, with an economy similar to Canada's and heavily dependent on fossil fuels, negotiated an 8 per cent increase of 1990 levels. As Harrison argued, Chrétien put the U.S. position as "the benchmark for preserving Canadian national honour" and did not follow lower level emission targets, supported by federal and provincial environment and energy ministers ("The Road" 11; Macdonald and Smith, "Promises" 120). However, the Americans set their ambitious targets higher knowing that they would never be ratified by Congress, and as such would never be implemented (Wells, *Right* 298-300). As a result of the personal decision of the prime minister, Canada accepted higher levels of reductions than the federal and provincial governments were prepared to take. As argued by Macdonald and Smith, "[i]t is impossible to escape the conclusion that the prime minister gave [premiers] private assurances that, yet again, Canadian rhetoric would in all likelihood not translate into action" (Macdonald and Smith, "Promises" 114-15).

Meeting Canada's emissions targets became even more difficult when, in 2001, the U.S. decided not to ratify the Kyoto Protocol. Canadian businesses immediately started arguing that the ratification would reduce the competitiveness of Canadian exports to the United States. Nevertheless, in 2002, the Chrétien government ratified the Kyoto Protocol. Chrétien supported the vote in the House of Commons despite the strong opposition from members of petroleum industry and the Alberta government, who complained that the accord would cost the Canadian economy billions of dollars. Some scholars, Heather Smith for example, argued that Chrétien converted to environmentalism at the end of his political career and decided to build his legacy on the Kyoto Protocol ("Political" 55). Kathryn Harrison maintained that it was prime minister's commitment to multilateralism, that drove him to ratify the Kyoto Protocol. Chrétien was aware that Alberta would not agree to the necessary reduction of emissions from fossil fuels. But having a strong and disciplined majority in the House of Commons, he preferred to choose his personal commitment to the Kyoto Protocol over electoral interests. What is more striking, Chrétien was repeatedly warned that he endangered Canada's international reputation because the country was bound to fail to meet the targets (Harrison, "The Road" 21). Smith speculated that the Chrétien government stayed in the Kyoto Protocol when the opposition from the U.S. Senate virtually ended U.S. participation in the agreement because "it allowed Canada to present an image of itself as a good and independent international environmental leader, thus challenging accusations of sabotaging negotiations in tandem with the United States" (H. Smith, "Political" 51-52).

The above explanation seems to be justified, as the next Canadian government, led by Paul Martin, presented the Kyoto Protocol as the most important element in the fight against climate change as well. Canada returned, at least rhetorically, to international leadership on climate change. Stéphane Dion, Paul Martin's minister of environment, served, for example, as president of the 11th "conference of parties," held in Montreal in December 2005 (H. Smith, "Political" 56). While Prime

Minister Martin publicly supported the tackling of global warming, he failed, however, at crafting a credible strategy that could secure achieving Canada's emissions targets. His government, similarly to his predecessor's, "relied almost exclusively on politically appealing but ineffectual voluntary programs and subsidies." The lack of the enforceable targets resulted in the continued rise of Canada's GHG emissions in the years following the ratification of the Kyoto Protocol, reaching 26 per cent above the 1990 baseline in 2007 (Harrison, "A Tale" 387). The reasons behind that failure were complex and included American influence through business lobbies. Nevertheless, the pressure from environmental NGOs and Canadian public opinion, strongly supportive of the Kyoto Protocol, forced the Chrétien and Martin governments to "give at least the appearance of action by developing policies to be implemented." In 2005, the Martin government introduced *Project Green,* called the greenest budget in Canadian history. However, it also did not impose new taxes and the obligatory regulatory controls planned for the industry were rather weak (Harrison, "A Tale" 387; H. Smith, "Political" 56). The 2006 federal election killed that plan, which nonetheless would not have been very helpful in lowering Canada's GHG emissions to the Kyoto levels.

The only consensus in the environmental polices in Canada since the Cold War has been based on the desire to present Canada's positive image and to play the leadership role. This consensus broke, however, as far as the GHG emission reduction implementation policies were concerned. All Canadian governments have fallen short of addressing the problem and Canada's emissions of greenhouse gases rose regardless of which party was in power. The explanation to this lies in the combination of Canada's geographic location and the structure of its economy.

Canada, as a sparsely populated, cold and northern country, with the economy heavily dependant on the extraction and export of fossil fuels, could not be easily transformed into a dream country of environmental activists without the support from most businesses and political actors on both federal and provincial levels. And it has been extremely difficult to strike such an agreement since the oil from Alberta's tar sands is "a major economic lever in Canada" and "one of the dirtiest, most carbon-intensive fuels on the planet" at the same time (Bratt, "Stephen" 489; Biello). The energy sector, as the *Globe and Mail* estimated it in 2014, is worth 10 per cent of Canada's GDP and around 25 per cent of Canada's exports, which is "more than retail, construction, agriculture and the public sector's contribution to the economy." Although there are periods in particular years when those numbers reach 30 and 40 per cent respectively (Jang and McCarthy).

When the Harper government came to power in 2006, Canada, in terms of meeting the Kyoto emission targets, was in a problematic situation and a number of available options for Harper, as Duane Bratt rightly argued, was limited to three. The first one was to play the same "game" as the previous Liberal governments, i.e. covering the lack of significant action with the rhetoric of importance of the climate change. The second one – introducing a real GHG emission reduction strategy aimed at reaching the Kyoto targets – entailed heavy political and economical costs. Harper chose the third option of abandoning "any pretence about carrying out meaningful action on climate change" (Bratt, "Stephen" 489). Or as Mark Jaccard puts it, the Conservatives simply "had no intention of dealing with climate change."

Harper's approach to the climate change was founded on the prolonged negligence of the climate change issue by the previous governments, but it was accompanied by the prime minister's and his ministers' disbelief in the real danger of the climate change. In 2002, in a fundraising letter, Stephen Harper compared the Kyoto Protocol to a "socialist scheme," based on "tentative and contradictory scientific evidence" that focused on carbon dioxide, which was "essential to life" ("Harper's Letter"). Later, some of Harper's cabinet ministers, including the one with the environment portfolio, questioned the very existence of climate change, calling it a "debatable" issue or claiming there was "no scientific consensus" over it. While doubting in greenhouse effect was rather incidental, the truth of the matter was that in Harper's highly selective approach to international affairs, economic interests prevailed clearly over tackling the challenges of global warming. Promoting the extraction of the so-called "dirty oil" from the tar sands in Alberta, Harper's major political support base, and constructing the Keystone XL pipeline, which would export that oil to the refineries in Texas and then, hopefully, to international buyers, were much higher on the government's agenda than curbing greenhouse emissions (Nikiforuk). Such an approach was especially visible after the 2008-2011 financial crisis. The public opinion's support for environmental issues, as seen in 2006, waned as the economy became the most important thing for Canadians. In the 2008 election, economy versus the environment was a defining campaign issue. Parties chose two different appeals in their platforms: the Conservatives emphasized the economy and the Liberals – the environment. Stéphane Dion's ill-received *Green Shift*, prompting introduction of a carbon tax system, did not have many chances with Harper's commitment to keep the books balanced (Nossal, "Primat" 8-9; Nossal, "Dion").

The results were obvious – GHG emissions grew despite new targets that had been announced several times. Canada was regularly handed with "fossil awards" by environmental critics at the United Nations climate conventions in 2007, 2009 and 2011, for obstructing discussions. The Canadian government also opposed the imposition of binding targets. Prime Minister Harper argued that the priority should be bringing all countries, including those exempted from the Kyoto Protocol, such as China and India, to a new agreement, that would in turn impose new binding targets. Without the U.S., the Kyoto Protocol covered only 15 per cent of emissions. Harper did not hide his *désintéressement*. For example, he did not attend the 2014 U.N. climate change summit of 127 world leaders in New York, instead sending Minister of Environment Leona Aglukkaq (Bratt, "Stephen" 489).

Initially, because the Conservatives formed a minority government in 2006, Harper had to weaken his vigorous opposition to the Kyoto Protocol, seeing that polls indicated the increased interest of the Canadian public in climate change. Thus, in 2007, the Harper government announced new GHG emission reduction targets of 20 per cent below 2006 levels by 2020 and between 60 per cent and 70 per cent below 2006 levels by 2050. The targets were similar to the ones the prime minister had spent many years mocking (Nossal, "Dion" 8). Ottawa also announced an implementation plan, *Turning the Corner*, although with regulations that did not place Canada on track of meeting the targets. Two years later, Ottawa signed the Copenhagen Accord, in which it committed to reduce its GHG emissions by 17 per cent below 2005 levels by 2020. This time the government chose to pursue the harmonisation of emission reduction policies and regulations with those of the United States, adopted under the Obama administration. At the federal level, the government indicated that it would pursue a "sector-by-sector regulatory approach" to meet its Copenhagen commitments (International Energy Agency 41).

Nevertheless, greenhouse emissions were increasing and when it was close to 2012, set in the Kyoto Protocol as the date by which the country was to meet its targets, Ottawa decided to withdraw from the Protocol on

December 9, 2011. Canada became the single country that pulled out of the only international binding agreement on climate change. It was also the first time Canada had ever withdrawn from an international treaty (Ibbitson, *Stephen* 343). The government cited the costs of meeting the Protocol's requirements as the main reason for the withdrawal. Peter Kent, environment minister, argued that:

> [...] under Kyoto Canada is facing radical and irresponsible choices if we are to avoid punishing multi-billion dollar payments [...] To meet the targets under Kyoto for 2012 [Canada would have to] remove every car, truck, ATV, tractor, ambulance, police car and vehicle of every kind from Canadian roads (qtd. in Simon).

The prime minister was even more open about the withdrawal. In the House of Commons, during the Question Period, he said: "What made absolutely no sense for this country was a Liberal government that signed the Kyoto protocols, signed what I quite frankly think were stupid targets and then had no plan after 10 years in office to even implement those" (qtd. in Proussalidis).

Canada was widely criticized for the withdrawal from the Kyoto Protocol. The country was dubbed "a beautiful nation turning itself into a corrupt petro-state." Germany, China, France, the small island nation of Tuvalu were concerned. Some countries, including India, were worried that Canada's decision might jeopardize future conferences. Australian government minister Greg Combet, however, defended the decision, saying that the withdrawal did not mean Canada would not continue to "play its part in global efforts to tackle climate change" ("Canada under Fire").

The Conservative government decided to ignore the international criticism. As John Baird, foreign minister, said in 2012: "I don't have many foreign ministers or many foreign governments who raise climate change with me. In eight months, maybe two or three times" (qtd. in Campbell, "John"). The government could afford ignoring the climate change thanks to a decreasing interest from the Canadian public opinion. Although 56 per cent of Canadians wanted Canada to sign the new international climate agreement, even if it meant job losses and higher prices, at the same time climate change was not seen as a "clear and present danger" at home (McCarthy). For example, the *Toronto Star*, the second largest Canadian daily, put the news about Canada's withdrawal from Kyoto on a rather distant fourth page ("Canada's Kyoto").

Regardless of the above, the government again changed its declared greenhouse gases emission target. In May 2015, Ottawa officially submitted to the UNFCCC its intention to reduce GHG emissions by 30 per cent below 2005 levels by 2030 ("Canada's INDC"). Yet, not many experts believed in the government's intention to meet this target (Jaccard). In fact, in 2015, Canada was the only country among 33 major economies with fewer climate change legislations than at the beginning of 2012 (Wilfert).

It is difficult not to agree with Kim Richard Nossal, who wrote in 2014 that what made Harper's climate change policies different from the policies of his predecessors was not feigned engagement in the implementation of regulations – all governments' record was mediocre, to say the least – but that he "abandoned the sort of principled stance against emissions," or, in other words, that he abandoned liberal internationalism as a cover to his actions (Nossal, "Primat" 8-9). Nevertheless, the results were similar.

The Harper government used various arguments to justify its approach to climate change. Firstly, the Conservatives indicated lack of ability of any federal government to implement full climate change policies without the consent of the provincial authorities as the implementation fell largely within their jurisdiction. And it was a contentious issue, especially after the 1980 National Energy Program, whose implementation "nearly tore the country apart" (Flannery). Secondly, the most common argument used by the Conservatives was that Canada's emissions were only a fraction of global emissions and, thus, whether Canada reduced its GHG emissions faster or slower – it did not significantly matter. Since the fossil fuel sector had been "a major economic engine in Canada," the Canadian government had to carefully consider the potential economic consequences of the proposals for combating climate change (Bratt, "Stephen" 490). Thirdly, the government indicated that the Kyoto framework was ineffective, insignificant and, if implemented, would threaten the economies of such countries as Canada. The framework, in the government's opinion, was dominated by radical environmentalists who scared citizens with apocalyptic visions of the future, whereas in fact it was "a massive wealth transfer from developed countries, who were not really expected to meet unattainable emission targets, to developing countries who were exempted or able to meet their targets as a result of economic decline precipitated by poor policy choices" (Boessenkool). Fourthly, Ottawa indicated the fact that the U.S. – Canada's largest trading partner – not only did not sign the Kyoto Protocol, but contrary to "the rhetoric of President Obama, shows no sign of reducing its own GHG emissions" (Bratt, "Stephen" 490). And finally, the Conservatives strongly argued that any future global agreement had to involve all major global emitters. They argued that Harper worked towards involving countries like China and India in a new climate action initiative that would not put Canada's economy at a comparative disadvantage (Boessenkool). Paradoxically, this argument was gradually becoming an increasingly common view in different parts of the world, which led to the adoption of the 2015 Paris Agreement (Swift, "Paris").

To sum up, we find consistency in the very selective application of climate change regulations across the entire spectrum of Canadian governments since the end of the Cold War. All the prime ministers have had their share in the failure to meet GHG reduction promises. And all have faced the same choice regarding the climate change policy: impose short-term costs and risks associated with the implementation of the promises for the long-term benefits or behave as usual and delay the implementation for as long as possible.

The Harper government did that calculation and apparently reached the conclusion that it was less politically costly to abstain from actions than to act on climate change. As Mark Jaccard accurately observed, such an approach was possible due to three reasons. Firstly, there were no compulsory policies in Canada, such as carbon taxes or cap and trade regulations. Secondly, climate change is an issue of global nature, which means that tackling it requires a joint action of the largest emitters to be noticed and effective. Last but not least, there is no global and independent "monitoring service that provides feedback about progress" (Jaccard; Wilt, "Conservatives").

Arctic sovereignty

The Arctic during the Cold War was perceived mostly from the security point of view. It was the shortest route for the Soviet bombers, and later intercontinental ballistic missiles, to potential targets in the United States and in Canada. To counteract Soviet threats, both countries built radar lines – the most recent one was the Distant Early Warning (DEW) Line in the northern parts of Canada and the U.S. – and deployed troops and other types of military equipment in the region (Bratt, "Stephen" 490). Apart from the security perspective, the Arctic resurfaced in Canadian politics only for short periods and quickly disappeared, as was the case with Prime Minister John Diefenbaker's *Northern Vision* in the 1960s (Isard).

Since the end of the Cold War, Canada's Arctic policy has undergone significant modifications. Firstly, in the late 1990s, the definition of continental security was broadened and human and ecological dimensions were added (Lackenbauer, "Mixed" 2). Secondly, the notion of sovereignty was expanded to also include cooperation with other Arctic countries and organizations. The result of that change was Canada's involvement of in the establishment of the Arctic Council, with permanent member states – Canada, Denmark, Finland, Iceland, Norway, Russia, Sweden, the U.S. – but also with Indigenous peoples' organizations as permanent observers. The Arctic Council has become the most important regional forum for institutional cooperation, for the protection of the environment and the sustainable development of the High North.

Such a way of articulating the Arctic policy – i.e. stressing the regional cooperation and human dimension of development – was clearly visible in the 2000 document entitled *Northern Dimension of Canada's Foreign Policy*, issued by the Jean Chrétien government. The strategy was based on four pillars: strengthening the security and well-being of all Canadians, including the residents of the North and Indigenous peoples; exercising and the strengthening of Canada's sovereignty in the Arctic; building a circumpolar region with a well-functioning and integrated economy; promoting the safety of the people living in the North and the sustainable development of these areas (Government of Canada, "The Northern").

Yet, by the mid-2000s, political preferences of Canadian society had undergone a profound change, which resulted in the emergence of a new narrative on the Arctic. On the one hand, climate change became a prominent issue, following debates that had swept through the media and the academic world that had warned about the growing evidence of the particularly negative impact of global warming on the polar regions. Another issue, which at some point almost dominated the political discourse, was Canada's sovereignty over the Arctic. The heated discussions were sparked by leaks about the activities of U.S. submarines in the waters of the Northwest Passage ("U.S. Sub May"). The debate was then extended to include additional Arctic issues related to sovereignty, such as, for example, the maritime boundaries in the North. Canada's dispute with Denmark over the status of a tiny and uninhabited Hans Island in the Nares Strait was particularly prominent (Loukacheva 194).

The growing interest of the Canadian public motivated politicians to include Arctic issues in their political programs. Already in 2005, Prime Minister Paul Martin declared that the Arctic, due to growing security threats, changes in global power and the global economy, was a priority for his government. The cabinet concluded that the next two decades could bring changes that would require new solutions to monitor and control Canada's territory and effective diplomacy. Significant challenges were identified, such as the opening of new transport routes, including the Northwest Passage, due to the melting of the ice sheet (Government of Canada, "A Role" 1-3). Those declarations initiated the practice of linking the issues of sovereignty and security in political rhetoric and strategic documents. The Arctic became an important element of the election platforms in the 2005 campaign. Major political parties were contending over what was the best solution for sovereignty crisis, which, according to many Canadians, would have a severe impact on Canada's future.

One of the politicians who provided voters with a clear vision for solving the Arctic problems was Stephen Harper. The strategists who helped construct the Conservative Party's platform determined that the Arctic would be the subject that would guarantee a success at the ballot box. Already during the election campaign, in December 2005, Harper promised an increase in military presence in the Arctic, which would provide protection against external threats to Canadian sovereignty (Harper, "Harper Stands Up"). In the electoral platform, Harper argued in a very simplistic manner that "[y]ou don't defend national sovereignty with flags, cheap election-rhetoric and advertising campaigns. You need forces on the ground, ships in the sea and proper surveillance. That will be the Conservative approach" (Harper, "Harper Election Platform"). The new rhetoric was a departure from the previously promoted human security issues and emphasized the potential of conventional forces (Lackenbauer, "Mixed" 3-4).

The Conservatives' 2006 election victory transformed those campaign promises into a coherent political strategy. By 2009, several documents had been published – they contained the most important elements of the new approach. All of them emphasized the need for active defence of the Arctic potential, which could in the future make the region a source of benefit for Canada and convert the country into an "Arctic superpower" (Boswell). The first phase of the Harper government's Arctic strategy was symbolically opened with Harper's declaration, declared alongside the plans of purchasing patrol vessels, in which he declared that "Canada has a choice when it comes to defending our sovereignty over the Arctic. We either use it or lose it" (Harper, "Prime Minister Stephen Harper Announces"). Under this approach, called "use it or lose it," the government pledged unprecedented CAD 5 billion to Arctic defence, including, among others, the construction of an icebreaker and a system of sensors to protect Canada's North from unauthorized submarine traffic, and the purchase of transport aircraft (Greenaway).

It is worth mentioning that linking sovereignty with its "exercising" was widely criticized by international law experts, who pointed out that, irrespective of actions or inactions, Canada's sovereignty over land and sea in the Arctic was not endangered (Macnab). Harper, however, believed that international agreements and treaties were not as important as the actual military presence in the North. In his view, if the Northwest Passage was transformed into a shipping route, Canada must be able to monitor it and provide law enforcement to counter illegal activities, such as pouring pollutants by ships or illegal fishing (Chase, "Myth").

Constant references to sovereignty and the announcement of the plan to increase military capabilities was intended to mobilize that part of the Canadian electorate which in previous years was convinced of the lack of adequate actions by the government ("Frozen"). It is also worth remembering that the choice of the Arctic strategy, combined with strong military accents, was a way to show independence from the United States and was calculated to gain the support of some anti-American-minded Canadians. That tactic was quickly noticed by American diplomats in Canada and Harper was faced with immediate criticism from the U.S. Ambassador to Canada, David Wilkins, who expressed a negative opinion on increasing Canadian military presence in the Arctic ("Harper Brushes").

The first phase of building Harper's Arctic policy should also be examined from the perspective of broader strategic objectives promoted by the Conservative Party. Canada's security strategy implemented after 2006 placed a strong emphasis on hard security, the capability to defend Canadian territory and maritime areas (Lackenbauer, "Mixed" 4). The *Canada First: Defence Strategy* warned:

> The government recognizes the challenges Canada's sovereignty in the Arctic could face in the future. In the coming years, sovereignty and security challenges will become more pressing as the impact of climate change leads to enhanced activity throughout the region. The defence of Canada's sovereignty and the protection of territorial integrity in the Arctic remains a top priority for the government (National Defence Canada, "Canada").

Focusing on the dangers posed by the Arctic military conflict allowed Harper to keep the public support for other defence projects.

Harper's rhetoric on the Arctic softened after the 2008 Ilulissat Declaration. In that document, five countries that border the Arctic Ocean (Russia, the United States, Canada, Denmark, and Norway) reaffirmed their commitment to working within an existing framework of international law to delimit their respective areas of jurisdiction over the seabed (Arctic Council, "The Ilulissat"). Since then, official statements have included more references to: international cooperation, international law, geological research, and the necessity to address the needs of people living in the northern regions. Military threats or sovereignty were mentioned less frequently (Cannon). In this more amicable international circumstances, the Department for Indian Affairs and Northern Development, in 2009, issued an official document containing a comprehensive federal strategy for the Arctic, entitled *Canadian Northern Strategy: Our North, Our Heritage, Our Future* (Indian and Northern Affairs Canada). It included elements of both domestic policy and foreign policy in the Arctic. The latter elements were also repeated in a more elaborate manner in 2010 in the *Statement on Canada's Arctic Foreign Policy. Exercising Sovereignty and Promoting Canada's Northern Strategy Abroad*.

At the rhetorical level, the two documents emphasized partnership and included the vision of the Canadian Arctic as an area inhabited by independent residents living in healthy and well-organized local communities, who manage their affairs and shape their future in a deeply-rooted tradition of respect for the environment. The cooperation between Canada and its neighbours in the Arctic was also highlighted. Military matters were also present, and the issue of strengthening sovereignty gained symbolic precedence. Actions aimed at realizing the vision of the *Canadian Northern Strategy* were grouped into four priority areas: Arctic sovereignty, supporting economic and social development, protecting the environment, and improving the management of the northern regions (Indian and Northern Affairs Canada 2). The 2010 *Statement on Canada's Arctic Foreign Policy* was even more outspoken in declaring as Canada's Arctic foreign policy objective a "stable, rules-based region with clearly defined boundaries" and an environment in which "dynamic economic growth and trade" can take place (Government of Canada, "Statement"; Robertson 107-108).

Although the *Canadian Northern Strategy* assumed that each of its four pillars was equally important and all were complementary to each other, the priority was given to promoting sovereignty (Government of Canada, "Statement" 4). Prime Minister Harper repeatedly stressed that this was the number one priority, which was "non-negotiable" ("Arctic Sovereignty"). Sovereignty in the Arctic was understood in a classical form as the exercise of authority, control and protection in a given area by the state. Such sovereignty required, firstly, resources to monitor what was happening throughout the North, and secondly, the ability to enforce and ensure compliance.

Consequently, several projects were included in the Arctic strategy, which were aimed at strengthening Canada's Arctic power. Among the most known were the exercises and manoeuvres conducted annually by the Canadian Army and police forces, such as "Nunalivut," "Nanook" or "Nunakput" (National Defence and the Canadian Armed Forces). Another example was Canada's participation in NORAD operations in the North. Among the investments, the *Canadian Northern Strategy* listed the establishing of the Canadian Forces Arctic Training Center at Resolute Bay in Nunavut. This facility was to serve as both a training base and a command centre for search and rescue operations. In 2013, the centre started its operations although its scale was reduced ("Military's").

As far as monitoring of Canada's Arctic area was concerned, two projects were the most important. In 2007, the RADARSAT-2 satellite system was launched, which enables tracking of vessels in the Arctic waters. The next phases include launching of three additional satellites in 2018 (Byers 66). After 2010, to monitor traffic in the Arctic waters, the Northern Canada Vessel Traffic Services (NORDREG) was made mandatory for all vessels over 300 tonnes (Kraska 228). However, this move had a serious gap. There was no compulsory reporting for smaller vessels, meaning that they could potentially be used by drug traffickers or smugglers of illegal immigrants (Riddell-Dixon, "Canada's Arctic" 2).

Much more serious problems were encountered by other projects related to the exercise of sovereignty. First, despite Prime Minister Harper's announcement in 2007, the construction of a port and a refuelling station at Nanisivik, Nunavut never materialized. The port was to be multifunctional and serve both the military and civilians. After several years, such extensive plans were substantially trimmed and currently only the refuelling station is being planned, working only during the summer months. After almost eight years, the construction of the base has not even started and the completion has been postponed until 2018 ("Arctic Naval").

Another problem was the failure to meet promises to increase patrolling capacity in the northern areas, as well as the ability to conduct search and rescue operations and research in the vast areas of the Arctic. Due to delays in the construction of an icebreaker named "*John G. Diefenbaker* for Canada's Coast Guard," which was announced as early as in 2007, Canada still does not have a vessel capable of operating in ice water. The currently used icebreaker, "Louis S. St-Laurent," will be withdrawn from service in 2017 – until that time a new unit will not be built (Riddell-Dixon, "Canada's Arctic" 2).

To maintain Canada's patrol capabilities, the *Canadian Northern Strategy* also mentioned the need to build modern patrol boats, able to sail in the Arctic waters throughout the whole year. Nevertheless, this project has also not been yet completed and in fact the vessels are able to operate in the northern waters only in summer (Milewski). The project was significantly scaled down, compared to what had been promised, even though experts have for years pointed out that Canada's capabilities in icebreaker operations are significantly smaller than Russia's (Jarratt and Thomson).

Also, in terms of search and rescue operations, Canada's capabilities were insufficient. Due to the growing traffic in the Arctic, coming from more frequent tourist visits, research units or ships and aircrafts associated with new economic projects and deliveries to the people living in the North, the need for search and rescue personnel was also growing (Koring, "Arctic"). The ability to carry out rescue and exploration operations was also important because Canada and other members of the Arctic Council signed a search and rescue treaty in 2011. It delimits regions for which particular countries are responsible (Arctic Council, "Agreement"). The treaty entered into force in January 2013 and is considered an important step towards securing the safety of the northern waters. It is also the first binding treaty signed within the Arctic Council. Its effectiveness will depend on how it will be implemented.

As part of the Arctic strategy, the Harper government also declared to expand and modernize the Canadian Rangers (Lackenbauer, "If It Ain't"). This voluntary formation, belonging to the Canadian Forces Reserve, composed mostly of the Inuit, provides symbolic Canadian military presence in the North, helps with reconnaissance, and assists in rescue and search operations. In 2011, Ottawa announced the strengthening of the Rangers by 750 people (up to 5,000) and by the introduction of more modern equipment and better training. Experts estimated that such an increase would bring only a slight change, given the vastness of the area where the formation operates (Riddell-Dixon, "Canada's Arctic" 2).

The exercise of sovereignty, as defined by the *Canadian Northern Strategy*, also meant having reliable sea maps of the Arctic. The exploration of the seabed in this region has not been completed. While international cooperation in collecting the scientific data required to map the continental shelf was positive, it was known that in some places claims of individual states would overlap, which may lead to long lasting disputes (Riddell-Dixon, "Canada's Arctic" 3).

Another element of great importance for the Harper government was the extension of the continental shelf beyond 200 nautical miles in the polar area, which was possible under Article 76 of the United Nations Convention on the Law of the Sea. Despite 10 years of research and CAD 200 million spent on research and mapping, Ottawa was not able to gather all the data necessary to make a submission to the Commission on the Limits of the Continental Shelf (CLCS). As a result, Ottawa filed only partial U.N. documentation in December 2013, claiming 1.2 million square kilometers. The government announced that it reserved the right to supplement the application for areas around the North Pole. Unofficial information from Canadian journalists indicated a significant difference of opinion between the expectations of the Conservative Party politicians and the officials preparing the request (Chase, "Arctic"). It was so deep that only Prime Minister Harper's personal intervention, at the last moment, caused that the claim was extended to include the North Pole (Chase, "Harper Orders"). The main reasons for that kind of action were fears of political consequences. The resignation from the claims to the North Pole, even in the absence of convincing scientific evidence, would have meant the loss of support for the Harper government.

Another difficult area was the issue of Arctic maritime boundaries. Out of all boundary disputes Canada had during the Harper government, the most important one was on the Beaufort Sea, which had long been a hotbed in Canadian-American relations. The delimitation of this border was of particular importance due to the deposits of natural gas and crude oil located in its vicinity. Without the agreement one could not start the exploitation of natural resources because the investment risk was too significant (Riddell-Dixon, "Canada's Arctic" 3). Nevertheless, there has been no progress in talks with the U.S. on that issue so far. Nothing has also changed in the dispute over Hans Island, claimed by both Canada and Greenland (Zilio, "Canada, Denmark").

The biggest problem for Ottawa is, however, the status of the Northwest Passage, i.e. a network of strategic straits forming the sea route, which is the shortest waterway linking Europe with East Asia. As early as in 1985, Ottawa unilaterally proclaimed its sovereignty over the waters surrounding the Arctic Archipelago. The United States, like the rest of the Arctic states (except Russia), did not recognize Canadian claims and still treats the disputed area as an international maritime route with freedom of navigation. Although, as argued by international law experts, the arguments of both sides contain some weaknesses and gaps, the increase in navigation plays in the U.S. advantage (Byers 127-130; Coates 205-207).

Harper's constant references to endangered sovereignty bear all the hallmarks of a concept of "securitization" (H. Smith, "Choosing" 925). It is defined as a method used by authorities to persuade public opinion to recognize a particular threat as a value that is situated high in the hierarchy, and to approve the commitment of more resources to address the issue. The Harper government used "securitization" in a specific way, as there was a large degree of confusion regarding potential threats to Canada's security in the Arctic. The governmental documents, for example, did not clearly show who or what was threatening Canada. Such a lack of precision gave the government a degree of flexibility and provided a possibility to change the message about threats based on particular political requirements (H. Smith, "Choosing" 935).

From this perspective Harper's foreign policy in the Arctic region was rhetorically different from previous approaches. For Franklyn Griffiths, Harper's "excessively dramatic" rhetoric created a form of "possession anxiety" or "sovereignty fetishism" (qtd. in Kinsman). Although the dangers to Canadian sovereignty in the Arctic were not clear, most governmental rhetoric attributed them to the Russians. After 2007 in particular, when Russia in a symbolic move planted a flag on the seabed at the North Pole (Chivers), Moscow became the most important source of fear in the Arctic. Russians were presented by Harper as potential antagonists who were "newly assertive" and behaved "increasingly aggressive." In such circumstances, Harper warned, Canada "must remain vigilant" (Harper, "The 2007").

This "fuzzy threat" rhetoric was enhanced by the fear of losing the prospects of Canada's economic development in the Arctic. Connecting sovereignty and security with economic issues was one of the hallmarks of the *Canadian Northern Strategy*, repeatedly emphasized by Prime Minister Harper (Harper, "Prime Minister Stephen Harper Announces"). According to this view, Canada had to be capable of exercising maximum sovereignty in its part of the Arctic because it could not afford to stay behind in the race for raw materials in this part of the world. The biggest threat in this area was the increasing number of foreign ships "dashing" in the Arctic waters. Dropping out of the Arctic rivalry would mean a loss of opportunity for economic development and, as a result, a loss of a major means to support and improve the well-being of Canadians.

The *Canadian Northern Strategy* was oriented toward the development of the economy of natural resources in northern Canada. This region was featured as "a huge oil, water and ocean inventory" and as one that had "energy and natural resource potential." The strategy indicated that the opportunities for the exploitation of natural resources in the Arctic were growing due to the increasing global demand and the difficulty of obtaining them from conventional sources. This provoked an upsurge in prices to the level that made mining in the North worthwhile. As a result of the global warming, the costs of operating in polar areas decreased, while the mining period, as well as possibilities of using the sea routes increased. In addition, new technologies, including satellite communication and seismic testing, facilitated better functioning and investments in polar conditions. The most important message coming from the environmental part of the *Canadian Northern Strategy* was the conviction of the government that climate change was a chance to transform the Arctic – that it was a catalyst for change. In the 2010 *Statement on Canada's Arctic Foreign Policy*, the government considered the climate change as more beneficial than risky, especially for the development of the mining industry. The strategy also emphasized most of all the richness of the Arctic natural resources, even though it also declared that "[a]s an emerging clean energy superpower, Canada will continue to support the responsible and sustainable development of oil and gas in the North" (Government of Canada, "Statement" 13).

Such a defined Arctic policy was met with considerable criticism, in particular from ecological organizations (e.g. Greenpeace). Critics pointed out to the fact that the government did not keep its environmental promises. They disapproved of how the National Energy Board, a federal agency that licenses the use of energy, granted drilling permits to petrochemical companies which did not fulfill specific environmental standards and endangered the Arctic coast with leakages and other ecological accidents ("Harper's Northern"; "Clyde").

A similar business-like attitude was visible in the Harper government's approach to the Arctic Council. Canada, during its chairmanship of the Council (2013-2015), intended to focus on the sustainable development of the extraction of natural resources, improved navigation safety, and the pursuit of sustainable community development ("Thematic"; "Looking"). The critics, including Mary Simon or Lloyd Axworthy, stressed that Ottawa had prioritized economic issues when chairing the Council. This was best evidenced by the establishment of the Arctic Economic Council. Although the forum's primary goal was to address the pressing issue of the creation of jobs for the northerners, it was also perceived as a channel of privileged access for multinational companies to national governments (Axworthy and Simon).

Other critics of Harper's Arctic policy were concerned with discrepancies between Ottawa's environmental declarations and actual actions, which were rather modest and always subject to other priorities. The 2009 *Canadian Northern Strategy*, for example, focused mostly on the extension of Canadian territorial waters protection from 100 to 200 nautical miles off the coast. This was achieved through the amendment of the 1970 *Arctic Waters Pollution Prevention Act*. The designation of the Lancaster Sound as a marine conservation area, in order to expand ecological protection, has not yet been formally completed. However, for observers with a realist approach to foreign affairs, such as John Kirton, such moves aimed at backing territorial claims amounted to "environmental custodianship" – they advanced Canadian values and interests and as such deserved appreciation (Kirton, "The Harper" 23-24).

Evaluating Harper's Arctic policy, one may perceive that priority was given to the initiatives promoting economic development, extraction of natural resources, and Canada's sovereignty in the North. In these areas, Harper's government managed to successfully implement more Arctic projects than his predecessors. Over the period of almost ten years, sovereignty was promoted to an unprecedented level as well as ideas of the development of the natural resources in the North. As Joël Plouffe puts it, "the 'North' made a central beam of Harper government's policies and public speeches." Critics argued, however, that this was at the expense of abandoning the commitments made by previous governments, and that Canada was failing to expand the number of ships capable of operating in the region. For Paul Heinbecker, Harper's Arctic defence policy was "window dressing." Other critical arguments stressed Canada's excessive focus on the military definition of security, its resource nationalism and limited co-operation (Plouffe; Byers 18). We argue that although the Conservatives had promised more than they were able or willing to deliver in the Arctic, they at least delivered a part of what had been promised. It was not so in the case of other Canadian governments.

Another characteristic of Canada's Arctic strategy was its continuity. Even the critics of Prime Minister Harper point out that while many of the promises remained only on paper, none of the priorities were abandoned. The prime minister's constant interest in the northern areas was also fascinating. Initially, Harper was motivated by the desire to attract voters and to some extent forced to take interest in the Arctic by the emergence of Arctic issues in the election campaigns. Harper apparently took the advice of Tom Flanagan – his principal mentor during the early election campaigns – who argued that Harper should concentrate on the Arctic, as it was one of those areas where the Conservative Party could show its different viewpoint clearly. This was, in Flanagan's opinion, a winning strategy because "polarized positioning is perfect for the next election." The Arctic was prominent in all Harper's election campaigns in: 2006, 2008, 2011 and 2015. In his last campaign in 2015, Harper warned that "[w]e share the Arctic with a hostile state, unconcerned with international norms such as respect for territorial integrity. […] Justin Trudeau's alarming naïveté, and Thomas Mulcair's dangerously ideological foreign policy, mean that they simply aren't prepared to keep Canada safe" ("Harper's Nunavut").

The presence of the Arctic among Harper's priorities, symbolized by his personal involvement in the North and annual visits, derived from the prime minister's desire to re-open the North of Canada and leave a lasting legacy on Canada's northern identity. His interest in the North seemed to be sincere and was not as short-lived as in the case of his predecessors (Lackenbauer, "Mixed" 2; Frenette).

It is worth noting – as highlighted by several observers, including Ken Coates – that Harper's Arctic policy evolved. In the initial phase, it was concentrated on the symbolic aspects of sovereignty – e.g. annual trips to the northern regions. Subsequently, the prime minister stressed the need to develop the economy of the North and to "integrate" it with the rest of Canada (Chase, "Myth"). As John Ibbitson wrote, comparing Harper's vision of the North with that of John Diefenbaker, Harper treated the Arctic as "a new Canadian frontier that should be developed and defended" (Ibbitson, *Stephen* 326).

The Harper government was not supportive of a multilateral approach to the Artic regions. Harper's policy towards the North was seen by some observers not only as a volte-face when compared with Canadian traditional internationalism and multilateralism, but also, paradoxically, as an antithesis to Barack Obama's Arctic policies. While the U.S. was attempting to actively influence the Arctic through regional bodies, Canada under Harper was skeptical of multilateral engagement with the Arctic neighbours in multilateral fora. As summarized by Joël Plouffe:

> Canada is more focused on domestic and continental issues that legitimatize the need for enhanced military capacities in the North since they have been, from a neocontinentalist perspective, neglected under the Liberals ("Stephen").

The Harper government thus neglected the role of multilateral co-operation, but it also downplayed the role of Inuit and First Nations communities in the Arctic (except that their very presence in the northern extremes of the country was useful in exercising sovereignty). This did not go unnoticed by other Arctic states and some critics, who warned of "Canada's willingness to isolate itself" from climate change issues and multilateral cooperation (Exner-Pirot 93). However, in our opinion, Harper pursued selectively chosen goals. We agree with John Kirton who suggested that Harper's Arctic policy was an example of putting national interests of sovereignty and territory above other elements of foreign policy, such as environmentalism or even good relations with the United States (Kirton, "The Harper" 16).

China

Harper's China policy was highly selective and based on rational and selfish calculations, particularly in the situations in which economic efficiency clashed with the human rights agenda. Even though on the rhetorical level the Harper Conservatives' election platform emphasized the primacy of values over interests in relations with China, in reality, especially after the 2008-2011 financial crisis, Ottawa abandoned a harsh rhetoric and assumed a more rational tone, associated with developing business opportunities.

In our opinion, Harper's approach to China was not remarkably different from the policies of previous governments. The focus on China had been a trademark of the Liberal government's foreign policy – with massive delegations (Team Canada) sent to China by Prime Minister Jean Chrétien with the mission to reinvigorate bilateral trade relations. But in reality, the People's Republic of China had occupied a special place on Canada's international relations agenda much longer, since the John Turner government (1984). China – a "strategic partner" of all Canadian governments after the Cold War – since 2003, has been Canada's second-largest trading partner, surpassing Britain and Japan (Canada is China's 13th largest partner). Although the Canadian economy is overwhelmingly linked with the U.S., between 1998 and 2007, imports from China grew by almost 400 percent and 6 per cent of Canada's total world trade was directed to China. Moreover, Canada's trade in natural resources has increasingly followed the direction of the Chinese economy (Tiagi and Zhou 2).

However, the question that has underpinned all the Canadian governments is associated with the extent to which Canada should engage with the Chinese communist regime, given the fact that human rights issues have been constantly prioritized by the majority of Canadians as a foreign policy concern. In 2016, 51 per cent of Canadians were willing to risk a loss of economic opportunities when a partner country violated human rights. Even more (76 per cent) were convinced that Ottawa should discuss issues related with human rights with that partner (Beck; Asia Pacific). In this situation, all governments had to assume flexible approaches to keep balance between business and human rights and to prudently navigate domestic debates on relations with China. This entailed using sophisticated ways of downplaying, tunneling or delinking human rights issues from business relations in order to avoid tensions with the Chinese communist regime, but sometimes also presenting a tough view on human rights violations. Before 2006, the Liberals usually followed a doctrine of quiet diplomacy when expressing their human rights concerns, although on certain occasions the Chrétien government also explicitly criticized the Chinese government for the suppression of the rights of Chinese citizens (Burton, "Canada's" 45). Nevertheless, as Charles Burton claims, after the Cold War Ottawa did not have much room for maneuver when dealing with Beijing if it wanted to make economic relations a priority. In fact, China was too powerful a nation to follow Canada's (or other nations') rules – Beijing set its own terms of relations.

The Liberals' open and business-oriented approach to China was harshly criticized by the Conservative Party. Stephen Harper as the leader of the opposition asserted, for example, that a thousand Chinese spies were active in Canada and that this issue should have been raised during Paul Martin's visit to China. Acute rhetoric continued to be manifested after the 2006 election. On several occasions the members of the government openly criticized China's human rights record. For example, Foreign Minister Peter MacKay rebuked the Chinese government for sponsoring the intellectual theft of Canada's technological secrets (Burton, "Canada's" 48). But the most famous words and gestures came from the prime minister himself. He bluntly declared that human rights should not be trumped by the "almighty dollar" and in 2007 he officially met with the Dalai Lama in the prime minister's office after the former had been awarded honorary Canadian citizenship. This contrasted with a private meeting the Tibetan leader had had with Prime Minister Martin in 2004. Additionally, until 2009, Harper did not bother to visit China – he even did not attend the opening ceremony of the 2008 Olympics in Beijing. Instead, the members of the Conservative caucus visited Taiwan. The prime minister met with the Dalai Lama for the second time in 2012 and reiterated his opposition to the practices of the Chinese regime against the Tibetans ("Richard"; Blanchfield, "Dalai").

Furthermore, under Harper, the Canadian-Chinese bilateral human rights dialogue came to a standstill. The annual meetings – initiated in 1997 by the Liberal Minister of Foreign Affairs Lloyd Axworthy – were a pillar of the Liberal government's approach of engaging the Chinese regime in quiet diplomacy discussions concerning human rights abuses in China. The Conservatives, however, did not see any signs of improvement in China's poor human rights record that would have resulted from that strategy. In a report submitted by the parliamentary human rights committee, they declared that the dialogue had had little impact besides being an alibi for Ottawa and Beijing for not properly addressing the concerns of the Canadian public about human rights in China (Burton, "Canada's" 49, 55).

The Conservatives' approach to China had its roots in a desire to pursue a policy clearly distinguishable from the Liberal past. In this pursuit, ideology played an important role. The most important element was the Conservative Party's disapproval of China's communist regime and the state-ruled economy. In the Conservative foreign policy, democratic governments, for example India's, were placed on the top of the trade agenda while regimes like China were deprioritized. This approach was, however, never met with the approval on the part of the specialists of the Department of Foreign Affairs and International Trade (Burton, "Canada's" 48). At the same time, the Conservative Party did not have their own specialists in Chinese affairs, as was evident with the appointment of David Emerson, a member of the official opposition Liberal Party, as minister of international trade and then minister of foreign affairs. He was known for his strong support for closer ties between Canada and China, and even though he did not succeed in compelling the Harper government to increase the involvement with China, he nevertheless was able to establish six new trade offices in Chinese cities (Burton, "Canada's" 46). For some time, however Harper did not fully realize the importance of China as a dominant player in energy, mineral and other commodity markets.

Supposedly, the government initially did not think that that the harsh rhetoric could deteriorate trade relations with Chinese state-controlled companies, as was evident, for example, in Jason's Kenney's answers to journalists' questions on possible negative consequences for Canada from China (Blanchfield, "Dalai"). This concern was not unfounded as other nations whose leaders met with the Dalai Lama faced threats of trade-related retaliation and restrictions associated with investment projects (Burton, "Canada's" 57; "China"). Canada, however, luckily avoided restrictions; Canada's ambassador to China was even permitted to visit the Tibetan Autonomous Region in 2011 and 2013 (Foreign Affairs Canada, "Ambassador").

However, after the initial years the Conservatives' commitment to look at China through the lens of human rights issues led the Harper government to face the contradictions of its own position. Most observers thought that Harper realized that it was impossible for Canada to keep the type of the rhetoric presented by the government and at the same time not to harm economic foundations and Canadian investors in China. Canadian businesses, but also Sino-Canadians who had voted for the Conservative Party, started to pressure Ottawa to formulate a more effective China policy that would balance human rights and economic ties (Ibbitson, *Stephen* 328).

What might have motivated Harper to change policies towards China was decreasing trade with the United States, which was a result of the financial crisis. The diversification of Canadian economic relations, one of Harper's government's priorities, coincided with the changing nature of the global economy and Canada's changing fortunes as an exporter of commodities. The Conservative government realized that any realistic foreign policy could not downplay the importance of China. China's economy was much larger and far more critical to ensuring Canada's future economic prosperity than that of any other developing nation, for example India. According to the International Energy Agency, the global demand for oil continued to rise, with the largest increase in China and simultaneous decrease in oil consumption in North America and Western Europe. Already in 2013, China surpassed the U.S. to become the world's largest importer of oil (Bratt, "Stephen" 490). Thus, the Harper government hoped to secure the world's largest market for

Canadian natural resources, in particular energy resources. Firstly, the government thought that suggesting that Canada might start to sell energy to China could make the negotiations with the Americans over the Keystone Pipeline easier. But then Harper's commitment to the idea of Canada as an "energy superpower" naturally aligned with improved relations with China (Nossal and Sarson 2). An additional issue, suggested by Kim Richard Nossal and Leah Sarson, was strong people-to-people links between China and Canada. This element, in fact, may become Canada's potent advantage in its relationship with Beijing, as the number of Canadians with strong personal or professional connections with China is growing (Nossal and Sarson 2).

Chinese-Canadian relations began to change in late 2008. After initial visits to China by Minister of Foreign Affairs Lawrence Cannon and Minister of International Trade Stockwell Day, Stephen Harper also finally went to Beijing in December 2009. He faced a rare public criticism on the part of Chinese Premier Wen Jiabao, who told Canada's prime minister that China had waited "too long" for his visit and that he was responsible for serious "problems of mutual trust." Nevertheless, the reopening initiated a series of efforts made "by Canadian politicians and industry officials to open up the Chinese market to oil and gas exports from Canada" (Bratt, "Stephen" 490). The term "strategic partnership" appeared in official statements ("Canada and China"). Two pandas were sent by the Chinese government to the Toronto (and Calgary) Zoos as a sign of a breakthrough. Ottawa also started to negotiate the Foreign Investment Protection Agreement with China, finally signed in 2012 and in force since 2014, to address the reluctance of Canadian businesses to invest in the Chinese market. The FIPA, although controversial – some critics point out that it grants too many concessions and possibly facilitates Chinese state's economic espionage activities – largely protects Canadian and Chinese investors from discriminatory practices by mandating national treatment and, what is important given the weak legal system of China, by making contract disputes subject to binding arbitration by a neutral third party outside of Canada and China (Bratt "Stephen" 491). Furthermore, a Canada-China Economic Complementarity Study was released by the Harper government in August 2012, which suggested the possibility of a free trade agreement between Canada and China (Foreign Affairs Canada).

Yet the Harper government was criticized, for example by Laura Dawson, for failing to engage in economic relations with China consistently:

> Despite warm initial overtures, Canada did not act on China's proposed high-level economic dialogue, which would have put Canada on the path to a bilateral free trade agreement such as was recently completed by Australia – a competitor to Canada in many respects. Quantitative analysis suggests that Canada stands to gain $7.8 billion in new exports annually by 2030, as a result of an FTA with China.

The reason for the Harper government's reluctance was the large amount of Chinese investments in the energy sector that started after 2011 and alarmed the Harper government (Lunn; Mas, "Delayed"). One of the most debated Chinese investments was the purchase of the Canadian oil and gas company Nexen by the China National Offshore Oil Corporation (CNOOC) (Ibbitson, "Harper"). The Harper government was reluctant to approve of that acquisition based on numerous assumptions. Firstly, CNOOC as a Chinese state-owned enterprise had access to state subsidies and cheap loans, which would give Nexen a competitive advantage (Bratt, "Stephen" 491). Secondly, the Chinese government could take advantage of CNOOC's presence in Canada to engage in economic espionage and the illegal transfer of Canadian technologies to other Chinese state companies. Thirdly, Chinese state-owned companies could try to contravene Canadian laws with bribery. And fourthly, there were fears that the Chinese state, invested with control over critical Canadian economic assets, would exercise:

> [...] undue political and economic leverage over decisions of the government of Canada [...] include[ing] Canada's ability to respond to Chinese human rights abuses domestically and the Chinese government's support for the regimes of undemocratic political dictators in the third world (Burton, "CNOOC's").

In 2014, a CBC article revealed the CNOOC case led to a significant rift within the cabinet over the economic engagement with China. Some ministers (including Jason Kenney and Peter MacKay) opposed CNOOC's purchase while other (especially John Baird and Ed Fast) not only backed the transaction but also a significant increase of the level of economic engagement with China. Harper's concerns concentrated around the threats of cyber espionage and cyber security, which evidently slowed down the prime minister's initial plans to intensify the trade relationship with China (Lunn; Mas, "Delayed"). While the government decided in December 2012 that it would approve CNOOC's purchase of Nexen, further transactions that could give state-owned companies access to Canada's oil sands were blocked (McCarthy and Chase). The prime minister bluntly stated that "[w]hen we say that Canada is open for business, we do not mean that Canada is for sale to foreign governments" (Harper, "Statement by the Prime Minister of Canada on Foreign").

The CNOOC's case illustrates Harper's priority of protecting Canada's security. This was an important factor in Chinese-Canadian relations, as Charles Burton suggested. Canada's security agencies were busy countering Chinese espionage. The fact that the Chinese companies Huawei and Lenovo were excluded from the governmental contracts in Canada as they might have been pressured by the Communist government to install back door access for Chinese security agencies in computers they sold is illustrative (Burton, "Canada's" 54).

In our understanding, Harper's China strategy clearly fit into the strategy of a typical selective power. Ottawa's approach was primarily based on the calculation of profits and losses. Harper wanted warmer economic relations with China but not at any cost. In his approach to China, he also drew from the Liberal experience of economic diplomacy. For example, the promotion of trade of energy resources had been part of the agenda of the Liberal predecessors. In October 2005, Natural Resource Minister John McCallum promoted the growth of oil sands exports to China as a means of diversifying Canada's energy sales (York). Reshaping or rapprochement are better words to describe Canada's China policy after 2008, when human rights issues were, to some degree, hidden from the public. This did not mean a total abandonment of the human rights dimension, as Ottawa did not stop criticizing China's human rights violations (Burton, "Canada's" 50). For example, Canadian diplomats raised issues associated with Tibet and religious freedom when China appeared before the U.N. Human Rights Council's Universal Periodic Review in 2013 (Hong, "Canada's"). The same happened when cabinet ministers visited China or received their counterparts in Canada. DFATD also regularly issued press release statements of concern "over Chinese government violence and arbitrary arrests against political protestors, democracy activists and human rights defence lawyers" (Burton, "Canada's" 55). In January 2014, the Ambassador of Canada to China, Guy Saint-Jacques, condemned the sentencing of a Chinese human rights defender Xu Zhiyong (Foreign Affairs Canada, "Statement on Sentencing"). The Harper approach was praised by the Dalai Lama for balancing value-based policy with the need to further economic ties with China ("Dalai").

Critics thought, however, that the government was inconsistent and its statements were not reflected in the policy – thus they were largely rhetorical (Hui). Nevertheless, the same tactic was used after the 2015 election. Ambassador Saint-Jacques's publicly reprimanded China's treatment of its own people in 2016, during Prime Minister Justin Trudeau's first visit to China (Vanderklippe and Stone). This happened two months after Chinese Foreign Minister Wang Yi publicly had rebuked a Canadian journalist after she asked him at a joint press conference with Canadian Foreign Minister Stéphane Dion in Ottawa about the Chinese government's detention of human rights advocates and a Canadian couple accused of espionage (Buckley).

In our opinion, in both phases of his China policy, Harper put Canada's interest first, although in each phase different aspects were stressed. In the first one it was the promotion of Canadian values in foreign relations, while in the second one it was the concentration on advancing the prosperity of Canadians through trade. But in fact those two elements had also been included in all Canadian foreign policy strategies towards China after the Cold War. As Charles Burton suggested, Harper's approach was consistent "with the norms that have governed Canadian China policy" since Prime Minister John Turner (Burton, "Canada's" 46). For example, in the 1995 *Canada in the World* publication, the three main objectives of Canada's foreign policy were listed. They were the following: the promotion of prosperity and employment, the protection of Canada's security within a stable global framework, and the projection of Canadian values and culture (Government of Canada, "Canada and the World").

We also consider important the fact that although the Liberal governments of Jean Chrétien and Paul Martin stressed the relations with China, the levels of trade remained low and Canada's market share of China's imports in goods and services actually declined, while under the Harper government they slightly increased (Statistics Canada, "Report").

This was mainly due to the growth of prices on the commodities that until today form most of Canada's exports to the People's Republic of China ("What Does"). In our opinion, two aspects are important in this context. Firstly, in the future Canada's natural resources may become important sources for Beijing to sustain China's economic growth. Secondly, Canadian economic and trade policies that prioritize investments in resource exploitation and in infrastructure to facilitate export to China and other Asian destinations – as a way to decrease dependence on the American market – would not cease to exist. This means that as long as Canadians firmly believe that commercial engagement with China must go in line with a wider commitment to promoting human rights, every Canadian government would face the extremely difficult task to strike a balance between economic interests and values. This would lead, in our opinion, to the similar situation Canadians witnessed during Harper's term in office. In other words, as Gerald Caplan wrote in his commentary for the *Globe and Mail*, "a foreign leader who wants to do business with China does exactly what Mr. Harper did and Mr. Trudeau is doing while pretending otherwise" ("On Foreign").

A value-based approach

Since the Second World War, Canada has belonged to a relatively small group of countries seriously engaged in promoting human rights and values (Lee). The legacy of John Humphrey, the main author of the *Universal Declaration of Human Rights*, has now lasted for decades, visible in Canada's 1960s immigration policy – based on points system, which promotes racially and ethnically unbiased criteria, such as education, language, and work experience, rather than race or ethnicity – and enhanced in 1971 by declaring multiculturalism as Canada's official federal policy. The protection of minority rights, including LGBTQ rights, and gender equality became the symbols of Canadian democracy – Canada was among the world's pioneers when it included women in military peacekeeping personnel in 1977 or legalized same-sex marriages in 2005.

Apart from this, Canada is known for promoting and spreading progressive values globally. But as Denis Stairs suggests, there is a hint of hypocrisy in in the way Ottawa does it. Stairs claims that "Canadian values are abandoned whenever a competing self-interest comes down the pike" (248). In other words, national interests usually trump values, but the official narrative tries to hide that fact under "the guise of value-based rhetoric." This type of inconsistency can be seen, for example, in climate policies (Lee 3). The shift in Canada's postwar policy towards South Africa under Prime Minister Mulroney, however, may be seen as an exception from the above rule. Instead of continuing trade and only symbolically condemning the regime, as it had been before Mulroney, Ottawa decided to combine diplomatic and commercial methods on the international forum to put pressure on the South African regime to drop apartheid policies. When apartheid ended, Canada worked towards reducing antipathy and the distrust of Canada's private sector towards the Nelson Mandela's South Africa (Freeman).

Nevertheless, values have often been promoted as necessary and foremost elements of Canada's foreign policy. After 1989, the clearest example can be found in the initiatives of Lloyd Axworthy, who served as minister of foreign affairs in the Jean Chrétien government between 1996 and 2000. Axworthy was able to persuade other countries to negotiate and sign a treaty banning landmines within one year. The 1997 *Convention on the Prohibition of the Use, Stockpiling, Production and Transfer of Anti-Personnel Mines and on their Destruction* (commonly referred to as the Mine Ban Treaty) has so far resulted in clearing mined areas in 29 countries (Schabas 142-154). Moreover, Axworthy was nominated for the Nobel Peace Prize in 1997 for his leadership in the so-called Ottawa Process. Another step in the realization of values-based foreign policy at the beginning of the 21st century was the creation of the International Criminal Court, in which Canada played a crucial role. Ottawa rallied global support for the idea of establishing a permanent tribunal with the jurisdiction to try acts of genocide, war crimes, and crimes against humanity. In effect, when the Rome Statute in April 2002 earned the required number of ratifications, the ICC was established.

Generally speaking, the Axworthy doctrine – built around the concept of human security – was designed as a response to changes after the end of the Cold War. It projected new ways of Canada's capacity for influence within the new global order. Using its ability to organize coalitions that "promote[d] the Canadian values of fairness, tolerance, and respect for the weak," Canada tried to become a global leader in the shaping of a new post-Cold War world order. This brought fruit in the form of the so-called

Responsibility to Protect (R2P) – an idea aimed at protecting civilians from genocide through international action. This concept, which emerged as a direct response to the horrors of Rwanda and the Balkans, was advanced during Canada's tenure on the U.N. Security Council in 1999-2000. In the context of R2P, the main dilemma was related to the clash between the concept of state sovereignty and the right of humanitarian intervention – the question was whether and when the protection of civilians in one state legitimized coercive actions of other states against that state. In September 2000, the Canadian government founded the International Commission on Intervention and State Sovereignty (ICISS), aimed at addressing the U.N. Secretary-General Kofi Annan's question "if humanitarian intervention is, indeed, an unacceptable assault on sovereignty, how should we respond to a Rwanda, to a Srebrenica – to gross and systematic violations of human rights that affect every precept of our common humanity?" (Council on Foreign Relations). A year later the ICISS issued a report in which the following principles of dealing with mass atrocities were listed: "prevent wherever possible; intervene wherever necessary; rebuild whenever the intervention ends" (Axworthy and Rock; See more in Foreign Affairs Canada, "The Responsibility"). In 2005, Axworthy's "Responsibility to Protect" doctrine was officially adopted at the United Nations World Summit.

For its supporters, the Axworthy doctrine presented "the most ambitious transformation effort in Canadian foreign policy history" and the creation of ICC was regarded as Canadian internationalism at its best. Louise Arbour, one of the foremost Canadian lawyers, summarized R2P as "the most important and imaginative doctrine to emerge on the international scene for decades" ("Gareth"). Others saw Axworthy's legacy as a proof that "that soft power assets such as issue-framing, networking and persuasion can produce meaningful changes in the behaviour of states" (Bernard Jr.). For its critics, the Axworthy doctrine was too radical as "a product of misguided idealism" and had no chances to be universally applied. As a matter of fact, the largest stockpiles of anti-personnel mines still remain undestroyed in those countries that have not ratified the convention, i.e. the United States, Russia, China, Myanmar, United Arab Emirates, Cuba, Egypt, India, Israel, and Iran ("Global").

As far as Harper's government is concerned, a more dogmatic approach to the application of principles in foreign policy was used. The plan of changing traditional characterization of Canada as "an honest broker" or "a middleman" was initiated in 2006. The Harper government sought a distinct Conservative foreign policy that would lead to the redefinition of Canada's position in the international system. In the Conservatives' view, excessive concentration on "helpfully fixing others' problems" and insufficient "advancing [of] Canada's own hard interests and fundamental values" threatened and diminished Canada's significance in the world. Past policies, according to the Conservative government, had not only been ineffective but they were also no longer applicable to the Canada of the day. Outward-looking needed to be replaced by inward-looking and Canada had no time for long considerations of nuances or gradual changes – there was time for direct action and changing fine distinctions into blunt moves (Heinbecker; Ibbitson, *Stephen* 322). According to the new prime minister's declarations, Canada would "no longer go along to get along" and would stop playing "a Boy Scout abroad" (Nikiforuk; M. MacKinnon, "Harper's"). The government announced that it was not enough "in this day and age, to say we get along with people [...] it's not just good enough to say, 'everybody likes us'" (qtd. in Whyte). The Conservatives thought Ottawa had an obligation to clearly and decidedly articulate the moral evaluation of international issues. The Harper government believed that Canadian values were so important that "moral ambiguity, moral equivalence are not options" (Chase, "Flaherty").

This type of reasoning, emphasizing values, recurred in Harper's speeches. For example, when he accepted the World Statesman award in 2012, Harper spoke about the uncertainty of the world, marked with dangerous changes for Ottawa: Canada's closest friends were facing troubled times, while states that were gaining power were not necessarily willing to share "Canada's ideals." In 2012, Harper said that democracy was in danger, as in Arab countries "[w]hat appears to some a hopeful spring for democracy quickly becomes an angry summer of populism" (qtd. in Campbell, "In Accepting"). For Harper, only values of freedom and human dignity that "Canadians and like-minded countries hold dear" constituted a "glimmers of hope," but even those values were under constant pressure from "rapid forces of change" (Campbell, "In Accepting"). This was a "narrative of danger" that emphasized, as Tom Keating puts it, "the prospects of a different design for international society, one less familiar, and perhaps less beneficial for Canadian interests" (Keating, "The Transition" 180).

Thus, the Harper government found itself under the moral obligation to defend the precious values. One of the opportunities to show Canada's new principled approach was the defence of democracy. Engagement in democratic development around the world stood on top of the Conservative government's agenda between 2006 and 2015. Stephen Harper strongly emphasized and kept long-term interests in the promotion of initiatives aimed at democratization and development around the world in accordance with the set of values he often spoke about, which were "freedom, democracy, human rights and the rule of law." For the Conservative government, in this sphere Ottawa had a potential to become a global leader (Kirton, "The Harper" 3).

Among the venues where the Harper government actively promoted such a stance was the Commonwealth. Ottawa became the biggest critic of the Commonwealth's formula, in particular its membership rules. Under Harper, Ottawa regularly expressed accusations that the Commonwealth had not pressured its members enough, Asian and African countries in particular, to fully implement the rule of law and stop violating democratic standards (De Souza, "Canada"). Canada even decided to boycott Commonwealth summits in countries that did not respect human rights. The best-known example of that tactic was the 2013 Commonwealth summit hosted by Sri Lanka. In November 2013, Stephen Harper had publicly declared he would skip the meeting organized by the country where human rights were regularly abused. Harper's move, based on the fact that the Sri Lanka government violated human rights of the Tamil minority, was followed by India and Mauritius (Gwiazda).

Harper's record on the defence of democratic values also included advocacy for homosexual rights abroad. He considered anti-homosexual laws as violating basic human rights. His government continued a long-established policy, initiated in 1960s by Pierre Trudeau, of accepting any "consensual acts between adults." On numerous occasions, legislations adopted by some countries against homosexual people were publicly chastised by Harper's ministers. For example, John Baird, Harper's minister of foreign affairs, regularly equated intolerance with hate that "breed[s] violence" ("Prime Minister Stephen Harper"). He repeatedly condemned those Commonwealth nations (41 of 54) that did not repeal laws against gay and lesbian sexual contacts (Payton, "Baird"). When in 2011 Nigeria considered toughening anti-gay laws, minister Baird argued that such a legislation would disregard basic human rights and that Canada "[t]hrough the Commonwealth and other forums [...] will continue to make this point in the most forceful of terms" ("John Baird"; Payton, "Commonwealth"). An introduction of anti-homosexual legislation in Putin's Russia was seen as the primary reason why the prime minister refused to attend the opening ceremony of the Sochi Olympic Games in 2014 ("Harper Joins").

In general, John Baird, who considered human rights as one of the most important aspects of his role as foreign affairs minister, believed that public condemnation of violations of LGBTQ rights was an accurate strategy as "diplomacy must be balanced with tough talk in the course of frank discussions" (Payton, "Commonwealth"). Ottawa used this tactic not only in the defence of the rights of homosexuals but also to emphasize its interest in the treatment of women around the world.

Freedom of religion

It was the condemnation of attacks on people practicing their faith that received the special attention of the Harper government. Harper treated freedom of religion as a fundamental right that was linked to democracy. He elaborated on the roots of his strong approach to the issue in an interview in 2013:

> [...] today, as many centuries ago, democracy will not find – democracy cannot – find fertile ground in any society where notions of the freedom of personal conscience and faith are not permitted. Former Prime Minister John Diefenbaker, who was one of the greatest human rights champions in our history, noted these realities when he introduced his original Canadian Bill of Rights. To remind you what he said: 'I am a Canadian, a free Canadian, free to speak without fear, free to worship God in my own way, free to stand for what I think is right, free to oppose what I believe wrong, free to choose those who shall govern my country. This heritage of freedom I pledge to uphold for myself and all mankind.' Indeed, it is 'this heritage of freedom' that Prime Minister Diefenbaker spoke of, that has drawn so many millions to our great country. And, it has been in defence of this heritage of freedom that so many Canadians have given their lives, in so many struggles against tyranny and oppression around the world (Harper, "PM Delivers").

For minister Baird freedom of religion was "an essential human right" – "one of the first things" in the Canadian Charter of Rights and Freedoms and the "front and centre in the U.N. Declaration of Human Rights" (qtd. in "Religious Freedom Office"). In numerous speeches, Baird criticized China for "raids against Roman Catholics and other Christians" and the persecution of Falun Gong practitioners, Tibetan Buddhists and Uyghur Muslims. Baird also singled out Egypt, where Coptic Christians were attacked, as well as Iran (Payton, "Commonwealth"). The Conservatives argued that there was an urgent need to undertake a more systematic action since assaults on religious freedom in various places in the world had been intensifying. Moreover, as they argued that religion was becoming an increasingly important factor in international affairs, Canada would have benefitted abroad if it had showed a strong dedication to the issue.

In its next step, the government declared to establish the Office of Religious Freedom (ORF). The decision was announced in the 2011 Speech from the Throne, but did not materialize until February 2013 (Harper, "The 2011"; Wallace and Wiseman). The ORF was modeled on the U.S. office of religious freedom and became a symbol of Harper's principled approach to foreign policy. The Conservatives believed Canada was uniquely positioned to protect and promote religious freedom worldwide as it was a pluralistic country "whose hallmark is toleration of diversity and respect for human dignity" (Harper, "PM Delivers"). This point of view was endorsed by specialists, such as Arvind Sharma from McGill University, who argued that Canada was a perfect place for that type of office as it was "a self-consciously multi-cultural society" that "define[s] religious freedom in a way which is inclusive, which takes the views of all the religions in the world into this view and not just the missionary religions" ("Christian").

The mandate of the ORF was to speak out against incidents of religious intolerance and persecution of religious minorities abroad, as well as to promote religious pluralism, dialogue and tolerance. One of the objectives of the ORF was also to train Canadian diplomats and prepare analyses and reports on violations against religious freedom in various countries. Andrew Bennett, a former civil servant and the dean of the Christian Augustine College in Ottawa, was appointed the head of the ORF – i.e. Canada's ambassador for religious freedom abroad. The office had had a 4-year mandate to 2015-2016 and a budget of CAD 17 million to finance international projects that assisted religious communities which faced intolerance or persecution in countries that Ottawa regarded to be of strategic interest (Global Affairs Canada, "Evaluation").

The establishment of the ORF, however, was met with harsh criticism in Canada. The main concerns were about the objectivity of the ORF, inclusiveness, transparency and lack of consultation with secular organizations. Although Bennett promised that the ORF would also monitor the treatment of atheists abroad, in practice the believers were the priority of the office (Chase, "New Religious-Freedom"). The creation of the ORF also drew accusations of blurring the line between the church and the state. Opponents were afraid that the office did not follow a balanced approach in the promotion of religious human rights and was dominated by the interests of one religion. This anxiety was fueled by the suspicion that the Conservative Party was excessively pro-Christian. The appointment of a Catholic to lead the institution did not help to dispel doubts. Additionally, the ORF was seen as a way to win support from ethnic voters as certain international crises could be picked to gain the favour of key diaspora groups at election time ("Christian").

The initial success of the ORF was releasing a Muslim leader Azath Salley from detention in Sri Lanka. Canada was one of the first countries to speak publicly in defence of his rights (Chase, "New Religious-Freedom"). On several occasions the ORF drew attention to individual cases of prosecution based on religion, as was the case of Raif Badawi, a Saudi blogger who had been sentenced to 1,000 lashes and 10 years in prison. The most important part of the ORF work was, however, funding projects abroad. Between 2013 and 2016, the office sponsored 20 projects of a total value of CAD 9.2 million, aimed at raising religious tolerance and fighting religious persecution in various countries, including: Indonesia, Nigeria, Ukraine, Pakistan, Myanmar, Iraq, Lebanon and Syria (Berthiaume, "Religious"; "Religious Freedom Is"). Bennett's office also bought or published materials on religious freedom that were distributed abroad (Solomon, "In Defence"). The ORF also provided training sessions on freedom of religion or "belief diplomacy" to Canadian diplomats (Global Affairs Canada, "Evaluation"). Bennett saw an increase of knowledge about the role of religious faith in international policy among the representatives of Canada's foreign service as a key element for the future (Berthiaume, "Sensitivity").

Most of the work of the ORF was aimed at long-term results. An evaluation of the ORF published by the Liberal government in 2016 informed that "substantive change in freedom of religion or belief was viewed as requiring long-term engagement" (Global Affairs Canada, "Evaluation"). The limited authority and budget of the office was a basis for questioning its impact. Additionally, some Canadian diplomats expressed criticism that the creation of the office politicized the issue of religious freedom and "hurt Canada's ability to advance it abroad by putting it into a silo" (Berthiaume, "Religious"). However, the activities of the office were met with the approval on the part of Jewish, Sikh and Ahmadiyya Muslim organizations. Amnesty International Canada appreciated Bennett's public interventions on both single instances and broader issues of religious persecution abroad and, in general, praised his idea to focus resources on a particular human rights concern (Berthiaume, "Religious").

A study published on the OpenCanada.org website revealed that Christian minority groups received almost twice as much of the support of the ORF when compared with Muslim and Jewish communities (Hemmat). The research also indicated that, from among the Muslim minorities, the small Ahmadiyya Muslim minority in Pakistan, but with a strong presence in Canada, received the most consistent assistance. Moreover, the ORF devoted special attention to Christian minorities in Pakistan and Coptic Christians in Egypt – both groups represent large number of immigrants in Canada. However, as "the ORF's focus on Egypt and Pakistan, and recent funding of projects in Indonesia and Burma, is a realistic reflection of persecution in the world," the engagement of the office in Ukraine – a country with one of the lowest rates of government restrictions and social hostilities at that time – seemed confusing as much as the ORF's absence in Afghanistan, Russia, and India (Hemmat). Moreover, even though Andrew Bennett proved to be competent and sensitive as head of Canada's Office for Religious Freedom, he was criticized for avoiding any engagement in the controversy regarding a ban on face coverings during citizenship ceremonies supported by the Harper government (Berthiaume, "Sensitivity").

Additionally, the ORF's policies were sometimes on a collision course with some of Canada's trading partners, especially China. Chinese officials were, for example, disappointed when religious persecution in China was singled out by Prime Minister Harper during the 2013 announcement of the new ambassadorial appointment (Chase, "New Religious-Freedom"; Chase, "Religious-freedom"; Hong, "How").

Even though the creation of the ORF was supported by the Liberal Party in 2013, the office was discontinued by the Trudeau government and closed in March 2016. Foreign Affairs Minister Stéphane Dion argued that religious freedom did not require a separate office because all human rights were "indivisible, interdependent and interrelated" (Zilio, "Liberals"; Zilio, "Canada's Religious"). The inclusion of the ORF within the structures of a new office of human rights that was created to promote "a comprehensive vision that includes all human rights" – acknowledged the difficulty of an activity that directly relates to religion in Canada's foreign policy. A more liberal part of Canadian society and political class tried to abstain from discussing religion, questioning the validity of religious freedom advocacy as the answer to violence and oppression (Levitz, "Conservative"; Hemmat).

However, despite criticism, from the perspective of the influence of Canada around the world, the office played a crucial role. Canada was praised as a leader in advancing religious freedom as part of human rights, as a country that "became a voice for the voiceless who were persecuted for daring to follow their conscience" (George and Swett). This assessment was supported even in an internal evaluation of the ORF, published by the Liberal government in 2016. The report acknowledged that efforts by the Conservative government to promote religious freedom around the world had been tainted by the perception of political interference. Nevertheless, the ORF positioned Canada as a welcome world leader on the issue. Prioritizing freedom of religion was relevant to "current geo-political developments in peace and security." Among like-minded countries – the report indicated that there were "more than the usual western allies" – and international organizations, Canada's position was recognized as a global leader addressing a gap on the world stage. As the internal review stated, "[o]ther likeminded countries received some positive benefits from working with Canada's leadership on freedom of religion or belief. Specific examples included the coordination of a contact group and a specific advocacy project to jointly *démarche* a country with high-levels of religious persecution" (Global Affairs Canada, "Evaluation"). The ORF was an important element of Canada's relations with selected countries, among them the Commonwealth members, as it allowed Ottawa to lead discussions and continue its active engagement for the cause of religious freedom. What is even more important from the selective power perspective is that with the creation of the ORF Canada could work through various avenues, including multilateral fora, for example with the U.N. Special Rapporteur on Freedom of Religion or Belief. All these activities elevated Canada to leadership in bringing awareness of the issues of religious freedom to more countries, demonstrating credibility and a constructive approach (Global Affairs Canada, "Evaluation").

The work of the office was spoiled by lack of regular communication and transparency about its goals and by concerns that the office was biased in its approach to which religions or countries it worked with. Even though the ORF tried to maintain a balanced approach to ensure its policies were not viewed as favouring any religion or group of stakeholders, some stakeholders interpreted the actions of the ORF as politically motivated. "Not surprisingly, the misperception that ORF was a political office was one of the challenges that the office continued to face" (Global Affairs Canada, "Evaluation").

Although the ORF can be seen as a pure element of the Harper electoral strategy attracting certain groups of ethnic voters, we see it rather as a pragmatically selected element of keeping balance between values and interests in foreign policy. The Harper government used the ORF as a means to position Canada as "a game changer" in the area that neither needed a large investment nor depended on "the military's display of strength, with or without allies, or trade liberalization initiatives" (Siebert 17). The main activities of the ORF offered DFAIT a possibility of using traditional soft power skills based on persuasion in both bilateral and multilateral diplomacy. Canadian Minister of Foreign Affairs John Baird could speak strongly of Canada "standing up against evil" and that its principled foreign policy was "not for sale" (qtd. in Levitz, "John"), and such statements were pragmatically calculated in order not to harm Canada's economy too much.

Respecting the territorial integrity of others

As Adam Chapnick rightly suggests, the most important (and known) element of the Axworthy doctrine – human security – was also the element which Stephen Harper rejected the most (Chapnick, "A Diplomatic"). The Harper government even decided to erase all mentions of human security from foreign policy documents. The reason for that was a fundamental difference between Axworthy and Harper in perceiving the role of the state in international relations. The Harper government emphasized the state's need to protect the very sovereignty in contrast to Axworthy's call for collective management of future challenges among state governments, non-state actors, and local populations.

The initiatives which the Harper government undertook after 2006 supported the idea of respecting territorial integrity and independence of the existing states. In reference to this idea, Harper made a declaration to the American audience that Canada's territory extended "200 miles out into the Arctic Ocean. No more, and no less" (Harper, "The Call"). This approach was consistent with the core conservative values and had already been featured in Canadian politics since the beginning of the 2000s, especially when in 2004 a U.S. submarine was spotted in the North Pole region, which ignited a new wave of interest in Canada's sovereignty in the Arctic, especially in the waters of the Northwest Passage.

A firm belief that the territorial rights of the existing states must be respected resulted in Harper's strong opposition to the militaristic policies of North Korea, Iran or Argentina. In 2012, during the Summit of the Americas in Cartagena, Canada protested vigorously when president Cristina Fernandez de Kirchner tried to get support from the summit leaders to Argentina's claim to the Falkland Islands. Stephen Harper even convinced the president of the United States that the support would conflict with the right of Falklanders to choose their own form of government (Ibbitson, *Stephen* 334-335).

Harper's defence of territorial rights stopped when violations of human rights were the case. In such situations Canada acted according to the R2P doctrine. Canada participated in the NATO-led intervention in Libya in 2011, helping to remove Colonel Gaddafi's regime from power. Another example was Syria. According to John Ibbitson, Harper lost confidence in Obama's human rights approach when in 2013 the president did not act decisively after Syrian president Bashar al-Asad had used chemical weapons, even though Obama had declared it "a red line" that the regime must not cross (Ibbitson, *Stephen* 335).

Focus on territorial integrity was also visible in Harper's relations with Ukraine and Russia. Contrary to the Pearsonian internationalism, Harper deliberately decided not to hide his criticism of Putin's Russia or the Yanukovych regime behind a tempered language. He was not willing to use a quiet diplomacy or play the role of a middle man, easing a dialogue between Moscow and Kiev. Although Harper and Putin started with friendly promises of cooperation in the Arctic, when they met in 2006 at the G8 summit in St. Petersburg, the Conservative prime minister, often described as a "Cold War warrior at heart," followed Canadian businesses' distrust of oligarchic Russia. Harper condemned Russia's invasion of Georgia in 2008, its involvement in Iran's nuclear weapons program, and Putin's support for the Assad regime in Syria's civil war. At the June 2013 meeting of the G8 in Enniskillen, Northern Ireland, Harper declared that Putin did not belong in the G8. "I don't think we should fool ourselves," he told reporters, "[t]his is G7 plus one" (qtd. in Ibbitson, *Stephen* 330). Foreign Minister John Baird went to Kiev during the protests against the Yanukovych regime on the Maidan square, and when President Yanukovych fled to Russia Stephen Harper quickly endorsed the new government and was the first Western leader to visit Ukraine. He proclaimed that "[w]hatever difficulties may lie ahead, whatever actions are taken by those who threaten Ukraine's freedom, Ukraine will never be alone, because Ukraine can count on Canada" (qtd. in Heinbecker).

After the Russian annexation of Crimea in 2014, Canada under Harper started to fulfill the prime minister's promises. Ottawa became a pioneer in sanctions against Putin's Russia: Canada's ambassador to Russia was ordered back home for consultations and the prime minister openly and publicly condemned Moscow with the harshest words of all G7 leaders (Bratt, "Stephen" 488).

Harper dealt with Russia's war on Ukraine in his most preferred way, i.e. through the means of international diplomacy and his direct contacts with the leaders of like-minded countries. Canada thus cooperated with other G7 states in boycotting the G8 summit that had been scheduled to be held in Sochi, and successfully insisted on expelling Russia from the G7 summit which was held in March 2014 in Brussels (Fisher). After Russian-supported Ukrainian separatists allegedly shot down a Malaysian civilian aircraft in July 2014, Harper reiterated his condemnation of the policies of Moscow. The Canadian prime minister even engaged in a personal quarrel with Putin during the G20 summit in November 2014 in Brisbane, Australia, saying to Russia's president that he would shake his hand only to send him a message that Russia "need[s] to get out of Ukraine" (Chase, "Harper Tells"). In an article written for the *Globe and Mail*, Harper cited Putin's lack of respect for democracy, international security and the rule of law as the reasons why "it is difficult to foresee any circumstance under which Mr. Putin's Russia could be readmitted to the family of G7 nations" (Harper, "Our Duty").

Harper's message to Putin was conveyed also via usually neutral fora, such as the Arctic Council. In 2015, while still chairing the organization, Canadian Minister of Environment Leona Aglukkaq declared that "Canada will use the Arctic Council ministerial meeting [to be hosted by Canada in Iqaluit in April 2015] as an opportunity once again to deliver our tough message to Russia for their aggression against Ukraine" (Weber). Russia did not send its Foreign Minister, Sergey Lavrov, to the meeting and it was widely speculated that this was due to Canada's uncompromising attitude to the Ukrainian crisis. In his remarks, the Canadian head of the delegation – Foreign Minister Rob Nicholson – did not mention Russia among Canada's Arctic neighbours ("Nicholson").

Such a confrontational approach of the Harper government was widely criticized in Canada. Heather Exner-Pirot argued that Canada should not have used a neutral venue for that type of rhetoric, saying: "Regardless of whether Canada's stance on Ukraine has been too tough or just right, using the platform afforded by chairing the Arctic Council to sermonize on the issue came across as tactless, and was in stark contrast to the response of the other Ministers represented" (91-92). Paul Heinbecker wrote that "[i]n responding to Russian aggression in Ukraine, the Harper government and its acolytes rode metaphorically into the Valley of Death. [...] The claims to leadership by Canada [...] went unnoticed by allies. The only way Canada was leading was in bluster." John Trent noticed that Ottawa did not have enough military capability to support its tough language (35), while Heinbecker gravely added that "[t]here is no prospect that any western government, including the Canadian government, will risk a third world war to defend Ukraine from Russia." Numerous commentators suggested that the hard line on Moscow played well with Canada's Ukrainian and Polish diasporas (Nikiforuk). Christopher Westdal, former Canadian ambassador to both Russia and Ukraine, even suggested that Harper's stance on Crimea was simply a way to get votes of Ukrainian-Canadians (Ibbitson, *Stephen* 331).

Canada's leadership in sanctions against Russia was clearly seen when other NATO countries joined Ottawa in sending military trainers to Ukraine (M. MacKinnon, "Canadian"). This decision was renewed even after the 2015 election in Canada (Fife and MacKinnon). The leadership was especially evident after the NATO summit held in Warsaw in 2016, when the establishment of the so-called Eastern Flank, in which Canada became a framework country in Latvia was decided. However, the direct economic help to Ukraine was limited, i.e. Canada assigned a CAD 200 million loan to support Ukraine, and other types of aid, such as training for horticultural farmers, were even scantier (Trent 35). In Harper's decisions there were elements typical of a selective power, such as pragmatically crafted decisions aimed at reaching the greatest possible results at the lowest cost. Harper's consistent opposition to the Russian invasion in Ukraine also helped to prove to the world that President Putin could not be treated as a regular, democratic head of state.

Middle East

Before we start to analyze the actual decisions of the Conservative government regarding the Middle East, it seems important to sketch a short history of Ottawa's policies towards this region. Since the creation of the state of Israel, the traditional and dominant Canadian approach has been based on keeping a balance between Ottawa's strong support of Israel and, at the same time, an ability to develop and keep working relations with the Arab countries. This was visible on various occasions when Ottawa worked towards the reconciliation of differences between Israel and the Arab world, especially when Ottawa was acting as an impartial "helpful broker" in the region, for example contributing to peacekeeping missions in conflicts between Israel and Egypt or Syria.

Under the Liberal Party, which governed for the greater part of the second half of the 20th century, Canada tried to keep a balanced approach by building its voter base among the growing Muslim immigrant population and, at the same time, not offending the Jewish voters. In foreign policy such an approach resulted in defending Israel's right to peace and the protection of its citizens, while also recognizing the Palestinian right to self-determination and supporting the creation of a Palestinian sovereign state. At the U.N., Ottawa adhered to the U.N. consensus, which meant supporting those votes in the United Nations General Assembly that criticized Israel for expanding its settlements on the occupied Palestinian lands, with the two-state solution as Ottawa's declared goal. This version of a balanced approach has become a pan-Canadian tactic, upheld by subsequent governments, supported by the academia and the media.

In the 21st century and in the post-9/11 world, Canada maintains that the balanced approach is a key to Canada's relations with the Middle East. Canada deployed soldiers in Afghanistan, in support of the U.N. resolutions, but at the same time the Jean Chrétien Liberal government kept a cautious distance from the U.S.-led war in Iraq. Nevertheless, even before, with the failure of the Oslo process and the subsequent terror attacks perpetrated by the Palestinian militant groups and the retaliatory actions on the part of the Israeli military, the Canadian Liberal government had become increasingly identified with European-like sympathy for Palestinians and the criticism of Israel. As Muslim countries kept their advantage in the U.N. voting pattern, the core element of Canada's cautious approach – adhering to the U.N. consensus – started to be associated with siding with the Arab countries. The Canadian approach was in strong contrast to that of the U.S.

Canadian policies towards the Israeli-Palestinian conflict and the peace process began to shift under the Liberal government of Paul Martin. With the appointment of pro-Israeli politicians to the cabinet, Canada's voting behaviour in the United Nations General Assembly changed, as Canada abstained from some votes that condemned the actions of Israel. This put Canada in the minority in the U.N. (Mackay 34).

As already discussed above, Harper repeatedly declared that Canada's foreign policy had to be guided by values. He believed there had been too many trade-offs between value-based positions and other vital foreign policy interests, especially when dealing with countries that violated human rights. Harper's government, contrary to the liberal internationalism, adopted a very principled approach in external affairs, in which normative foreign policy goals took precedence and in which there was little space for compromises between values and other goals (Schönwälder). Such an approach gradually softened with Harper's time in office – as visible in relations with China – but stayed unmoved regarding the firm friendship for Israel. The Conservatives' commitment to Israel culminated in Harper's visit to Israel in January 2014, when the prime minister promised in the Knesset that "through fire and water, Canada will stand with you" (Harper, "The Special"; Ivison, "'Through'").

As suggested by Harper's biographers, including John Ibbitson, Canadian prime minister's support for Israel had its roots in his father's highly principled and favourable view of Israel, which he managed to implant in his son's mind (Ibbitson, *Stephen* 326). From his early childhood Stephen Harper had deeply believed – some even likened it to religious conviction – in the role Israel played in Middle East as the only democratic state in the region, surrounded by hostile regimes that ultimately may also become Canada's enemies (Bratt, "Stephen" 490). In May 2008, Harper declared Canada's support for Israel saying that "those who threaten Israel also threaten Canada, because, as the last war showed, hate-fuelled bigotry against some is ultimately a threat to us all, and must be resisted wherever it may lurk" (qtd. in Nossal, "Primat" 9-10). Harper elaborated more on his view on the relations between democracy and the defence of Israel in an interview in 2011:

> Israel [is] essentially a Western democratic country that is an ally of ours, who's the only state in the United Nations whose very existence is significantly questioned internationally and opposed by many, including by the other side of that particular conflict […] [T]hose who most oppose the existence of Israel and seek its extinction, they are the very people who, in a security sense, are immediate – long-term but also immediate – threats to our own country (qtd. in Whyte).

The second element of Harper's attitude towards the Middle East was his conviction that anti-Semitism had not been eliminated in the world. The prime minister believed that "new anti-Semitism" was on the rise and it was "the mutation of the old disease of anti-Semitism" that "targets the Jewish people by targeting Israel" and "selectively condemns only the Jewish state and effectively denies its right to defend itself, while systematically ignoring – or excusing – the violence and oppression all around it" (qtd. in Payton, "Stephen"). There were also other reasons for Ottawa's support of Israel, among them the most important was Israel's military response to terrorism (Bratt, "Stephen" 490).

Given the above elements, Canada, according to Harper, was under the moral obligation to support Israel, even at the price of being isolated on the world scene. It simply was "right to do so" (Harper, "The Special"). Thus, accordingly, under Stephen Harper Canada shifted its traditional policy in the Middle East, abandoning the traditional role of an intermediary and adopting a strong pro-Israel stance.

When the Harper Conservatives won the election in 2006, they obviously reversed many of the positions of the Chrétien Liberal government, although they kept in line with the Martin government's approach. It is, however, important to emphasize that the main aspects of Canada's official government policy towards the Israeli-Palestinian conflict had not changed that much. For example, Ottawa condemned Israeli settlements in the occupied territories and was fully supportive of a two-state solution, with the creation of a Palestinian state and with guarantees for Israel's security. The most visible element of Harper's new approach was the change of rhetoric. Canada's tone became less nuanced, with more vocal support for Israel and lesser confidence in U.N. institutions (Mackay 35). Harper's symbolic actions were in stark contrast to past Canadian actions and were mostly covered with the rhetoric referring to the importance of values of democracy. From this perspective, it seemed there was a gap between the official government policy and its rhetoric.

The pro-Israeli rhetoric became evident as soon as Harper went to attend his first G8 summit. The prime minister declared there that Canada stood firmly behind Israeli incursion into Lebanon. Even though this move was criticized by other NATO members, Harper believed that Israel had the right to defend itself and that "Israel's response under the circumstances has been measured" (qtd. in Ibbitson, *Stephen* 326). Ottawa also refrained during the Gaza wars from criticizing Israeli military tactics, even after an independent U.N. commission and respected non-governmental organizations had documented possible Israeli and Palestinian violations of international law. The Harper government called the Israeli response "balanced." At the same time Ottawa criticized Palestinians for using "indiscriminate and inaccurate rockets" (Heinbecker; Trent 32). This type of unconditional vocal support for Israel from the Conservative Party never abated.

Then came other changes. Ottawa limited the funding of NGOs that promoted human rights in the Middle East and even dismantled the Rights and Democracy council, one of the world's most recognized organizations (Trent 32). Harper also announced that Canada would not participate in the 2009 Durban Review Conference, considering the event as exploited by radical groups for anti-Israel campaigning. A similar justification was presented in 2014 to explain Ottawa's boycott of a U.N. conference in Geneva on the situation in the Palestinian areas (Bratt, "Stephen" 490). Between 2006 and 2015, Canada altered the

U.N. voting patterns on Palestine, joining the U.S., Australia and several other countries in principled opposition to the votes which criticized Israel. The Harper government believed that this was due to the U.N.'s bias against Israel that Jewish nationalism was singled out on the U.N. fora (Hessey). Moreover, Ottawa cut all diplomatic contacts with the elected Palestinian Authority in 2006, referred to Hamas as a terror organization and suspended development assistance when Hamas won the election (Burgman). The Harper government kept this stance throughout his whole tenure. In 2011, Canada blocked a G8 leaders' statement that urged peace talks on Israel. Ottawa also campaigned against the recognition of Palestine as a non-member observer state in the U.N. and, in 2012, Canada became one of only nine countries to vote against a U.N. resolution which granted Palestine that status (Saunders; Campbell, "John"; Bratt, "Stephen" 490). Canada voted similarly against Palestinian accession to the International Criminal Court. There were also symbolical gestures, such as the meeting between John Baird and an Israeli cabinet minister in East Jerusalem in 2013. This was a deliberate break with international customs and an offence to the Arab world ("Palestinians").

Another element of the new Conservative Middle East policy revolved around Canada's tense relations with Iran – a country that was perceived by Harper "as the most significant threat to global peace and security in the world" (qtd. in Robertson 112). Ottawa criticized Iran's nuclear program, its support for terrorism, anti-Israel activities and abuse of human rights. In 2012, the Harper government suddenly terminated diplomatic relations with Iran, closed Canada's embassy in Tehran, and expelled Iranian diplomats from Canada. Baird explained that decision saying that Iranian leaders "routinely threaten the existence of Israel, engage in racist anti-Semitic rhetoric and incite genocide" ("Canada, Slamming"). Canada implemented all the U.N. sanctions against Iran and adopted additional unilateral measures (Juneau). Canadian sanctions against Iran remained in place even after the 2013 Iranian nuclear framework deal, as the government was "deeply skeptical" of Iranian intentions and actions. Minister Baird justified the decision on the grounds that Iran's "past actions best predict future actions, and Iran has defied the United Nations Security Council and defied the International Atomic Energy Agency. Simply put: Iran has not earned the right to have the benefit of the doubt" (qtd. in McKenna, "Canada"). Ottawa's scepticism and economic sanctions stayed unchanged also two years later when the five permanent members of the U.N. Security Council, together with Germany, reached an agreement on Iran's nuclear weapons program (Bratt, "Stephen" 489). However, the hostility of the Harper government toward Tehran became more nuanced in 2015, reflecting a growing concern about the instability that was caused by the expansion of ISIS in the Middle East (Boessenkool). Nevertheless, Ottawa maintained a distinctly harsher tone than its closest allies.

Harsh rhetoric and cutting diplomatic ties with Iran, which limited the ability to conduct an independent and eyewitness assessment of events, was in sharp contrast to previous Canadian positions and was widely criticized by the Canadian diplomatic corps, among others by Ken Taylor. Taylor was the Canadian Ambassador to Iran in the 1970s. His behaviour at the height of the Iranian Revolution in 1979 became symbolic in a way. He was able to smuggle six U.S. diplomats out of Iran after they had narrowly fled the U.S. Embassy taken over by a crowd of demonstrators (Bratt, "Stephen" 489). Those who disagreed most strongly with the Harper approach quit their jobs (M. MacKinnon, "Harper's").

It is clearly visible that the Conservative Middle East policy showed the rising assertiveness in advancing Canada's own interests and values and was noticed internationally. Such an approach transgressed the rules of a middle power – as a middle power Canada could not afford to make a controversial decision and still be a relevant actor in trying to bring stability to the region. Petrelekas and de Kerckchove aptly singled out a decision to end diplomatic relations with Iran as "a clear example of the Government's blending pragmatism and a principled approach by taking a measure which would further express its support for its Israeli ally and friend, while reinforcing its condemnation of Iran on its human rights record and its nuclear policy" (15).

This assertiveness towards Iran was possible since Iran presented only a marginal threat to Canadian interests. The costs of such a policy were also negligible – Canada's small trade with Iran would have been impaired because of sanctions anyway. Iran did not retaliate against Canadian interests. Nevertheless, the government faced an allegation of inconsistency or even hypocrisy – on the one hand, Ottawa claimed that its approach to Iran was based on the principles of human rights, but on the other it approved the sale of weapons to Saudi Arabia – a country whose human rights record was very poor (Juneau).

Harper's pro-Israel policy was accused of being crafted to reap Jewish votes for the Conservative Party. In fact the approach of the Conservative government toward the Middle East was supported by a larger group of Canadians. In a 2012 survey, 48 per cent of the society believed that the federal government's policy in the Israeli-Palestinian conflict "[struck] the right balance" (Martin). Nevertheless, the Harper government ignored Canadians' growing unease with Israel's conduct. In 2013, 57 per cent of Canadians viewed Israel's influence in the world as mainly negative (Ditmars). An even larger contradiction with broad public opinion can be observed with the Harper government official policy that supported the two-state solution for the Israel-Palestine conflict. In 2011 a majority of Canadians supported Palestine's bid for statehood. More importantly, although many evangelical Christians – a support base for Harper's government – were traditionally pro-Israel, at the same time they fundamentally opposed a two-state solution (Ditmars). Lastly, Harper's policy could also be harmful for the Conservative Party since Muslims in Canada outnumber Jews by almost three to one. However, Canada's Arab population, due to its internal divisions and less organized structures, was not as able to influence Ottawa as a powerful interest group as their Jewish Canadian counterparts (Mackay 37).

The Middle East policy of the Harper government supports the view that Canada stopped being an honest broker in the Middle East. Harper limited Canada's capacity as a mediator, and perhaps Joe Clark, former prime minister of Canada, was right when he remarked that Canada's "traditional reputation for even-handedness" in the Middle East had been limited as "other countries in the region regard the Israeli-Palestinian conflict to be the litmus test of fairness and credibility" (Clark, "Canada"). At the same time, it can be said that in many aspects the Canadian position on the conflict between Palestinians and Israel followed a policy based on realism. Harper's supporters argued that when under Paul Martin Canada sought to play a role as a mediator, it did not produce a positive impact and Canada lost the trust of the Israeli government, which "objected to what it viewed as a moral failure of Europe as well as Canada, in the wake of mass terror and suicide bombing" (Nikiforuk). Instead of being an objective observer, the Harper government chose to take a stand. John Baird admitted this when he remarked that Canada was "not a referee. We have a side. The side is freedom. The side is human rights. The side is open economies" (qtd. in Berthiaume, "Canada").

This stance reflected a general transformation of the Canadian society, which no longer saw its country as a "middle power." The default position of Canada during the Cold War era and immediately after was no longer applicable in time of terrorism and the declining U.S. position. Ottawa could no longer position itself in the middle between the rich North and the poor South and build its image on the fact of being praised and courted by the majority of the U.N. member states for keeping in line with the policies that garnered the support of the U.N. majority. As in the 21st century Canadian foreign policy became an important battleground in an international ideological debate on the Israel-Palestine conflict, Ottawa could not pretend that Canadians were only peacekeepers. As Frank Dimat from B'nai Brith Canada suggested, as "the world has changed [...] Canadian foreign policy has changed with it" and the Conservative government decided to ally itself with Israel "on the frontline of the war against Islamic radicals" (qtd. in Ditmars).

Such a tactic obviously generated some costs. Canada was no longer seen by the Arab nations as an honest broker and did not receive the voting support in the U.N. which it had received from the Arab countries in the past. The lack of such support contributed to the lost battle for a seat as a non-permanent member of the United Nations Security Council in 2010. However, the lost seat could not be solely attributed to Canada's rhetoric and actions towards the Israeli-Palestinian conflict, as the Harper government had also been more critical of the United Nations as a whole.

It is worth emphasizing that, apart from the change in rhetoric, the Trudeau government has not reversed the main elements of the Conservative approach to the Middle East. During the 2015 election campaign, Trudeau's statements, for example on Gaza, were similar to those of the Conservatives, even though an open letter published in 2014 called for a change (Canadians for Justice and Human Rights in Gaza; Ditmars). In his speeches at Canadian synagogues, Trudeau declared that the Liberal party "will have Israel's back" because it is "the only real democracy in the Middle East," sharing "the very values and ideals that define Canada: values of openness, respect, compassion, that seek for justice, search for peace" (qtd. in Zerbisias). Such a message was effective because it brought victory in many ridings with a significant number of the Jewish population (Zerbisias). Thus it was obvious that the official support of the Trudeau government for Israel and the two-state solution would remain unchanged (Caplan, "Trudeau"; Bonokoski).

But, as under Harper, little effort to go beyond declarations also occurred under Trudeau (Hessey). For example, in its very first statement on Israel-Palestine conflict, the Trudeau government expressed its opposition to the Palestinians using the U.N. institutions to advance their cause (Woodley). The Trudeau government also maintained Harper's voting patterns at the U.N. Small changes, such as renewing Canadian funding to the U.N. Relief and Works Agency for Palestine have occurred, but the general line and much of the language remains similar. The Liberal government tactically delayed condemnation of the announcements concerning the expansion of Israeli settlements and did not condemn Israel's brutality or offered sympathy to Palestinians who were suffering (Caplan, "Trudeau"). As of February 2017, Trudeau also has not restarted diplomatic relations with Iran. To sum up, we see Trudeau's approach to the Middle East constitutes more of a shift in tone than a significant change based on action. Canada's support and friendship for Israel is maintained at the same high level.

Arms sale

Harper's principled approach to foreign policy was clearly seen in his tactic of boycotting or using economic sanctions against countries that violated human rights. Sometimes, as was the case with Iran, Canada's hard-line approach differed from other countries. On other occasions, for example with North Korea or Myanmar, Ottawa's reactions were consistent with the behaviour of other Western states. However, during Harper's tenure, the difficulty of bringing together value-based and interest-motivated foreign policy became very clear. This problem was particularly exposed when values collided with economic interests. We already mentioned Canada's troubled relations with China, but Ottawa's contradictory approach to human rights was apparent also in various cases concerning arms sales to other countries. The most controversial case, which galvanized the Canadian public opinion, was the arms contract with Saudi Arabia – a country with a known record of human rights abuses – announced in 2014 (Fitzgerald; Freedom House).

In Harper's economic and foreign policies, Saudi Arabia was a country of focus. Under Harper's strategy of "economic diplomacy," diplomatic service was linked with private industry interests and its task was also a promotion of business contracts. Although most official documents remain secret, WikiLeaks revealed some information on how Ottawa had for several years approached Riyadh offering lucrative contracts (Chase "Leaks"). This tactic resulted in the signing of the largest advanced manufacturing contract in Canadian history in 2014, which involved the sale of an undisclosed number of Light Armoured Vehicles (LAVs) to Saudi Arabia. Initially, Ottawa announced that the value of the contract was CAD 10 billion, but subsequently this amount grew to CAD 15 billion. The transaction was championed by International Trade Minister Ed Fast as a major success for Canadian diplomacy and an important step for Canada's economy, supporting "500 local Canadian firms" with 3,000 jobs for over 14 years, mostly in Ontario, where the light-armoured vehicles were to be designed and assembled (Chase and Blackwell).

However, a number of problematic issues were embedded in the contract. Firstly, the tightening of economic and security ties with the Arab Gulf monarchies after 2011, as part of Harper's strategy of increasing the sales of arms, was met with substantial criticism in Canada (Vucetic, "A Nation" 3, 5-6; Klassen, "Joining Empire: Canadian"). In light of the value-based rhetoric – as evident in 2012 when minister John Baird declared in Washington that Canada was not "selective in which basic human rights we defend, nor can we be arbitrary in whose rights we protect" – the fact that in the wake of the civil war in Libya, Saudi Arabia became a close ally of Ottawa's Middle East policy and a significant customer of Canadian arms, was a basis for accusations of selectivity and arbitrariness (qtd. in Payton, "Religious"; Engler).

For the Harper government, selling arms to Saudi Arabia was a pragmatic choice that had to be made, given the fact that Saudi Arabia was a powerful regional ally in the Middle East and that the Saudi government could have easily bought similar LAVs from other suppliers. Thus the Harper government calculated rationally, although coldly, not to subordinate Canada's economic and strategic interest to the rhetoric that most probably would have not changed the policies of the regime in Riyadh anyway (Black).

As a matter of fact, Canada has been selling LAVs to Saudi Arabia since the late 1980s, and a noticeable growth of arms exports occurred after the 9/11 attacks. For example, according to the information which was revealed by journalists, in three separate deals in 2006, 2009 and 2011, Saudi Arabia bought LAVs from Canada for a total value of around

CAD 8 billion (Webster). Saudi Arabia also had other business contracts with such Canadian companies as Bombardier and SNC Lavalin and participated in the exercises of the Canadian navy and air force (Chase and Fife, "Saudi Arabian"; Jabir and Hussain). However, after it was revealed in the Canadian press that in March 2011, the Saudi army had suppressed the Arab Spring protests in Bahrain using its existing fleet of Canadian-made LAVs, the sale of arms became the object of public scrutiny (Webster). Nevertheless, it came as no surprise that the contract for the sale of military equipment, including LAVs to Saudi Arabia, reverberated widely in Canada – even more so when it was revealed that with this contract Canada became the second largest arms exporter to the Middle East in 2015 (Chase, "Canada").

In this public mood, the deal, which was a special transaction concluded between a Canadian company and a foreign government, became scrutinized by journalists. They exposed that, as a result of the decrease in defence spending in the United States after the recent financial crisis, Canadian defence exports were bound to seek new markets and those in the Middle East looked particularly promising. As exporters turned towards this region, they were backed by the Canadian Commercial Corporation (CCC), a Crown corporation established to help defend exporters with "a long track record of stewarding defence deals" (Webster). Moreover, the Canadian government also actively lobbied for the contract. Several members of Harper's cabinet visited Saudi Arabia. The prime minister even wrote a personal letter to King Abdullah to assure him that Canada was committed to the deal. As disclosed by WikiLeaks, executives from the CCC spent the Christmas of 2013 in the Middle East waiting for the opportunity to get the monarch to sign the deal (Chase, "The Big"). Coincidentally, around the time of the visits, Ottawa also closed the Canadian embassy in Iran, Saudi Arabia's arch-enemy. On the other hand, Riyadh made its own investments in Canada, such as donations to private Islamic schools in Canada (Webster). Additionally, when the Harper government lobbied for the contract, it defeated French and German competitors. For the government officials, such as Adam Taylor, an aide to the minister of trade, it proved that "Canada was playing the game in a competitive world where others are playing the game more fiercely and with better results" (Chase, "The Big"). However, according to Paul Christopher Webster, a *Globe and Mail* journalist, Germans refused to sell 800 tanks to Saudi Arabia in 2014 after a human rights review and subsequently suspended all arms sales to the country. Ottawa simply used the vacuum space created by the German withdrawal (Webster). The information was revealed only in 2017, but the Canadian public had already had suspicions as to how the government's economic policy actually worked.

These suspicions were reinforced, as mentioned above, by the fact that Canadian-made weaponized armoured vehicles were to be sold to a country that was roundly condemned for an abysmal record on human rights as a result of its appalling treatment of women, dissidents and prisoners. Critics argued that the contract on LAVs was "un-Canadian," shameful for a country "whose icons include peace makers such as Lester B. Pearson and Roméo Dallaire" (Chase, "The Big"). However, what outraged the Canadian public was the fact that the Trudeau government decided to fulfill the contract with Saudi Arabia in 2016, which is discussed in Chapter 4.

Obviously, with so much secrecy around the contract, it is extremely risky to make final judgements about it. Nevertheless, the arms sale deal with Saudi Arabia may be treated as another example of the selective power behaviour of Canada. Selling arms to countries that violate human rights has been typical of the Canadian governments since 1989. According to research done by Srdjan Vucetic, "Canada's support of international human rights tends to hit a hard wall when it comes to the arms trade." Although Canada sold substantially less military goods to buyers with poor human rights records than, for example, the Netherlands or Sweden, nevertheless human rights considerations almost never stopped Canadian authorities from issuing export permits. Usually "economic and strategic considerations" turned out to be paramount and the authorities only declared to "monitor" the use of military equipment (Vucetic, "What" 12-13). Another research work by Naël Shiab revealed that in the past 25 years Canada sold CAD 5.8 billion worth of weapons to countries with a deeply questionable human rights record.

From this perspective, the Harper government's record on arms sale did not differ substantially from previous governments. Canada did not sell more arms abroad under the Conservative governments than under the previous Liberal governments. This consistency of Ottawa's behaviour applies also when one compares the Harper decade with the period when Lloyd Axworthy was minister of foreign affairs in the Chrétien government in 1996-2000 (Vucetic, "A Nation" 16). The same argument also applies to the Liberal Justin Trudeau government. As summarized by Anna Stavrianakis, most states use "a realist explanation" in which "seemingly normatively progressive regimes serve as rhetorical cover for material or strategic interests." Nevertheless, this "hypocrisy and instrumental or functional pursuit of material interests," has also been a feature of Canadian governments since the Cold War (Stavrianakis 844-845). However, as Aaron Karp argues, in arms trade, a government of every exporting country must "acknowledge the contradictions of their foreign and security policies":

> the gap between the goals of a peaceful world, the possibilities of inter-state war, and the everyday reality of armed conflict and hybrid war, between the desire to transform the world and the imperative to support friends and slow the spread of chaos, between moral purity and messy realities (qtd. in Chase, "As Canada").

Official development assistance

The official development assistance (ODA), as foreign aid policy in Canada is called, is intended to contribute to the economic and social development of poor regions, to implement human rights and to strengthen the bilateral economic and political ties between Canada and the assisted states. Canada has a large and internationally praised system of providing development assistance abroad, as presented in Chapter 1.

The Harper government inherited the official development assistance policy that had been the subject of severe long-standing criticism from many Canadian and international institutions, OECD among others (Anderson, Brown, and Jean 135). Among the ranks of critics there were also politicians from the Conservative Party. They blamed Ottawa for the ineffectiveness due to excessive fragmentation of aid, subsidies for states that were corrupt and the absence of far-reaching strategies. All of these elements resulted in the wasting of the taxpayers' money (Harris and Manning 293-328). Since 2006, the Harper government was committed to introduce thorough reforms to the Canada's ODA, although Ottawa did not issue an official ODA policy review between 2006 and 2015. Therefore, Harper's vision of foreign aid reform has to be reconstructed from various public speeches and publications. Initially, there was not much change comparing Harper's policies with those of his Liberal predecessors, as the government constantly repeated the importance of making a difference in people's lives through aid and Canadian generosity. What Stephen Harper announced in the United Nations in 2010 could have been repeated by any Canadian prime minister: "It is essential that we strive to make a significant, actual difference in the lives of the world's most disadvantaged people. Who, seeing his neighbour distressed, will pass by on the other side of the road?" (Harper, "Prime Minister Harper Highlights").

During its first few years in power, the Harper government accepted the commitments of the previous Liberal governments of Jean Chrétien and Paul Martin to increase the ODA budget on an annual basis and double support for Africa. Although the Conservatives kept the list of priority countries that had been adopted in 2005, they focused most of the resources on Afghanistan due to the presence of Canadian troops in the province of Kandahar, where Canada commanded the Provincial Reconstruction Team. Since 2005, the amount of money directed to Afghanistan increased more than 100 per cent a year until 2008 (in the 2005-2006 fiscal year it was CAD 101 million, in 2006-2007 – CAD 229 million, in 2007-2008 – CAD 345 million) (S. Brown, "The Instrumentalization"). The visibility of Canadian troops in Kandahar was used by many scholars to suggest that the desire for prestige and the craving for an increase of Canada's international reputation were the driving forces for the Conservatives to reform the ODA (S. Brown, "Aid"; Kirton, "Harper's" 47).

However, the symbolic prestige was not the only driving force of the foreign aid reforms. As the government continuously emphasized the need for greater accountability of spending, a turn towards economic self-interest began. The financial restrain became even more pressing when the 2008-2011 financial crisis hit Canada's economy. To increase the effectiveness of Canadian aid programs, in 2009 Ottawa reduced the number of potential recipients of Canadian development assistance. This was done by the drawing up of a list of 20 regions and "countries of focus" to which 80 per cent of funds were allocated. The list of priority recipients was changed another time in 2014 and included 25 countries to which 90 per cent of bilateral aid would flow. New countries added to the list were Benin, Burkina Faso, the Democratic Republic of Congo,

Jordan, Mongolia, Myanmar and the Philippines (Foreign Affairs, Trade and Development).

What was important, on the new list poor African countries were replaced by wealthier ones in Latin America and the Caribbean, where Canada could promote its commercial interests. The idea behind that was to make foreign aid "more efficient and effective" and to "improve the quality and value for money." But it also brought side effects as Canadian foreign aid became more and more instrumentalized, privatized and "recommercialized" (Mackrael, "'Huge"; S. Brown, "Aid"). This meant that a link between aid and commercial interests was enhanced. After 2011, the prime minister and subsequent ministers of international development supported special funding deals between the government, NGOs and Canadian private mining companies to assure that "Canadians themselves benefit from foreign aid" (S. Brown, "Aid"). Internal reviews of aid programs conducted by the CIDA clearly indicated that Canadian "commercial interests have become a key consideration in determining how much aid a developing country will receive" (Mackrael, "Commercial").

As suggested in research conducted by Stephen Brown, although using the ODA for self-interests did not set the Harper government apart from its predecessors, unique consistency in driving foreign aid to benefit Canada was exceptional ("The Instrumentalization" 18). However, such an approach to the official development assistance should not be surprising since it was clearly in line with economic neo-liberalism preferred by the prime minister. The reduction of state intervention in the economy, openness toward the private sector and requiring that funds for aid be spent on Canadian products and services marked Harper's new approach. As Brown summarized, "Canada's version of aid effectiveness is clearly 'a distinct, more narrow version' of the internationally endorsed agenda that concentrates on internal organizational issues and accountability to Canadian taxpayers" ("Aid").

This was particularly evident in countries where Canadian NGOs managed developing projects which were co-funded by CIDA and Canadian extractive companies. Such projects were seen by critics as "subsidizing mining companies' corporate social responsibility programs" (Mackrael, "'Huge"). Nevertheless, the importance of the mining industry for Harper's agenda did not recede. At the 2012 Summit of the Americas in Cartagena, Harper applauded the benefits of the mining sector for Canada:

> Looking to the future, we see increased Canadian mining investment throughout the Americas, something that will be good for our mutual prosperity and is therefore a priority of our Government. We are prepared to share our expertise in this area because, as part of our Americas' strategy, we are striving to promote prosperity, democracy and security throughout our hemisphere. A couple of examples, the Canadian International Development Agency (CIDA) is funding the Andean Regional Initiative for promoting effective social responsibility. This initiative aims to help local governments and communities implement related development projects for the benefit of people living near mines or other development activities. Also, last year I announced the establishment of the Canadian International Institute for Extractive Industries and Development to bring together the best in government, private sector, academia and civil society expertise to help our developing country partners secure the greatest possible benefit from their natural resources (Harper, "Statement by the Prime Minister of Canada in Cartagena").

The culmination of the process of commercialization and instrumentalization of Canadian foreign aid occurred in 2013, when the responsibilities of the CIDA were taken over by the newly created Department of Foreign Affairs, Trade and Development. Although the government maintained that poverty reduction was still the key priority of Canada's aid activities, the critics suggested that the merger undermined the very purpose of foreign aid, not to mention that it weakened Canada's development commitments and served mostly private interests. The instrumentalization of the ODA, maintained the opponents, was indicative of the lack of strategic and long-term thinking of benefits Canada could obtain from a stable world and reduced "Canada's ability to use its soft power to influence the global order" (S. Brown, "The Instrumentalization" 18).

An additional element of transformation of the ODA that was widely criticized was the securitization of aid. Two elements were involved in this concept: the first one made security a requirement to deliver international assistance; the second linked international development with international trade (S. Brown, "The Instrumentalization"). This concept was announced as early as in 2007. In the Speech from the Throne, the government declared that Canada's capacity to "make a difference" was exposed most in Afghanistan – a place where Canadians, as part of "the United Nations-sanctioned mission," not only fulfilled a "noble and necessary" goal, but also comprehended that "development and security go hand in hand. Without security, there can be no humanitarian aid, no reconstruction and no democratic development." But the government also emphasized that "[t]he best hope for fostering development and our common security in the hemisphere and beyond is through bolstering international trade" (Harper, "The 2007"). The connection of development and security was also emphasized in 2008, when Ottawa declared transformation of Canada's military mission in Afghanistan "to focus on reconstruction and development" and praised "[t]he hard work and heroic sacrifices of Canada's men and women in the field – military, diplomatic and development" (Harper, "The 2008"). Similar statements, linking military elements and humanitarian aid, were reiterated in 2010 and in 2011 (Harper, "The 2010"; Harper, "The 2011"). Moreover, the concept of securitization was not limited to Afghanistan only. In the 2010 Speech from the Throne, the Harper government praised the Canadian army's assistance to Haiti after an earthquake had destroyed much of the country in 2010, saying that:

> [i]n Haiti, the Canadian Forces have taken the lessons learned in Afghanistan and put them to use in very different circumstances. Their speed and effectiveness in deployment were and are unsurpassed in the world (Harper, "The 2010").

In the first years of Harper's term in office, the prime minister upheld what he had promised during the election campaign – mainly adopting Paul Martin government's commitment to raise ODA by 8 percent annually. In 2010, Canada reached the G8 pledged target of doubling ODA – a rare achievement among G8 countries (Kirton, "Vulnerable" 138). That achievement was covered by the subsequent budgetary cuts and was judged by critics as a temporary performance. On the one hand, the austerity policy brought real budgetary savings, but on the other hand it provoked the criticism of Canada. Important institutions distributing or monitoring aid to poor countries (OECD, the World Bank, Oxfam and many non-governmental organizations) reacted negatively to the reform of Canadian aid policy and significantly reduced Canada's position in the rankings of the most generous donors ("Canada Development" 14). This negative perception was reinforced by the undelivered promise of keeping ODA at CAD 5 billion annually (Kirton, "Vulnerable" 138). According to data provided by OECD Development Assistance Committee (DAC) Canada's ODA dropped below CAD 5 billion already in 2012 (USD 4.76 billion), stayed below in 2013 (USD 4.54 billion) and in 2014 (USD 4.30 billion), only to grow above CAD 5 billion in 2015 (USD 5.43 billion) (Organisation for Economic Cooperation and Development, "Total").

According to the above-mentioned data, it is clear that although Canada continued to spend considerable amounts of resources on development aid, the ODA was severely impacted. An aid budget freeze, cuts and a policy of underspending started after the financial crisis and did not end until Harper's lost election of 2015. As a result, not only was Canada's ODA spending never restored to the pre-2008 levels, but in 2014 it dropped to 0.24 per cent of Gross National Income (GNI), the second lowest level in Canada's history (Greenhill and McQuillan; Organisation for Economic Cooperation and Development, "DAC").

Nevertheless, we argue that the financial and institutional aspect of Canada's ODA policy under the Harper government needs to be put into a wider perspective. Firstly, it is important to note that whereas in the two decades, from 1975 to 1995, Canada's contribution to development never dropped below 0.4 per cent of GNI, it also never reached the OECD target of the ODA volume, which was 0.70 per cent GNI. This included years with some of the largest budget surpluses in Canadian history. The lowest level of development assistance in Canada's history – 0.22 per cent – was reached in the fiscal year of 2000-2001 under the Liberal government (Greenhill and McQuillan). Thus we must distinguish between the rhetoric and figures on actual spending on ODA during the Harper government. As summarized by Greenhill and McQuillan: "The difference in spending between the periods before 1995 and after 1995 is much more significant than the differences between political parties during each period. [...] The key difference in spending levels is, therefore, not partisan: it is periodic."

Still, when in 2002 Jean Chrétien committed Canada to doubling its international assistance to Africa by 2011 and three years later Paul Martin pledged to increase development assistance by CAD 500 million over two years, it was only the Harper government that met those commitments.

Moreover, as already mentioned, Canada succeeded in doubling its aid in nominal terms between 2001 and 2010 (Greenhill and McQuillan; S. Brown, "Aid").

Secondly, in a situation of fiscal pressures, foreign aid has always been cut more than domestic government spending, and Ottawa has been reluctant to reverse this. Balancing the budget generally has priority in Canada over the official development assistance. This inconvenient truth applied not only to the Harper government (in the period 2010-2014), but to the Chrétien government as well (1995-2001) (Greenhill and Wadhera). What is even more striking is that the first budget of the Liberal Trudeau government kept Canada's ODA commitments at lower levels (0.26 percent of GNI) than the average for the Harper era (0.30 per cent) (Greenhill and Wadhera).

Thirdly, since the end of the Cold War, each Canadian government has tried to introduce some reforms to foreign aid, usually adding or refining elements implemented by its predecessors. For example, under Paul Martin, Canada integrated aid more closely with other foreign policy instruments and reduced the number of recipient countries. Stephen Harper followed the pattern and integrated Canada's aid further (S. Brown, "Aid"). Moreover, the government emphasized that the effectiveness of foreign aid had started earlier. For example, the much-criticized focus on Latin America and the promotion of the interests of Canadian private mining companies had been introduced during the tenure of the Liberal predecessors. Long before Harper the Canadian ODA had been connected to "non-development-related interests" or instrumentalized (S. Brown, "Aid"). Finally, the reduction of the recipients and the concentration on sectors had started long before the Harper government. For example, in 2002, Jean Chrétien announced the intention to bolster the impact of the ODA by concentrating on "a limited number of the world's poorest countries." This direction was continued by Paul Martin (S. Brown, "Aid").

Fourthly, the merging of CIDA with the Department of Foreign Affairs and International Trade, although controversial, was not without rational grounds. As Robertson argued, there was a discrepancy between DFAIT and CIDA in regard to how they considered their missions or between foreign policy objectives and the way development assistance was delivered (Robertson 106-107). As CIDA had developed a level of independency, backed by large budgets, its civil servants not only thought that "long-term development goals should not be subject to short-term diplomatic imperatives," but also acted independently from ambassadors or high commissioners. This resulted, on some occasions, in the fact that CIDA-funded projects were recognized by a host country's government as interfering in its domestic affairs (Robertson 106-107). From this perspective, the take-over of CIDA by the DFAIT was in line with the Conservative government's desire to inject a "business" perspective into development. The Harper government also believed that Canadian investments should also "promote Canadian values, Canadian business, the Canadian economy, benefits for Canada" (Mackrael, "Fantino"). Moreover, this shift in approach to foreign aid was followed by other countries, for instance Britain or Australia (Robertson 106-107).

Fifthly, as presented for example by François Audet and Olga Navarro-Flores, the Harper government's shift in Canadian official development assistance was supported only partially by the declared goals of increasing the role of the private sector, downsizing of the government and improving the program's efficiency. Some decisions resulted either from electoral concerns or were influenced by a Conservative ideology (Audet and Navarro-Flores 189-190). What is also important, and was briefly mentioned in the introduction to this chapter, the Conservative Party saw the Liberal internationalism as a kind of "bias" that needed to be removed. From that perspective, the "injection" of the Conservative ideology could be interpreted as only replacing one "bias" with another. The Harper government remained in the "mainstream economic development discourse in which ODA is an instrument of economic self-interest" (Audet and Navarro-Flores 188-189).

And lastly, according to the OECD review of the Canadian development policy, published in 2012, Canada was one of the best institutionally prepared countries to provide humanitarian and development assistance and a country with "an exemplary record in meeting its international commitments." The OECD praised, for instance, Canada's "field presence in partner countries," "support for research for development," "significant and strategic support for the multilateral system," "whole-of-government approach" and "good track record as a constructive partner within the development co-operation and humanitarian communities" (Organisation for Economic Cooperation and Development, "Canada" 9). What is also important, the OECD mentioned the unprecedented share of untied ODA – it increased from

80 per cent in 2010 to 93 per cent in 2014 (Organisation for Economic Cooperation and Development, "Canada" 18; Organisation for Economic Cooperation and Development, "DAC"). The organization highlighted some of ODA initiatives in which Canada took part:

> It was the first donor to disburse its funds for the L'Aquila Food Security Initiative (a pledge worth USD 1.1 billion). It doubled its aid to Africa between 2005 and 2010 (reaching USD 2.1 billion in 2008/09 and again in 2009/10). And at the 2010 G-8 Summit in Muskoka, Canada committed USD 1.06 billion of new funding for maternal, newborn and child health – 80% of which will go to sub-Saharan African countries ("Canada" 14).

The OECD also applauded Canada's response to the devastating earthquake in Haiti, where Canada was among the first and largest donators ("Canada" 22). On the humanitarian front, Canadians did more than their share in the fight to contain the Ebola outbreak in West Africa in 2014 (Ibbitson, *Stephen* 342). The OECD opinion stands in contrast with the critics who indicated the decrease of Canada's soft power capacity due to changes in the official development assistance.

After the last financial crisis, in the Conservative government's rationale, the economic stability took precedence over any other function of the state. To be able "to make a difference" in people's lives, Canada's economy and Canadian companies – private ones in the government's desired scenario – had to be financially viable. In other words, without a stable source of money, the long-term and effective foreign aid would not have been possible. The Harper government's record on expenditure on official development assistance is mixed as the ODA undertook deep cuts between 2010 and 2014. Nevertheless, as we already mentioned, Canada's engagement in the official development assistance should always be judged using a longer perspective. In fact, Canada's deep global engagement can be observed only when one looks at a period prior to 1989 (Greenhill and McQuillan).

Security, whether in military or economic dimension, was at the top of the prime minister's agenda and using development to provide greater security for Canadians was an important motivation for Harper in defining his ODA policies. Paradoxically, such an approach was in line with the long-held conviction among Canadian elites that fighting poverty would benefit Canadians as it contributes to the elimination of radical ideologies, terrorism and extremism. What is striking to many observers when assessing the level of bilateral aid is that the Harper government spent a significantly higher proportion of its aid in low-income countries (37 percent) during its nine years in power (2006-2014) than the Liberal governments of Jean Chrétien and Paul Martin had done (24 per cent) during their nine years (1997-2005) (S. Brown, "The Instrumentalization").

International organizations

As discussed in Chapter 1, since the end of the Second World War Canada has been actively involved in a large number of multilateral organizations. Under the liberal internationalism, multilateralism was seen as a way of leveraging Canada's moderate status on the world stage. Yet, under the Harper government, Canada's fervour for joining almost every "international club" became more selective. Ottawa behaved cautiously when choosing international clubs through which it wanted to manifest Canada's external activity. As prime minister Harper famously stated, Canada stopped "fund[ing] talk shops any more" (qtd. in Whyte). For many observers of Canadian foreign policy, Ottawa, under the Conservative government, acted as if multilateralism was no longer a favoured method of the realization of Canada's interests in the world. They suggested that Canada participated in multilateral institutions only when they served its interests. They also cited Prime Minister Harper's skepticism towards the effectiveness of such bodies. Tom Keating wrote of Harper's general "disregard for the conventions and processes of international society along with international institutions and multilateral diplomacy" (Keating, "The Transition" 178). His list of examples included, among others: the withdrawal from the Kyoto Protocol; the failure to obtain a seat in the U.N. Security Council; the criticism of La Francophonie and the Commonwealth; the opposition to observer status for Palestine at the U.N.; the withdrawal from the 1994 Convention to Combat Desertification. Other critics warned of Canada's diminished support for many NGOs and funds for public diplomacy (see Polachová and Fiřtová). As Harper on many occasions expressed his disapproval of various multilateral fora, some scholars, such as Colin Robertson, indicated Harper's strong preference for unilateralism, writing that he "applied unilateralism whenever possible, and multilateralism when necessary" (109). John Ibbitson put it this way: "Wherever two or three nations were gathered together in the name of diplomacy, Canada was absent" (Ibbitson, *Stephen* 341). Robert Fowler, the former Canadian ambassador to the United Nations, was even more open when described the behaviour of the Harper government as a "departure from global citizenship" (qtd. in "Tories").

However, what stood behind Harper's disregard for large multilateral fora was his strong confidence that they failed to set viable and deliverable goals and to establish accountability. In the prime minister's view, they were becoming more and more irrelevant in the globalized world, as they were setting "implausible targets [...] that are never met" (Ibbitson, *Stephen* 340). In such an attitude, there were no ideological presumptions, but rather cold and rational calculation whether an organization was capable of delivering a given goal or meet a certain target or not. When Harper was convinced that a multilateral body was the best way – and sometimes the only one – to reach a desired end, he used that venue. For example, while Harper did not regard the Commonwealth of Nations or La Francophonie as particularly trustworthy fora, in December 2014, former Governor General of Canada Michaëlle Jean was elected as head of La Francophonie and the Canadian government publicly supported her push for a greater economic focus of the organization (Mackrael, "Michaëlle"). A similar rationale applied to Harper's attitude towards the United Nations. Obviously, it was disrespectful of the prime minister to miss several annual U.N. General Assemblies, choosing instead to visit "a plant supplying iconic Tim Horton's coffee shops." Yet when Stephen Harper was convinced that multilateral backing was essential for reaching a goal in external affairs, he would go and speak to the U.N. to promote his vision and get support from as many states as possible (Drohan). This was the case of the Muskoka Initiative he presented during the U.N. General Assembly in September 2014 in New York. Both these examples stood against frequent accusations that Harper totally ignored international institutions.

Harper's attitude towards multilateralism, though different from the previous Canadian governments, was a change more in tone than in substance. In other words, he did not reject all aspects of multilateralism (Drohan; Bratt, "Stephen" 488). His government distinguished between those international organizations that it opposed and those it supported.

After 2006, Ottawa showed growing skepticism, even distrust, of large, multilateral bodies, especially those that that were able to impose political decisions on their members, even when those members did not support them. This category included, among others, the United Nations, La Francophonie or the Commonwealth. Moreover, it may seem legitimate to think, as suggested by Tom Keating, that among the Conservative elites there was a belief that those bodies not only stopped playing "a constructive role in managing international order," but also did not leverage "Canada's own role in that process." The logical assumption was that Ottawa should not "worry about devoting any Canadian resources to cultivating or sustaining them or indeed a Canadian role in them" (Keating, "The Transition" 179). However, it is also worth remembering that Canada under the Harper government continued to be the fifth most generous contributor to the U.N. budget (2012-2015), a significant growth in the ranking from the period of 2003-2005, when it was 10th (United Nations, "Top Ten" 2006; United Nations, "Top Ten" 2016).

As John Kirton or Duane Bratt indicated, there were types of multilateral bodies that were regarded as important and deserving a level of trust from the Harper government. They included international organizations with a smaller membership structure, more exclusive, grouping democratic, developed and "like-minded" states, with traditional Westphalian handling of sovereignty of states, which took decisions only after unanimous agreement had been reached, and which were regarded as geopolitically important. Usually, they were bodies able to manage the global financial and economic system, like the G8, G20 or OECD, but also organizations of military importance, mainly NATO (Kirton, "Canada as a Principal Financial"). As rightly suggested by Bratt, Ottawa was convinced that "smaller groups [...] give Canada more leverage than is the case with larger ones such as the U.N." ("Stephen" 488).

When analyzing La Francophonie, it is impossible to prove Harper's total disregard for that institution. Apart from being a forum of a dialogue and cooperation with other Francophone states, it served as the body where Canada could build its prestige. As Stephen Harper declared, La Francophonie gave Canada's bilingual and multicultural nature a chance to be noticeable on the international stage (Robillard). For this reason – and because of the impact La Francophonie had on Quebec – Canada continued to be the largest budgetary contributor to La Francophonie after France. Ottawa did not stop shaping activities of the forum, taking part in its summits, working in its agencies, contributing to its programs and funds, despite its internal disputes and the fact that La Francophonie, like the Commonwealth, was split by divisions between democratic and non-democratic countries – the fact that even today translates into the ineffectiveness of both international bodies and the limited impact they have on the contemporary international system.

The Harper government's criticism of multilateral organizations such as the Commonwealth or La Francophonie was based on the fact that they did not subscribe to Harper's vision of the role of such values as "freedom, democracy, human rights and the rule of law" in foreign policy. We already mentioned Harper's boycott of the Sri Lankan summit in 2013, based on the treatment of the Tamil minority. Harper explained in 2013 that if the Commonwealth desired "to remain relevant it must stand in defence of the basic principles of freedom, democracy and respect for human dignity, which are the very foundation upon which […] [it] was built" (qtd. in Bratt, "Stephen" 488). The Canadian prime minister also lectured leaders of French speaking countries on the role of the core values. During the summit of La Francophonie in the Democratic Republic of the Congo in 2012, the Canadian prime minister warned that he might not attend future summits because of the participation of non-democratic countries (Bratt, "Stephen" 488; "Harper calls").

Harper's critics, such as Colin Robertson, argued that Harper's tactic of distancing Canada from multilateral bodies prevented Canadian prime minister from building personal relationships with foreign leaders that could leverage Canada's international position. Michaëlle Jean was in fact the only Canadian backed vigorously by Harper for an international leadership position (Robertson 109). At the same time, however, the G8 (later G7) and G20 summits, which dominated Harper's attention, served for him as venues to keep personal contact with the most powerful and like-minded counterparts. The longer Prime Minister Harper attended the meetings of both organizations, the more his position, in his opinion, as a leader of a key country was elevated. We agree with John Kirton that this was of particular importance as in the 21st century, the G8 and G20 became the most relevant fora for global diplomacy and governance, substituting the role of the U.N. and other multilateral institutions ("Canada as a G8" 3).

Another element connected with Harper's Canada's transformed attitude toward multilateralism was the fact that part of the Canadian identity comes from the way Canada is seen by other international actors. Before Harper, this image had been reinforced by Canada's strong support and contribution to international order through multilateral institutions. Nevertheless, Harper represented a different intellectual background – the political culture of Canada's West instead of the liberal internationalism represented by the Liberal Party. With deeply held disregard for "moral relativism," his opinion of multilateral bodies, shared by many Conservative supporters in Canada, was extremely low. The Conservatives' stance in that regard was rightly summarized by *National Post* commentator Rex Murphy, who wrote in 2010 that "no self-respecting country" would feel "embarrassment" associated with losing a vote in an institution you do not respect. The United Nations, whose members included: Chavez's Venezuela, autocratic China, Iran, Libya, Sudan or Saudi Arabia, which do not respect human rights, "should not and [were] not able to evoke respect." In Murphy's opinion, looking for "external confirmation" of a country's "moral stature" was a sign of the lack of confidence in its own ideals (Murphy). In Harper's vision of international affairs, Canada, a key country in the world, was not only capable of making decisions that mattered globally; its new, assertive international image was acknowledged by other actors and internalized by Canadians so deeply that it did not need an outside endorsement.

With this idea in mind it is easier, in our opinion, to understand Harper's approach to international organizations. Most critics wrongly argued that Harper limited traditional – and sacred – Canadian support for multilateralism, undermined the foundations of international cooperation and the peaceful resolution of disputes. For example Roland Paris, recognized Harper's departure from "multilateral approach to international affairs" (275). We rather think that Harper's line of reasoning was directed against the conviction that the interests of Canada, a middle-sized country, had always been served best by a traditional, liberal internationalism. As John Kirton rightly argues, "the close historical association between Canada and international institutions has led many to assume that Canadian foreign policy has been all about multilateral organizations, and to overlook important policy developments in other areas" (qtd. in Welsh, "Canada and the World" 364). In our opinion, Harper could easily subscribe to the following idea: "Without effective multilateral bodies, and without strong Canadian presence in them, Canada would risk subjecting itself to the wishes of more powerful states that may not act in accordance with its priorities" (Welsh, "Canada and the World" 365). The Harper government was not "turning its back on international society" as a whole, but rather applied a highly realistic approach to world affairs, marked by lack of interest in "the seamstress job that some previous governments had welcomed" (Keating, "The Transition" 178).

The United Nations

Strong commitment to multilateralism has made Ottawa reluctant to the solutions that are clearly unilateral. This tendency has not changed significantly even after the end of the Cold War. For example, Ottawa has repeatedly demanded that military interventions be undertaken on behalf of the international community and with its consent. Also, Ottawa has sought to work out agreements above political and ideological divisions, persuading China and Russia, for example, to support the resolution condemning war crimes in Darfur. At the same time, Canada has refused to participate in military operations unauthorized by the United Nations or NATO (for example in Iraq in 2003).

The vision of Canada as a "valued-added nation in the international system" that always backs a collaborative and consensus-based approach was praised during Lloyd Axworthy's tenure as minister of foreign affairs. On the other hand, Harper's vision, as already described above, emphasized values and principles over unity, consensus, or the "honest broker" role. This was especially evident in Harper's Canada's attitude to the United Nations. This largest international organization was not even mentioned in the 2006 Conservative Party election platform (Conservative Party of Canada, "Stand Up"). There were several causes of Conservatives' skepticism towards the U.N.

Firstly, after the Cold War, especially after 2000, the United Nations criticized various areas of Canadian internal politics, such as: Quebec's language policy, Canadian labour laws, the poor conditions of living of Indigenous peoples', gender inequalities, and the inefficiency of social programs for Indigenous children. Ottawa was also accused of repeated extraditions of alleged war criminals to countries where deportees could not count on fair trials. Repetitive stigmatizations of Canada by the United Nations damaged relations between Ottawa and the organization.

Canada began to gradually reduce its activity in the U.N. and withdraw its support for the United Nations. As a result, for instance, Ottawa's approach to peacekeeping changed (discussed in the next subchapter).

As a matter of fact, long before Harper, the United Nations had been stringently criticized in the Canadian press and by Canadian politicians. Most of the objections were in line with the criticisms formulated in other Western countries. The U.N. was portrayed as an ineffective body, whose indolence was caused by its internal divisions and the divergences of interests between developing countries and rich countries. Some voices coming from the House of Commons even urged Ottawa to focus on activities within more effective organizations – for example NATO – or even to withdraw from the U.N. structures (Burney and Hampson, *Brave*). From Canada's perspective, unilateral actions of such superpowers as the United States, China and Russia were seen as particularly detrimental to the international law. Also, the construction of the U.N. Security Council was harshly criticized as blocking the effectiveness of U.N. actions, and was perceived as an anachronism of the Cold War era. In addition, the press in Canada widely commented on a number of U.N.-related absurdities, including, for example, the election of Muammar Gaddafi's Libya to the U.N. Human Rights Council (2010) or the appointment of North Korea to serve as president of the Conference on Disarmament (2011). The critics also pointed out that various dictators, such as former Iranian President Mahmoud Ahmadinejad, used the United Nations venues to spread hate speech. Therefore, even Canadian diplomats judged the United Nations as "dysfunctional, [...] ineffective, [...] and often corrupt" ("Can Canada").

The Harper Conservatives eagerly exposed U.N. failures to further strengthen negative attitudes towards the institutions grouping non-democratic countries, such as Iran or Russia, whose governments regularly violated human rights and were generally regarded as enemies (Bratt, "Stephen" 488). Harper's aversion to the United Nations was manifested in several ways. The prime minister, for example, addressed the U.N. General Assembly only three times (out of nine opportunities he had). Sometimes he deliberately showed his disrespect for the U.N. by speaking at the time of the U.N. General Assembly in other venues located in New York (Slater, "Harper in New York"). Harper's ministers regularly depicted U.N. bodies and conferences as a "charade," a "hatefest" or a "talkfest." John Baird, in his famous 2011 speech to the U.N. General

Assembly declared that "Canada does not just 'go along' in order to 'get along'" (qtd. in Wherry, "Canada"; Galloway; "Tories"). A deep disregard for the U.N. was also evident in Canada's not even trying to pretend that it acted as a team player. Such behaviour contributed to the perception of Canada as a rather problematic country, not willing to "yield even on certain things to create a consensus." Ottawa's inflexible stance usually did not help to change a situation or push the agenda further, but rather created internal tensions that ultimately worked against Canada's image. This is what happened in the context of a planned reform of the U.N. Commission on Human Rights, which Ottawa disrupted, taking a firm stand that states that violated human rights should not be able to gain seats (M. MacKinnon, "Harper's").

Not surprisingly, such an approach backfired when in 2010, for the first time in its history, Canada failed to secure a seat in the U.N. Security Council. Lawrence Cannon, minister of foreign affairs, commented that the lost bid was due to the "attachment to [our] values," but most experts did not agree ("Cannon Blames"). The criticism in Canada was enormous. The defeat was widely attributed to the fact that Canada was "turning its back on the UN" (Burney and Hampson, "No More"; Ibbitson and Slater). According to Prosper Bernard Jr., the world was putting "Canada on notice that it was not living up to the world's expectations." Doug Saunders observed that "Canada said things, but just wasn't there" (qtd. in Bernard Jr.). For Joe Clark, Brian Mulroney's minister of foreign affairs, "hostile" treatment of the U.N. set Harper apart from both the Liberal and Progressive Conservative governments (Clark, *How* 29). The opposition parties blamed Harper's foreign policy for the lost bid. Most of the critics also argued that Canada's reputation declined because of the failed attempt to win the seat. It seems, however, that the negative effect on Canada's reputation because of the failure to secure the UNSC seat might have been overestimated. In international rankings for the period 2005-2015, attitude towards Canada did not change substantially (Schönwälder; Gilmore, "Has Harper").

In reality, as Colin Robertson rightly argued, the failure could not be attributed only to the Conservatives' policies and their negative perception of the United Nations. Robertson indicated other possible reasons: a late and amateurish campaign or the fact that Canada was in a coalition with the European Union countries (109). The prime minister only indirectly admitted that the campaign had been clumsy. At the same time, he put more blame on his government's loyal support of Israel. As Harper elaborated, the support for Israel had been made a condition under which the Conservative government agreed to continue the UNSC campaign, which was started by the previous Liberal government. After the lost bid, Harper repeated the arguments of the critics of the U.N., and bitterly said that being a member of the body that was ultimately controlled by its five permanent members was not a goal "worth selling out the most important foreign policy positions of the government" (qtd. in Levi).

Nevertheless, after the failure to win the seat, Harper's suspicion of the United Nations turned to open hostility. The prime minister avoided the U.N. General Assemblies for three years (2010-2013). The negative rhetoric also intensified. John Baird, for example, echoed his prime minister's blunt criticism of the U.N., exclaiming that "Canada's principled foreign policy is not for sale for a Security Council seat" (qtd. in Levitz, "John"). He also told the U.N. General Assembly in 2012 that "the United Nations must spend less time looking at itself, and more time focused on the problems that demand its attention." He added that Canada "cannot and will not participate in endless, fruitless inward-looking exercises. Canada's Permanent Mission to the United Nations will henceforth devote primary attention to what the United Nations is achieving, not to how the U.N. arranges its affairs" (Baird; Campbell, "Too Much").

Baird's statement exemplified a problem the Conservative government had with the rhetoric. The apparent lack of willingness to use a more neutral wording brought harmful effects to the image of Canada, which covered more positive developments. Prime Minister Harper, for instance, co-chaired the U.N. Commission on Information and Accountability for Women's and Children's Health; John Baird changed his earlier negative opinion on the U.N. and in February 2015 agreed to co-chair, alongside former Australian Prime Minister Kevin Rudd, a commission reforming the U.N.'s World Health Organization. Rudd called Baird "a pragmatic internationalist," who "speaks with a high degree of credibility from a realist perspective: he wants to see the U.N. function and function effectively" (qtd. in Ibbitson, *Stephen* 342).

Two observations seem to be of particular importance in this context. The first one was authored by Duane Bratt. He argued that from a strategic point of view Harper could afford playing down the importance of the United Nations because two priority areas of his government

– security and economics – did not "feature strongly in the agenda" of the organization, in contrast to environmental and social issues (Bratt, "Stephen" 488). Moreover, Harper's lack of respect for the U.N. may be understood better given the fact the Security Council was apparently at a low point in its history, exemplified by the fact that the U.S. under President Barack Obama did not consult the body when, in 2014, the Americans began bombing northern Iraq. Also, the UNSC was inefficient in its response to Russia's illegal actions in Ukraine.

The second observation was formulated by Derek Burney, former Canadian ambassador to South Korea and the United States. He pointed out to the difference in political preference between the Harper's Conservatives and the previous Canadian governments. Burney admitted that he was "always troubled by these the-world-needs-more-Canada analyses" and proposed to focus more on discussing foreign trade and spend "less time fretting about foreign aid" (qtd. in M. MacKinnon, "Harper's"). For Harper, foreign trade and the issues related to global economy, finances and trade systems were priorities in his foreign policy agenda. They were also matters that required, in Harper's opinion, close international and multilateral cooperation. But he preferred to discuss those issues with like-minded countries or on the fora that were more elitist, less divided and also less inclusive than the U.N.

Institutions of global governance

The G7/G8 and G20 fora are the most important and most efficient multilateral institutions managing the global economy. Canada, as a member of these both influential and rich clubs has the unusual opportunity to influence the global governance. Therefore, G8 and G20 summits are regarded by many scholars as the most useful for Canadian diplomats and foreign policy makers.

The G7/G8 is a relatively small club of well-connected heads of government, who deliberate in a generally friendly atmosphere. Although economically smaller than the other G7/G8 countries, Canada has made meaningful contributions to G7/G8's development, playing a constructive role in discussing such issues as collective security and often initiating certain debates and summit declarations. Initially, Canada fought against the economic protectionism by promoting trade liberalization and the reduction of tariff barriers. But soon the agenda of the summits went far beyond the strictly economic sphere and started to cover political and even military issues. Much to the credit of Canadian prime ministers, Pierre Trudeau in particular, the G7 launched a debate on energy security, environmental issues, denuclearization and international crime and terrorism. Brian Mulroney, as already mentioned, was known at the G7 summits for his strong condemnation of South African apartheid and vocal criticism of the massacre of students at Beijing's Tiananmen Square. In 1994, another Canadian prime minister, Jean Chrétien, initiated and hosted the G7 meeting devoted to economic aid to Ukraine. A year later, in response to the releasing of sarin on the Tokyo metro, the first G7 discussions on international terrorism were held in Ottawa. During the Denver summit, held in 1997, the Canadian government successfully persuaded the G7 leaders to support the Ottawa Treaty banning the production and use of anti-personnel mines. In 2001, Canada also organized the first meeting of the so-called Global Health Security Initiative, an organization set up by the G7 and Mexico to monitor and respond to biological and epidemiological risks (Kirton, "Canada as a G8" 3-18; Kirton, *Canadian* 300-303; Kirton, "Vulnerable" 212-218).

During the Harper period, the G7/G8 summits were also influenced by Canada's agenda. For example, at Harper's first summit in 2006 in Sankt Petersburg, Ottawa fashioned, against Russia but with the support of the U.S., the final wording of the G8 statement, where – at Ottawa's insistence – the references to the attacks on Israel were included. At the 2007 German summit, however, Canada received unprecedented criticism – U2's leader Bono called Ottawa a "laggard" – for its unwillingness to commit more money to the development assistance for Africa ("Bono"). Two years later, however, at the 2009 summit in Italy, Canada changed its stance and became the first G8 member to keep its 2005 commitment to double aid to Africa (Kirton, "Canada as a G8" 22).

During the most recent financial crisis, the G20 was elevated to the role of the most important forum for discussing global economic matters. The forum, in fact, has deep "Canadian" roots as the very idea of establishing the G20 is attributed to Canadian Minister of Finance (later Prime Minister) Paul Martin. Owing to his joint initiative with the U.S. Secretary of the Treasury Lawrence Summers, in December 1999, the representatives of the EU countries and the largest regional powers in Asia, Latin America and Africa were invited to join the debates with the G8 leaders. This laid the foundations for the forum of the world's 20 largest economies. In comparison to the G8, the G20 forum, better reflects the global demographics and is more representative of the increasingly polycentric structure of international economic relations (Smith and Heap 8). In the G20, unlike in the G8, Canada no longer serves as a peripheral partner with the smallest economy and the lowest population. That change was even recognized as Canada's achievement by the Paul Martin government in a review of Canada's foreign policy published in 2005 (Government of Canada, "A Role" 27).

Initially, unlike in G8 meetings, the key discussants in G20 summits were finance ministers and national bank governors, not the presidents or prime ministers. However, since 2008, the G20 summits of the heads of state or government have also been organized. Canada has been heavily involved in the G20 decision-making process regarding, among others, the rules which determine the functioning of banks, investment funds, the economic development or the financial reserves of the International Monetary Fund. During and after the 2007-2008 financial crisis, Canada has frequently been at the forefront of the debates, being a key member providing ideas and support in containing the financial crisis. The research undertaken by John Kirton shows Canada's rising importance at the G20 summits (Kirton, "Vulnerable" 140-141). Since the first G20 summit, held in Washington in 2008, Ottawa has successfully presented its economic and fiscal solutions to handle the crisis, including the free market approach, the need to resist protectionism and the necessity to improve banking oversight. Under the Harper government, Canada's influence on the G20 debates was particularly evident. Ottawa succeeded in influencing the decisions of other members, which could be treated as a triumph of Canada's "soft power" and diplomacy (Kirton, "The Harper" 4). As the ensuing financial crisis deepened the vulnerability of Washington, Canada used the relatively favourable condition of its own economy and acted as a global leader, able to oppose unwelcome solutions, build coalitions and compromise to achieve its priorities.

There is no doubt that the participation of Canadian prime ministers and ministers in the meetings of the leaders of the world's largest economies, on the one hand, has built the prestige of Canada and Canadian politicians. On the other hand, it has also helped establish close personal relations with world's leaders, and offered a chance to gain insider knowledge of the planned political moves of major international players. It has also leveraged Canada's influence in debates on the most important global economic, security-related and political issues. Former Canadian Prime Minister Jean Chrétien argued, for example, that the participation in the G7 forum not only allowed Canada to play the role of a global leader and the reformer of international economic and financial institutions, but also created opportunities for the more effective promotion of democratic values in the world (Kirton, *Canadian* 298).

For Harper, the summit diplomacy offered a possibility to sit "at the table and drive discussion" in the "real" assemblies that group "friends and like-minded allies" (qtd. in Campbell, "Stephen'"; see Whyte). According to his vision of global governance, presented in a speech at the World Economic Forum in Davos in 2010, the G8 and G20 were "lifeboats" protecting the world from serious economic and political crises. The two fora had, however, separate roles to play. According to Harper, the G20 should focus its interests and actions on strictly economic issues such as "financial sector reform, stimulus programs and global trade and growth strategies" (Harper, "Statement by the Prime Minister of Canada at the 2010"). While the G8 should deal primarily with "non-economic matters," such as "promoting democracy, development, peace and security," tackling terrorism, fighting against environmental threats, and working for nuclear disarmament (Smith and Heap 12, 15).

This leads us to the new element of the Harper doctrine or his new approach to the world order – to a concept which is referred often to as "enlightened sovereignty." Stephen Harper – as the prime minister of a stable, democratic, politically predictable and economically sound country that had proven its leadership in responsible governance – saw himself in a position to lecture other leaders on numerous global issues. He advised that all nations must accept shared responsibility for the world by changing their own policies at home in such a way as to contribute to the global welfare. Harper stressed that – without waiting for others to go first – the countries should implement policies regulating banks, reducing trade restrictions, lifting protectionist barriers, and improving the health of children (Campbell, "Stephen"). When he presented his vision at the 2010 G8 summit in Muskoka, he prophesized a new future:

> But ladies and gentlemen, in that brief parting of the veil, I saw world leadership at its best, a glimpse of a hopeful future – one where we act together for the good of all. The world we have been trying to build since

1945. The world we want for our children and grandchildren (Harper, "Enlightened" 6-7).

Harper envisioned a new kind of world leadership, in which the leaders would work collectively for the common good and not concentrate only on "narrow self-interest in sovereignty's name." All countries should agree, he claimed, for a new "enlightened sovereignty," which would be "a natural extension of enlightened self-interest" and would promote "mutual-interest in which there is room for all to grow and prosper" (Harper, "Enlightened" 6-7). To avoid "the terrible experience with trade in the 1930s," states should reconsider all policies obstructing business relations. In his vision, the global economy was more than a zero-sum game. He believed that "the rising tide of recovery must lift all boats, not just some." Therefore, Harper openly appealed to the G20 countries to act jointly and not rely only on "the structure of global institutions" (Harper, "Enlightened" 6-7). While "enlightened sovereignty" remained a rather vague concept, it was clearly a voice of leadership calling to cede some power that one had in order to act together to meet common recognized values.

Apart from the G7/G8 and the G20 summits, Harper also attended other meetings that offered opportunities to establish direct relations with the top global actors. The Nuclear Security Summits (2010, 2012, 2014) are a good example. They were meetings devoted to the protection of nuclear installations against terrorist attacks (Bratt, "Stephen" 488). Although Harper declared that Canada wanted these gatherings to "serve the broader interests of the entire global community," the prime minister's preference for "the power of direct dealings and summit diplomacy" over the U.N. was, however, criticized as the indication of contravening the crucial elements of the Pearsonian internationalism (Harper, "Prime Minister Harper Highlights"; Nossal and Sarson 2).

To sum up, Harper's tactic towards the most important institutions of global governance brought Canada tangible practical benefits. Ottawa's ability during and after the 2007-2008 financial crisis to significantly influence world politics in a preferred direction was a derivative of the Harper government's wise strategy. Obviously, this was possible due to Canada's specific economic and political profile and favourable conditions – the declining influence of the U.S. during the financial crisis and the growing power of China. Nevertheless, Canada's place among the world powers, as recalled by Smith and Heap, was competed by other fast-growing states, such as: China, Brazil, Russia or India, and Harper's foreign policy agenda helped to secure Canada's place among the world powers.

And lastly, the active participation in the G7/G8 and the G20 had been a priority long before the Conservative Party ascended to power. Through these fora Ottawa had been able to advance its interests – whether economic, social or security-related ones – but also share its values and preferences. Both institutions had elevated Canada's international position and put Ottawa at one table with the most important world powers. It is highly likely that the activity in both fora will remain a prominent goal for subsequent Canadian governments, as is already evidenced by Justin Trudeau's approach. He used his first appearance at the G20 summit in Turkey not only to start his international career, but also to present his global agenda ("Trudeau's Global"). This is primarily because both G-groups are effective institutions, capable of providing various responses to problems that the increasingly globalized world is facing.

The military, security and peacekeeping

Since the mid-1990s, Canada's approach to U.N. peacekeeping missions has changed considerably. From one of the largest suppliers of forces to peacekeeping operations – Canadian troops constituted as much as 10 per cent of all peacekeeping military personnel – Canada has dropped to the bottom of the contributors' list, sending few soldiers to missions (Shephard). The reasons behind this trend are related to the collapse of the bipolar configuration of powers after the Cold War, but also to the fact that, with the rise of terrorism after 9/11, the nature of dangers in the globalized world is now different. Moreover, what had a negative effect on Canadian military strategy towards peacekeeping were Canadian traumas connected with taking Canadian troops as hostages in Kosovo, the powerlessness of the U.N. mission in Rwanda, which was commanded by a Canadian General Roméo Dallaire, and a shock after the so-called Somalia Affair of 1993 (Murray and McCoy 181). As a result, at the beginning of the 21st century the traditional peacekeeping of the 1960s and 1970s became more and more irrelevant, either as a Canadian goal or as a tool effective in solving the world's conflicts. In the early 1990s,

Ottawa had between 4,000 and 5,000 troops in U.N. peacekeeping operations. In 2005, there were only 312 Canadians dispatched (Bratt, "Implementing" 22). Such a huge decrease had been completed well before the Conservative Party won the 2006 election. For that reason, the tense relations Canada had with the U.N. under Harper had rather little impact on Canada's low rank among peacekeeping nations. The Conservative government simply continued the previous policies and, as of September 2015, Canada had as few as 115 personnel dispatched to the peacekeeping missions, including only 18 troops (United Nations, "Ranking" 2).

The decreasing importance of peacekeeping in Canada's military doctrine coincided with the stabilization of the political situation in Europe, which lowered the risk to the security of Canada and other NATO members. Ottawa, as the first NATO state, announced the closure of military bases in Europe and in 1994 the last group of Canadian troops returned to Canada. The next step was the reduction in size of the Canadian army, as well as the cuts to the overall military budget, including the resources spent on supporting NATO initiatives. This was the result of a simple observation that NATO's importance for Canadian security fell with the fall of the Soviet Union. On the other hand, the transformation of NATO after 1989 towards the organization of a more political than military nature was appreciated in Canada (Zyla, "Years" 22-26; Jockel and Sokolsky 326).

To better understand the Canadian defence policies under Harper, especially their selective nature, one should examine the change in Canada's military expenditure in the post-Cold War years. In that period, according to Greenhill and McQuillan, Canada's spending as a per cent of GDP was below the average for G7 countries – for most years Canada was second last to Japan. In 2000, as result of major cuts in the 1990s, defence spending reached a historical low of 0.89 per cent of GDP. Some reversals of the cuts were made under Prime Minister Martin, but in 2006 the Canadian military expenditure reached only 1.1 per cent of GDP, which – save Spain and Luxembourg – was the lowest ratio among NATO countries (Greenhill and McQuillan). One of the reasons for this low military spending was the increased criticism of the Canadian military policy by the left-wing politicians and organizations. They accused Ottawa of an unreflective support for the U.S. military ventures and generating excessive spending on defence. According to the critics, the military policy was funded at the expense of other important areas, such as education, health care and social services (Jackson and Jackson, 554). Simultaneously, Ottawa was regularly criticized for cutting military spending and not engaging sufficient resources to NATO while at the same time benefitting from its collective defence guarantees. Such a behaviour was largely possible because, from a strategic point of view, Canada was considered a secure country, mostly thanks to the security umbrella of the U.S. – the largest military power in the world. Thus, Ottawa saw no strategic rationale for massive investments in the defence systems. Instead, Canadian politicians preferred to play the role of intermediary honest brokers, presenting as collaborative attitudes as possible or, if needed, to focus on such types of military activities abroad that were better received domestically.

However, judging Canada's involvement in NATO only by the money it spends on the military ignores Canada's huge contribution of financial and human capital to NATO's military operations. Canada sent one of the largest military contingents to the Balkans, to the NATO-led peacekeeping missions in Bosnia and Herzegovina (1995) and later in Kosovo (1999). At the peak moment, there were almost 4,000 Canadian soldiers in the former Yugoslavia (Jockel and Sokolsky 329).

Nevertheless, while still in opposition, the Conservative politicians described the Chrétien and Martin era as the "decade of darkness" for the Canadian Army. They promised that, if elected to govern, they would restore a more balanced approach to the military spending and rebuild Canada as an important player in NATO. Such declarations were in line with one of the pillars of Harper's conservative worldview – the emphasis on the prominence of the military, which was seen as a break from the Liberal past, especially from the Axworthy doctrine (Drohan). As already mentioned, Harper's government questioned the assumption that Canada should lead the world using its unique capacity of soft power. Instead, for the Conservatives, it was the military capacity that was a much more important element of external affairs as it made other states take the country seriously. In Harper's vision, Canada – "a brave warrior" – was obliged to actively use armed forces abroad to defend key values in accordance with its proud military past (Boessenkool). Canada needed to focus on hard power and on military reinvestment in order to be treated seriously and to be able to provide a "meaningful action [...] that produces real results" (Harper, "Prime Minister Harper Highlights").

The much-criticized "militarization" of Canada or, as others described it, the increase in investment in the military sphere, was, therefore, a logical consequence of Harper's worldview, in which Canada, was to be "at its most influential" and had to have "the capacities to act" when "called upon" (qtd. in Whyte). For the Harper government, such a concept of global leadership prevailed over the traditional assumption that Canada might be only a mere middle power.

Such ideas stood in clear opposition to Canada's more traditionally perceived foreign policy "roles." During Harper's tenure, the Conservatives deliberately and persuasively tried to shift the narrative of national history and identity in favour of the image of Canada as "a principled warrior." The very idea as well as certain actions standing behind it – including yellow ribbon campaigns, war commemorations, recruitment drives, the "Highway of Heroes" ceremonies celebrating fallen soldiers – were widely criticized in Canada and depicted as a "state-orchestrated cultural revolution," aimed at promoting a new "culture of militarism" (McKay and Swift 280, 284; Klassen, "Joining Empire: Canadian"; Gabryś; Drohan). An apparent dislike for liberal internationalism led the Conservatives to such moves as closing the Pearson Peacekeeping Centre in Ottawa in 2013 (Willick). According to the research by Roland Paris, however, the Conservatives' hope to change the historical narrative was unsuccessful. As of 2014, in various polls, Canadians "continue[d] to express an overwhelming preference for the liberal internationalist role over Prime Minister Harper's alternative" (Paris 305).

As mentioned before, the Conservatives promised to increase military investments. In the 2006 Conservative election platform, *Stand up for Canada*, they wrote of a need of a "complete transformation of military operations and defence administration" and the increase of military budget by CAD 5.3 billion to 20 billion in five years (Conservative Party of Canada, "Stand" 44). In 2008, the Harper government also presented the *Canada First Defence Strategy*. It was an ambitious plan of equipment acquisitions and overall military spending exceeding a total value of CAD 490 billion in two decades. The procurement plans included the purchase of aircrafts, ships, and the development of infrastructure in northern Canada, including a port and a military base in Nanisivik in Nunavut (National Defence Canada, "Canada").

Most of all these bold announcements of rebuilding the Canadian army proved to be impossible to deliver. Some problems resulted from the government's preoccupation with the war in Afghanistan, other included those of ideological and budgetary nature (Brewster, "The Strange" 122). Equipment procurements became politically contentious issues. After the 2008 economic crisis, the government decided that balancing the budget must be a priority. This profound change in Harper's approach became particularly evident after 2011 and it coincided with Canadians' pervasive perception that safety and security had to be judged more from an economic perspective, not only from a physical security standpoint. Calculating losses and profits and trying to strike a balance between debt and deficit reduction on the one hand and international activities on the other, the Harper government decided that economic factors trumped all other considerations.

Thus, the exigency of keeping spending under control, combined with additional procedural problems in the Department of National Defence (DND), resulted in a large reduction of previously announced projects. For example, budgetary cuts, planned in the government's *Strategy Review and Deficit Reduction Action Plan*, lowered the defence appropriation by CAD 2 billion per year compared to what had previously been projected for 2014 (Brewster, "The Strange" 125). According to Greenhill and McQuillan, in 2013 and 2014, spending on national defence as a percentage of GDP was the lowest in the last decade. In 2014, it fell to 0.99 per cent of GDP, which ranked Canada last among the G7 countries in terms of military expenditure. In 2015 and 2016, the military budget stayed at roughly the same low level (Greenhill and McQuillan; World Bank, "Canada - Military"). The situation was grave enough for the Parliamentary Budget Officer Kevin Page to warn about the "impending affordability gap," which could cause a "reduced defence capability in the future" (qtd. in Greenhill and McQuillan).

Also, as a result of unresolved backlogs and other procedural problems related to "defence bureaucracy," various procurement projects were delayed. They included the planned purchases of maritime helicopters and of 65 F-35 stealth fighters. The latter plan proved to be Harper's symbolic failure. The plan was announced in 2010, but was delayed due to the political debates over the costs of the project, which, according to the government, should not exceed CAD 16 billion for the planes and their lifetime support. However, both the Parliamentary Budget Office and the auditor general questioned that figure, insisting that the lifetime cost should have rather been estimated at around CAD 45 billion. But the most politically dangerous accusation against the Conservative government was that they had not prepared "the requisite staff work to assure taxpayers the F-35 was the best choice" (Brewster, "The Strange" 124). With the plan being potentially risky and politically damaging, the Conservatives decided to postpone the decision on the replacement of the existing CF-18s with F-35s, originally scheduled for 2014-15, until after the 2015 election. The issue undermined the Conservatives' promises regarding the military and weakened their reputation as a party of "prudent managers of the public purse" (Brewster, "The Strange" 125).

The situation in the Royal Navy was equally unpleasant. After almost ten years of the Conservative management, the government was not able to deliver its own National Shipbuilding Procurement Strategy. As a result, Canada, as of 2017, did not have a so-called blue-water navy, i.e. the one capable of navigating in deep waters of open oceans (Gilmore, "The Sinking").

In fact, only several original equipment projects were successfully delivered by the Harper government. The list included the purchases of C-17 Globemaster transport planes, C-130J Hercules and CH-47F Chinook helicopters and different types of armoured vehicles for the army (Brewster, "The Strange" 126). C-17s enhanced Canada's ability to dispatch the Disaster Assistance Response Team (DART) at a moment's notice. As a result, Ottawa was able to provide a swift response to the earthquake in Haiti in 2010 and to Typhoon Haiyan in the Philippines in 2013. The government also claimed before the 2015 election that it was on track to properly deal with a two-decade old backlog relating to the replacement of CH-124 Sea King helicopters by CH-148 Cyclones. Nevertheless, by the early 2017, the old equipment has still not been substituted. In general, as indicated by the Parliamentary Budget Office in 2015, Canada's military budget was too small for the military structure Canada had, and none of the major defence purchasing projects included in the government's 2008 *Canada First Defence Strategy* were completed (Brewster, "The Strange" 127; Gilmore, "The Sinking").

However, Canada's low military spending was not only a result of the decisions made by the Harper government. Unworkable defence procurement systems and the relative ease to cut military budgets had been typical of all post-Cold War Canadian governments. Harper differed from his predecessors only by the fact that he openly admitted dropping the long-term plans of military purchases. Before the delayed military procurements and the cuts to Canada's defence budget became the issues widely debated in the 2015 election campaign, they had been matters of concern for the Canadian allies. The U.S. and Britain pressured Harper to increase military budget to meet NATO's two per cent of GDP spending goals. To face that pressure, however, Ottawa acted typically for a selective power. Having calculated profits and losses, Harper declared at the 2014 NATO leaders' summit that Canada was willing to engage in the military mission against the Islamic State and stand up to the Russian aggression in Ukraine, but will "do so on a budget" (Brewster, "The Strange" 126).

In Harper's decisions to send troops abroad one could observe a large degree of calculation and highly selective attitude. Such an approach, as argued by Christian Leuprecht and Joel J. Sokolsky, has in fact long been a part of Canada's strategic culture. This sort of pragmatism – or "expediency," as both authors call it – although constantly present, is, however, usually camouflaged by Canadian leaders. The "language of realpolitik" is rarely present in Canadian public discussions when it comes to the explanation of Canada's defence policies (Leuprecht and Sokolsky 546). Leuprecht and Sokolsky argue that Ottawa, instead of answering Robert S. McNamara's famous question "How much is enough?," rather prefers to carry cost and profit analyses based on another, slightly modified question: "How much is *just* enough?" And for Canada "just enough" is usually the amount of military spending that secures Canada "a seat at the diplomatic table or multilateral military headquarters" (546). Such an approach to allied commitments, as David Haglund and Stéphane Roussel claim, "guarantees that Canada will almost always prefer to undertake less of an effort than its great-power partners want it to, but not so little as to be eliminated altogether from their strategic decision-making" (11). Thus, Canada's defence and security policies, especially after the Cold War, have been deliberately designed to gain as much influence as possible without engaging excessive funds or manpower. This did not change under the Harper government, when Canada's involvement in military missions was rather moderate. For example, in order to fight effectively on a combat mission in Kandahar in 2011, Canada would have needed to deploy much more than 3,000 troops that were eventually sent there.

Another element worth mentioning is Harper's strong belief that Canada's main security and defence priorities were aligned with the ones of Washington. Such a pro-American attitude was particularly evident

during a debate over Canadian participation in the war in Iraq in 2003.
While Chrétien's Liberal's government decided that Canada would not
support the U.S.-led intervention, Harper backed president George
Bush's decision (Harper and Day). He passionately argued for helping
the ally, stating in the House of Commons that "[w]e should not leave
it to the United States to do all the heavy lifting just because it is the
world's only superpower" ("Iraq War"). Harper reiterated his support
during the 2006 election campaign, when he promised to improve the
relations with the United States after the years of skepticism or even anti-
American attitudes that had been presented on certain occasions by both
the Liberal governments of Chrétien and Martin. On a military ground,
the improvement resulted not only in the closer cooperation and the
enhancement of interoperability with the U.S. and NATO forces, but also
in Canadian strong support for the U.S. fight against terrorism (Klassen,
"Joining Empire: Canadian").

The Harper government did not stop Canada's engagement in NATO-
led military operations, believing in NATO's abilities to act fast and
efficiently. Stephen Harper wanted to show that Canada was a willing
and active partner and an ally in the global security. In fact, during his
term in office, Canada took part in all NATO-approved missions. Thus,
as John Ibbitson rightly points out, although the Harper government was
heavily criticized for the lack of traditional support for multilateralism,
Canadians under his leadership were on the front lines (Ibbitson, *Stephen*
342). This was in line with Harper's vision that "[a] handful of soldiers is
better than a mouthful of arguments, for the Gaddafis of this world pay
no attention to the force of argument" (qtd. in Robertson 104).

One of Harper's first decisions as prime minister was to continue
fighting in Afghanistan. This mission embedded the most essential
elements of Harper's visions and beliefs with regard to foreign policy: good
bilateral relations with the U.S. and a strong military. In Afghanistan,
Canada was also supporting its most important military alliance – NATO
(Bratt, "Mr. Harper" 11, 13). Last but not least, Afghanistan was also
a place where Canada could manifest its leadership role in defence of
universal and global interests and values (Kirton, "The Harper" 14).
During his trip to Afghanistan in 2006 Harper declared:

> Canada is not an island. We live in a dangerous world. And we have to show
> leadership in that world. [...] Your work is about more than just defending

Canada's interest. It's also about demonstrating an international leadership role for our country. I want Canada to be a leader. [...] Finally, but no less important, is the great humanitarian work you're doing. Of course, standing up for these core Canadian values may not always be easy at times. It's never easy for the men and women on the front lines. And there may be some who want to cut and run. But cutting and running is not your way. It's not my way. And it's not the Canadian way ("Address by the Prime Minister to the Canadian Armed Forces").

Since the beginning of the 21st century, many foreign policy scholars indicated that Canada's global influence was falling (Cohen; Hillmer and Appel Molot). From that perspective, as was aptly argued by Duane Bratt, Afghanistan should be considered as a way to "reengage Canada on the world stage" ("Mr. Harper" 11). The type of leadership rhetoric Harper used was perhaps not so different from the rhetoric of the previous governments. But the Conservatives did not stick to words only. In the early years of their tenure, they also invested serious resources in the mission in Afghanistan.

Canada was engaged in Afghanistan since October 2001, when the Chrétien government deployed special forces and 750 regular troops to support the U.S.-led operation aimed at killing and capturing Al-Qaeda and Taliban members. It was Canada's first "full-scale war" operation since the Korean War, with soldiers being "deployed into an explicit ground war" (Bratt, "Mr. Harper" 4). In 2003, Prime Minister Chrétien decided to join NATO's International Stabilization Assistance Force (ISAF) and sent 1,700 ground troops to Kabul. In May 2005, Paul Martin's government moved the Canadian Forces to the province of Kandahar, where, since February 2006, they served as the Provincial Reconstruction Team. The province was believed to be the most dangerous Afghan region and Canadian troops had significant "combat responsibilities" (Bratt, "Mr. Harper" 4).

Under the Harper government, Ottawa invested heavily in the Afghan mission, the number of troops was nearly doubled to almost 3,000 to fight the guerilla war. Canada, along with the United States and the United Kingdom, was the most important participant of the Afghan mission, bearing the financial costs of up to CAD 2 billion per year. Human costs were enormous. Until the mid-2014, 158 Canadian Forces personnel, two civilian contractors, a diplomat and a journalist were killed in Afghanistan ("These Are"). Canadian fatalities were third highest after the United States and United Kingdom.

In order to show Canada's long term engagement with Afghanistan, the Harper government pledged an average of CAD 200 million a year as an official development assistance to that country (Kirton, "The Harper" 14). For Harper, the move promoted Canadian values – through "rebuilding" and "reconstruction." Canada helped reduce poverty. Harper claimed that thanks to Canadian efforts "millions of people are now able to vote; women are enjoying greater rights and economic opportunities that could not have been imagined under the Taliban regime; and of Afghan children who are now in school studying the same things Canadian kids are learning back home" (Harper, "Address by the Prime Minister to the Canadian Armed"). Such a rhetoric resembled Paul Martin's 2005 *International Policy Statement*, in which Canada's foreign policy was declared to be based on three pillars: physical security, economic prosperity, and the promotion of Canadian values (Government of Canada, "A Role").

Canada's mission to Afghanistan was extended twice – in May 2006 – to 2008, and again in 2008 – to 2011. However, as the number of fatalities in Afghanistan was growing, the Harper government's enthusiasm for the mission eventually faded. The public and the opposition parties began to present the mission as too costly and inefficient, as it failed to defeat the insurgency as well as achieve other goals, such as democratization or economic development. After more than a decade, Afghanistan was hardly a safer place, as the power of warlords and drug traffickers was growing (Klassen, "Joining Empire: Canadian"). The criticism in Canada was also inspired by the revelations about Canadian soldiers who had allegedly handed detainees to Afghan security personnel by whom they were tortured ("Harper Grilled"). As a result of the rising public disapproval, the Canadian mission in Afghanistan transitioned from a combat to a training one in 2011, and three years later, it ended on March 31, 2014.

The fact is that after the financial crisis, Harper's interest in the Afghan mission waned and his government started to concentrate on economic aspects of international relations, with the goal of providing fiscal and financial security for Canadians. As a consequence, Canada returned to its traditional strategic culture, i.e. to more selective and more pragmatic policies towards overseas military missions and engagement with NATO.

The result of that was the Conservative government's refusal to extend Canada's mission in Afghanistan beyond 2014. Harper thought that Canada had done more than its share there and that NATO allies had not been helpful enough to the Canadians in Kandahar during the hard times of war against the Taliban guerrilla rebels (Paris 279; Brewster, "Defence"; Ivison, "Crimea"). The strategy of cost-and-benefit calculations was also visible when Canada withdrew from two NATO surveillance programs in 2013 – the Airborne Early Warning and Control (AWACs) and the Alliance Ground Surveillance. In both cases Ottawa cited budgetary reasons (Taber, "NATO"). Ottawa also limited its participation in the Libya mission only to air strikes in order to avoid the troubles of a potential full-scale military land intervention against the Gaddafi regime. On the other hand, the government swiftly took advantage of the fact that Canadian Lieutenant General Charles Bouchard commanded the NATO-led Libya mission to build Canada's international prestige. Financial prudence was also the reason why Canada offered only logistical support to the French peacekeeping troops in Mali. Ottawa also rejected the U.N.'s requests to lead the peacekeeping mission in Congo twice, in 2008 and 2010 (Campbell, "Canada Rejects").

Harper was also skeptical over supporting the rebel forces in Syria, seeing too many radical elements within their ranks. Thus, initially Canada limited its offer only to humanitarian aid to Syrian refugees displaced by the civil war (Ibbitson, *Stephen* 390). However, in the course of time, Harper was becoming more and more convinced that "Islamic extremist terrorism" was a serious threat to Canada and that Ottawa needed to take more responsibility and "contribute more" to support its allies, most importantly the U.S., in fighting terror (qtd. in Whyte). His stance was reinforced by a shooting on the Parliament Hill in 2014, in which a lone attacker, with links to Islamist extremists, killed a Canadian soldier at the National War Memorial and managed to go inside the federal parliament buildings. The prime minister called the shooting "a terrorist attack" and stated clearly in the House of Commons that he was "resolved to fight" terrorism both at home and abroad (Chase, "Harper Vows"). Thus, when ISIS was established in June 2014, Ottawa was promptly engaged – firstly by deploying its special forces to train the Kurds; later, in October 2014, Canadian fighter jets were sent to Iraq; finally, in March 2015, the air operation extended to Syrian territory. What is important, unlike earlier military missions, that one was supported by both NATO and the U.N., and Canada was fighting ISIS in an *ad hoc*, U.S.-led, but multinational coalition (Bratt, "Stephen" 491).

Harper's decision to send Canadian troops to fight against ISIS proved Harper's strong belief that Canada's defence interests were closely aligned with the United States. On the other hand, as it was with all the missions Canada had taken part in after 2011, Harper made sure the Canadian contribution was modest and politically manageable. After Kandahar, Ottawa did not want to be engaged in a ground campaign. Thus, a highly specialized contingent (70 special forces trainers and six fighter jets) but very limited in size represented exactly, as Murray Brewster argued, "the perfect kind of low-cost, high-publicity war" that the Conservative prime minister valued (Brewster, "The Strange" 132).

Although Canadian public opinion was generally supportive of the military campaign against ISIS, the Liberals in the 2015 election campaign declared to end the air combat component of the mission (Anderson and Coletto; "Chronology"; "Most"). The Trudeau government fulfilled that promise, but nonetheless preserved and expanded other components of the operation, such as aerial surveillance, training and medical aid. Since 2016, Canadian special forces have also been spotted in the front lines (Cullen; Campion-Smith, "Justin").

Altogether, the Harper government's defence and security policies were clearly very selective, based largely on the calculations of benefits and costs of a given decision. After early enthusiasm for increasing military spending the Harper government returned to the post-Cold War traditional strategy of military budgets at minimal levels that were acceptable for Canada's allies. Other priorities, most notably the reduction of the deficit, prevailed over the financial needs of the Canadian Army. The result was that when the Liberals took power after Harper, Trudeau's government was advised by the Parliamentary Budget Officer to find between CAD 33 billion and 42 billion "to put Canada's military as a whole back on a sustainable footing" (Gilmore, "The Sinking").

Critics, Joe Clark among them, argue that the Harper government used the war in Afghanistan to beef up Canada's profile as "a war-fighting nation." He claims that this was done, for example, through various "photo ops" involving cabinet members and Canadian troops in Afghanistan. For Joe Clark, such an emphasis on the military aspects was in a stark contrast to a steady and deliberate decline of the funding of the military, as well as Canada's diplomatic and development capacity ("Canada").

Obviously, Harper intended to present Canada in "a more macho" role in the world and generally wanted to reshape Canada's international position. His strategy of engaging Canada's troops in the U.S.-led military missions had some positive results. Canadian efforts were noticed and appreciated in Washington (Stewart). Moreover, as Brewster suggests, after the war in Afghanistan the Canadian Army was profoundly transformed – it was reasonably well-equipped and had battle-tested soldiers ("The Strange" 132). Canada under Harper was not afraid of being active on global issues in "distant, dangerous theatres overseas" (Kirton, "The Harper" 15), even if it entailed military engagements as it was in Afghanistan, Libya or in the operations against ISIS. But the Harper government selectively decided about the exact venues of Canada's involvement. The preference was generally given to those foreign military operations that could result in enhanced security or economic cooperation with most effective partners, such as: the U.S., G8, G20 or NATO (Brewster, "The Strange" 132). In assessing international engagements it was important to always keep a cold, calculating and cautious eye. Those undertakings that were domestically popular and could be conducted at a relatively low cost were supported, according to the utility-maximizing rule, which sought "to maximize the foreign policy political payoff of expeditionary operations while minimizing investment in defence" (Leuprecht and Sokolsky 553). But when certain engagements entailed an excessive burden, Canada was ready to diminish its role in them or even withdraw.

4. Canada in international relations under Justin Trudeau

In October 2015, the power shifted from Harper's Conservatives to the Liberal Party of Canada, led by Justin Trudeau, the son of former Prime Minister Pierre Elliott Trudeau (1968-1984). As the *Guardian* suggested, the sweeping and surprising victory of the Liberals – the party won an overall majority, receiving almost 40 per cent of the popular vote – "ended the divisive reign of the Conservative prime minister, Stephen Harper" (Murphy and Woolf). Although it has been only several months now (as of February 2017) since Justin Trudeau took the prime ministerial office, he has already demonstrated himself as an active player on the international stage and his government has set new priorities of Canadian foreign policy. One of Justin Trudeau's major electoral promises was to rebuild the international image and reputation of Canada. In Trudeau's opinion, it had been heavily tarnished by the policies pursued by Stephen Harper's Conservative government. Trudeau's accusations against the Conservatives primarily concerned their unilateral policies towards various countries and regions, the Middle East in particular, which resulted in Canada leaving its traditional middle-power role. For Liberal critics, Canada under Harper had become egoistically introvert and ceased to function as a promoter of openness, compromise solutions and multilateralism in international relations. Neither was it ready or willing to take responsibility for the maintenance of global peace, for the provision of foreign aid to developing countries nor for tackling the greenhouse effect. Therefore, the new Liberal foreign policy strategy was mainly founded on the concept of reconstructing Canada's reputation by reengaging the country in solving the most pressing global problems such as the refugee crisis, climate change, the promotion of human rights or dialogue with developing countries.

Obviously, too little time has passed since the Liberals came to power to be able to make a comprehensive assessment of Canada's current international position. Nonetheless, the new foreign policy doctrine has been clearly outlined by the Liberal cabinet. Beyond doubt, in many aspects it significantly differs from the policies pursued by predecessors, but also from the attitudes presented internationally by many other states of the so-called West. Moreover, Trudeau's external policies have already been widely discussed in the opinion-forming newspapers and magazines, both Canadian and foreign ones. Therefore, it is crucial to address the change introduced by Trudeau's ascension to power. This chapter presents the main objectives of the current foreign policy of Canada. It analyzes the specific international actions of Canada and how they are perceived abroad. The examined issues are presented through the prism of the changes and new elements that have been introduced by the Trudeau government to the discourse on Canada's international role and position. This chapter thus aims to assess whether today's Liberal foreign policy is truly innovative or should rather be regarded only as the return to traditional international roles played by Canada after the Second World War. But there are other important questions addressed below: a) does the Liberal foreign policy significantly differ from what was pursued by the Harper government?; b) has Canada become a less selective power under Trudeau than it was under Harper?

Foreign policy in the 2015 Liberal campaign platform

The 2015 Canadian federal election, held on October 19, 2015, was in many ways exceptional. It completely reshuffled the Canadian parliamentary scene, giving Liberals a victory whose scale had not been forecasted by experts or pollsters. At the same time, it ended nearly a decade-long Conservative dominance over the Canadian federal politics and brought the political career of Stephen Harper, one of the longest-serving prime ministers in Canada's history, to a halt. Expecting, as it had been suggested by the pre-election polls, the close race of the three major contending parties (Liberals, Conservatives, and the New Democratic

Party), the pundits and the media were stunned at the extent of the Liberal triumph. Not only did the Liberals take 184 of the 338 seats in the House of Commons, but they also won all ridings in three federal territories and all the seats in the Atlantic provinces. Therefore, post-election newspapers and magazines wrote about "an unexpected majority government" and the "Liberal gains that […] turned into an outright sweep" (Geddes, "How the Liberals took").

Overshadowed by domestic issues, Canadian external affairs were not a key item of the pre-election debates. In the 88-page Liberal Party's document entitled *Real Change: A New Plan for a Strong Middle Class*, in which the party's campaign platform was unveiled, the chapter specifically devoted to foreign policy, tellingly entitled *Renewing Canada's Place in the World and Strengthening Our Security*, was no more than four pages long. Combined with the sections on such global issues as climate change, trade, refugees and development assistance, less than one tenth of the document altogether went anywhere beyond domestic matters (Liberal Party of Canada 64-71). This does not mean, however, that foreign policy was not debated in the campaign or that it was an entirely marginal topic. In fact, external matters were frequently addressed by the major contenders. On September 28, 2015, the Munk Centre hosted a federal election debate fully devoted to foreign policy issues, the first such event in Canada's history (Naylor). In addition, global and external affairs were widely discussed in the Canadian media.

As far as the realm of foreign affairs is concerned, the Liberal campaign platform was based on accusations of misconduct and ill-management against the Conservative government. On the whole, the major fault ascribed to Stephen Harper was, as Matthew Bondy put it, "not merely imprudence, but a disregard for the nation's best traditions of global conduct." Therefore, liberal critics gave Harper's policies different pejoratively-sounding names – "ideologically conservative, incoherent, a betrayal of a proud foreign policy tradition," to mention just a few (Ibbitson, "The Big" 5). "Canada has a proud tradition of international leadership, from helping to create the United Nations after the Second World War, to the campaign against South African apartheid, to the international treaty to ban landmines" – pronounced the Liberal Party's official campaign document. However, "under Stephen Harper, our influence and presence on the world stage has steadily diminished" – it was further stated in the next paragraph (Liberal Party of Canada 68).

The document presented a long list of the Liberal accusations and Harper's failures, including, among others:

- the inability to work constructively with other nations, turning Canada's back at the United Nations and other multilateral organizations;
- weakening Canada's diplomatic service and military, considerably limiting Canada's involvement in peacekeeping initiatives and doing it at the worst moment "[a]s the number of violent conflicts in the world escalates, demand for international peace operations has never been greater;"
- destroying Canada's reputation as a humane and open country by refusing to resettle more refugees and by cutting Canadian aid programs to developing states;
- running "the largest trade deficit in Canadian history" (Liberal Party of Canada 67-71).

A catalog of Liberal commitments, of which one promise seemed to be of particularly crucial and symbolic value – to "restore Canada as a leader in the world, not only to provide greater security and economic growth for Canadians, but because Canada can make a real and valuable contribution to a more peaceful and prosperous world" – was equally robust (Liberal Party of Canada 68). To that end, the Trudeau Liberals declared to:

- "recommit to supporting international peace operations with the United Nations" by providing professional personnel and peacekeeping trainers, to "contribute more to the United Nations' mediation, conflict-prevention, and post-conflict reconstruction efforts," transforming Canada's military contributions to humanitarian support and training missions (in Iraq, for instance);
- "immediately" admit at least 25,000 Syrian refugees through both government and private sponsorship and to contribute financially to the United Nations High Commission for Refugees to help fight the refugee crisis;
- increase funds for poverty reduction outside Canada;
- actively combat climate change by taking proper action, such as introducing a carbon tax, both at home and abroad;
- lift visas for Mexicans, to continue to participate in the NATO initiatives – operations: REASSURANCE and UNIFIER – in Central Europe;

- promote economic openness and free trade with established partners and emerging markets;
- increase Canada's foreign aid activity;
- continue to promote Canadian sovereignty in the Arctic, although more through supporting local communities, working with multilateral partners, and focusing on science and research than solely through investing in the development of the infrastructure in the High North;
- go on with supporting sanctions against Russia for its invasion on Ukraine (Liberal Party of Canada 39-40, 66-71).

Rhetorically, the Liberal election campaign was a success. It was best evidenced in Justin Trudeau's performance at the aforementioned foreign policy leaders' debate organized at the Munk Centre. He demonstrated there what one could call a comprehensive and clear vision of foreign policy, though based strongly on the rejection of Harper's strategies and rhetoric. As the media and academic pundits commented after the debate, Trudeau was "sharp and aggressive" and "did well to highlight Harper's diplomatic failures" ("Munk"). He proved effective in making his point, his arguments were solid, his idea of foreign policy conduct seemed coherent, and he himself looked prime ministerial and well suited for the leadership role. Such an image was an overall contradiction to how the Conservatives wanted to present Justin Trudeau publicly. In their campaign, they had indicated his young age, numerous gaffes, inexperience and lack of skills, which, put together, proved that he was "just not ready" for the job of Canada's prime minister. A viral Conservative campaign ad that had been running on the Internet and television depicted Trudeau as a celebrity with "nice hair," who "says things before thinking them through" and whose key policy would be legalizing marijuana yet he himself "has some growing up to do." The ad went viral and for some time, as the polls showed, was effective among the public (Woods; Caplan, "Is Trudeau"), though – given Trudeau's eight-year experience as an MP and two-year service as the leader of the Liberal Party – it was not a fair assessment of Trudeau's political record (Russell). It was thus during the three televised leaders' debates, especially during the one devoted to foreign policy, where Justin Trudeau proved that he had enough statesmanship to contend for power and, eventually, to get hold of the helm of Canada. While it is difficult to assess how Trudeau's good performance influenced the election results, he was appreciated by the viewers of the debate. In a CBC online voter-engagement survey, he was perceived the winner of the debate. Overall, 46 per cent of respondents thought so, compared to 37 per cent feeling that Stephen Harper won and 7 per cent voting for Thomas Mulcair, the leader of the New Democrats ("Vote").

Most importantly, however, the arguments presented by Trudeau in the debate were very much representative of the rhetoric the Liberals had used throughout the campaign to disavow Harper's foreign policy legacy. Essentially, the Liberals claimed that Harper's Canada, having ignored such issues as peacekeeping, multilateralism, development assistance, or compromise building, was no longer a "helpful fixer" in international relations (Kelly 23). They accused the Harper Conservatives of transfiguring Canada's foreign policy, of introducing "a transformation from all that has gone before," of bringing about the change so radical and disruptive that the Liberals coined the entire period of Harper's prime ministership a "big break" (Ibbitson, "The Big" 5), a "culture shift" (Ibbitson, "Tories'" 2013), "a foreign policy U-turn" (Schönwälder), or a "revolution in Canadian foreign policy" (Klassen "Joining Empire: Canadian"). Generally speaking, the Liberal criticism of Harper, as some political experts noticed, went along the catchy slogans: that "Canada has zero influence" as it "has drifted from the game of global governance," that "Harper has been all talk," that he had been "using security as a scare tactic" and therefore had a goal of "securitizing everything from the Arctic to the Keystone pipeline," that the relations with the U.S. were "at an all-time low," that, in the environmental context, "Canada is an international pariah," and when it comes to the Arctic, Harper's policies "were a sled with no dogs" ("Munk").

What could have been seen as problematic in the Liberal campaign rhetoric had to do with the references to the so-called traditional ways of pursuing Canada's foreign affairs, which Harper had seemingly rejected. The critics of the Liberal stance implied that what the Liberal Party perceived as customary and traditional in Canadian foreign policy was a narrowly understood liberal internationalist approach, symbolized by Canada's middle-power role and distinguished by the legacy of the Liberal prime ministers of the past – Louis St-Laurent, Lester B. Pearson, Pierre Trudeau. These where the "great internationalists" who were responsible for involving Canada "heavily in activities such as peacekeeping, dispute resolution between countries, and in multilateral institutions such as the United Nations" (Kelly 23; Appel) and "whose liberal legacy still looms large in Canada" (Bondy). The truth is that Canada's postwar political scene has been dominated by the Liberals. Putting aside Joe Clark's and Kim Campbell's terms in office – both lasted less than a few months in 1979/80 and 1993 respectively – before Harper, there had been only two Conservative prime ministers since 1945: John Diefenbaker (1957-1963) and Brian Mulroney (1984-93). Although the legacies they left behind in foreign policy were important as they included, for example, the establishment of NORAD and NAFTA, they could not be compared to the footprint left by the Liberal prime ministers, who had governed Canada much longer than their Tory counterparts.

Some authors, such as Bricker and Ibbitson, even claim that a small group of liberals of the St. Lawrence River Valley, representing urban elites of Toronto, Montreal and Ottawa, have dominated the Canadian academic discourse, its economy, media, even culture (7-26). Gerry Nicholls calls this liberal group "urban downtown elites" and claims that it comprises "all those columnists, artists and professors out there who consider themselves intellectually and morally superior to the ill-educated rabble inhabiting the untamed suburban and rural wild lands." These elites, Nicholls maintains, disregarded and hated Conservatives, and Harper in particular, simply because they were "not part of their culture." While Nicholls' opinion is an overstatement, there is, clearly, a temptation among journalists, politicians, even scholars to associate Liberal heritage, also in foreign policy, with the Canadian tradition or, colloquially speaking, with typically Canadian ways of doing things. At the same time, there is an inclination to treat Conservative policies and narratives as "un-Canadian," as a break from the customary conduct or as the rejection of the usual practices (J.M. Smith).

Obviously, the Liberal view of Harper's legacy, as presented above, was one-sided and unsympathetic. It does not mean, however, that it was entirely inaccurate. The Liberals were correct in pointing out that Harper's approach to foreign affairs was far from what had been embraced by his predecessors in terms of security, immigration or trade policies. They were also right to highlight Harper's new narrative about Canada's external affairs. Indeed, as Matthew Bondy claimed, under Harper, "Canada's foreign policy adopted a harsh tone, putting a greater emphasis on hard power over soft power and elevating economic diplomacy and free trade to the top of the agenda." Similarly, Gerd Schönwälder argued that:

Gone is the Canadian penchant for dialogue, negotiation and compromise, which were formerly expressed in decades-long support for multilateralism, the search for fair and equitable solutions to the world's problems, and such Canadian-inspired institutions as international peacekeeping. [...] Billed as more "principled" than before, Canadian foreign policy has acquired a much sharper edge, taking sides (as in the Israel-Palestine conflict), putting more emphasis on the use of force (as in Afghanistan), and sometimes obstructing (as opposed to facilitating) key international negotiation processes, particularly around climate change.

Brent Kelly lamented that "Canada's foreign policy has become more nationalistic, more interventionist (when it serves national interests), more and more militaristic." Canada led by Harper, he contended, "lost much of its credibility as a peace-loving, pacifistic middle power" and started to play a role of a "US strongman wannabe" (27). Jerome Klassen went further in his assessment of Harper's achievements, calling his policies "a new grand strategy of armoured neoliberalism: a fusion of militarism and class warfare in Canadian state policies and practices" ("Joining Empire: Canadian"). Another author, John Ibbitson, criticized Harper's legacy more or less along the same lines, though in a slightly less radical way:

Prime Minister Stephen Harper's three Conservative governments have pursued a foreign policy so unlike what came before that it could be called the big break. What was elitist became populist; what was multilateral became self-assertive; what was cooperative became confrontational; what was foreign affairs became an extension of domestic politics. What was peacekeeping, foreign aid, collective security – you name it – became a relentless focus on trade agreements. The big break – or the Conservative transformation of Canada's foreign policy – has been heavily criticized by academics, former diplomats, politicians and journalists, but it has also had a few defenders ("The Big" 5).

However, what the Liberals and some of their supporters failed to notice, or perhaps preferred to omit, was Harper's international economic successes and the fact that Canada's reputation did not suffer significantly under his prime ministership. As Matthew Bondy noticed:

Though Harper has been the object of unusual animus from his own country's elites and his domestic political opponents for "staining" Canada's international good name, in 2015 the Reputation Institute reported that Canada is the most admired country in the world.

"Responsible conviction": Trudeau's foreign policy doctrine

The Liberals made plenty of declarations in the election campaign. Among this "dense thicket" of over 200 promises, as *Maclean's* calculated (Geddes, "The Trudeau"), an undefined but significant number of declarations referred to foreign policy. Typically for policy pledges in campaigns, they were mostly very general, sometimes sketchy, ideas. In broad terms, the Liberal plan assumed that "[f]oreign policy will be more open and Canada will be more willing to work with others in a multilateral context" (Ivison, "Where"). The question was, however, how that plan could be transformed into practical actions and foreign policy decision-making. Would the Liberals be able to deliver the most ambitious promises regarding climate change, the refugee crisis, the support for multilateral organizations and the U.N. peacekeeping? Would there be, indeed, the "real change now" in the conduct of external affairs, as the Liberals promised in their election slogan, or would it only be the Conservatives' antagonistic tone that would disappear? Last but not least, would the long list of political plans be put together to form a coherent broader strategy or philosophy, perhaps even a new Liberal foreign policy doctrine? "The short answer is, we simply don't know. The suspicion is, neither do the Liberals." – wrote John Ivison, the *National Post*'s skeptical columnist, several days after Justin Trudeau had taken the prime ministerial office ("Where").

Naming Stéphane Dion as Canada's foreign minister did not resolve the doubts over the prospects of foreign policy under the Liberals. While Dion had already been a veteran politician – he had served as an MP since 1996, then held intergovernmental affairs and environment portfolios in the Liberal cabinets of Jean Chrétien and Paul Martin, and had even been the leader of the Liberals in 2006-2008 – he had had no experience in managing foreign affairs. As such, he was definitely not "an obvious choice to be Canada's top diplomat and all the high-level schmoozing and wheeling-and-dealing associated with the position" (Sevunts). In the beginning, his vision was largely unknown, so political analysts could only formulate hypotheses about the future shape of Canada's foreign policy. Some of them, such as Paul Heinbecker – on a very general level, but otherwise quite rightly – predicted that Canada would focus more on reengaging with the world through multilateral diplomacy, more constructive involvement in the climate change talks, peacekeeping, and less-biased Middle East policies (Sevunts). These were, however, only forecasts and suppositions.

A clear and coherent Liberal stand on external affairs was presented by Stéphane Dion no sooner than in March 2016. Addressing the audience at the "Canada in Global Affairs, New Challenges, New Ways" international conference, held at the University of Ottawa, Dion unveiled the guiding principles and a roadmap for foreign policy under the Trudeau government. Since Dion's statement had all the features of the announcement of government's fundamental international policy, it was immediately dubbed by political commentators a doctrine; more specifically – a doctrine of "responsible conviction" (Connolly, "Dion"; Blanchfield, "Dion"; Robson). In the formulation of his philosophy, Dion was inspired by the writings of Max Weber, a German sociologist and historian.

In his lecture of 1919, entitled *Politics as a Vocation*, Weber made a distinction between the ethical standards in politics founded on *convictions* and the ones based on *responsibility*. A politician driven by the pure *ethics of conviction* perceives politics as a vocation and himself as a moral actor who "should commit himself to the cause entirely and must not allow himself to be diverted by influences and temptations external to the cause" (Enderle 85). In other words, he is a politician whose actions and behaviour are determined by his firm convictions, on which he never compromises, regardless of the outcome. Politics based on ethical convictions is therefore nothing more than simply "concentrating on the objectives of political action while ignoring its means and consequences." In Weber's view, the antithesis to such an approach was the politics founded on the *ethics of responsibility*, which referred to making political decisions based always on the expected or foreseeable consequences. No doubt that Weber preferred responsibility over absolute internal conviction, though in his ideal and typical model he combined the two ethics, demanding from politicians that they be both passionate and realistic, or rather showing "a passionate commitment to a realistic cause" (Enderle 86).

Stéphane Dion adopted Weber's vision. Similarly to Weber, he opted in favour of the *ethics of responsibility* and rejected the *ethics of conviction*. He considered the latter as reckless and overidealistic, comparable – as he stated – only to pacifists who are ready to "recommend unilateral disarmament in the face of the enemy" and "advocate non-violence at all times," despite the fact that such uncompromising "Gandhi's pacifism" is not always workable ("Stéphane"). Like Weber, he decided to combine both the ethics of conviction and the ethics of responsibility to formulate a new concept. He called it the *ethics of responsible conviction,* though in fact it was Weber's old idea, which was only given a new name. Dion explained his vision as follows:

> Max Weber did not claim that those who support the ethics of responsibility lack conviction. But since this is how he is often misinterpreted, I prefer to go beyond his rigid distinction to create a more syncretic concept – the ethics of "responsible conviction." This formulation means that my values and convictions include the sense of responsibility. Not considering the consequences of my words and actions on others would be contrary to my convictions. I feel I am responsible for the consequences of my actions. [...] [M]y guiding principle will be responsible conviction. One of the convictions that drives me is the sense of responsibility. I will make my decisions by taking into account their foreseeable impact on others ("Stéphane").

The ethics of responsible conviction, according to Dion, would allow the Liberals to conduct a foreign policy that would be far better than Harper's, both for Canada and the world. "Canadian foreign policy has lacked responsible conviction in recent years," he claimed. It had been a policy dominated by dogmas and moral relativism and less focused on defining realistic goals and delivering results. It was, in Dion's opinion, a failed approach partly based on wrong convictions, partly on ill-thought-out strategies of achieving goals, and partly on idealism, which made Canada's foreign policy appear to be out of touch with the real world. Also, the Harper government, Dion claimed, usually failed to assess the consequences of the chosen methods, which resulted in a progressing isolation of Canada in international affairs. The Liberal policies were to be completely different. "Armed with its strong convictions, mindful of the consequences of its words and its actions," the Liberal government was planning to run the policies that would be more realistic, more principled, more empathic, and more engaged with the world; "more fair-minded and determined" ("Stéphane"). More responsible and more convincing.

According to Stéphane Dion, it was the ethics of responsible conviction that inspired the Trudeau government to adopt three general objectives to be achieved in the realm of foreign policy:

- making Canada a leader of international efforts to combat climate change;
- increasing Canada's support for United Nations peace operations and its mediation, conflict-prevention, and post-conflict reconstruction efforts;
- championing the values of inclusive and accountable governance, peaceful pluralism and respect for diversity, and human rights, including the rights of women and refugees ("Stéphane").

All these objectives, in Dion's opinion, derive from the Liberals' firm convictions and reflect Canadian values. More importantly, however, these ideals and beliefs are tempered with responsibility, in the sense that the goals are realistically defined and can be responsibly achieved, serving the interests of both Canada and its allies.

The doctrine of responsible conviction obviously raised many questions. Was it the announcement of a real change in the conduct of Canada's foreign policy or, possibly, it was only a rhetorical hoax aimed at enabling the Liberals "to say what sounds good, do what's easy, and deny any apparent contradiction?" (Robson). Is this doctrine new indeed or, as John Robson suggested in the *National Post*, it is merely a package of "unconnected proposals that poll well but share no fundamental linkage other than an eagerness to please?" Has this doctrine made a difference or perhaps, in a closer look, there has been no radical change in how Canada has dealt with the outside world? Is Trudeau's foreign policy agenda less selective and more open to the outside world than Harper's? And how, if at all, does Trudeau's Canada fit in the model of a selective power? The following part of the chapter attempts to address these questions by assessing Dion's words against the Trudeau government's actions in various areas of international relations.

Return to multilateralism

In the aforementioned foreign policy leaders' debate, Justin Trudeau confirmed the promise to change the conduct of Canadian foreign policy so that Canada could again serve as a more "constructive and positive" player in international relations, because – as he put it – "Canada has an important role to play on the world stage and should be a strong partner." Trudeau reiterated Liberals' accusations against Harper of the ill-thought-out foreign policy strategies and of the mismanagement of Canadian external affairs. He harshly criticized Harper's militaristic, hard-power approach to the Middle East crisis, based – in Trudeau's opinion – on "quick fixes," "easy solutions," and "dropping bombs" in northern Iraq instead of training and equipping local forces "so they can defeat ISIS on the ground." He thus signaled a shift that would later materialize, i.e. Canada's departure from military involvements and replacing them with training and humanitarian missions. "Sending in Western troops is not always the best possible outcome and indeed often makes things worse," he said. Canada, according to Trudeau, should rather focus its efforts to "reengage and revitalize the United Nations' peacekeeping" and "refocus and support peacekeeping operations around the world." Given Canada's historic role in establishing the modern U.N. peacekeeping forces, the very fact that under Harper "Canada has nothing to contribute to that conversation" was for Trudeau particularly "disappointing," especially that peacekeeping has been something he thinks Canada "can do differently and often better than anyone else." Canada, said Trudeau in the debate, needed first and foremost to "take leadership role in multilateral organizations," engage with international partners and be able to "offer solutions to the world." The success in foreign relations would only be achieved, Trudeau stated, if Canada worked closely with other allies and international organizations. Harper's tactics of just "talking loudly and strongly," was, according to Trudeau, counter-effective as it led to Canada having "a diminished voice on the world stage" and losing its former impact on multilateral institutions. Canada, Trudeau assured, "needs to engage positively on the world stage" ("Federal").

In a key change, announced in the Trudeau foreign policy doctrine by Dion, Canada was supposed to return to its longstanding middle-power role of an "honest broker." Dion promised to reengage Ottawa with the world, "on a quest for peace, security, sustainable development, respect for diversity and human rights, peaceful pluralism, and justice for all" ("Stéphane"). The goal was to be achieved by increasing Canada's involvement in multilateral organizations, the United Nations in particular. Under Harper, Dion suggested, Canada had voluntarily "isolated itself" from "the whole range of multilateral venues," including the U.N., OECD, Organization for Security and Co-operation in Europe (OSCE), the International Atomic Energy Agency and a few other organizations. Such an approach had had "no positive consequences" for anyone – Canada's international role had diminished and the opportunity of "effecting positive change" was lost ("Stéphane").

With these remarks, Dion, obviously, referred to Harper's distrust of such multilateral organizations as the U.N., the Commonwealth, or La Francophonie (discussed in the previous chapter). For the Liberals, such an approach was pure preachiness, which in the long-term perspective served against the Canadian interests. There was a cumulative cost – declared Stéphane Dion while he was announcing the Trudeau foreign policy doctrine – to Canada's absence from the United Nations and "to our failure to convene, chair, and host multilateral meetings." Disengagement meant "forgoing the potential for dialogue and confidence-building" within the global system of the collective security. No benefit for anyone. Dion admitted that "keeping open channels with authoritarian regimes" gives no pleasure. But a realistic and pragmatic foreign policy needs to deal with the world as it is – "highly imperfect" and not "made up of nothing but exemplary democracies." Improvement of the world can be achieved only through involvement, never through withdrawal. Without speaking frankly to authoritarian regimes, claimed Dion, there is no hope that the values Canadians hold dear – such as "democracy, human rights, peace, justice and sustainable development" – will ever be successfully promoted. For Dion, having strong faith in certain ideals does not make these ideals delivered. One should also have the strategy of promoting their values and this can be done only by acting responsibly in multilateral organizations, by demonstrating leadership not using an antagonistic tone; by having a practical and positive impact, and "acting together in a complementary fashion with our allies ("Stéphane").

Unsurprisingly, the reengagement with the U.N., the most multilateral international organization, plays a key role in Trudeau's doctrine. "[T]he U.N. is an imperfect institution, but it is the one we have, and we must not neglect it if we want to advance our objectives," declared Stéphane

Dion. He promised that "the Trudeau government will ensure that Canada resumes its position in the U.N., from the Commission on the Status of Women to the Security Council," because – on the one hand – "[o]ther countries, including democracies similar to ours, are asking us to return" ("Stéphane"), and – on the other hand – because Canada, as any other country which is not a major power, has a vested interest in supporting the organizations which set certain global rules and make international relations more predictable and stable.

Therefore, Justin Trudeau embraced the first possible opportunity to declare the return of Canada to its traditional policies of internationalism and multilateralism. "We need to focus on what brings us together, not what divides us," stated the Canadian prime minister in his first speech at the United Nations General Assembly on September 20, 2016. "For Canada that means re-engaging in global affairs through institutions like the United Nations." Trudeau promised to revive Ottawa's constructive involvement in the global problem-solving initiatives. "It doesn't serve our interests – or the world's – to pretend we're not deeply affected by what happens beyond our borders," he said. On behalf of Canadians, he pledged to work actively with other U.N. partners on the issues of refugee crisis, climate change, peacekeeping and economic and gender equality. "We're Canadian and we're here to help," he declared at the very end of his address, which received him cheers, applause and the wide coverage in international media (Trudeau, "Prime Minister Justin Trudeau's Address"). Trudeau's promises were in stark contrast with the policies of Stephen Harper, who had preferred to focus on internal politics and reluctantly took part in the U.N. General Assemblies, even skipped them deliberately from time to time (Austen, "Justin").

Peacekeeping and military missions

The military, as mentioned in Chapter 3, was important for Harper as a symbol of Canada's reimagined history. He reinstated the prefix "Royal" to the official names of the air force and navy and willingly embraced every possible occasion to celebrate Canada's military history. That, however, did not result either in significantly increased expenditures on the army or in Canada's more active involvement in peacekeeping operations. Quite the opposite, Canada's participation in the U.N. peacekeeping, as already discussed, reached an all-time low under Harper, though – as explained above – it was not the prime minister's sole fault. Such a policy, however, made Canada appear more like a militaristic and interventionist hard power than a pacifistic middle power.

For the Liberals, support of the U.N. peacekeeping is an important element of their external affairs agenda and constitutes an essential part of their political identity. After all, it was Lester Pearson, the Liberal prime minister, who invented modern U.N. peacekeeping. Therefore, peacekeeping was included as one of the key points of the foreign policy doctrine announced by minister Dion and supported by the proclamation that "Canada must be a fair-minded and determined peace builder" ("Stéphane"). The pledge was then repeated by Prime Minister Trudeau in his address to the U.N. General Assembly, where he committed his government "to expanding Canada's role in United Nations peacekeeping operations" (Trudeau, "Prime Minister Justin Trudeau's Address").

After the victorious election, the Liberals confirmed this recommitment on international forums. In September 2016, at the London U.N. peacekeeping summit, Canada's Defence Minister Harjit Sajjan declared the deployment of up to 600 Canadian Armed Forces personnel for future U.N. peace operations. The exact scope of the future deployments as well as the specific locations were to be determined in the future, "based on discussions with the U.N. and Canada's partner nations, as well as an assessment of where Canada can best make a meaningful impact." One of the most frequently mentioned places, though yet-unconfirmed, has been Mali, where there is already a French-led U.N. mission. But other locations in Africa, including the Central African Republic or South Sudan, have also been discussed (Berthiaume, "Political"; Pugliese). Sajjan also announced "Canada's intention to host a major United Nations conference on peacekeeping in 2017." The exact date of the U.N. Peacekeeping Defence Ministerial, as the conference is officially named, was to be decided later. Earlier, at the end of August 2016, Stéphane Dion, Minister of Foreign Affairs, had promised to give CAD 450 million to a newly started initiative by the Global Affairs Canada called the Peace and Stabilization Operations Program. The initiative's aim is to "help better protect civilians, including the most vulnerable groups, such as displaced persons, refugees, women and children" (National Defence Canada, "Minister").

The Liberals' clash with the Conservatives over peacekeeping has been ideological since Harper's ascension to power. The Tories claim that the U.N. has failed to manage peace support operations on too many occasions, including Rwanda or Bosnia, to be trusted as a reliable peacekeeping institution. Hence, for them, the most effective missions are those commenced in collaboration with close political allies, such as the U.S.-led military operation against the Islamic State in Iraq and Syria, or the missions led by the organizations grouping politically similar countries, such as NATO (Berthiaume, "Political"). The Liberals, on the other hand, apart from treating the U.N. peacekeeping as their own brainchild and thus being sentimentally linked to it, have generally advocated for more institutionalized multilateral peacekeeping initiatives and expressed no enthusiasm to spontaneously created coalitions of a small number of states. Therefore, they have favoured the U.N. as the most proper organization through which the global peace should be kept or made. Justin Trudeau explained the Liberal stand in an open editorial he published on the *Huffington Post Canada*'s blog just before the election:

> We are a country with a great deal to offer – it is time for us to reclaim our place. […] To become, once again, an active and constructive member of the United Nations and other multilateral organizations would magnify Canada's voice in international affairs. Shouting from the sidelines, as the Harper Conservatives have done for years, marginalizes Canada. That's not leadership. Because the United Nations remains the world's largest provider of such [peacekeeping] missions, it deserves our special attention ("The World").

He accused Stephen Harper of scorning the U.N. peacekeeping as revenge for his government's failed bid to win a Security Council seat for Canada in 2010. He claimed Harper's Canada had turned its back to the global community at the worst possible moment, when the "[d]emand for peace operations has never been greater, and the U.N. has never been busier" as "the number of violent conflicts in the world has tripled since 2008." Canada, wrote Trudeau, "must provide the U.N. with the expertise and capabilities it needs to respond to this unprecedented challenge" ("The World").

Compared with the Conservatives, the Liberals have far less confidence in the effectiveness of military operations in keeping peace. They claim, as Trudeau did in the *Huffington Post*'s editorial, that peace operations nowadays differ from those in the past – they are "more fluid" and thus require much more than "monitoring fixed ceasefire lines." Non-military means can be more useful. For this reason, the Trudeau government promised to withdraw Canada from the bombing operations in Syria and Iraq and "contribute more to U.N.'s mediation, conflict-prevention, and post-conflict reconstruction efforts." The withdrawal from military involvement was to be compensated with Canada's increased participation in investment and foreign aid programs or training and humanitarian missions. Thus, instead of combat battalions, Canada has willingly offered training equipment and civilian police and military training personnel, especially French-speaking officers so needed on peacekeeping missions in Africa. Moreover, Canada is also ready to contribute its "specialized capabilities, such as engineering companies to repair infrastructure, aircraft to ferry supplies and peacekeepers, signals teams to provide communications, mobile medical facilities, and mission planners." In other words, the new Liberal government considers Canada's soft power – i.e. the strength of Canadian values, the capability of serving as a good example and "providing hope to millions of ordinary people who wish, above all, to live without the threat of being killed or driven from their homes" (Trudeau, "The World") – as a much more efficient means of promoting peace than soldiers involved in combat missions. A militaristic approach is not Canadian, as Trudeau once stated. "We are a nation of diverse people – with roots in every corner of the world – living peacefully together. It is part of what makes us Canadian," he declared (Trudeau, "The World").

In practical terms, however, little has been achieved (as of February 2017) in increasing Canada's participation in peace operations, apart from the fact that Ottawa's rhetoric regarding the U.N. itself and its peacekeeping efforts has changed considerably and is now much friendlier and more welcoming. Statistical data, however, remained unchanged. In December 2016, Canada had 105 personnel in the U.N. peacekeeping missions, including only 19 troops, allocated to U.N. peace missions, which ranked it 66th among the 125 contributing countries. It was exactly the same rank as at the end of September 2015, three weeks before the Harper Conservatives lost power (United Nations Peacekeeping).

As for the so-far most concrete issues, Canadian Chief of Defence Staff Jonathan Vance, reminding the U.N.'s past failures in Bosnia and Rwanda, has declared that Canada will agree to deploy its soldiers only if they are under the Canadian command (Berthiaume "Canada's peacekeeping"). Such a declaration rather proves that the Liberal government is as distrustful of the U.N. commanding abilities as Conservatives. In actuality, even the very pledge of only 600 personnel for peace operations from the party that has declared to revive Canada's peacekeeping leadership sounds very modest. In the early 1990s, when Canada was in fact a peacekeeping leader, its commitment exceeded 3,000 troops (Chase, "Defence"). As Walter Dorn, a professor specializing in the study of Canada's participation in the U.N. peacekeeping, suggested, Canada cannot hope to "get the top leadership positions" in peacekeeping without making "substantial contributions to the missions" (qtd. in Blanchfield, "Liberals").

To be fair to the Liberals, however, Trudeau had said that soldiers would be replaced by high-level experts on missions. Also, it is worth noticing that Canadian peacekeeping efforts are not limited to the U.N. missions solely. In September 2016, there were over 800 Canadian troops deployed in Iraq and Kuwait; Ottawa also had about 400 soldiers training in Poland and Ukraine. Furthermore, Ottawa has agreed to deploy military equipment and a 450-strong battle group to a Canada-led multinational NATO force in Latvia (Blanchfield and Berthiaume). As for the latter, the Trudeau government is in fact continuing the policies pursued by Harper, whose government was strongly supportive of strengthening NATO's eastern flank in Europe in order to counter aggressive Russian policies in the region. These NATO obligations, undoubtedly, put limitations on the number of troops that Canada can dispatch for U.N. deployments. Nonetheless, the reappearance of Canada in U.N. peacekeeping was strongly emphasized in the Liberal foreign policy agenda, and so far the Trudeau government's record in transforming that election promise into reality has not been impressive. Only a few declarations have been made. Defence Minister Harjit Sajjan, for instance, promised to make the deployment decision by the end of 2016 (Chase, "Defence"). The Liberals also declared to send a group of diplomats and military men on a fact-finding "reconnaissance mission" to Mali and other African countries in August 2016 ("Feds"; Chase, "Liberals"). As for now, however, the Liberal government has neither indicated the specific location for Canadian peacekeepers nor given the precise schedule of deployment. Even the U.N.'s insistence on Canada to urgently send troops and equipment to its mission in Mali did not help ("Canadian troops"). In January 2017, as the media reported, the Canadian government opted not to make any definitive pronouncement of new engagements in the U.N. peacekeeping due to the election of Donald Trump as President of the United States. As one author implied, Ottawa was seeking "to get a better handle on what the Trump administration's arrival means for Canada's defence priorities" and wanted "a better sense of the Trump administration's expectations before making a decision." Officially, the defence minister said the government needed more time for discussion and analyses in order "to be able to maximize our impact on the ground" ("Canadian peacekeepers"). Earlier, new rumors had even emerged of a plan for a joint Canadian-Mexican peace mission in Colombia (Chase, "Defence").

All of the above issues raise questions about the Trudeau government's real intentions and objectives. The Conservative critics accuse the Liberals of idealizing both the U.N. and their own motives for pursuing deeper involvement in the peacekeeping operations. They claim that the "ultimate goal here is to achieve a seat at the U.N. Security Council when it becomes available" (Berthiaume, "Political"). All this, the Conservatives claim, makes the Liberal policies look cold, cynical and calculated. The Liberals, naturally, reject the accusations, saying that their support for the U.N. peace operations is purely altruistic – i.e. that they are driven by the will of making the world more peaceful and stable (Berthiaume, "Canada's peacekeeping"). Even if such is their cause, their policies have not gone far from Harper's very selective approach to peacekeeping. It is just that the priorities and, most of all, the rhetoric have been set differently. But, as Stéphane Dion admitted in an interview:

> We need to be very selective. We need to have a clear view about where we will be the most effective in co-operation with others [...] The requests come from everywhere. From the French, from the British, from the U.S. – everybody has an idea about what Canada should do. [...] If we add all these requests, I think the minister of finance will have a tough time (qtd. in Blanchfield, "Liberals").

The January 2017 decision to delay the deployment of Canadian peacekeepers to Africa might indicate that Canada, despite the Liberals' declarations in the election campaign, will act very carefully in order not to provoke or alienate the new Trump administration. It seems highly unlikely that, should the situation demand it, Canada would be ready to sacrifice good neighbourly relations with the U.S. to peacekeeping. There is always "the calculation you have to do," admitted Prime Minister Justin Trudeau during a meeting with the editorial board of the *Toronto Star* in December 2016. What he had in mind was achieving the desired results of peacekeeping missions, i.e. bringing peace and stability, and at the same time minimizing the risk to Canadian peacekeepers. With the new American president, however, Trudeau's calculations would also need to take into account the U.S. reactions and expectations (Campion-Smith, "Canada"). That includes Canada's involvement in NATO. Donald Trump had called NATO "obsolete" and demanded more military and financial commitment from other NATO members or threatened to scale back American contributions to the alliance. The Canadian Prime Minister's reaction was to stand in defence of NATO and voicing Canada's support for it. However, he refused to declare the increase in Canada's military budget. And Ottawa is a typical underperformer in NATO. Its military budget is only at around half of the 2 per cent threshold required by NATO from its members, which ranks Canada at a distant 23rd place among 28 member states. In a long-term perspective, Canada might not be able to remain defiant over American pressures. Should the Trudeau government be compelled to boost military expenditures by the Americans, the question will emerge whether Canada has enough means to contribute to the U.N. peacekeeping ("Trudeau affirms"). David Perry, an expert at the Canadian Global Affairs Institute, interviewed by *Maclean's*, had already raised this matter:

> [Trudeau's government] inherited a situation where there is not nearly enough money to go around, and it's a situation they have to deal with. If they're not prepared to put in more funding, then they're going to have to make some tough decisions about how to lower the expectations of what they want the armed forces to do (qtd. in Friscolanti, "Liberals").

Should that happen, we might see the Liberals being constrained and, in fact, very selective about Canada's participation in peacekeeping missions. In actuality, the very excerpt from Justin Trudeau's statement on peacekeeping, saying that "when a government considers deploying our men and women in uniform, there must be a clear mission and a clear role for Canada," is formulated vaguely enough to enable the government to act very selectively about Canada's peacekeeping and procrastinate the decision of deploying the troops for as long as it is needed (Trudeau, "Statement by Justin Trudeau").

Immigration policies and refugees

In a country like Canada, where around 300,000 newcomers are accepted yearly and where over 20 per cent of the total population is foreign-born (Statistics Canada "Immigration"), immigrants have a profound impact on both domestic and foreign policies, let alone election results. No wonder, thus, that political parties in Canada always must consider the so-called "immigrant factor" in their political programs, also when they take positions toward such issues as immigration, refugees, or policies towards certain countries, regions or international organizations.

An irritant, perhaps most important, for Canadian visible minorities was Harper's policy towards immigration. Admittedly, the Conservatives did not remove the 50-year old, Canada-invented points-based system. Nor did the Tories limit the immigration quotas. On the contrary, under Harper, Canada even increased the limit for newcomers from 265,000 to 285,000 a year – a move after which the *Economist* labeled Canada as being "enlightened on immigration" and named the ruling Conservatives "the only right-leaning party in the Western world firmly in favour of it" ("Canada's immigration"). However, the policy changed and the immigration priorities shifted. Economic and commercial factors began to prevail. The process of – to use Harper's own words – "re-orienting our immigration over the last several years to make it more focused on economic needs and focused on more long-term labour market needs" gained momentum in 2015 (qtd. in Mas, "Immigration"). The result was that, following the policies of Australia and New Zealand, preference in Canada was given to those who had already been offered employment and obligation was put on an employer to prove there had been no eligible Canadians applying for the job. Effective April 2015, the so-called "4 and 4" rule was implemented. According to it, immigrant workers had their visas issued for four years, after which they were obliged to leave Canada and were not allowed to return to work for four years. Also, a limit was placed on the number of applications and the list of preferred occupations was created so that immigrant workforce could better serve the needs of the Canadian labour market (Lenard). The critics raised many objections to the altered system, suggesting, among others, that it would be more susceptible to fraud and discrimination, that it would be an employer-led program and as such could easily turn into the "privatisation of [the] immigration policy." This, in turn, would pave the way to making the fate of immigrants fully dependent on the caprices of private entrepreneurs ("Canada's immigration"). Others complained that "immigrants are now evaluated simply in terms of the benefits they bring to Canada in the short-term, and not their ability to integrate more broadly into the Canadian economy and society over a life-time" (Lenard). Last but not least, the critics thought there was a danger that the new policy would come at the expense of refugees or families brought to Canada by immigrants already enjoying permanent resident status. No wonder, thus, that the Conservative approach to immigration gained little popularity among the new arrivals, especially that the new policies were accompanied by a harsher Conservative rhetoric towards immigrants and refugees.

On a few occasions, Harper declared that Canada would not be "chasing headlines" (Levitz, "Opening") and was not going to "open the floodgates and airlift tens of thousands of refugees out of a terrorist war zone without proper process" (Momani). Earlier, in 2012, Jason Kenney, at the time serving as Canada's citizenship and immigration minister, announced that Canada's "generous asylum system has been abused by too many people making bogus refugee claims." He accused refugees of taking advantage of Canadian generosity and compassion and promised far-reaching reforms (Kenney). In a most controversial change, in 2012, the federal government cut the refugee health-care funding, refusing, for example, to provide care to rejected refugee claimants unless their health condition posed a risk to the public. The decision was widely criticized by immigrant, medical and charity organizations and, eventually, in 2014, was struck down by the Federal Court of Canada as unconstitutional, "cruel and unusual" (*Canadian Doctors*; Payton, "Federal"). The ruling forced the Harper government to restore the funding, but did not prevent it from appealing the court's decision. Before the appeal was heard, however, the Conservatives lost power in Ottawa. Also – despite the calls from NGOs, immigrant organizations and the U.N. to significantly increase the number of Syrian refugees admitted to Canada – the Harper government set the refugee quotas at a rather low level

(Mas, "Immigration"). In 2014, for instance, Chris Alexander, Kenney's ministerial successor, agreed to take in only 1,300 refugees from Syria ("Canada's immigration"). Last but not least, the Harper administration created a list of the so-called "safe countries," such as Hungary or Mexico, whose nationals' applications were generally taken for granted as groundless (Lenard).

It was only in September 2015, a few weeks before the election, that the Harper government firmly confirmed the earlier promise given to the U.N. to accept 10,000 more refugees from Syria over the following three years and fast-track refugee applications from Syrians and Iraqis. The government had also promised to launch a private sponsorship program to bring refugees to Canada and to send additional personnel to missions abroad ("Canada's refugee"). But this was done largely at the insistence of the public opinion, deeply shocked at a touching photo, published on front pages around the world, of a dead three-year old Syrian boy named Alan Kurdi, whose corpse had been washed ashore on a beach in Turkey (Hall, "Harper Wants"). Together with his mother and elder brother, both also drowned, he had been travelling on an overloaded boat to the Greek island of Kos, from where the family hoped to head to Canada to join a relative living in Vancouver. Alan's surviving father blamed "the authorities in Canada" for the death of his family, implying that because of the restrictive Canadian rules his family's permission to settle had been rejected (Donnelly). While it was soon revealed that the accusations were false, as the Kurdi family had neither officially requested to receive a refugee status in Canada nor had been registered with the U.N. as refugees, the Harper government was put on the defensive ("Government says").

The Alan Kurdi case exposed Harper's immigration and refugee policies to fierce attacks from the opposition parties and visible minorities, in particular Muslim Canadians. They accused the prime minister of islamophobia, anti-Muslim bigotry, and the lack of compassion by refusing to help those affected by wars (Siddiqui). Harper's approach to immigrants also raised questions abroad. Attracted by Alan Kurdi's death, the media from across the world focused their attention on Canada's migration policies, presenting Harper's reforms in a rather unfavourable light. *Al Jazeera*, for instance, quoted former Prime Minister Jean Chrétien claiming that Harper's policies had "tarnished almost 60 years of Canada's reputation." The very title, as well as the rest of *Al Jazeera*'s article, suggested clearly that, once-welcoming Canada had had in fact become "a haven no more" for the refugees (Hashem). A similar tone was used in the *Independent*, a left-wing British daily, where Stephen Harper's Conservatives were claimed "to have forgotten a cherished tradition about refugees" and their policies were described as "weird" and "fear-mongering" (Fisk, "In Canada"). Another British daily, the *Guardian*, accused the Harper government of running "fortress-style border policies at home" and participating in the "wars abroad [which] are a lethal contribution to a global refugee crisis." "Canada has more than one refugee death on its hands," one could read in the title (Lukacs). The *Economist*, alluding to Harper's "tougher line on refugees and elderly people wanting to join their families in Canada," named Canada a "no country for old men" and characterized the Conservatives as generally "hard-nosed about letting in refugees and immigrants' family members" ("Canada's immigration"). The *New York Times*, referring to Canada's refugee policies, accused Harper's administration of slow handling of the Syrian refugee claims and wondered "why Mr. Harper's office took the step against Syrians in particular" (Austen, "Syrian"). Even in the Israeli press, usually sympathetic to Harper, it was noted that Canada had become "less welcoming to refugees under Harper" (Gilles). These and similar comments on Canada in the international media left a scar on the country's image abroad. As one Canadian author claimed, Harper's immigration and refugee policies "have broken Canada's reputation as a welcoming country, undermining its character as a fair, open and compassionate society" (Lenard). But such opinions stood in the opposition to Harper's own assessment of Canada's repute. According to Prime Minister, Canada was "the most admired country in the single world, respected as never before" (Omar).

Moreover, Harper's administration proposed two controversial legislations that did not gain the Conservative Party much sympathy among the visible minorities. One of them, called Bill C-24 or the *Strengthening Canadian Citizenship Act*, passed in June 2014, was an anti-terrorist law of a specific kind, aimed at bolstering Canada's national security. The law allowed Canadian citizenship to be revoked from convicted terrorists or those convicted of treason or espionage, provided they held citizenship of another country. The Tories defended the law claiming that "heinous crimes" are "fundamentally incompatible with Canadian values" and those who commit them in fact "choose to forfeit their Canadian citizenship." The provisions of the law, according to the government officials, were fair and just as they allowed for the revocation of citizenship "in accordance with all the principles of natural justice, due process, and constitutionally enshrined safeguards" (Fine). Such arguments did not convince opponents, among whom one could find visible-minority representatives, opposition parties, immigration lawyers or security experts, who vocally expressed their disapproval, dubbing the law as unusual, cruel, unfair, arbitrary and unconstitutional. The law was regarded by many security pundits as counter effective and unreasonable – they could not understand why the state would "strip citizenship from known extremists" and deport them instead of having them under control at home (Friscolanti, "Liberals"). More importantly, however, the critics claimed that Bill C-24 unfairly stigmatized dual nationals as it did not apply to those holding only Canadian citizenship. Since those who hold double or multiple citizenships are mostly immigrants, the law appeared to have a discriminatory, anti-immigrant nature. That left the impression that dual nationals were "less Canadian," one of the immigration lawyers said, and accused the Conservatives of passing the laws whose effect amounts to creating "two classes of citizens" (Friscolanti, "Tories"). The Conservative government, wrote another critic, "has worked to undermine the post-World War II consensus that citizenship is a right, arguing that instead it ought to be treated as a privilege" (Lenard).

Another controversial rule introduced under Harper touched on a particularly delicate issue of identity. In December 2011, the Citizenship and Immigration Canada issued an operational guideline titled *CP 15: Guide to Citizenship Ceremonies*, which required that "[c]andidates for citizenship wearing a full or partial face covering must be identified" and to do that "they will need to remove their face covering during the taking of the oath" (qtd. by Saint-Cyr). In practice, the new rule sanctioned a ban on wearing face veils by Muslim women while receiving their citizenships. Arguing in support of the new regulation, Stephen Harper told media that it was consistent with Canadian values to "reveal yourselves to Canadians" by presenting your face "when you join the Canadian family in a public citizenship ceremony" (qtd. in MacCharles and Spurr). On another occasion, while addressing the parliament, he called the practice of face veiling "contrary to our own values," "rooted in a culture that is anti-women" and "unacceptable to Canadian women" (qtd. in Chase, "Niqabs"). The critics, Canadian Muslims in particular, immediately accused Harper of toying with islamophobia, instilling hate by "pitting the country against Muslims" and inspiring, this way, the rise of racism and discrimination. Many Muslim women interviewed by the press admitted that, because of the debate, they feared about their security. The National Council of Canadian Muslims blamed Harper's divisive policies for reportedly more attacks on Muslim women and religious centres. In general, Harper was criticized for stigmatizing Islam, politicizing face veiling and resorting to politics of fear in order to win the election. His government's decision to ban face coverings was widely perceived as "playing politics with the rights of minorities" (MacCharles and Spurr).

One immigrant from Pakistan, named Zunera Ishaq, launched a legal battle against the new regulations after she was refused citizenship when, at a citizenship ceremony, she had objected to removing a niqab, a veil covering most of her face. In the courts, she argued that, since face veiling was mandatory to her faith, the new rules violated her religious freedoms (Quan). Her case went through multiple court instances until she finally won the fight. In September 2015, the Federal Court of Appeal lifted the government's ban on face coverings, declaring that "the change in policy applicable to women who wear the niqab, that requires them to unveil to take the oath of citizenship, was unlawful." The court ruled it conflicted with the already existing regulations made under the *Citizenship Act* of 1985. The government, the court ruled, had no authority to adopt the citizenship rules without amending the act itself and voting the changes in the parliament. The court obliged the authorities not to delay the process of granting citizenship to Mrs. Ishaq (*Canada (Citizenship and Immigration) v Ishaq*). While Ishaq obtained her citizenship in October 2015, the Harper Conservatives remained uncompromising on the "niqab issue." Not only did they decide to appeal the ruling to the Supreme Court, but also, if re-elected, to adopt a new law banning face veils from the federal public service (MacCharles and Spurr). However, with the election of Justin Trudeau, the new Liberal government withdrew the appeal from the Supreme Court, which ended the case (Mas and Crawford).

As it was with Alan Kurdi's death, Canada's "niqab debate" was widely discussed in international media, often with little sympathy to Harper. A columnist in *New Yorker*, for instance, wrote that, should the veil ban been upheld, Muslim women's "basic human right will have been violated" and suggested that "special restrictions directed at their faith alone" were signs of islamophobia and cultural relativism (Gopnik). The *Washington Post*, in turn, while admitting that "Canada is an impressively, resolutely multicultural country, with a historically progressive approach to immigration," quoted a number of opponents of Harper's veil policies, including Naheed Nenshi, a Muslim mayor of Calgary, who called Harper's approach to face coverings "disgusting" (Tharoor). The *Independent* accused Harper's Conservatives of being "prone to linking all things Islamic to 'security' fears" and having an "obsession with Muslim practices" (Fisk, "Niqab"). "Muslim-bashing is an effective campaign tactic," reported a columnist in the *Economist*, referring to the Conservatives' election strategy ("Canada's election"), while the *New York Times* wrote about "the Conservative Party's scapegoating of Canadian Muslims" and branded the Conservatives' approach as "anti-Muslim campaign," clearly indicating that Canada was having its own "Trump Moment" (Patriquin).

In the campaign race, as one of the authors wrote, "Trudeau's stand for diversity played far better than Stephen Harper's appeal to a narrower sense of identity" (Geddes, "The Trudeau"). Generally speaking, Justin Trudeau presented himself as Harper's antithesis, especially on the issues of multiculturalism and immigration policies. At the same time, he wanted to be seen as a continuator and a vigorous defender of Pierre Trudeau's legacy. Multiculturalism, declared an official federal policy by his father, was his father's key political achievement for Justin Trudeau. It had played a critical role in transforming Canada into what it is today – "the country strong not in spite of its diversity but because of its diversity" ("Federal"). Once becoming prime minister, Justin Trudeau defended Canadian multiculturalism vigorously, also on international forums. In November 2015, for instance, addressing the audience in the Canada House in London, UK, Trudeau boasted that, in Canada, diversity was "the air we breathe" and "there is no doubt that we're a better country – a stronger, more successful country – because of it." "We're open, accepting, progressive and prosperous," he exclaimed (Trudeau, "Diversity"). A year later, in his address to the U.N. General Assembly, in December 2016, he declared that "in Canada we see diversity as a strength, not a weakness" (Austen, "Justin"). Harper's policies, in Justin Trudeau's eyes, were a contradiction to Canadian multicultural heritage. To understand

Trudeau's attitude to Harper's legacy, it is worth analyzing Trudeau's statements from the foreign policy leaders' debate.

What the Liberals attacked particularly fiercely in Harper's policies was Harper's response to the refugee crisis. Trudeau claimed the Conservatives had merely paid "lip service" to the efforts to help refugees, without ever reaching any substantial targets. Facing an enormous tragedy as the one in Syria, stated Trudeau in the debate, it was the Canadian government's duty to help refugees resettle in Canada. Not only because it was humanitarian, but also because it would make the economy grow and "help our communities flourish." Canada, Trudeau declared, had resettled tens of thousands of humans and had "always benefited from being an open nation that helped people in the crisis situations." Therefore, for Trudeau, Harper's uncompromising plan to admit no more than 10,000 new Syrian refugees over three years was shy, not to say un-Canadian, as it damaged the international image of the country and broke with the long history of Canadian openness and hospitality to immigrants. Hence Trudeau's strong and emotional statement during the debate:

> Mr. Harper, we stand here tonight just a few blocks from Ireland Park. Ireland Park was where, in 1847, 38,000 men, women and children, fleeing the famine, arrived on the shores of Toronto. There were 20,000 citizens of Toronto at that time. And they accepted 38,000 refugees, who proceeded to contribute to this country, to this city, and to who we are today. Canada has always done more. It's not about politics, it's about being the country that we have always been. Not only are you reneging on our duties as Canadians, not only are you failing us, but the entire world is looking at Canada and saying: "What is going on? You used to be a country that welcomed human beings, that appreciated diversity." People in crisis, people in distress wished to help build the better and brighter future for their children. Our community gave them this opportunity; that's what we were as a nation. And yet now Mr. Harper talks about nothing but security. We need to do the bare minimum. But he [S. Harper] talks about resisting the tyrants and dictators. But you know who is resisting these tyrants and dictators? The families who are fleeing for their lives, who are resisting the violence on the ground. They come to Canada and what are you doing when they get here? You're taking away their healthcare. That's not the generous nation that we've been in the past ("Federal").

In Trudeau's judgement, accepting more refugees – he confirmed Liberal Party's promise to resettle 25,000 Syrian expatriates – was one of the best ways for Canada to prove that it was ready to contribute productively to fighting humanitarian crises and bringing relief to global tensions ("Federal").

The Liberals also vehemently opposed Harper's idea of revoking Canadian citizenship from dual nationals convicted of terrorism. As Trudeau claimed in the debate, it was the introduction of a "two-tiered citizenship," based on a scheme by which one "can be judged differently by our systems of laws and rights, because their parents were born in a different country." This led him to use an impassioned tone to issue a warning against such a solution. Later on, it was one of the most frequently quoted statements of the debate. Pointing to Stephen Harper, Trudeau said:

> Particularly from this prime minister, who has made a habit of calling out First Nations groups, environmental groups as terrorists, we should be very worried that any prime minister would have the ability to revoke citizenship from people. It's a slippery slope that belies what Canada is. A Canadian, is a Canadian, is a Canadian. [...] You devalue the citizenship of every Canadian in this place and in this country when you break down and make it conditional for anyone. We have a rule of law in this country and you can't take away citizenship if you don't like what someone does. You can't do that! [...] We're not a country dominated by fear, we're a country of laws and rights ("Federal").

"Playing the politics of fear" was one of the most frequently repeated accusations by Liberals against Harper. As Trudeau sarcastically said in the debate, "Mr. Harper wants us to be afraid that there's a terrorist hiding behind every leaf and rock around us and we need to be afraid. And that's why he's there to protect us" ("Federal").

The Trudeau government has fulfilled its promise to resettle thousands of Syrian refugees. The first government plane of newcomers to arrive in Canada in December 2015 was personally welcomed by the prime minister at Toronto Pearson International Airport. Trudeau used the greeting ceremony as one more occasion to promote Canada's diversity and tolerance, telling the media just before the refugees' landing that accepting immigrants on such a large scale can be done only because what it means to be a Canadian is defined "not by a skin colour or a language or a religion or a background, but by a shared set of values, aspirations, hopes and dreams that not just Canadians but people around the world share" (Battersby).

While initially the government had failed to stand up to its pledge to bring 25,000 Syrian refugees by the end of 2015 (Nicolaou), the overall number of expats from Syria admitted to Canada considerably exceeded the promised quota. From November 2015 to January 2017, according to the government data, over 40,000 Syrian expats were resettled into 350 communities across Canada. The government's commitment to relocate Syrians is also continuing in 2017. In order to be able to evacuate such large numbers of Syrians and integrate them into Canadian society, the Liberal government adopted a sophisticated refugee relocation program involving provincial, territorial and local authorities, NGOs, social networks, but also private sponsors. As for the latter, almost a third of all Syrian refugees have come to Canada not as government-assisted refugees but thanks to a private sponsorship scheme (Citizenship and Immigration Canada, "#WelcomeRefugees"). Under this program, either Sponsorship Agreement Holders (SAHs), which are larger groups or incorporated organizations properly experienced and sufficiently staffed, or so-called "Groups of Five" (G5), i.e. five private individuals, agree to provide more than two (SAH) or just one refugee (G5) "with care, lodging, settlement assistance and support for […] 12 months starting from the refugee's arrival in Canada or until the refugee becomes self-sufficient, whichever comes first" (Citizenship and Immigration Canada, "Guide"). Canada's success in running a mixed system of government and private refugee sponsorship attracted the attention of international partners. The chief of the United Nations refugee agency presented the Canadian system as a model for the world to follow (Harris, "Extraordinary"). The result of this increased interest was a refugee conference held in Ottawa, in December 2016, jointly by the United Nations High Commissioner for Refugees and the Canadian government. Attended by over 90 representatives of several countries, interested in replicating Canadian solutions, the conference effected in the launch of the Global Refugee Sponsorship Initiative. Its aim is "to train and advise other countries on how to establish programs that allow private individuals and groups to finance, facilitate and support refugees coming to the country" (United Nations High Commissioner for Refugees).

Apart from that, Justin Trudeau has repeatedly appealed to the international community to engage more actively in helping refugees. In September 2016, he co-chaired a U.N. conference on refugees and migrants. Seated beside Queen Rania Al-Abdullah of Jordan, a country that – alongside Turkey and Lebanon – has accepted the most Syrian refugees, Trudeau promised a contribution of CAD 64.5 million to support the victims of humanitarian crises around the world ("Trudeau Tells").

Canada's refugee policies have been a success so far and, as such, have made headlines around the world. But enhancing the country's repute abroad, the Liberal government did not indulge in complacency or self-congratulations. In order to fill the demographic gap and, most of all, the shortage in the working-age labour force, the Trudeau government has also opened the doors to Canada for economic immigrants. As Immigration Minister John McCallum noticed: "Canada is an aging country, so we are in need of new blood because Canadians aren't having enough babies and so the labour force growth depends very much on the entrance of immigrants" (qtd. in Dharssi). As a consequence, since Trudeau came to power, Canada has admitted a record number of immigrants. In the year 2015/2016, 320,932 newcomers were accepted. According to a Statistics Canada's release, "the country had not received such a large number of immigrants in a single annual period since the early 1910s during the settlement of Western Canada." This, in turn, contributed to the highest upsurge of the country's total population recorded in one year. "[A]n increase of 437,815 or 1.2% during the year 2015/2016 […] had not been recorded since 1988/1989," wrote Statistics Canada in its 2016 demographic estimates ("Canada's Population Estimates: Age and Sex, July 1, 2016."). By 2021, the Liberal government is considering boosting the quota of accepted immigrants to 450,000 a year. Canadians seem to be supportive of this move. According to surveys, 80 per cent of Canadians think that immigrants have a positive impact on their country's economy ("The Last"). The public opinion is also largely sympathetic to refugee resettlements. Thousands of Canadians have offered their sponsorship for newcomers, crowds have rallied on the streets and expressed support for them in social media.

Contrasted with Europe and the United States, where protectionist and nationalistic sentiments are on the rise, Canada appears to be showing outstanding openness and tolerance for immigrants. The United Nations, as was mentioned before, has even on a few occasions presented Canada's immigration and refugee programs as models for the rest of the world. But experts argue that, given the country's specifics, Canada's policies are not easily exportable outside. "What works in Canada may not work elsewhere," warns Michael Ignatieff, former leader of the Liberal Party (qtd. in "The Last"). First and foremost, Canada's geography is unique, which in the context of pro-immigration and pro-refugee sympathies is essentially important. Separated from Asia and Africa by vast oceans and from Latin America "by a wall the size of the United States," Canada will never experience massive inflows of either refugees arriving to its shores in overloaded boats or illegal immigrants sneaking through its land border. In fact, illegal immigration – unlike in the U.S. or Europe – has never been a big issue in Canada. In such circumstances, as one of the *Economist*'s columnists wrote, "[i]t is easier to be relaxed about immigration" ("Canada's Example").

Most importantly, however, those who present Canada's refugee and immigration policies as pure altruism and philanthropy, based solely on humanitarian grounds, compassion and unselfish motives, present a romanticized and somewhat distorted image. While undoubtedly Canada is, as mentioned, an exceptionally hospitable country for newcomers nowadays, its immigration policies still are – as they have always been – very careful and, most of all, highly selective. In the past, the restrictedness of Canadian immigration laws and the government's non-welcoming approach were responsible for one of the most shameful parts of the country's history. To mention a few of these dark episodes – Canada had outlawed immigration from China, refused to accept Jews escaping Nazi Germany, turned away Punjabis, interned Ukrainians, Germans, Italians or the Japanese. In reality, as late as until 1960s, immigrants had been admitted on the basis of ethnic and racial criteria (*The History*). First preference was given to immigrants from Britain, then it was extended to Western Europeans. In the first decades of the 20th century, facing a desperate shortage of farmers in the Prairies, Canada opened its doors to newcomers from Central and Eastern Europe. However, it was only after the Second World War that non-Europeans could come *en masse* to Canada.

But, to keep balance, Canada also had its moments of pride and glory when it, for instance, accepted thousands of asylum-seekers from Uganda, Vietnam, and Kosovo. There were even earlier successes, enumerated by Justin Trudeau in his address at the Canada House in London in

November 2015: "The Underground Railroad. The *Charter of Rights and Freedoms*. The *Multiculturalism Act*. The *Official Languages Act*. The welcoming of Ismaili Muslims. The freedom for Jews and Sikhs, Hindus and Evangelicals to practice their religion as they choose" (Trudeau, "Statement by Justin Trudeau").

There is also a famous Canadian points system, which Trudeau forgot to mention, effective since 1962, by which the ethnicity-based qualification of immigrants was finally dropped. The point system made Canadian immigration rules race-blind, more transparent and democratic, but it did not remove Canada's selective approach. Obviously, Canada is an immigrant country. Since its foundation, Canada has been built and shaped mostly by the subsequent waves of newcomers. In fact, for the last two decades, immigration has been a much bigger source of the country's population increase than natural growth (Statistics Canada, "Population Growth"). Therefore, it is hardly surprising that no major force on the present Canadian political scene calls for the substantial limitation – let alone complete abolition – of immigration.

But Canada is very picky about whom it takes. The points system gives preference to immigrants with specific trades, qualifications, work experience, or language skills. By assigning points to would-be immigrants, the government basically selects those who are needed and can be easily integrated. Each government, be it Harper's or Trudeau's, has run a selective immigration system, although specific policies varied in such details as quotas or preferred professions. Frequently, however, they remained quite similar even if declared otherwise. Take Harper's and Trudeau's attitudes to immigration policies, for instance. In the campaign, the Liberals accused the Harper government that all the policies it was running, immigration programs included, were subjected to achieving one leading goal – financial profits. They even claimed that the Tories' foreign policy, in general, amounted to little more than merely "economic diplomacy." In the context of immigration, such a claim was not very difficult to prove. The Harper government did in fact – as was already discussed – alter immigration rules and began fast-tracking immigrants with job offers and qualifications and experience that were on demand. Since they came to power, however, the Liberals have not significantly changed that system. In actuality, they have promised to introduce an immigration reform that would go relatively along the same lines. "Canadians are generous, but that generosity is not unlimited," admitted the Liberal Immigration Minister John McCallum announcing his reforms plans. "Canadians will accept immigration, but largely for economic reasons." Therefore, "the emphasis will be more on immigrants who can quickly contribute to the Canadian economy" (qtd. in Geddes, "How the Liberals are taking"). As the statistical data for 2016 suggests, under Liberals, immigration continues to be perceived as a force that can fill the demographic gap. Similarly to previous periods, the age of almost all immigrants admitted to Canada in 2016 was less than 50 (Kirby, "Canada's"). Despite some Liberal modifications in Canada's migrant policies – such as scrapping the abovementioned "4 and 4" rule – what has really changed is not the overall strategies or key priorities, but the number of accepted newcomers and the rhetoric, which – compared to Harper's years – creates more convivial and welcoming atmosphere around the newcomers. The ruling Liberals, for instance, hold no plans of regulating religious outfit or scrapping citizenship from dual national convicts; they do not blame refugees or immigrants for abusing Canadian generosity; nor they intend to test them on Canadian values. Rhetorically, the change is indeed significant. But putting this aside, Canada's immigration program is as selective as it has always been.

To some extent, similar conclusions can be drawn regarding the refugee policies. The major difference between the Liberals and Conservatives is refugee quotas and the rate of resettlement. The Liberal government has already relocated four times more Syrian refugees to Canada than the Conservatives had promised to relocate over the three-year period. Undoubtedly, this constitutes an accomplishment that deserves credit and appreciation. Nonetheless, the large numbers of resettled Syrians should not outshine the fact that Canada's refugee program is highly selective. The Liberal government, for instance, has not rescinded Harper's aforementioned "safe country" list, which designates the citizens of certain countries as ineligible to seek asylum in Canada (Nerenberg). Moreover, when it comes to Iraqi and Syrian refugees, not only are they subjected to a very detailed screening, which – given the circumstances – seems natural, but under the government-assisted relocations specific, most persecuted and defenceless groups are favoured: women, families with children or gay, lesbian, transgender and bisexual persons – those who, strictly speaking, are the least likely to pose a security threat once in Canada. At the same time, single – especially young – adult men are, in principle, not relocated. Thus, while other countries are criticized for their arbitrary and discriminatory plans of selecting refugees basing on their religion – giving preference to Christian Syrians, for example – "Canada is thought to be unique in explicitly prioritising based on gender or sexual orientation" (Nicolaou).

Human rights advocates, usually enthusiastic about the Canadian approach to immigrants and refugees, see this particular aspect of Canada's refugee policy as problematic. Amnesty International (AI), for instance, in a statement on its website says openly that "it is a mistake for the [Canadian] government to outrightly eliminate single men from the possibility of resettlement or only focus on single males who are members of the LGBTI community." While the organization calls it "a huge challenge" and "noble" act that "exceptional resources" are being placed by Ottawa to help Syrian refugees, it reminds Canadian officials that "it is critical that we do not discriminate against refugees," "identify those who are the most vulnerable" and "not engage in decision-making that stigmatizes." "Profiling single men unfortunately only serves to feed into negative stereotypes which already exist, and risks stigmatizing an entire population as individuals who are to be feared," the AI statement says (Nafzinger). The above reaction proves that the selectiveness of Canadian migration-related policies may cause controversies even among those who usually brand Canada as an exceptionally hospitable and helping country.

But in the world that is increasingly inclining towards different sorts of populisms and particularisms, a relevant question is whether Canada's proverbial openness and tolerance for newcomers can be taken for granted. Being widely considered a bastion of liberal democracy and progressive values, Canada does not exist in a vacuum or in isolation from other state actors. In fact, as close as behind its southern border, empirical evidence has been just provided of how immense the political power of anti-immigrant arguments can be and what enormous political profits it can bring. Were politicians in Canada tempted to play an anti-immigrant card, would Canadians stay immune to their argumentation? The first test for Canada is coming with the Conservative Party leadership contest. Some of the candidates there – such as Kellie Leitch – on a few occasions have already retorted to an anti-immigrant rhetoric to the extent that makes even their fellow Conservative colleagues fear that the party might be "hijacked" by "negative and irresponsible populism" (Harris, "Irresponsible"). So far, though, as the most recent federal election or 2014 election in Quebec suggest, the majority of Canadian voters have denounced politicians whom they see as openly railing against immigrants. But will this trend continue if, for instance, the refugee resettlement program goes less smoothly than was previously projected?

As for the time being, relocating Syrians and other evacuees to Canada has been presented – quite fairly and deservedly – by the Liberals as a success story. Ottawa has accepted newcomers in large numbers and in a very short time, and the resettlements have generally been met with welcoming attitude from Canadians, who have eagerly offered to cover the refugees' expenses under the private sponsorship schemes. Thus, the initial Liberal goal to revive Canada's international reputation by being a hospitable nation has been achieved. The biggest struggle, though, is about to begin, as lots of effort and resources would yet need to be put in place in order to integrate the newcomers into the Canadian economic and social realities. The financial sponsorship, as was mentioned, expires after 12 months since the refugee's arrival; beyond that period, newcomers are expected to take responsibility for their home budgets. Will Canadians' patience and hospitality survive untouched if refugees fail to contribute to the Canadian economy and, instead, become a long-term burden for Canada's welfare system? Will Canadians be ready to spend generously on language classes, healthcare, job training, social assistance or housing for refugees if Canada faces an economic crisis? Questions of this kind seem to bear particular relevance in the context of the presidency of Donald Trump, whose remarks on revolutionizing NAFTA and the U.S. trade relations have already placed Canada in the sphere of economic uncertainty (see below).

As a matter of fact, resentments against some immigrant groups are rising in certain Canadian regions. Chinese millionaires, for instance, are blamed for making Canadian large cities unlivable and unaffordable by flooding Vancouver's and Toronto's housing markets with their capital and inflating real estate prices there to the level that is out of reach for average citizens. The province of British Columbia even introduced a 15 per cent property tax for foreigners buying residential properties in the Vancouver area to tackle the so-called "affordability crisis" (J. Gordon; Stiem). Also, as recent polls show, more and more Canadians feel increasingly insecure about the large immigration quotas and expect the government to lower them. In January 2016, a quarter of the surveyed respondents considered immigration levels too high. While a significant majority (59 per cent) still thought the quotas were just right, the proportion of those who opposed was on the rise (Curry).

Last but not least, Donald Trump's uncompromising stance on immigrants has a large potential to affect Canadian immigration policies. In fact, the Trump travel ban for the citizens of seven Muslim-dominated countries and the U.S. plans of massive deportations of illegal immigrants, have already caused problems on the Canadian border. The police and border services have reported an increased number of immigrants from the U.S. crossing to Manitoba and Quebec illegally (Macdonnell). It still remains to be seen how Ottawa will exactly address the new American policies. One of the possible outcomes is that Canada's refugee and immigration policies would need to be transformed to please American partners. This, in turn, could result in Canada becoming even more strict and selective – and thus less open – towards migrants. In fact, the Liberal government, officially citing huge backlogs as the reason, has already announced, for 2017, a cap of only 1,000 applications for Syrian and Iraqi refugees privately sponsored by "groups of five" (Brach).

Environmental and energy policies

In the televised pre-election debate, Justin Trudeau promised that his policies on climate and environment would be the exact opposite to Harper's. He made climate change a top priority of his agenda and declared that his government, in collaboration with the governments of the Canadian provinces and territories, would work constructively to fight climate change by introducing a carbon tax and investing CAD 20 billion in ten years in green, sustainable infrastructure, including the public transit system, which would reduce greenhouse gas emission ("Federal"). In actuality, profound changes in environmental policies were one of the most frequently repeated electoral declarations by the Liberals. The promise to "develop real climate change solutions, consistent with our international obligations to protect the planet" was included in the Liberal Party's official campaign document (Liberal Party of Canada 39). "Making Canada a leader of international efforts to combat climate change" was also, as mentioned, the key part of Trudeau's foreign policy doctrine ("Stéphane"). Furthermore, on numerous occasions, including in his address to the United Nations General Assembly in September 2016,

Prime Minister Trudeau has declared his intention to work constructively with international partners to tackle the greenhouse effect. Given all the above, no wonder that before the election the critics of the Harper government claimed that Canadians were not only going to vote on a new government, but were "also choosing whether to save the planet" (Dembicki).

Evidently, it was easier for Trudeau to proceed with more ambitious environmental policies than for Harper. The political costs of combatting climate change were definitely lower for the Liberals than for the Conservatives. Unlike Harper, Trudeau had only few votes to lose in the Prairie Provinces, particularly in Alberta, a major producer of fossil fuels in Canada. In fact, voters there have not supported the Liberals in federal elections since Pierre Trudeau introduced his National Energy Program in 1980, aimed at imposing more control and taxes on the oil industry, which alienated large swathes of Albertans. Hence, as one author wrote, "the Trudeau name – so much of an asset in other parts of the country – is kryptonite in Alberta" (Hirsch 33).

Practically speaking, various aspects of Canada's climate policies have changed diametrically after Liberals' ascension to power. In November 2015 in Paris, Trudeau took part in the U.N. climate change summit (the so-called COP21). In his address, he passionately announced Canada's readiness to accept the role of a global leader in the fight against climate change and presented COP21 as "an opportunity to make history" by signing "an agreement that transitions to a low-carbon economy that is necessary for our collective health, security, and prosperity" (Fekete). In the summit, Canadian delegates were positive and constructive actors; Canada even joined the so-called High Ambition Coalition, advocating for an ambitious deal and advanced measures to be adopted in order to limit the growth of average global temperature (Government of Canada, "Canada at the 21st"). Without hesitation, Ottawa also committed itself to reduce its carbon emissions by 30 per cent – i.e. below the 2005 levels – by 2030. In December 2015, Canada signed the Paris climate deal and ratified it the following year ("Canada's Climate"). Everything went swiftly and surprisingly smoothly compared to Harper's dealings with the Kyoto Protocol. On top of this global deal, Canada and the U.S. issued a *Joint Statement on Climate, Energy, and Arctic Leadership*, where they committed themselves, among others, to curb methane emissions, the use of hydrofluorocarbons and limit oil and gas exploitation in the Arctic (U.S. White House, "U.S.-Canada").

Furthermore, in the election campaign, Trudeau also declared to depart in a long-term perspective from coal-fired electricity and limit Canada's reliance on fossil fuels in general. To reduce air pollution and help Canada meet its climate commitments, the government announced a plan to introduce a market pricing on the country's carbon emissions. The Liberals declared to synchronize their policies with the ones of the provinces and territories. To that end, they promised to establish a federal funding scheme to assist the provinces and territories with their pursuit of clean air policies (Wells, "Justin"; Fekete). In October 2016, the government announced the emissions-reduction plan, which all the provinces and territories will be forced to adhere to. By 2018, the plan will introduce, pan-Canadian pricing regulations on greenhouse emissions at a minimum level of CAD 10 per tonne, which by 2022 is planned to increase to CAD 50 per tonne. While the revenues will stay in the provinces and territories and each jurisdiction will be allowed to choose its own way of reaching the targets, those who will fail will have carbon prices imposed on them by Ottawa (Trudeau, "Prime Minister Justin Trudeau delivers").

The move is a bold step as many jurisdictions object to the new solutions either because, like British Columbia or Alberta, they already have their own carbon tax schemes in place, or, like Quebec and Ontario, have adopted a cap-and-trade system and prefer to keep the federal government out of their provincial policies. Some provinces, including Newfoundland and Labrador or Nova Scotia, have rejected the federal government's plans by occasionally leaving negotiations with Ottawa (Proudfoot). They fear the new scheme will ruin their economies, which are largely dependent on the energy sector. Saskatchewan's Premier Brad Wall, whose province has no carbon tax, refused to accept the federal plan straight away, calling it a "betrayal." Wall claimed Saskatchewan's economy would not be able to carry the burden of the Trudeau government's climate policies ("Canada's Climate"). The Liberals seem, however, adamant in proceeding with the national carbon pricing policy, though its details are still under discussion. This might serve as an indicator that the Trudeau government treats fighting climate change seriously. Canada's policy is also praised by the U.N. and presented as a model for other countries to follow (Panetta, "A Carbon"). Stephen

Harper used to say that "the reason governments do carbon taxes is not so they can reduce emissions, but so they can get more tax revenue in the government's pocket" (qtd. in Reguly). Justin Trudeau believes carbon pricing can change behaviour and, as such, can be an effective way of greenhouse emissions reduction. This is yet another difference between Trudeau and Harper.

Also, Canada's climate policies have undergone a noteworthy – even ostentatious – change on the rhetorical level. Canada's officials express no doubts that global warming is induced by humans. Unlike the Conservatives, they do not dismiss the efforts to reduce air pollution as "job killing" (Dembicki). Instead, they prefer to present Canada as a leader of global combat against the greenhouse effect and, to that end, they have accepted the U.N.'s offer to host the World Environment Day in Canada on June 5, 2017 (United Nations Environment Programme). Generally speaking, the Liberals like to present their policy as significantly different from that of Harper. "My predecessor wanted you to know Canada for its resources," said Justin Trudeau in his speech at the World Economic Forum in Davos in 2016. The statement was an intentional – even if veiled – criticism of both Harper's preoccupation with making Canada's fossil fuels more exportable and his reckless approach to environmental concerns. Trudeau, in contrast, wants to be seen as being guided by more soft-power-like priorities: "I want you to know Canadians for our resourcefulness," he declared in Davos, by which he meant not the abundance of natural resources but certain Canadian sociocultural features, such as diversity, creativity, high-level education or political and economic stability (qtd. in Press).

In its entirety, Canada's reengagement in climate change talks should not be perceived solely through the prism of progressive ideas or purely altruistic motivations. While, undoubtedly, the Liberal government is concerned about the greenhouse effect and has genuine intentions to contribute positively to solving global environmental problems, Canada's return to the discussion table is also inspired by more selfish motives.

First and foremost, in the reinvolvement the Liberals appear to see a swift and effective method of improving Canada's international image and reconstructing its damaged reputation. As Trudeau claimed in the election campaign, under Harper, Canadians were perceived as "absolute laggards," frustrating the whole world, and "obstructionists in the bargaining process on climate change" ("Federal"). His purpose, thus, is to replace a notorious brand of a climate blocker with a more positive one – of a climate progressive. The ultimate goal, however, is not only to gain international praise or put an end to "hunkering down in disapproving isolation." By reengaging in climate change talks, Canada seems to be aiming at a much bigger win – at boosting its rank in the global hierarchy and at becoming – or, at least, at being regarded as – a global leader in the promotion of environmental protection, sustainability and awareness. As Jeremy Kinsman, a former Canadian diplomat, argues, climate change issues give Canada a chance to locate itself again "in the forefront of nations" ("Seven"). In his article in *Foreign Policy*, Mathew Bondy is equally hopeful when he contends that "[b]y bringing Trudeau's progressive environmental views" to international fora, Canada has a capacity to "affect a tectonic shift in global climate politics."

Secondly, while changing many aspects of Canada's climate policies in substance not in words only – plans to cap carbon emissions or playing a constructive role at the COP21 are good examples – the Liberals, like their Conservative predecessors, continue to address environmental issues selectively. Quarrels over the Keystone XL pipeline illustrate this point clearly. In the election campaign the Liberals harshly criticized the Harper government for "narrowing the entire relationship with the United States to a single point around the Keystone XL pipeline" (Simon and McLaughlin). The fact was that the Harper government actively lobbied in the U.S. for the extension of the pipeline, calling it a "complete no brainer" and presenting the opposing environmental groups as "radicals" trying to "hijack" Canadian economy (Dickinson). All in vein, however, as in February 2015 the Obama administration vetoed a bill passed in the U.S. Congress approving the pipeline, and in November 2015 rejected the project altogether. Announcing his decision, Obama stated that the U.S. "must transition to a clean energy economy" and the Keystone XL pipeline, based on "shipping dirtier crude oil into our country," was an obstacle to meet such a goal. He saw no profits for the U.S. in the approval of the project. The pipeline, he said, "would not make a meaningful long-term contribution to our economy," "would not lower gas prices for American consumers," and "would not increase America's energy security." Most importantly, however, Obama argued, "this project would have undercut" America's global leadership in combatting climate change (U.S. White House, "Statement").

Trudeau's reaction to the rejection was rather muted. In a surprisingly short statement, he expressed his government's disappointment, but at the same time he declared that "the Canada-U.S. relationship is much bigger than any one project" and that he was hoping for "a fresh start with President Obama to strengthen our remarkable ties" and to work "to combat climate change, adapt to its impacts, and create the clean jobs of tomorrow" (Trudeau, "Statement by the Prime Minister"). Until the end of Obama's term in office it was not worth raising the issue again, especially that all Democratic presidential candidates, including Hillary Clinton, the election favourite, opposed the pipeline (Labott and Berman).

The situation changed when, in January 2017, Donald Trump was sworn in as U.S. President. The Republicans had been supportive of the Keystone project – its approval constituted the party's official line. Trump had personally, on numerous occasions, expressed his intentions to allow the pipeline construction. On January 24, 2017, in one of his very first decisions as president, Donald Trump signed an executive order permitting the Keystone XL project to be reconsidered. He invited the TransCanada Corporation, the pipeline operator and the owner of the Keystone XL, "to promptly re-submit its application" and promised that final decision would be made "within 60 days" (U.S. White House, "Memorandum"). The move was immediately praised by Justin Trudeau, who admitted pressing on Trump in phone calls to announce the decision swiftly. Trudeau argued the project was all good news for Canadians and Americans – it would lead to "economic growth and good jobs for Albertans," he said (qtd. in Tasker, "Trudeau"). He also assured the Keystone would not translate into Canada's departure from its own climate change goals. These, in Trudeau's opinion, were not at risk because of the caps and taxes on emissions his government and provincial authorities were planning to implement. Other cabinet ministers assumed a similar tone ("Liberals Applaud"). The U.S. president was equally enthusiastic, claiming the investment would create thousands of construction jobs in the U.S., although he warned that some terms of the deal might be renegotiated to guarantee that the pipeline is constructed using the U.S.-made steel (Tasker, "Trudeau"; "Donald Trump Backs").

If everything goes well, as it seems to be the case, with other approving procedures – the Keystone XL still needs to be accepted by Nebraska – the pipeline will be completed. It might in fact – as suggested by the federal and Alberta governments – bring measurable profits to the budgets on both sides of the border, create new jobs and revive Canada's oil industry, recently hit by low crude prices. But the Keystone's revival will also have immediate negative repercussions. It has already undermined Justin Trudeau's – and thereby Canada's – credibility as a genuine advocate of environmental protection. It also brings a sharper focus to the integrity of Ottawa's climate policies and raises multiple questions: how can the Trudeau government proceed with the transition to a low-carbon economy when, at the same time, it is developing projects meant to exploit and ship the "dirty" oil across the continent?; how is Canada going to curb its greenhouse gas emissions effectively without starting to reduce investments in high-emitting fossil fuel infrastructure?; are Canada's COP21 climate commitments still relevant after the approval of Keystone?; how can the government portray itself as a climate leader when it proceeds with the oil pipeline investments regardless of their damaging impact on the environment? As for the latter, major climate organizations and government agencies have warned against the destructive effect pipelines would have on climate change combat. It is enough to look into the American assessments of Keystone XL's environmental impact to understand the problem (see U.S. Department of State; U.S. Environmental Protection Agency).

Pipelines have also been vehemently opposed by all major environmental organizations. Greenpeace, for instance, calls them "brazen crony capitalism" and the "[p]rojects that trample Indigenous treaties and rights, while endangering the lives and drinking sources of hundreds of thousands of people" (Coleman). The Natural Resources Defense Council, an NGO headquartered in New York City, dubs the Keystone a "dangerous project" and claims its potential approval would undermine "decades of environmental policy as well as commitment to public engagement and transparency." But it also hopes it will eventually be blocked by "the coalition of Native Americans, ranchers, landowners, clean energy businesses, student activists, Nobel Laureates, scientists, and many many others" who "will be making their voices heard" (Swift, "Significant"). The World Wildlife Fund, in turn, asserts that the project "not only would degrade and fragment wildlife habitat, [but] it would also open the door to accelerating oil and gas development and the potentially devastating impacts of pipeline spills" (World Wildlife Fund). Similar conclusions are drawn by Canada-based organizations. The Pembina

Institute and the Suzuki Foundation, for example, have long criticized the Canadian government's policies of pipeline expansions, claiming that they undermine climate actions and degrade ecosystems (Lemphers; Bryant).

Trudeau's Liberals seem to ignore the above opinions and present the same economic arguments the Harper government formulated in support of the pipeline extension. They claim, as was mentioned, that the pipelines will contribute to job creation and boost Canadian exports. The government's argumentation has, in fact, been largely based on the reasoning presented by Canada's National Energy Board in March 2010, when NEB approved the Keystone XL (National Energy Board, "Reasons").

While, indeed, developing pipelines might have a positive impact on the Canadian economy, climate scientists prove clearly that the greenhouse effect can only be fought by limiting and, eventually, departing from fossil fuel use. Thus, in the context of pipeline expansion, it is dubious, not to say senseless, to present Canada as a climate leader, which the Liberals frequently do. And even if, as suggested by the *New York Times*, Trudeau's support of the pipelines was a step he had to take in order to convince skeptical Alberta to his national carbon-pricing program (Austen and Krauss), it still tarnishes his reputation as an environmentally friendly politician.

Trudeau's relationship with the Aboriginal communities in Canada and the U.S., the most fervent opponents of the pipelines, is already very tense. Trudeau's government, on the one hand, has repeatedly called for the reconciliation with Indigenous people and has been an outspoken advocate "for a renewed, nation-to-nation relationship with Indigenous Peoples, based on recognition of rights, respect, co-operation, and partnership, […] engagement and participatory capacity of Indigenous groups in reviewing and monitoring major resource development projects" (Trudeau, "Minister"). But when it comes to energy projects – not only the Keystone or other oil pipelines, but also hydro energy investments in British Columbia and Newfoundland and Labrador – Ottawa has played down Aboriginal environmental concerns and challenged the protesters, or has been challenged by them, in courts. As a consequence, Indigenous confidence in the Liberals' good will and decent intentions has largely been lost. For many Aboriginal leaders – as Roland Willson, Chief of West Moberly First Nation, put it – it appears that "this Liberal government is no different than the previous Harper government. They're just sneaky" (qtd. in Gilchrist). Angered by Ottawa and allied with environmental activists, NGOs and farmers, First Nation communities are ready to enter the fight against the federal government and block the construction of the pipelines.

All of the above elements combined create an impression that the Trudeau government remains reluctant to take action to reduce the greenhouse effect if Canada's finances or vested economic interests are at stake. In this narrow regard, Liberals' attitude to global climate issues does not vary much from Stephen Harper's stance. Assessing words against practice, the Liberal government is much better at communicating widely strong messages about ambitious climate targets than actually putting verbal declarations into actions. The major obstacle for actions is that fossil fuels are vital to Canada's economy, which makes it difficult to resign from their exploitation and expansion. This, in turn, slows down the process of adjusting Canada's economy to a low-carbon energy model. For the economies of specific provinces, the exploitation of fossil fuels is even more important. In Alberta, for instance, the energy sector, mostly oil and gas production, generates almost one third of the budget (Jang and McCarthy). Hence, giving up large sections of the energy sector for the sake of the cleaner climate would pose a real risk for Canada's entire economy and puts constraints on actions of all Canadian governments, be it Conservative, Liberal or even today's government of Alberta, run by the left-wing New Democratic Party. This results in what can be observed today – a somewhat inconsistent, and at the same time highly selective, policies on climate pursued by the ruling Liberals.

On the one hand, where this bears relatively low immediate costs for Canada, the Trudeau government is strongly supportive of international initiatives combatting the greenhouse effect: the Liberals present Canada as an environmentally aware country, they willingly accept climate change commitments and declare climate targets would be met. They also claim the reduction of greenhouse gas emissions does not have to imperil the economic growth. On the other hand, in the areas where a bigger price is attached to environmentally friendly policies, Ottawa is reluctant to change a very selective approach of the olden days. For instance, fossil-fuel subsidies, which the Liberals had previously promised to remove over the "medium term," are included in the 2016 budget. According to a new pledge, they will be eradicated only by 2024. The carbon-emissions reduction goal that Canada adhered to at the COP21 is another example.

Ottawa, as discussed in this and in the previous chapter, agreed to cutting its emissions by 30 per cent by 2030. But this, as a matter of fact, is exactly the same target as under Harper (Gurney). Now, the Liberals claim the goal was well defined, it was just that Harper never had a plan to achieve it. In the campaign, however, they had called such levels an unsatisfactory minimum (Proudfoot).

The Liberals also, as discussed above, are following the footsteps of their predecessors and refuse to stop developing oil and gas infrastructure. In actuality, they are no less vocal supporters of constructing oil pipelines than the Harper government. Their intentions and motivations are also similar. Like the Conservatives, they believe Canada is an energy-resource powerhouse and as such should be able to use its natural wealth for the benefit of its economy. Thus, similarly to Harper's policies, they approve the extension of pipelines that would link Alberta's oilfields with the Pacific and Atlantic ports in Canada and the U.S. Such investments, as Trudeau once stated, "give traditional Canadian energy resources access to international markets." To that end, the Trudeau government has not only continued Harper's lobbying mission in the U.S. for the Keystone XL, but also, in November 2016, gave a formal approval to two more projects: Kinder Morgan's Trans Mountain pipeline, connecting Edmonton with Burnaby, British Columbia, and Enbridge's Line 3 pipeline from central Alberta to Manitoba and then to the U.S. Midwest. It is estimated in Ottawa that, when completed, the investments would at least double the capacity of the existing infrastructure, "generate billions of dollars in government revenue at all levels" and create thousands of new jobs (Trudeau, "Prime Minister Justin Trudeau's Pipeline"). The approval was issued in spite of the opposition from numerous environmental activists, some regional authorities, First Nations communities and scientists, but, most importantly, despite the negative impact of the projects on the natural environment. According to the assessment presented by the Environment and Climate Change Canada, a governmental department, each of the pipelines would contribute to "annual carbon pollution that would be equivalent to about five or six million cars on the roads" (De Souza, "Trudeau"). Should these forecasts be accurate, it will make it virtually impossible for Ottawa to meet its own climate change commitments. Currently, as many NGOs inform, including the Climate Action Network, Canada may not be on track to meet its Paris Accord promises, as it would require policies much more rigorous than those imposed anywhere in Canada today (Wilt, "Why").

Canadians, however, were reassured that the approval had been based "on rigorous debate, on science and on evidence" and that "a price on carbon and strong environmental protection in place" would neutralize the potential negative effects of the pipelines. Even if such is the case, it is still evident that the government's decision to approve the pipelines was guided mainly by economic motives. "There isn't a country in the world that would find billions of barrels of oil and leave it in the ground while there is a market for it," admitted Prime Minister Trudeau (Trudeau, "Prime Minister Justin Trudeau's Pipeline). On another occasion, he confessed that he "can't make a choice between what's good for the environment and what's good for the economy," and "can't shut down the oil sands tomorrow." At the same time, however, he acknowledged oil sands must be eventually "phased out" (qtd. in Austen and Krauss). But once the latter remark was met with angry reactions from the oil industry and Alberta politicians and regular voters, he backtracked on the comment, saying he "misspoke," "said something the way I shouldn't have said it." He assured he would "not run against Alberta" and the jobs provided by the oil industry (qtd. in Krugel, "Trudeau"). That was not, obviously, sending a clear and consistent message to the public about the pipelines. Because of the contradictory announcements Trudeau had made on oil sands, one author was tellingly asking in the title of his article whether Justin Trudeau was a "climate leader or charlatan?" (King). At one of the gatherings in Alberta, Trudeau was openly called "either a liar or confused, or both" by a man from the audience (Austen and Krauss).

There is every reason to believe that the fossil fuel sector will not suffer under Trudeau but rather that it will be further expanded. The Trudeau government already approved, despite criticism from scientists and climate experts from Canada, the U.S. and Australia (Kassam), the Pacific NorthWest LNG project, one of Canada's largest resource development projects. It includes building a natural gas pipeline and a liquefied natural gas facility near Prince Rupert in British Columbia. The project is designed to ship LNG to markets in Asia. LNG offers an opportunity for Canada's energy industry. The International Energy Agency projects the growth of the world demand for natural gas by 46 per cent by 2040, driven primarily by the rapidly expanding Asian economies. Canada, with around 20 LNG terminals planned on the West Coast, wants to become a player in the world market with access to those new markets where demand is growing (McMillan).

Constructing new infrastructure and extending the existing ones sends a clear signal that Canada is going to continue to rely on crude oil and gas and ship them across the southern border, but also that Canadians are seeking new markets for their fossil fuels. In the U.S., where the production of oil and shale gas is flourishing, demand for Canada's crude is relatively low; while the Canadian domestic market is too small. The pipelines are, thus, needed to make Canada's oil exportable to markets beyond North America. Should that happen, the oil production would most likely rise. It is doubtful if, in such circumstances, Canada would be able to meet the targets of its own carbon pricing scheme and fulfill the COP21 climate accord.

Obviously, Canada's energy strategy will be very much dependent on the dynamics of the market. With low prices, the big and costly development projects cannot make economic sense. But at the same time there is no other way than to develop energy resources in Canada in a responsible way. Canada has been an energy producing country and it will continue to be one for some decades to come (Bambury).

Although Trudeau tends to present himself as an advocate of a transition from fossil fuels to a clean energy economy, his environmental record does not necessarily entitle him to such claims. His government's approach to climate is highly selective, erratic and inconsistent. On the one hand, Trudeau declares his unequivocal support for curbing greenhouse gas emissions. On the other hand, he asserts that pipeline extensions are needed for economic growth which, in turn, will generate funds for environmental protection. Such an attitude lacks logic, climate experts claim. They compare it to practicing "a diet by eating a lot of ice cream" (de Trenqualye). It looks as though the policies of the Trudeau government on oil exploitation and pipelines have not changed radically since Harper. The economy still appears to prevail over environmental issues and, once facing a choice between cleaner air and job creation, or between being environmentally sustainable or economically advantaged, Ottawa chooses the latter. In fact, Stephen Harper had also stated that Canada needed to scale down its dependency on fossil fuels. He even signed an end-of-meeting statement at the G7 meeting in 2015, calling for an end to fossil-fuel use by the global economy by 2100 and reducing greenhouse-gas emissions by 2050 as much as 70 per cent from 2010 levels ("Think" 15). Harper's message thus was similar to Trudeau's – using fossil fuels in Canada would have to stop, but only at some point of time in the future. The difference between both prime ministers was the timeline of decarbonization – Stephen Harper believed that this would happen closer to 2100 than 2050. But Harper and Trudeau were similarly skeptical when it comes to imposing a burden and responsibilities to their commitments (Jaccard, Hein, and Vass 5).

The hardest test for Trudeau's climate policies, however, is yet to come and is related to Trump's presidency. Donald Trump has already announced further pipeline expansions and the U.S. withdrawal from the Paris climate deal. Also, his administration seems to have no plans of limiting the exploitation of resources in the Arctic or imposing carbon taxes or caps on emissions. Given that the economies of both countries are closely linked and, actually, Canada's economic well-being depends highly on the policies south of the border, Trump's reluctance to combat climate change may bring Canada's own environmental commitments to naught. As evidenced by history, when Canadian climate policies are incompatible with the American ones, Canada finds it extremely difficult to fulfill its own pledges and targets, and often retreats. Such was the case with the Kyoto Protocol: Ottawa had ratified the agreement, made certain commitments, but then found an excuse not to act because the U.S. had not joined the deal. Now, when Canada and the U.S. declare divergent approaches to climate issues, there is a risk that American policies will force Canada to backtrack on its own goals, including carbon price and capping emissions. Prof. Kathryn Harrison, an expert on climate, explains it as follows:

> It's much easier for Canada to do things to mitigate climate change if the U.S. is matching actions, because the Canadian and U.S. economies are so tightly integrated. We now know that's not going to be the case. If we impose a higher carbon price than the U.S., there will be pushback from the business community and some provinces that are concerned about competitiveness impacts. It will be a real challenge on the regulation of motor vehicles – which make up almost 30 per cent of Canada's greenhouse gas emissions – because the North American motor vehicle market is so integrated (qtd. in de Trenqualye).

The Trump administration is not interested in, not to say it is hostile to, discussing environmental issues or even recognizing climate change as a problem. It would be, therefore, naïve for Ottawa to expect a meaningful collaboration with the U.S. in the protection of the natural environment in the upcoming years. In bilateral relations, Washington, as Donald Trump's election campaign has already indicated, will most likely prioritize economic and security issues – such as: trade, growth, benefits, jobs, investments or border controls – over environmental ones. For Canada, that would mean combatting climate change alone in North America, which would considerably increase the costs of Canadian environmental policies. Certain sectors of the Canadian economy would inevitably suffer. Carbon caps or taxes, for instance, if imposed only in Canada, would put American manufacturing and industries at a competitive advantage. Would Canada be ready for such a sacrifice in order to fight climate change? To what extent are Canadians prepared to pay for environmental protection? Will environmental awareness eventually prevail over economic calculations in Canada's selective policy-making? This remains to be seen.

The economy

"Interest trumps values, when the economic well-being of Canadians is at stake," wrote John Ibbitson about the conduct of Canadian foreign policy. He suggested that values-based diplomacy prevails in Canada only where it does not entail major economic sacrifices ("The Big" 13-14). In other words, in Canada's selective and realistic approach to external affairs, whenever there is a conflict between interests and values in foreign policy, the latter rarely win. Ibbitson made these remarks about Harper's management of external affairs, although in the context of the present plans of pipeline expansions, his observations can be assumed to be as relevant for the Liberals as for the Conservatives.

Stephen Harper, when in power, was chastised by his adversaries for his government's economic policies. He was said to have "adopted a harsh tone" and was bashed for his preference of "hard power over soft power" (Bondy). He faced criticism for defining foreign policy objectives selectively and narrowly, in particular for making economic benefits and free trade top priorities of his foreign policy agenda and being careless about other dimensions of external affairs, such as environmental protection or peacekeeping.

Rhetorically, the Liberals have presented a diametrically different vision of foreign policy. Their policymaking was to be guided – as Stéphane Dion declared while presenting the Liberal foreign policy doctrine – more on convictions, responsibility, less on cold economic calculations, preachiness or uncompromising moralistic tones ("Stéphane"). Yet despite those declarations and many genuine divergences, some aspects of the Liberals' foreign policy have not changed remarkably since Harper's Conservatives lost power. In no other sphere is it more evident than in Canada's external economic relations, where Liberal and Conservative viewpoints are surprisingly similar. Both political camps, for instance, present a highly realistic approach to economic relations with the United States, being fully aware that the stability and good condition of the Canadian economy is mostly dependent on a deep and friendly relationship with the southern neighbour and that the unimpeded access to the American market is a key to Canada's economic wellbeing. To that end, the Conservatives and the Liberals alike have long promoted freedom, openness and expansion of bilateral trade, called for the removal of economic irritations and barriers between the two countries, especially in the sectors Canada has a vested interest to develop, and fought against American protectionist sentiments and initiatives.

Accordingly, both the Conservatives and the Liberals have made continuous efforts to ensure that security measures adopted by the U.S. after the 9/11 attacks do not impede the movement of people and commerce across Canada-U.S. border. The Trudeau government continues the policies favouring openness on the border, rejecting and tackling protective, and more frequently nationalistic, sentiments emerging in the U.S. Since they won the election, the Liberals have actively lobbied in Washington to convince the U.S. Congressmen to adopt a legislation that would speed up movement of goods and people through the Canada-U.S. border. Their efforts brought positive results in December 2016, when the American Congress passed the so-called preclearance bill, which allows for the construction of new pilot facilities and the extension of the existing sites for faster screening of travelers; the law also permits the U.S. customs officers to operate, carry weapons and interview travelers in Canada. All this is aimed at accelerating travel across the border. The law was generally met with a warm welcome in both countries as it ended a long process which had involved both the U.S. Democrats and Republicans as well as the Harper and Trudeau governments. The Canadian ambassador to the U.S. called the law "a win-win for enhanced security and prosperity on both sides of the border" (Panetta, "Canadian"). A similar bill is expected to be passed with broad support in Canada's House of Commons in spring 2017.

The Liberal administration, like their Conservative predecessors, have repeatedly warned the Americans that revising free trade agreements and raising border barriers such as taxes, increased duties, tariffs and customs fees or limitations on people and imports allowed to cross the border would have a damaging effect on the bilateral trading relationship. For Justin Trudeau, relations with the Obama administration were relatively unproblematic in terms of the economy and bilateral trade, climate change, refugee crisis. In all these areas Obama and Trudeau worked together as natural allies. Troubles for Canada – some call them "a major reset with Washington" (Blanchfield, "Trudeau") – started with the ascension of Donald Trump to prominence in the Republican Party and then to the U.S. presidency. Trump's "America-first" and anti-NAFTA announcements, articulated in the election campaign, were particularly disturbing for Ottawa. He called NAFTA – a free trade agreement between the U.S., Mexico and Canada, established in 1994 – "one of the worst economic deals ever made by our country or frankly any other country" and promised to start consultations with Canada and Mexico with the ultimate goal of either amending or abolishing NAFTA ("Donald Trump's Complete").

Anti-trade rhetoric is nothing new in the U.S. presidential election. In fact, it often resonates well among large swaths of both right and left-wing American voters, including anti-globalists, the unemployed or the factory workers in the U.S. Midwest. Hence it is often used by both Democratic and Republican candidates in the campaign trail. Skepticism towards NAFTA and other free trade deals, even promises of their renegotiations, had been expressed before Trump, among others, by Hillary Clinton or Barack Obama. The latter, in the 2008 campaign, even dubbed NAFTA a "mistake," "an unfair deal," and an agreement which was "devastating" the American economy (Solomon, "Is NAFTA").

With Trump, however, it looks as if it is much more than mere political opportunism, wrangling or simply saying "anything, anytime, anywhere" (Solomon, "Is NAFTA"). He seems to be a true believer in the damaging impact the present (NAFTA) and future free trade deals

(TPP) have or will have on America's economy. Trump appears to be truly convinced that "protection will lead to great prosperity and strength." In his inaugural address as president, he referred to the vision of "America First," which he had presented throughout the whole campaign. Without ever mentioning Canada or NAFTA, Trump declared a policy that was threatening Canadian vested interests. "For many decades, we've enriched foreign industry at the expense of American industry," he said, but "[f]rom this day forward, a new vision will govern our land. From this day forward, it's going to be only America first." In practice, it meant that – to use Trump's own words – "[e]very decision on trade, on taxes, on immigration, on foreign affairs will be made to [...] protect our borders from the ravages of other countries making our products, stealing our companies and destroying our jobs." Trump's "America first" vision was declared to be based on two "simple" principles: "buy American and hire American" (Trump, "Inaugural"). In more practical terms, Trump promised to review the U.S. bilateral trade partners, especially those running trade surpluses with the U.S., and to thoroughly revise the economic relationship with those who use foul and unfair trade practices. Given the ongoing softwood lumber dispute (discussed in Chapter 3) and the very fact that Canada's exports to the U.S. exceed imports by "about $34 billion to $45 billion," all the above declarations were received in Ottawa as particularly alarming, even though they were directed less against Canada than, for instance, China or Mexico, whom Trump had branded as the countries that "are killing us on trade," and with whom in fact the U.S. has much bigger trade deficits than with Canada (Markusoff).

Nonetheless, Trudeau took Trump's statements seriously and reacted promptly. In January 2017, several days before Trump's inauguration, he shuffled his cabinet so that trade pundits and skilled negotiators were elevated to more prominent governmental positions. One of the changes involved the appointment of Chrystia Freeland, a trade expert and an experienced negotiator of CETA, as Canada's foreign minister. These moves prove clearly that, with Trump in the White House, preserving access to the U.S. markets for Canadian producers and goods has become an issue of the highest priority in Canada's foreign affairs.

The overall Canadian strategy of tackling Trump's plan seems to be putting all hands available on deck, i.e. involving provincial premiers and other prominent politicians to reach out to Americans and lobby for Canada with the authorities there of both the federal and state levels, and start convincing Americans that an open and free trade relationship between the two countries is of crucial importance not only to Canada, but also for the economic well-being of particular American states and the U.S. as a whole. To that end, both prior to and after President Trump's inauguration, Canadian politicians of various regions and party colors, were making rounds in the U.S. states' capitals and toured Washington. Their message to the U.S. partners was along the same lines as the already quoted Trudeau's declaration made to the U.N. General Assembly – "We need to focus on what brings us together, not what divides us" (Trudeau, "Prime Minister Justin Trudeau's Address"). In bilateral contacts with Americans, thus, Canadian negotiators and politicians started to omit controversial and potentially antagonizing issues, such as refugees, immigration, transcontinental free trade, climate change or environmental protection. Instead, they have brought a sharper focus to matters where there is common ground and goals and to the areas where both countries could complement each other, specifically to natural resources and energy sphere (the aforementioned Keystone XL pipeline), the fate of middle class or jobs creation. As Evan Solomon put it, Canadian ministers and diplomats have repeated "the political mantra" that "35 U.S. states and nine million Americans depend on trade with Canada, that we don't have a sizable trade deficit with the U.S. or that Canadian workers are not paid less than U.S. workers." The key argument was, however, that "the U.S. and Canada are totally integrated and the U.S. will do damage to themselves if they hurt Canada" (Solomon, "Why Canada").

So far, it seems Trudeau's approach is wise, thoughtful and, most importantly, effective. As Jason Markusoff writes, "Canada at present sits on Donald Trump's nice list – or is, at least, far off his declared enemies list." Not a small achievement, given Trump's overwhelmingly protectionist rhetoric and the fact that Justin Trudeau is commonly perceived as an antithesis to almost everything Trump stands for. For the time being at least, Canadians have been reassured by Stephen Schwarzman, Trump's economic advisor who visited Canada in January 2017, that "Canada's held in very high regard," that the bilateral trade "is very much balanced and is a model for the way trade relations should be," and hence "that's not the kind of situation where you should be worried" (Markusoff). "Don't worry, be happy. It's not us, it's Mexico, right?" – as one columnist wrote in *Maclean's* (Solomon, "Why Canada").

The renegotiations of NAFTA are only about to start and their results can be hardly forecast at the moment. However, what is very likely, Mexico would become a target for a much more intensified anti-immigration and anti-free trade campaign in the U.S. than Canada.

What is, however, certain and evident in this whole U.S.-Canadian economic context is the fact that under Trudeau, just like under both his Conservative and Liberal predecessors, the highest priority is assigned to stable, mutually beneficial commercial relations with the U.S. Upon them, no doubt, Canada's well-being is mostly founded. The U.S. is Canada's largest trading partner, receiving three quarters of Canadian exports. Therefore, in Canada's highly selective foreign policy, whether conducted by the Liberals or Conservatives, the American aspects prevail over, not to say overshadow, all other dimensions. Trudeau's management of foreign affairs is no exception here. His agenda might in many ways be different from, even contradictory to, specific policies, initiatives or priorities of the incumbent U.S. president. In such circumstances, Ottawa would emphasize commonalities not divisions, would use its diplomatic skills and avoid confrontations – all this would be aimed at not putting bilateral relations, and at the same time Canada's economic and political security, at excessive risk. Canada, simply put, cannot risk alienating the U.S. And Justin Trudeau's politics is revolving exactly around this goal – he does not ignore the ideological gap that separates him from Trump, but he also does not expose it. Except, perhaps, for two incidents: first, when he congratulated the participants of women's marches in Canada – held in January 2017 in solidarity with women marching against the Trump presidency across the U.S. – on supporting women's rights and keeping his own government "inspired" (Gajanan); second, when he declared Canada's gates would remain open for refugees, including the citizens of the countries included in the aforementioned Trump's travel ban. Otherwise, Trudeau is treading rather cautiously, acting diplomatically, bearing in mind a famous quote from his father, which can serve as one of the best illustrations of the Canadian dilemma with the southern neighbour, and a very accurate portrayal of Canada's position in relation to the U.S.: "Living next to you is in some ways like sleeping with an elephant. No matter how friendly and even-tempered is the beast, if I can call it that, one is affected by every twitch and grunt" (qtd. in Thompson and Randall 250). Some diplomats and experts caution Trudeau Jr. not to forget these words and remember that as friendly as possible relations with the U.S. should always be Canada's foreign policy top priority, pursued, if necessary, at the expense of all other issues, including the relations with other countries. In other words, they advise Trudeau to run an even more selective and calculative foreign policy and, for instance, stop insisting that Mexico continues to form a part of NAFTA. In this context, it might be worth quoting Derek Burney, Canada's former ambassador to the U.S. and one of the major negotiators of NAFTA, who had this piece of advice for Trudeau: "We should not indulge in ridiculous posturing – like getting together with Mexico to defend our interests, when Canada has very different economic interests than Mexico. It is a fundamental error to conflate them" (qtd. in Solomon, "Why Canada"). It only remains to be seen whether – should the occasion arise – Canada would be ready and willing to sacrifice Mexico in order to boost its own economy and secure its interests. Such a policy would be the ultimate evidence that Canada fully deserves a brand of a "selective power."

But even without such proof, Canada's foreign policy behaviour can be easily classified as selective, i.e. highly selectively focused on the economy and profits. Obviously, the desire to keep friendly U.S.-Canada relations untouched is sincere in Ottawa and provincial capitals. But, at the same time, Trudeau's Canada is trying to make use of the uncertainty that surrounds the U.S. after the election of Donald Trump to its own advantage and economic benefits. Universities and university organizations, for instance, hope to attract more U.S. and international students alienated by or not admitted to the U.S. because of Trump's more restrictive immigration policies. Should this plan succeed, the income from tuition fees and the positive impact foreign students have on the economy and global links could partially compensate Canada for potential losses caused by the failure to negotiate the softwood lumber agreement and protective economic and immigration policies of the Trump administration. According to the CBC, which gained access to the research conducted for Global Affairs Canada, in 2014, "the combination of tuition, housing and discretionary spending by international students was greater than Canadian exports of softwood lumber, financial services or wheat. They contributed roughly as much to the economy as exports of automotive parts." This share can increase even more as Canadian universities, mostly from Ontario, have seen a significant rise of interest from international students. The number of American-only applications to the University of Toronto, for instance, almost doubled ("Could").

Time will show if this trend will persist and whether, in the long-term perspective, it will translate into economic profits for Canada. For the time being, the impression has been created that – as it was put in the *Economist* – "Canada is more open to foreign talent than the United States" ("Vancouver"). Another impression is that, among the wide selection of foreign policy areas, economy matters most. Not much difference compared to Harper's conduct of foreign affairs.

This is particularly visible in the fact that both the Liberals and the Conservatives fervently support Canada's participation in transcontinental, regional and bilateral free trade agreements, considering them as drivers for the Canadian economy and vital tools for diversifying Canadian trade and decreasing Canada's economic dependence on the U.S. Stephen Harper, admittedly, had outstanding achievements in this field, as discussed in Chapter 3. The Conservatives even claimed that had it not been for the Tory governments, Canada would have been a free-trade laggard. The Conservative Party of Canada's website declared the following:

> The Liberals claim to support free trade, and are happy to let our Conservative government do the hard work of finalizing this deal. But despite decades in power, the Liberals have almost no record on free-trade. Jean Chrétien is the only non-Conservative *ever* to conclude *any* free-trade agreements for Canada. Prime Minister Harper's Government has since improved half of the agreements concluded by Chrétien in order to bring them up to 21st century standards (Conservative Party of Canada, "Harper").

Even the Liberals seemed to acknowledge Harper's free-trade efficiency. In the campaign, Justin Trudeau promised to continue Harper's efforts and go on with signing free trade agreements and attract foreign investments in Canada. He declared, though, to do it in an even better way than his predecessor, by presenting more transparency in negotiating international trade deals, such as the Trans-Pacific Partnership or the Comprehensive Economic Trade Agreement with the European Union. He also promised to make trade deals a genuine driver for the Canadian economy, something he claimed Harper had failed to achieve. As Trudeau pointed out, despite finalizing numerous free trade agreements, Harper had "the worst rate of export growth of any prime minister since World War Two" ("Federal").

For Harper, and Trudeau alike, TPP and CETA definitely played a crucial role in stabilizing Canada's global economic posture and providing Canada's manufacturers steady and safe access to both transatlantic and transpacific markets. Canada's negotiations over the two agreements started under the Harper prime ministership and had they both succeeded, they would have granted Canada, as the Harper government estimated, "preferred access to more than 60% of the global marketplace and benefit every sector of the Canadian economy" (Conservative Party of Canada, "Harper").

Initially, the Harper government refused to join the talks over TPP, a free trade deal among a dozen of Pacific Rim countries, including Canada, that had been negotiated since 2006. Ottawa feared that the agreement would be too demanding when it came to the protection of intellectual property and would not serve the best interests of Canadian agriculture, especially of dairy and poultry producers. However, when the global economic crisis erupted in 2008 and the U.S. and Mexico joined the negotiations, the Harper government decided it was better for Canada to be a part of the deal. The negotiations led through a long and bumpy road, but they were completed on October 5, 2015, two weeks before the federal parliamentary election in Canada. The Harper government boasted that the agreement would provide Canadian producers admission to the "market of almost 800 million consumers with GDP of $28 trillion – over 14 times the size of Canada's economy," including giving the "access to new markets where we don't currently have free-trade agreements – like Japan, the world's 3rd largest economy." The Conservatives also argued that TPP would strengthen NAFTA, and that "every sector and region of Canada will benefit from the preferential access the TPP will create – lobster and salmon fishing, the wine industry, mining, manufacturing, financial services, forestry and agriculture" (Conservative Party of Canada, "Harper").

In the election campaign, Justin Trudeau was less enthusiastic about TPP than Stephen Harper. At first, Trudeau claimed he had to study the deal thoroughly and put it under review prior to making any definite decision over it ("New Zealand"). In January 2016, however, the Liberal government announced there was no room for renegotiations or Canadian veto and the decision was only a "yes" or "no" decision" about what had been negotiated for Canada by Harper (Marowits). A few days later, the Liberals declared their intention to sign the deal, which happened in

February 4, 2016, although they abstained from openly announcing they would support subsequent ratification. "Just as it is too soon to endorse the TPP, it is also too soon to close the door," stated, rather vaguely, Chrystia Freeland, International Trade Minister at the time (qtd. in Blatchford, "Canada Will"). At the moment of signing, the TPP was the biggest trade deal ever negotiated by Canada. Had it come into life, it would have covered almost 40 per cent of the global economy ("New Zealand"). But after Donald Trump's assumption of the presidential office in the U.S. it seems the TPP will not have a chance to take effect in the upcoming years. In his protectionist attitudes to trade, Trump campaigned against TPP with even more hostility than against NAFTA, and pledged to remove the U.S. from the deal immediately after winning the presidency ("Trump Sells"). He did as he promised. In his first decision as president, he signed an executive order officially withdrawing the U.S. from the TPP. In order for the TTP to come into force, at least six countries representing 85 per cent of the GDP of all 12 members have to ratify it. These requirements can be no longer met after the U.S. withdrawal (Shum). Thus, in order to survive, the TPP would now need to be renegotiated in a new formula – without the U.S. The Liberals have never rejected the TPP. Nor have they openly denounced Harper's negotiating accomplishments. But, admittedly, they have also not been as vocal and enthusiastic supporters of it as their Conservative predecessors. They rather chose to tread more warily over the issue, mostly because many Canadian voters had doubts about the agreement, less because they were TPP's opponents themselves. Their decision to sign the TPP seems to suggest they were supportive of the agreement, though, obviously, their stance towards TPP was less clear than the Conservative one.

But with CETA, another of Canada's landmark free trade deals, the Liberals and Conservatives were equally clear in their support. The negotiations had begun and ended under Harper. They started in 2009 and the text of the agreement was published in September 2014. In the 2015 campaign, the Conservatives presented the deal as one of their major economic achievements, which according to their estimates, "could increase Canada's income by $12 billion annually, equal to increasing the average Canadian family's annual income by $1,000." Once implemented, CETA and the TPP combined, the Conservatives argued, would make Canada a real trading nation. The ratification of CETA was left for 2015 and 2016 and both the EU and Canadian officials expected the deal to come into force by that time.

Instead of a smooth implementation, however, CETA faced fierce opposition in many parts of Europe, where it was met with large street protests. A complex ratification process (all EU member states, but also regional authorities in some countries, are required to ratify it separately in order to make it fully implemented) could not start. The opponents mostly feared that the agreement would open the EU market to Canadian GMO food and that Canada would flood Europe with its cheaper and less ecological beef and crops; that the mechanism of solving disputes between investors and states, known as the investor-state dispute settlement (ISDS) mechanism, adopted in CETA, would put big private companies and the banking sector in a privileged position, allowing them to sue governments for compensations if they found that the laws in a particular country were blocking them from making profits. The anti-CETA protesters simply believed that, as Mike Blanchfield put it, "big multinationals were intent on bulldozing the laws and regulations of sovereign countries in a broad range of areas including food safety, the environment and labour." There were also fears that some of these controversial provisions could be copied to the Transatlantic Trade and Investment Partnership (TTIP), a free trade deal project that was being negotiated at that time between the European Union and the U.S. and later dumped by the Trump administration. The opponents claimed that TTIP would have had an even more damaging impact on Europe given that the U.S. is a ten times larger economy than Canada. Most of these concerns were exaggerated – CETA does not allow for imports of GMO products to Europe, the ISDS mechanism has been amended, and Canada is only a 35-million country, which compared with 500-million EU makes it a too minor partner to be scared of the revolutionizing effect CETA might have on the EU. Nonetheless, the formal enforcement of CETA was blocked by certain European actors who hold veto power over CETA. At the last stage the deal was gridlocked by the opposition from Belgium's Wallonia, whose authorities feared that the influx of Canadian agricultural products – mainly beef and dairy – would put Walloon farmers at a disadvantage. Wallonia had to be appeased by the adoption of specific explanatory provisions addressing their doubts ("CETA Impasse").

All these ratification problems intensified in 2016, when Trudeau was already an occupant of the prime ministerial office in Ottawa.

Interestingly, despite repeated accusations in the campaign that Harper had commercialized Canada's foreign policy and made Canada look egoistic in global economic affairs, the Liberals seem to have put on the same shoes the Conservatives wore before and are as devoted and passionate defenders of CETA, or free trade in general, as their predecessors. Debating with the Europeans over CETA, the Liberals even resorted to the same narrative the Conservatives had used, presenting Canada as a progressive, open, pro-free trade country, whose visions "at a time when so many other countries are closing their doors, are saying they are not interested in foreign investment, are saying they are not interested in trade" – as Canada's international trade minister said – are built on a belief "in being open to the global economy" (qtd. in Banerjee). Canada's trade-friendly attitudes, the Liberals claim, are rooted in the country's history. "We have always been dependent on trade with the world. So an anti-trade argument really doesn't get very far in Canada from the get-go," argues Prime Minister Trudeau ("The Last"). By this he is in fact repeating, almost word by word, the argumentation of the Harper government, who claimed that "Canada has always been a trading nation. Our Conservative Government knows that trade creates jobs and fuels the economy" (Conservative Party of Canada, "Harper").

It is too early to predict whether the tactics of promoting an open-door, progressive economic agenda will pay off and work effectively with CETA. This has been partially successful so far. Canada's skillful, but also emotional (see: Wells, "Freeland"), approach to the negotiations with the EU paid off. After Wallonia withdrew its objections, CETA was formally signed on October 30, 2016. It will provisionally – i.e. without the investment protection and the investor-state dispute settlement system, but with most tariffs and duties lifted – enter into force once it has been ratified both by Canadian and the European parliaments (the former is expected to vote in February 2017). Trudeau asserted that the signing of CETA showed Canada's leadership and proved that Canada was "an example to the world of how we can move forward on trade deals that do genuinely benefit everyone" (qtd. in "Christie"). Yet for its full implementation, all EU member states must end their ratification procedures separately, which is highly likely to take years and, given the vast opposition in some countries, is not even certain to ever be completed (Waldie).

Regardless of the final result, the CETA issue, just like the TPP, makes one thing apparent – the Trudeau Liberals have as selective a taste in foreign policy as the Harper Conservatives. Similarly to their forerunners, they prioritize the economy. Stable and beneficial commercial relations with the largest global economies, based on openness and free trade, seem to occupy the highest position on the Liberal list of Canada's foreign policy priorities.

The Harper government, as was mentioned, was accused by its critics of the commercialization of Canada's foreign policy and of presenting an egocentric approach to global economic affairs by selfishly pursuing "national economic interests at the expense of the international" (Kelly). By thoroughly analyzing some aspects of Trudeau's economic policies, the same assertion can actually be made about the Liberals. Presenting the Liberal foreign policy doctrine, for instance, Stéphane Dion, Canada's foreign minister of the time, promised to base Canada's actions on what he dubbed "responsible conviction," which he declared "must not be confused with some sort of moral relativism [...] or the lack of strong convictions" ("Stéphane"). Yet, observing the Liberal government's stance in reference to various international issues, some of their policies and attitudes seem to be alarmingly close to moral relativism. John Robson of the *National Post* enumerates a few seemingly hypocritical and contradictory positions of the Trudeau government:

> It [the government] approves of sanctions on North Korea but not Iran. It wants to defeat Middle East terrorism with special forces but not bombs. It wants to sell arms to Saudi Arabia while disapproving of doing so, a decision reached after apparently weighing dead Yemeni civilians and oppressed Saudis against the political cost of lost Canadian jobs and an upset Saudi government. Dion's most recent justification for the Saudi sale – that if Canada doesn't provide the arms, someone else will – suggests neither responsibility nor conviction.

This leads Robson to the conclusion that Dion's entire rhetorical argumentation regarding responsibility and convictions in international affairs is in fact nothing more but "just a convenient means of justifying whatever actions the government should choose to take," and that actually Dion's declarations represent no political doctrine or logically defined and linked ideas "other than an eagerness to please." While Robson has a point when he observes that Trudeau's government is much keener than Harper's on satisfying Canadian voters and the international community with verbal declarations and big promises, he at the same time seems to underestimate the role profits and commercial interests play in the Liberal foreign policy agenda. Speaking more precisely, economic arguments appear to be crucial considerations for the Liberal government, overshadowing all others, before making ultimate decisions concerning foreign policy actions or inactions. Stéphane Dion, for example, explaining why Canada would not give up a contract on arms sales to the Saudis (discussed in Chapter 3), concluded under the Harper government, argued as follows:

> Cancelling this $15 billion contract could result in Canadian taxpayers having to pay costly penalties and damage the credibility of the Government of Canada's signature. This would have a ripple effect in an industry on which 70,000 jobs in Canada directly depend, including many veterans. At least two-thousand workers, primarily in London, Ontario, would be out of a job. Similar equipment would almost certainly be sold to Saudi Arabia by a company in another country. Riyadh does not care if the equipment comes from a factory in Lima, Ohio, or Stirling Heights, Michigan, rather than one in London, Ontario ("Stéphane").

Nonetheless, the deal can also be judged from a human rights perspective, as suggested by Lloyd Axworthy, who urged the government to review the transaction, calling it "immoral and unethical." However, the Trudeau Liberals framed the Saudi deal as a *fait accompli* and said that they could not alter it. They also said that they were "not aware of any evidence that combat vehicles exported to Riyadh in the past had been used to violate human rights" (Chase, "As Canada"). Definitely, the contract with Saudi Arabia included economic interests in a politically important region, as there was a possibility that the production would be moved to another country if Ottawa cancelled the deal (Chase and Fife, "Cancelling Saudi"). Furthermore, the termination of the transaction would negatively impact Canada's relations with Middle Eastern states, which could limit Canada's access to military facilities in the region. Furthermore, as it was argued by Craig Stone, Canada's reputation as a trusted country would be at stake, which would not serve well "for other business development, military and commercial, and opportunities around the world for trade" (qtd. in Chase, "As Canada").

Speaking of sanctions against the Iranian regime, Stéphane Dion also had economic concerns. "Canada's severing of ties with Iran had no positive consequences for anyone," he said and suggested that "unilateral sanctions maintained by Canada alone would be ineffective against Iran, and would have negative consequences for many Canadian families and businesses." He also claimed that severing diplomatic ties with Iran by Harper bore no fruit. In fact, it put Canada at an economic disadvantage to other countries. "Is it right to need to count on Italy to protect our interests in this country?" – Dion asked rhetorically. In his further statements he said that the Liberals "take no more joy than our conservative friends in keeping open channels with authoritarian regimes" and "would like to live in a world without weapons" or, more generally, "would like it if the world were made up of nothing but exemplary democracies." But responsible decision making "must take the real world into account," which is "highly imperfect, and to improve it we must engage in it with our eyes open, not withdraw from it" ("Stéphane").

Such declarations do not only prove that, as Robson suggests, there might be a fine line between the notion of "responsible conviction" and moral relativism the Liberal government so much rejects. They also make it evident that on Canada's foreign policy priority list national economic interests prevail over moral values, human rights concerns or climate issues. In this regard, the Liberals' list does not appear to be remarkably different from Harper's. Especially that, when it comes to political practice and real decisions, Dion's words have been put partly into life. Canada indeed did not cancel the arms sales deal with Saudi Arabia and is going to start deliveries of light-armored vehicles there after the Federal Court decided in January 2017 that the government's decision to export weapons to Saudi Arabia was legal (Harris, "Federal"). Also, the Liberal government, following the footsteps of its NATO allies, including the U.S., lifted sanctions on Iran (Tasker, "Iran"). Moreover, some of the foreign investment promotion and protection agreements that have so far been completed or entered into force under the Liberal rule, and are listed on the Global Affairs Canada's website, are deals with countries that have rather dubious human rights and democratic records. The list includes, among others, Cameroon, Senegal, Mali, and Côte d'Ivoire (Global Affairs of Canada, "Trade"). But the Liberal government also signaled that it might seek a free trade deal with China (Fife). Therefore, in this respect there seems to be very little – if any – difference between the Liberals and the Conservatives. The Liberals continue to focus relentlessly on free trade and investment deals with other countries and, continuing a very selective approach to foreign affairs, they prioritize the economy over other spheres of international relations.

Obviously, there is nothing incorrect or peculiar for a government to stand on guard of national commercial and trade interests. It is rather an entirely natural and expected behaviour. What may seem to be odd in the Liberals' conduct of foreign affairs, however, is rather their tendency to hide economic motives under the cover of the rhetoric that overexposes such issues as global peace and security, multilateralism, or responsibility and respect for human rights, openness, tolerance. Naturally, it is a part of a soft power use strategy. The Trudeau government is aware that the skillful use of soft power by Ottawa's diplomats and politicians and the positive opinions, impressions, perceptions and imaginations of Canada that are held abroad are crucially important tools that help achieve foreign policy goals and promote Canada's interests globally. As a matter of fact, the Liberal government in general, and Prime Minister Trudeau in particular, have already demonstrated their high skills in using soft power and creating a positive image of Canada. As a result, the world has again been gripped by Trudeaumania, bringing back to life the memories of Justin Trudeau's father, who also enjoyed a global celebrity status and whose photographs, like Justin's today, were massively published and commented around the world. Like Pierre Elliott in the past, Justin Trudeau is now being profiled in the media as a women's idol, a caring father and husband, animal lover, environmental activist, LGBTQ rights advocate, a sporty figure, even a pop culture star. But, as the *Economist* argues, "Mr Trudeau owes his celebrity to more than glamour." Indeed, he is far better than Stephen Harper – "a prickly Conservative, who in ten years as prime minister conducted an ideologically charged foreign policy" – in using soft power and rhetorical tools. "Mr Trudeau replaces a scowl with a smile," writes the *Economist* ("Canadian Foreign"). His Canada talks friendlier, looks kinder, and seems to be more willing to cooperate and contribute globally. Most importantly, however, for the progressives around the world, Justin Trudeau – and Canada, consequently – serves as "a happy contrast to what is happening in other rich countries, where anger about immigration helped bring about Britain's vote for Brexit,

Donald Trump's nomination and the rise of populist parties across Europe" ("The Last"). The liberally-oriented media portray Canada as an "example to the world," "a citadel of decency, tolerance and good sense." In the world of rising populisms, nationalisms and anti-immigrant sentiments, they write, "in an age of seductive extremes," "in this depressing company of wall-builders, door-slammers and drawbridge-raisers, Canada stands out as a heartening exception, [...] it remains reassuringly level-headed" ("Canada's Example"; Lawson).

Undoubtedly, the Trudeau government is seriously concerned about all the humanitarian and climate matters it raises on the occasion of various international debates and summits – i.e. the refugee crisis, global peace and security, women's equality, LGBTQ rights, sustainable development, rule of law, promotion of democracy, religious and individual freedoms, tolerance, tackling the greenhouse effect etc. But on the other hand, Trudeau recognizes that both Canada's international success and his own political well-being and popularity among voters are to the largest extent dependent on Canada's global economic achievements – on creating jobs, on defending the interests of Canadian entrepreneurs, on providing commercial opportunities for Canadian exporters, on guaranteeing trade surpluses etc. Since the rhetoric is frequently different from the actual behaviour and decisions, as shown in this chapter, Trudeau's use of soft power, his efficiency in building positive images, his ability of speaking nicely, and his indisputable personal charisma – these are all means intended to help Ottawa achieve economic goals. This also means that those skills can often be applied to convey, in a delicate manner, a message to the outside world that Canada would avoid or postpone certain costly engagements or decisions (see: contribution to peacekeeping), or that it would continue pursuing certain profitable initiatives, despite the fact that they contradict earlier commitments (the expansion of oil infrastructure). Economic calculations, based on a simple rule that more profits should be incurred than losses suffered, are still a key factor determining Canada's foreign policy decisions and actions.

Conclusion

This book is published in 2017, a year that marks sesquicentennial anniversary of Canada's becoming a self-governing political entity. The anniversary is a reminder of a 150-year long evolution of Canada's international positions and roles. Throughout that period, Canada has gone through a long path of development: from a dominion whose external affairs were controlled by London, to an increasingly autonomous actor on the international stage after the First World War, then a key member of the Allied coalition during the Second World War and a self-defined middle power during the Cold War, to the position that we call a selective power, that is a country that has a capability to influence a global agenda in certain areas. Generally speaking, over time, Canada's rise in international affairs has been marked by its growing assertiveness resulting from an increased self-identity on the international stage and more precisely defined and premeditated goals and interests. This has helped Canada gain the global significance, achieve more meaningful status, even become a 'trend-setter' in certain periods and sectors of international relations.

There has been a multitude of theories formulated to describe and determine Canada's international position. The most significant ones are discussed in the chapters above. Our opinion is that they no longer can be treated as relevant depictions of Canada's global roles and stature. The classifications of Canada, as either a satellite or a foremost power, or even a middle power, seem to be too archaic nowadays, as they do not assume a sufficiently realistic approach to the changes that have occurred in the international system since the end of the Cold War and to the new ways, venues, and attitudes that subsequent Canadian governments have chosen to pursue Canada's interest and international goals. Some of these theories, a middle-power framework in particular, perceive Canada's foreign policy idealistically, focusing on Canada as an altruistic helpful-fixer of global problems, whose actions are primarily based on soft power use and who is either incapable or unwilling to use its hard power potential.

In our attempts to define Canada's global place, position and capacity, we were looking for permanent elements in Canadian foreign policy conduct. Thus, we focused on those long-term strategies or essential foreign policy objectives that are independent from temporary rhetoric or verbal declarations, which change every time a new government is elected and are not necessarily followed by political actions or decisions. While words, statements and gestures are important as they create a certain atmosphere, which may have a cooling and helpful impact on external affairs practice, they can also serve as a cover for genuine motivations and intentions. Therefore, our research is primarily based on the analysis of political practice, as we concentrate on decisions and their outcomes. Such an approach may appear immensely realistic, but at the same time, we hope, it helps shed more light on the pragmatic aspects of Canadian foreign policy and demythologize idealistic visions of Canada as a participant of the global system that is inspired by mostly unselfish motivations.

A closer examination of Canada's post-Cold War international behavior, in particular Stephen Harper's and Justin Trudeau's conducts of external affairs, leads us to the conclusion that Canada's foreign policy can be characterized as increasingly inward-looking, hard-interest based, rational, highly realistic and selective. This, in turn, drives us to redefine Canada's position in the international system and offer a new, selective-power perspective.

In our reasoning, Canada falls into a category of a selective power based on five premises:

Firstly, Canada's foreign policy is heavily economy-oriented. Economic arguments, calculations of losses and profits, appear to be crucial considerations for governments of either party color, determining ultimate foreign policy decisions. Stable commercial relations with the U.S. are of particular importance. In the highly realistic approach to economic relations, the strength and the good condition of the Canadian economy is mostly dependent on the unimpeded access to the American market, which is a guarantor of Canada's economic well-being. However, a pragmatic and future-oriented approach to economic international policy requires Canada's participation in various types of free trade deals and foreign investment agreements with other partners than the U.S. in order to decrease Canada's trade dependence on the southern neighbour, diversify its trade, and enhance its economic security. Canadian economic successes – Canada went through the 2007-2008 financial crisis relatively untouched – and its high positions in international economic rankings are often presented by Canadian politicians, and are recognized abroad, as evidences of Canadian effective and skillful economic management.

Discussing the economy, Canada's comparative advantage has been built on the abundance of natural resources, especially energy resources, in particular fossil fuels. They are vital to Canada both as the sources of Canada's economic wealth, which Canadians are unwilling to stop exploiting, and as the determinants of the roles Canada intends to play in a resource-short world, which is that of an energy-resource powerhouse and a stable commodity supplier. Adopting such roles means that Canada must constantly balance between a desire to grant its energy resources access to international markets and fulfilling international environmental obligations. In practice it means that Canada needs to address environmental issues selectively, tackling climate change in such a way that neither imperils the use of its natural wealth for the benefit of its economy nor puts Canadian businesses at a disadvantage.

Obviously, foreign policy in practice is always a balance between interests and values, between ideals on one side and realpolitik and economic gains on the other. Having said that, we do not intend to suggest that Canada abstains from promoting universal values globally. As a matter of fact, Ottawa has long been one of the most devoted promoters of democracy and fervent defenders of human rights. However, we observe that Canadian leaders have become increasingly pragmatic and flexible, less dogmatic and more economy-motivated, in terms of how they adjust their ideals to the real world.

Also, Ottawa pursues a limited version of value-based and morally justified approach. Rhetorically, all governments preach the importance of such values as democratization, defence of gay rights or other human rights, but at the same time the methods and venues used for that purpose reflect a deliberate and carefully crafted choice.

Secondly, we interpret Canadian behaviour towards international, or more broadly, multilateral institutions as a selective approach. In general, a restraint towards some of the multilateral institutions in Canada flows out of the need to channel its resources and stay involved only in those fora that are perceived as effective, efficient and profitable at a particular period of time. In other words, Ottawa seems to depart from the conviction that it needs to be highly active at every possible multilateral institution and rather tends to concentrate on a limited number of international venues by making a deliberate, selective choice. For us, this strengthens Canada's features of a selective power.

Thirdly, Canada presents a highly pragmatic approach to its international military and security obligations. Ottawa favours participation in initiatives led by organizations that are perceived as resourceful, operative, influential and like-minded, for instance NATO or G7. Foreign policy is generally based on the primacy of effectiveness and oriented towards achieving results, sometimes even at the expense of the quality of the decision-making process. However, the scope of Canada's engagement is always dependent on the calculations of losses and profits. Where it is deemed beneficial for its security interests or prestige, Canada eagerly takes part in military missions aimed against the biggest global threats, as it was in Afghanistan or Libya. But also when the opportunity arises to avoid or postpone some expenditures, Canada readily uses it. Canada's low spending on the military and defence, well below the NATO's 2 per cent of GDP threshold, is the best example. On the other hand, Canada reluctantly involves itself in the projects which are managed by multilateral organizations and which are long-term, cannot bring immediate results and expose Canada to risk and financial costs. For instance, Canada has considerably limited its participation in U.N.-led peacekeeping missions.

Fourthly, Canadian widely praised immigration and refugee programs are also based on carefully defined and highly pragmatic criteria. Basic policies in that regard have not changed for decades. The very idea of the points system upon which Canada's immigration system is founded is selective as it favours immigrants who can easily integrate, can contribute to Canada's economy and would not be a burden for Canadian taxpayers. Also, the refugees Canada accepts in large numbers are cautiously screened and preference is given to specific groups from specific countries.

Last but not least, what has been a permanent feature of Canada as a selective power is a skillful and conscious use of soft power and rhetorical tools, which are applied to serve strictly and clearly defined purposes.

This is particularly evident under the Trudeau government, which uses an amicable rhetoric both to achieve economic and political goals (like, for example, developing trade relations and attracting foreign investments), and to create a positive image of Canada as a country that is approachable, sympathetic, and ready to collaborate and work constructively for the benefit of the international system. Among the roles Canada aspires to play are those of a stable and reliable provider of natural resources, especially energy resources, and a promoter of a free market approach.

Having said all the above, it must be stated clearly that Canada in its selective approach to foreign affairs, i.e. in the pursuit of its economic and political security interests, is restricted by the dependence on the United States. In every decision it makes, in almost every step it takes, Canada cannot risk alienating the U.S. and endangering bilateral relations. That applies to almost every sphere of Canada's international activity, be it economic affairs, immigration and refugee policies, or environmental issues. Given Canada's geopolitical position, stable relations with the United States will for a long time remain the top priority in the Canadian foreign policy agenda. The selective power theory, in our opinion, aptly describes Canada's place on the contemporary international scene. It apprehends the fact that Canada has a potential to play a leadership role in particular spheres of external affairs and that, in fact, Ottawa is able to make a global difference, especially that Canada, even when pursuing its own interests, usually acts globally without harming or impeding other states.

Bibliography

Documents

"A Climate Change Plan for the Purposes of the Kyoto Protocol Implementation Act – 2007." *Environment Canada*. 2012. Web. 12 Jan. 2017.

Arctic Council. "Agreement on Cooperation on Aeronautical and Maritime Search and Rescue in the Arctic." 2011. Web. 2 Mar. 2012.

Alberta Energy Regulator. "ST98-2015: Alberta's Energy Reserves 2014 and Supply/Demand Outlook 2015-2024." 2015. Web. 2 Nov. 2016.

Foreign Affairs Canada. "Ambassador of Canada Visits Tibet." 2013. Web. 2 Apr. 2016.

"Annexation Manifesto" [Oct. 11, 1849]. *Canadahistory.com*. Web. 10 Mar. 2014.

Arctic Council. "The Ilulissat Declaration." 2008. Web. 2 Mar. 2012.

---. "Thematic Articles Highlighting Arctic Council Accomplishments under the Canadian Chairmanship." 2015. Web. 4 May 2016.

Baird, John. "Speech to the United Nations: Full Text of Speech Delivered at the UN October 1st, 2012." *Huffington Post*. 2012. Web. 1 June 2014.

Canada (Citizenship and Immigration) v Ishaq, 2015 FCA 194.

"Canada and China Broaden Strategic Partnership." *Office of the Prime Minister*. 2010. Web. 3 Oct. 2013.

"Canada's INDC Submission to the UNFCCC." *United Nations*. 2015. Web. 4 July 2016.

Canadian Doctors for Refugee Care v. Canada (Attorney general), 2014 FC 651.

Cannon, Lawrence. "Notes for an Address by the Honourable Lawrence Cannon, Minister of Foreign Affairs, on Canada's Arctic Foreign Policy." *Foreign Affairs Canada*. 2009. Web. 3 Oct. 2011.

Citizenship and Immigration Canada. "#WelcomeRefugees: Key Figures." 2017. Web. 30 Jan. 2017.

---. "Guide to the Private Sponsorship of Refugees Program – 2. Private sponsorship of refugees program." 2016. Web. 30 Jan. 2017.

Conservative Party of Canada. "Harper Announces Successful Conclusion of Trans-Pacific Partnership Negotiations." 5 Oct. 2015. Web. 27 Jan. 2017.

---. "Stand up for Canada: Conservative Party of Canada Federal Election Platform 2006." 2006. Web. 21 Jan. 2017.

Council on Foreign Relations. "International Commission on Intervention and State Sovereignty: Responsibility to Protect Report." 2001. Web. 8 May 2015.

"Donald Trump's complete convention speech, annotated." *Los Angeles Times*. 21 July 2016. Web. 23 Jan. 2017.

Food and Agriculture Organization. "Food and Agricultural Commodities Production/Countries by Commodity." 2015. Web. 26 July 2016.

---. "Canada-China Economic Complementarities Study." 2013. Web. 4 May 2015.

---. "Statement on Sentencing of Law Professor Xu Zhiyong." 2014. Web. 3 May 2016.

---. "The Responsibility to Protect: Report of the International Commission on Intervention and State Sovereignty." 2001. Web. 4 May 2015.

Foreign Affairs, Trade and Development. "Where We Work in International Development." 2014. Web. 20 Dec. 2015.

Freedom House. "Freedom in the World 2016: Saudi Arabia." 2017. Web. 2 Feb. 2017.

Global Affairs Canada. "Evaluation of the Office of Religious Freedom." 2016. Web. 4 Dec. 2016.

---. "Trade and investment agreements." 2016. Web. 27 Jan. 2017.

Foreign Affairs, Trade and Development Canada. "Global Markets Action Plan: The Blueprint for Creating Jobs and Opportunities for Canadians through Trade." 2013. Web. 4 June 2016.

Government of Canada. "A Role of Pride and Influence in the World. Canada's International Policy Statement." 2005. Web. 2 Mar. 2011.

---. "Canada and the World." 1995. Web. 3 Apr. 2011.

---. "Canada at the 21st Conference of the Parties." 15 Dec. 2015. Web. 20 Jan. 2017.

---. "Statement on Canada's Arctic Foreign Policy. Exercising Sovereignty and Promoting Canada's Northern Strategy Abroad." 2010. Web. 3 Apr. 2011.

---. "The Northern Dimension of Canada's Foreign Policy." 2000. Web. 3 Apr. 2011.

Harper, Stephen. "Address by the Prime Minister at the Canada-UK Chamber of Commerce." 2006. Web. 3 Feb. 2016.

---. "Address by the Prime Minister to the Canadian Armed Forces in Afghanistan." 2006. Web. 3 Feb. 2016.

---. "Harper Election Platform." 2006. Web. 3 Feb. 2016.

---. "Harper Stands Up for Arctic Sovereignty. Address by the Hon. Stephen Harper, P.C., M.P. Leader of the Conservative Party of Canada." 2005. Web. 3 Feb. 2016.

---. "Notes for an Address by the Right Honourable Stephen Harper, Prime Minister of Canada to the APEC Business Summit." 2007. Web. 3 Feb. 2016.

---. "PM Delivers Remarks on the Establishment of the Office of Religious Freedom." 2013. Web. 3 Feb. 2016.

---. "Prime Minister Harper Highlights Canada's Role on the World Stage." 2010. Web. 3 Feb. 2016.

---. "Prime Minister Stephen Harper Announces New Arctic Offshore Patrol Ships." 2007. Web. 3 Feb. 2016.

---. "Statement by the Prime Minister of Canada in Cartagena, Colombia." 2012. Web. 3 Feb. 2016.

---. "Statement by the Prime Minister of Canada on Foreign Investment." 2012. Web. 3 Feb. 2016.

---. "Statement Made by Prime Minister Stephen Harper at the World Economic Forum." *Global News*. 2012. Web. 3 Feb. 2016.

---. "Statement by the Prime Minister of Canada at the 2010 World Economic Forum." 2010. Web. 3 Feb. 2016.

---. "Text of Harper's Speech: The Prepared Text of Prime Minister Stephen Harper's Address to the United Nations General Assembly on Thursday." *Globe and Mail*. 2006. Web. 12 Oct. 2011.

---. "The 2007 Speech from the Throne." 2007. Web. 3 Feb. 2016.

---. "The 2008 Speech from the Throne." 2008. Web. 3 Feb. 2016.

---. "The 2010 Speech from the Throne." 2010. Web. 3 Feb. 2016.

---. "The 2011 Speech from the Throne." 2011. Web. 3 Feb. 2016.

---. "The 2013 Speech from the Throne." 2013. Web. 3 Feb. 2016.

---. "The Call of the North." 2006. Web. 3 Feb. 2016.

---. "The Special Relationship between Israel and Canada." *National Post*. 21 Jan. 2014. Web. 3 Feb. 2016.

Indian and Northern Affairs Canada. "Canada's Northern Strategy. Our North, Our Heritage, Our Future." 2009. Web. 2 May 2012.

International Energy Agency. "Energy Policies of IEA Countries: 2015 Review Canada." 2015. Web. 5 June 2016.

International Hydropower Association. "Canada." Aug. 2015. Web. 26 July 2016.

International Monetary Fund. "World Economic Outlook Database: Report for Selected Countries and Subjects." Apr. 2016. Web. 15 June 2016.

"Joint statement by the Prime Minister of Canada and the President of the United States on softwood lumber." *Prime Minister of Canada*. 29 June 2016. Web. 21 Jan. 2017.

Kenney, Jason. "Speaking notes for The Honourable Jason Kenney, P.C., M.P. Minister of Citizenship, Immigration and Multiculturalism. Immigration, Refugees and Citizenship Canada." 16 Feb. 2012. Web. 28 Jan. 2017.

Liberal Party of Canada. "Real Change: A New Plan for a Strong Middle Class." 2015. Web. 15 Jan. 2017.

Marshall, Katherine. "How Canada Compares in the G8." *Statistics Canada*. 2005. Web. 21 Jan. 2017.

"Muskoka Declaration: Recovery and New Beginnings G8 Summit, 25-26 June 2010." 2010. Web. 6 July 2016.

National Defence and the Canadian Armed Forces. "Operations in the North." 2017. Web. 2 Jan. 2017.

National Defence Canada. "Canada First: Defence Strategy." 2008. Web. 2 Oct. 2011.

---. "Minister Sajjan Reaffirms Peace Operations Pledge at UN Defence Ministerial." 8 Sep. 2016. Web. 24 Jan. 2017.

National Energy Board. "2012 – Estimated Production of Canadian Crude Oil and Equivalent." 2012. Web. 2 Feb. 2017.

---. "2014 Natural Gas Exports and Imports Summary." June 2016. Web. 14 June 2016.

---. "2015 Oil Exports and Imports Summary." 2017. Web. 2 Feb. 2017.

---. "Canada's Energy Future 2013 – Energy Supply and Demand Projections to 2035 – An Energy Market Assessment." 2013. Web. 4 May 2015.

---. "Crude Oil Exports – Summary by Type and Destination – Volume (m³/d) – From 2016-01 To 2016-03." 2016. Web. 14 June 2016.

---. "Reasons for Decision: TransCanada Keystone Pipeline GP Ltd., OH-1-2009." Mar. 2010. Web. 25 Jan. 2017.

Natural Resources Canada. "Exploration and Mining in Canada: An Investor's Brief." Feb. 2016. Web. 26 July 2016.

North Atlantic Treaty Organization. "The North Atlantic Treaty." 2016. Web. 28 Sept. 2016.

Organisation for Economic Cooperation and Development. "Canada Development Assistance Committee (DAC) Peer Review 2012." 2012. Web. 20 Oct. 2016.

---. "DAC Member Profile: Canada." 2016. Web. 20 Oct. 2016.

---. *Education at a Glance 2013: OECD Indicators.* Paris: OECD Publishing, 2013. Web. 26 July 2016.

---. *Education at a Glance 2016: OECD Indicators.* Paris: OECD Publishing, 2016. Web. 26 Feb. 2017

---. "Total Flows by Donor (ODA+OOF+Private) [DAC1]: Open Data - Total ODA by Type of Aid [DAC1]." 2016. Web. 15 July 2016.

Statistics Canada. "Canada's Population Estimates: Age and Sex, July 1, 2015." Sept. 2015. Web. 26 July 2016.

---. "Canada's Population Estimates: Age and Sex, July 1, 2016." Sept. 2016. Web. 31 Jan. 2017.

---. "Figure 1 Population Growth Rate (in Percentage) of the G8 Countries, 2001 to 2006 and 2006 to 2011." 2015. Web. 20 Jan. 2017.

---. "Immigration and Ethnocultural Diversity in Canada." 15 Sep. 2016. Web. 26 Jan. 2017.

---. "International investment position, Canadian direct investment abroad and foreign direct investment in Canada, by North American Industry Classification System (NAICS) and region." 20. Feb. 2017. Web. 24 Feb. 2017.

---. "Population Growth: Migratory Increase Overtakes Natural Increase." 28 Sep. 2016. Web. 31 Jan. 2017.

---. "Report – Trade Data Online – China – Canadian Trade Balances." 2016. Web. 4 Feb. 2017.

---. "Table: Merchandise trade: Canada's Top 10 Principal Trading Partners – Seasonally Adjusted, Current Dollars." Web. 14 June 2016.

Strengthening Canadian Citizenship Act, [Bill C-24]. 2014. Web. 29 Jan. 2017.

Trudeau, Justin. "Diversity is Canada's Strength: Address by the Right Honourable Justin Trudeau, Prime Minister of Canada." 2015. Web. 31 Jan. 2017.

---. "Minister of Indigenous and Northern Affairs Mandate Letter." 2015. Web. 27 Jan. 2017.

---. "Prime Minister Justin Trudeau's Address to the 71st Session of the United Nations General Assembly." 20 Sep. 2016. Web. 24 Jan. 2017.

---. "Prime Minister Justin Trudeau delivers a speech on pricing carbon pollution." 3 Oct. 2016. Web. 31 Jan. 2017.

---. "Prime Minister Justin Trudeau's Pipeline Announcement." 30 Nov. 2016. Web. 31 Jan. 2017.

---. "Statement by Justin Trudeau Regarding the Extended Mission in Iraq and Syria." 24 Mar. 2015. Web. 29 Jan. 2017.

---. "Statement by the Prime Minister of Canada on the Keystone XL pipeline." 6 Nov. 2015. Web. 31 Jan. 2017.

Trump, Donald. "Inaugural address: Trump's full speech." *CNN*. 21 Jan. 2017. Web. 27 Jan. 2017.

U.S. Department of State. "Record of Decision and National Interest Determination: TransCanada Keystone Pipeline, L.P. Application of Presidential Permit." 3 Nov. 2015. Web. 25 Jan. 2017.

U.S. Environmental Protection Agency. "Comment Letter." 2 Feb. 2015. Web. 25 Jan 2017.

U.S. White House. "Memorandum for the Secretary of State, the Secretary of the Army, the Secretary of the Interior: Construction of the Keystone XL Pipeline." 24 Jan. 2017. Web. 30 Jan. 2017.

---. "Statement by the President on the Keystone XL Pipeline." 6 Nov. 2015. Web. 31 Jan. 2017.

---. "United States-Canada Beyond the Border: A Shared Vision for Perimeter Security and Economic Competitiveness: Action Plan." Dec. 2011. Web. 21 Jan. 2017.

---. "U.S.-Canada Joint Statement on Climate, Energy, and Arctic Leadership." 10 Mar. 2016. Web. 30 Jan. 2017.

U.S. International Trade Commission. "USITC Votes to Continue Investigations on Softwood Lumber Products from Canada." 6 Jan. 2017. Web. 21 Jan. 2017.

United Nations Association in Canada. "The Canadian Contribution to United Nations Peacekeeping." 2007. Web. 20 May 2016.

United Nations High Commissioner for Refugees. "Global Refugee Sponsorship Initiative promotes Canada's private refugee sponsorship model." 2016. Web. 30 Jan. 2017.

United Nations Development Programme. "Canada: Briefing Note for Countries on the 2015 Human Development Report." 2015. Web. 20 Jan. 2017.

United Nations Peacekeeping. "Troop and police contributors archive (1990-2016)". 2016. Web. 22 Jan. 2017.

United Nations. "Background for International Day for the Preservation of the Ozone Layer – 16 Sept." n.d. Web. 3 Jan. 2017.

---. "Charter of the United Nations." n.d. Web. 24 June 2016.

---. "Human Development Report 2015: Work for Human Development." 2016. Web. 26 July 2016.

---. "Ranking of Military and Police Contributions to UN Operations." 2015. Web. 3 Jan. 2017.

---. "Top Ten Providers of Assessed Contributions to United Nations Budgets and of Voluntary Contributions to United Nations Funds, Programmes and Agencies, Including the Standing Peacebuilding Fund." 2006. Web. 3 Jan. 2017.

United Nations Environment Programme. "Canada to Host World Environment
    Day in 2017." 21 Sep. 2016. Web. 24 Jan. 2017.
United States Census of Bureau. "QuickFacts: United States." 2016. Web.
    15 June 2016.
United States Energy Information Administration. "International." 2015. Web.
    26 July 2016.
---. "International Energy Outlook 2016." 2016. Web. 12 Dec. 2016.
---. "U.S. Imports from Canada of Crude Oil and Petroleum Products." 2017.
    Web. 3 Mar. 2017.
World Bank. "Canada – Military Expenditure (% of GDP)." 2017. Web. 1 Feb.
    2017.
---. "Canada – Central government debt, total (% of GDP)." 2017. Web. 1 Feb.
    2017.
Zaretskaya, Victoria. "As Japan and South Korea Import Less LNG, Other Asian
    Countries Begin to Import More." *U.S. Energy Information Administration.*
    2016. Web. 3 Jan. 2017.

Books and Book Chapters

Audet, François, and Olga Navarro-Flores. "The Management of Canadian
    Development Assistance: Ideology, Electoral Politics or Public Interest?"
    Rethinking Canadian Aid. Eds. Stephen Brown, Molly den Heyer, David
    R. Black. Ottawa: University of Ottawa Press, 2014. 179-194. Print.
Blanchfield, Mike. *Swingback: Getting Along in the World with Harper and
    Trudeau.* Montreal: McGill-Queen's University Press, 2017. Print.
Bratt, Duane. "Stephen Harper and the Transformation of Canadian Foreign
    Policy." *Europa World Year Book.* 2017. 486-495. Print.
---. *The Politics of CANDU Export.* Toronto: Toronto University Press, 2006.
    Print.
Brebner, John Bartlet. *North Atlantic Triangle: The Interplay of Canada, the
    United States and Great Britain.* New York: Columbia University Press, 1958.
    Print.
Brewster, Murray. "The Strange Voyage: Stephen Harper on Defence."
    The Harper Factor. Eds. Jennifer Ditchburn, Graham Fox. Montreal–
    –Kingston–London–Chicago: McGill-Queen's University Press, 2016. 117-
    133. Print.
Bricker, Darrell, and John Ibbitson. *The Big Shift: The Seismic Change in
    Canadian Politics, Business, and Culture and what it Means for Our Future.*
    Toronto: Harper Collins Publishers, 2013. Print.

Brimelow, Peter. *The Patriot Game: Canada and the Canadian Question Revisited.* Toronto: Key Porter Books, 1988. Print.

Brooks, Stephen. *Canadian Democracy.* Don Mills, ON: Oxford University Press, 2012. Print.

Brown, Robert Craig. *Canada's National Policy, 1883-1900.* Princeton, NJ: Princeton University Press, 1964. Print.

Brown, Stephen. "Aid Effectiveness and the Framing of New Canadian Aid Initiatives." *Readings in Canadian Foreign Policy: Classic Debates and New Ideas.* Eds. Duane Bratt, Christopher J. Kukucha. 3rd edition. Don Mills, ON: Oxford University Press, 2015. Print.

Burney, Derek H., and Fen Osler Hampson. *Brave New Canada: Meeting the Challenge of a Changing World.* Montreal–Kingston: McGill-Queen's University Press, 2014. Print.

Buteux, Paul. "NATO and the Evolution of Canadian Defence and Foreign Policy." *Canada's International Security Policy.* Eds. David B. Dewitt, David Leyton-Brown. Scarborough: Prentice Hall Canada, 1995. 153-170. Print.

Byers, Michael. *Who Owns the Arctic?: Understanding Sovereignty Disputes in the North.* Vancouver: Douglas & McIntyre, 2010. Print.

Canada's Foreign and Security Policy. Soft and Hard Strategies of a Middle Power. Eds. Nikola Hynek, David Bosold. Don Mills, ON: Oxford University Press, 2010. Print.

Chambers, Tom. *Canadian Politics: An Introduction.* Toronto: Thompson Educational Publishing, 1996. Print.

Chapin, Paul. *Security in an Uncertain World: A Canadian Perspective on NATO's New Strategic Concept.* Ottawa: Canadian Defence and Foreign Affairs Institute, 2010. Print.

Clark, Joe. *How We Lead: Canada in a Century of Change.* Toronto: Random House Canada, 2013. Print.

Coates, Ken, et al. *Arctic Front. Defending Canada in the Far North.* Toronto: Thomas Allen & Son, 2008. Print.

Cohen, Andrew. *While Canada Slept: How We Lost Our place in the World.* Toronto: McClelland & Stewart, 2003. Print.

Cooper, Andrew F. "Niche Diplomacy: A Conceptual Overview." *Niche Diplomacy: Middle Powers after the Cold War.* Ed. Andrew F. Cooper. New York: St. Martin's Press, 1997. 1-24. Print.

Creighton, Donald. *Canada's First Century.* Toronto: Macmillan of Canada, 1970. Print.

Dawson, Laura. "Canadian Trade and Investment Policy under the Harper Government." *The Harper Factor.* Eds. Jennifer Ditchburn, Graham Fox.

Montreal–Kingston–London–Chicago: McGill-Queen's University Press, 2016. 160-176. Print.

Donaldson, Gordon. *The Prime Ministers of Canada.* Toronto: Doubleday Canada Ltd., 1997. Print.

Doxey, Margaret. "Canada and the Commonwealth." *Making a Difference? Canada's Foreign Policy in a Changing World.* Eds. John English, Norman Hillmer. Toronto: Lester Publishing Ltd., 1992. 34-53. Print.

Dyck, Rand. *Canadian Politics: Critical Approaches.* Scarborough: Nelson, Thomson Canada Ltd., 2004. Print.

Elliot-Meisel, Elizabeth R.B. "A Grand and Glorious Thing... the Team of Mackenzie and Roosevelt." *Franklin D. Roosevelt and the Formation of the Modern World.* Eds. Thomas C. Howard, William D. Pederson. Armonk, NY: M.E. Sharpe, 2003. 138-156. Print.

Evans, Paul. "Asia Power Shift: Ready or Not?" *Canada Among Nations, 2009-2010: As Others See Us.* Eds. Fen Hampson, Paul Heinbecker. Montreal––Kingston: McGill-Queen's Press, 2010. 115-121. Print.

Ewart, John Skirving. *The Kingdom Papers.* Ottawa: Paper Press, vol. 1, 1912. Web. 17 Dec. 2016.

Gabryś, Marcin. "Canada's Politics of Memory during Stephen Harper's Terms in Office." *Re-Imagining the First World War: New Perspectives in Anglophone Literature and Culture.* Cambridge: Cambridge Scholars Publishing, 2015. 269-286. Print.

Gheciu, Alexandra. "Reconciling Different Logics of Security Provision: The Case of NATO." *Routledge Handbook of Diplomacy and Statecraft.* Ed. Brian J.C. McKercher. London: Routledge, 2012. 252-263. Print.

Granatstein, John. *Canada's Army: Waging War and Keeping the Peace.* Toronto: University of Toronto Press, 2011. Print.

Haglund, David G. *The North Atlantic Triangle Revisited: Canadian Grand Strategy at Century's End.* Toronto: Canadian Institute of International Affairs, 2000. Print.

Hale, Geoffrey. *So Near Yet So Far: The Public and Hidden Worlds of Canada-US Relations.* Vancouver: University of British Columbia Press, 2012. Print.

Harris, Mike, and Preston Manning. *Vision for a Canada Strong and Free.* Vancouver: Fraser Institute, 2007. Print.

Hart, Michael. *From Pride to Influence: Towards a New Canadian Foreign Policy.* Vancouver: University of British Columbia Press, 2008. Print.

Hilliker, John, and Donald Barry. *Canada's Department of External Affairs*, vol. 2: *Coming of Age, 1946-1968.* Montreal: McGill-Queen's University Press, 1995. Print.

Hilliker, John. *Canada's Department of External Affairs*, vol. 1: *The Early Years, 1909-1946.* Montreal: McGill-Queen's University Press, 1990. Print.

Hillmer, Norman, and Maureen Appel Molot, eds. *Canada Among Nations 2002: A Fading Power.* Don Mills, ON: Oxford University Press, 2002. Print.

Hillmer, Norman. "The Anglo-Canadian Neurosis: The Case of O.D. Skelton." *Britain and Canada: Survey of a Changing Relationship.* Ed. Peter Lyon. London: Frank Cass, 1976. 61-84. Print.

Holloway, Steven Kendall. *Canadian Foreign Policy: Defining the National Interest.* Peterborough, ON: Broadview, 2006. Print.

Ibbitson, John. *Stephen Harper.* Toronto: Signal, 2015. Print.

Imperial Relations in the Age of Laurier. Eds. Ramsey Cook et al. Toronto: University of Toronto Press, 1969. Print.

Jackson, Robert J., and Doreen Jackson. *Politics in Canada: Culture, Institutions, Behaviour and Public Policy.* Toronto: Pearson Prentice Hall, 2009. Print.

Keating, Tom. *Canada and World Order: The Multilateralist Tradition in Canadian Foreign Policy.* Toronto: McClelland & Stewart, 1993. Print.

Kirton, John. "Canada as a Principal Summit Power: G-7/8 Concert Diplomacy from Halifax 1995 to Kananaskis." *Canada Among Nations 2002: A Fading Power.* Eds. Norman Hillmer, Maurine A. Molot, Don Mills, ON: Oxford University Press, 2002. 209-232.

---. "Harper's 'Made in Canada' Global Leadership." *Canada Among Nations, 2006: Minorities and Priorities.* Eds. Andrew F. Cooper, Dane Rowlands. Montreal: McGill-Queen's University Press, 2006. 34-57. Print.

---. *Canadian Foreign Policy in a Changing World.* Toronto: Thomson Nelson, 2007. Print.

Klassen, Jerome. *Joining Empire: The Political Economy of the New Canadian Foreign Policy.* Toronto: University of Toronto Press, 2014. Print.

Laxer, Gordon. "Superpower, Middle Power, or Satellite? Canadian Energy and Environmental Policy." *Canada's Foreign & Security Policy: Soft and Hard Strategies of a Middle Power.* Eds. Nik Hynek, David Bosold. Don Mills, ON: Oxford University Press, 2010. 138-161. Print.

Legault, Albert. "Some Aspects of Canadian Diplomacy in the Area of Disarmament and Arms Control, 1945-1988." *Making a Difference? Canada's Foreign Policy in a Changing World.* Eds. John English, Norman Hillmer. Toronto: Lester Publishing Ltd., 1992. 163-182. Print.

Levant, Ezra. *Ethical Oil: The Case for Canada's Oil Sands.* Toronto: McClelland & Stewart, 2010. Print.

Lunn, Janet, and Christopher Moore. *The Story of Canada.* Toronto: Key Porter, 2007. Print.

MacLaren, Roy. *Commissions High: Canada in London, 1870-1971*. Montreal: McGill-Queen's University Press, 2006. Print.

Malcolm, Andrew H. *The Canadians*. New York: Times Books, 1985. Print.

Massie, Justin. "A Special Relationship? The Importance of France in Canadian Foreign Policy." *Canada Among Nations 2008: 100 Years of Canadian Foreign Policy*. Eds. Robert Bothwell, Jean Daudelin. Montreal: McGill-Queen's University Press, 2009. 235-270. Print.

McKay, Ian, and Jamie Swift. *Warrior Nation: Rebranding Canada in an Age of Anxiety*. Toronto: Between the Lines, 2012. Print.

Nossal, Kim Richard. *The Politics of Canadian Foreign Policy*. Scarborough: Prentice Hall Canada, 1997. Print.

Poy, Vivienne, and Huhua Cao. *The China Challenge: Sino-Canadian Relations in the 21st Century*. Ottawa: University of Ottawa Press, 2011. Print.

Reid, Escott. "The Birth of the North Atlantic Alliance." *Canadian Foreign Policy Since 1945: Middle Power or Satellite?* Ed. Jack Granatstein. Toronto: Copp Clark Publishing, 1973. 56-59. Print.

Riendeau, Roger. *A Brief History of Canada*. Markham: Fitzhenry and Whiteside Ltd., 2000. Print.

Robertson, Colin. "Rising Power: Stephen Harper's Makeover of Canadian International Policy and Its Institutions." *The Harper Factor*. Eds. Jennifer Ditchburn, Graham Fox. Montreal–Kingston–London–Chicago: McGill-Queen's University Press, 2016. 97-115. Print.

Roussel, Stéphane. "Contemporary Canadian Foreign Policy: A Middle Power in a Great World." *Routledge Handbook of Diplomacy and Statecraft*. Ed. Brian J.C. McKercher. London: Routledge, 2012. 131-142. Print.

Sartry, Roger. "The Interplay of Defence and Foreign Policy." *Canada Among Nations 2008: 100 Years of Canadian Foreign Policy*. Eds. Robert Bothwell, Jean Daudelin. Montreal: McGill-Queen's University Press, 2009. 111-141. Print.

Schabas, William A. "Canada's Contribution to International Law." *Canada Among Nations 2008: 100 Years of Canadian Foreign Policy*. Eds. Robert Bothwell, Jean Daudelin. Montreal: McGill-Queen's University Press, 2009. 142-158. Print.

Sinclair, Scott, and Stuart Trew. "What Trade Agreements Have Meant for Canada." *Canada after Harper: His Ideology-fuelled Attack on Canadian Society and Values, And How We Can Now Work to Create the Country We Want*. Ed. Ed Finn. Toronto: James Lorimer & Company Ltd., 2015. 113-130. Print.

Skelton, Oskar Douglas. *General Economic History of the Dominion, 1867-1912*. Toronto: Publishers' Association of Canada, 1913. Print.

Smillie, Ian. "Foreign Aid and Canadian Purpose: Influence and Policy in Canada's International Development Assistance." *Canada Among Nations 2008: 100 Years of Canadian Foreign Policy*. Eds. Robert Bothwell, Jean Daudelin. Montreal: McGill-Queen's University Press, 2009. 183-208. Print.

Smith, Goldwin. *Canada and Canadian Question*. Toronto: Macmillan, 1891. Print. .

Stacey, Charles Percy. *Canada and the Age of Conflict: A History of Canadian External Relations*, vol. 2: *1921-1948, The Mackenzie King Era*. Toronto: University of Toronto Press, 1981. Print.

The History of Immigration and Racism in Canada: Essential Readings. Ed. Barrington Walke. Toronto: Canadian Scholars' Press, 2008. Print.

Thompson, John H., and Stephen J. Randall. *Canada and the United States: Ambivalent Allies*. Athens, GA: University of Georgia Press, 2008. Print.

Trent, John E. *Harper's Canada*. Ottawa: Canadian Electronic Library. 2015. Web.

Waite, Peter B. *Canada 1874-1896: Arduous Destiny*. Toronto: McClelland & Stewart. 1971. Print.

Walz, Jay, and Audrey Walz. *Portrait of Canada*. New York: American Heritage Press, 1970. Print.

Wells, Paul. *Right Side Up: The Fall of Paul Martin and the Rise of Stephen Harper's New Conservatism*. Toronto: McClelland & Stewart. 2006. Print.

Welsh, Jennifer. "Canada and the World: Beyond Middle Power." *The Oxford Handbook of Canadian Politics*. Eds. J.C. Courtney, D.E. Smith. New York: Oxford University Press, 2010. Print.

---. "Canada, North America and the Commonwealth." *The Contemporary Commonwealth: An Assessment 1965-2009*. Ed. James Mayall. London: Routledge, 2010. 157-171. Print.

Wight, Martin. *Power Politics*. London: Continuum, 2002. Print.

Academic articles

Bernard Jr., Prosper M. "Canada and the International Criminal Court: A Case for Renewed Commitment." *Policy Options*. Apr. 2011. Web. 19 Apr. 2015.

Bernstein, Steven, and Christopher D. Gore. "Policy Implications of the Kyoto Protocol for Canada: An Overview." *Isuma: Canadian Journal of Policy Research* 2.4 (2001): 16-35. Print.

Berzins, Christopher. "Let's Hear It for Being Average: Canada's Moral Exceptionalism May Not Be Getting the Job Done." *Literary Review of Canada* 17.4 (2009): 7-9. Print.

Biello, David. "How Much Will Tar Sands Oil Add to Global Warming?" *Scientific American*. Jan. 2013. Web. 5 June 2016.

Blencowe, Andrew. "In Search of an Identity: The Case for Niche Diplomacy in Canadian Foreign Policy." *Atlantic International Studies Journal* 5 (2009). Web. 4 Apr. 2016.

Boessenkool, Ken. "How Harper's Philosophy Transformed Canada for the Better." *Policy Options*. 2015. Web. 4 Apr. 2016.

Bondy, Matthew. "Justin Trudeau Is Putting the 'Liberal' Back in 'Canadian Foreign Policy'." *Foreign Policy.* 21 Oct. 2015. Web. 16 Jan. 2017.

Brown, Stephen. "The Instrumentalization of Foreign Aid under the Harper Government." *Studies in Political Economy: A Socialist Review* 97.1 (2016): 18-36. Print.

Burton, Charles. "Canada's China Policy under the Harper Government." *Canadian Foreign Policy Journal* 21.1 (2015): 45-63. Print.

Chapnick, Adam. "A Diplomatic Counter-Revolution: Conservative Foreign Policy, 2006-11." *International Journal* 67.1 (2011): 137-154. Print.

---. "The Canadian Middle Power Myth." *International Journal* 55 (1999-2000): 188-206. Print.

Cleland, Mike. "Canada as an Energy Superpower: How Clean, How Powerful, How Super?" *Policy Options*. 2007. Web. 3 Mar. 2011.

Dembicki, Geoff. "How Canada's Election Will Decide the Fate of the World." *Foreign Policy.* 15 Oct. 2015. Web. 31 Jan. 2017.

Dorn, A. Walter. "Canadian Peacekeeping: Proud Tradition, Strong Future?" *Canadian Foreign Policy Journal* 12.2 (2005): 7-32. Print.

Drohan, Madelaine. "Wolverine Diplomacy: Making Sense of the Harper Government's Foreign Policy." *Literary Review of Canada*. 2015. Web. 4 Sept. 2016.

Enderle, Georges. "The Ethics of Conviction Versus the Ethics of Responsibility: A False Antithesis for Business Ethics." *Journal of Human Values* 13.2 (2007): 83-94. Print.

Exner-Pirot, Heather. "Canada's Arctic Council Chairmanship (2013-2015): A Post-Mortem." *Canadian Foreign Policy Journal* 22.1 (2016): 84-96. Web. 4 Jan. 2017.

Frenette, Yves. "Conscripting Canada's Past: The Harper Government and the Politics of Memory." *Canadian Journal of History* 49.1 (2014): 49-65. Web. 4 Apr. 2016.

Gecelovsky, Paul. "Constructing a Middle Power: Ideas and Canadian Foreign Policy." *Canadian Foreign Policy Journal* 15.1 (2009): 77-93. Web. 4 Apr. 2016.

Greenhill, Robert, and Celine Wadhera. "Assessing Canada's Global Engagement Gap – Second Edition." *OpenCanada.org.* 2017. Web. 1 Feb. 2017.

Greenhill, Robert, and Megan McQuillan. "Assessing Canada's Global Engagement Gap." *OpenCanada.org.* 2015. Web. 5 Dec. 2016.

Haglund, David G., and Tudor Onea. "Sympathy for the Devil: Myths of Neoclassical Realism in Canadian Foreign Policy." *Canadian Foreign Policy Journal* 14.2 (2008): 53-66. Print.

Haglund, David G., and Stéphane Roussel. "Is the Democratic Alliance a Ticket to (Free) Ride? Canada's 'imperial Commitments,' from the Interwar Period to the Present." *Journal of Transatlantic Studies* 5.1 (2007): 1-24. Web. 5 Dec. 2016.

Harper, Stephen. "'Enlightened Sovereignty': A Road Map to Muskoka and Toronto." *Policy Options.* 2010. Web. 3 Feb. 2016.

Harrison, Kathryn. "A Tale of Two Taxes: The Fate of Environmental Tax Reform in Canada." *Review of Policy Research* 29.3 (2012): 383-407. Web. 5 Dec. 2016.

---. "The Road Not Taken: Climate Change Policy in Canada and the United States." *Global Environmental Politics* 7.4 (2007): 92-117. Web. 5 Dec. 2016.

Heinbecker, Paul. "Foreign Posturing How Does Harper's Foreign Policy Stack Up?" *Literary Review of Canada.* 2015. Web. 4 Dec. 2016.

Hemmat, Samane. "Evaluating Harper's Office of Religious Freedom." *OpenCanada.org.* 2015. Web. 10 Oct. 2016.

Hessey, Krista. "The Canadian Government's Double Take on Israel." *OpenCanada.org.* 2016. Web. 1 Feb. 2017.

Hirsch, Todd. "Battling ghosts: Can a Trudeau win in Alberta?" *Policy Options.* Nov. 2012. Web. 21 Jan. 2017.

Hynek, Nikola. "Canada as a Middle Power: Conceptual Limits and Promises." *Central European Journal of Canadian Studies* 4.1 (2004): 33-43. Print.

Ibbitson, John. *The Big Break: The Conservative Transformation of Canada's Foreign Policy.* Waterloo: Centre for International Global Innovation. CIGI Papers 29.7 (Apr. 2014). Web.

Jockel, Joseph T., and Joel J. Sokolsky. "Canada and NATO: Keeping Ottawa in, expenses down, criticism out… and the country secure." *International Journal* 64.2 (2009): 315-336. Web. 5 Dec. 2016.

Keating, Tom. "The Transition in Canadian Foreign Policy through an English School Lens." *International Journal* 69.2 (2014): 168-182. Web. 5 Dec. 2016.

Kelly, Brent. "Changes to the Canadian Foreign Policy Agenda: From Liberal Internationalist to Neo-Realist." *The Lyceum* 1.1 (2000): 22-31. Print.

Kinsman, Jeremy. "Arctic Sovereignty: Fear and Loathing Over Santa's Workshop." *OpenCanada.org.* 2014. Web. 3 Mar. 2015.

Kirton, John. "Canada as a Principal Financial Power G-7 and IMF Diplomacy in the Crisis of 1997-9." *International Journal* 54.4 (1999): 603-624. Web. 5 Dec. 2014.

---. "Vulnerable America, Capable Canada: Convergent Leadership for an Interconnected World." *Canadian Foreign Policy Journal* 18.1 (2012): 133-144. Web. 5 Dec. 2014.

Klassen, Jerome. "Joining Empire: Foreign Policy under Harper." *Canadian Dimension* 49.4 (Sept./Oct. 2015). Web. 22 Jan. 2017.

Kraska, James. "The Northern Canada Vessel Traffic Services Zone Regulations (NORDREG) and the Law of the Sea." *International Journal of Marine and Coastal Law* 30 (2015): 225-254. Print.

Lee, Steve. "Canadian Values in Canadian Foreign Policy." *Canadian Foreign Policy Journal* 10.1 (2002): 1-9. Web. 5 Dec. 2014.

Leuprecht, Christian, and Joel J. Sokolsky. "Defense Policy 'Walmart Style': Canadian Lessons in 'not-so-grand' Grand Strategy." *Armed Forces & Society* 41.3 (2015): 541-562. Web. 5 Dec. 2016.

Lyle, Greg. "Canadians Conflicted on Canada as an Energy Superpower." *Policy Magazine*. 2013. Web. 4 Dec. 2015.

Macdonald, Douglas, and Heather A. Smith. "Promises Made, Promises Broken: Questioning Canada's Commitments to Climate Change." *International Journal* 55.1 (1999/2000): 107-124. Web. 5 Dec. 2015.

Macdonald, Laura, and Jeremy Paltiel. "Middle Power or Muddling Power? Canada's Relations with Emerging Markets." *Canadian Foreign Policy Journal* 22.1 (2016): 1-11. Web. 5 Dec. 2016.

Macnab, Ron. "'Use It or Lose It' in Arctic Canada: Action Agenda or Election Hype?" *Vermont Law Review* 34.3 (2009): 3-14. Print.

Massie, Justin. "Canada's (In)Dependence in the North American Security Community: The Asymmetrical Norm of Common Fate." *American Review of Canadian Studies* 37.4 (2007): 493-516. Web. 5 Dec. 2015.

Mulroney, Brian. "Walk the Talk on Energy." *Policy Options*. 2014. Web. 8 Sept. 2016.

Murray, Robert W., and John McCoy. "From Middle Power to Peacebuilder: The Use of the Canadian Forces in Modern Canadian Foreign Policy." *American Review of Canadian Studies* 40.2 (2010): 171-188. Web.

Paris, Roland. "Are Canadians Still Liberal Internationalists? Foreign Policy and Public Opinion in the Harper Era." *International Journal* 69.3 (2014): 274-307. Web. 5 Dec. 2015.

Polachová, Barbora, and Magdalena Fiřtová. "Canadian Identity: Issues of Cultural Diplomacy (1993-2012)." *TransCanadiana* 7 (2014-2015): 81-103. Web. 5 Dec. 2015.

Potter, Evan H. "Canada in the Commonwealth." *The Round Table* 96.4 (August 2007): 447-463. Print.

Pratt, David. "Canadian Grand Strategy and Lessons Learned." *Journal of Transatlantic Studies* 6.1 (2008): 61-78. Web. 5 Aug. 2015.

Rhéaume, Charles. "Cautious Neighbour Policy: Canada's Helping Hand in Winding Down the Vietnam War." *Cold War History* 11.2 (May 2011): 223-239. Print.

Riddell-Dixon, Elizabeth. "Canada at the United Nations 1945-1989." *International Journal* 62.1 (2006-2007): 145-160. Print.

Ross, Douglas A. "Canada's International Security Strategy: Beyond Reason But No Hope?" *International Journal* 65.2 (2010): 349-360. Print.

Rudderham, Melissa A. "Canada and the United Nations Peace Operations: Challenges, Opportunities, and Canada's Response." *International Journal* 63.2 (2008): 359-384. Print.

Segal, Hugh. "Grappling with Peace." *International Journal* 65.2 (2010): 331-338. Print.

Smith, Gordon S., and Peter C. Heap. "Canada, the G8, and the G20: A Canadian Approach to Shaping Global Governance in a Shifting International Environment." *The School of Public Policy SPP Research Papers* 3.8 (2010): 1-27. Print.

Smith, Heather A. "Choosing Not to See. Canada, Climate Change, and the Arctic." *International Journal* 65.4 (2010): 931-942. Print.

---. "Political Parties and Canadian Climate Change Policy." *International Journal* 64.1 (2008): 47-66. Print.

Smith, Jordan M. "Reinventing Canada: Stephen Harper's Conservative Revolution." *World Affairs* 174.6 (2012). Web. 22 Jan. 2017.

Stairs, Denis. "Myths, Morals, and Reality in Canadian Foreign Policy." *International Journal* 58.2 (2003): 239-256. Web. 15 Dec. 2014.

Stavrianakis, Anna. "Legitimising Liberal Militarism: Politics, Law and War in the Arms Trade Treaty." *Third World Quarterly* 37.5 (2016): 840-865. Web. 3 Jan. 2017.

Vucetic, Srdjan. "What Joining the Arms Trade Treaty Means for Canada." *OpenCanada.org.* 2017. Web. 3 Jan. 2017.

Wallace, James C., and Richelle Wiseman. "The Promise of Canada's Office of Religious Freedom." *The Review of Faith & International Affairs* 11.3 (2013): 52-60. Web. 5 Dec. 2015.

Way, Laura. "An Energy Superpower or a Super Sales Pitch? Building the Case through an Examination of Canadian Newspapers Coverage of Oil Sands." *Canadian Political Science Review* 5.1 (2011): 74-98. Print.

Zyla, Benjamin. "NATO and Post-Cold War Burden Sharing: Canada 'the Laggard'?" *International Journal* 64.2 (2009): 337-359. Web. 5 Dec. 2015.

---. "Years of Free-Riding? Canada, the New NATO, and Collective Crisis Management in Europe, 1989-2001." *American Review of Canadian Studies* 40.1 (2010): 22-39. Print.

Newspapers and Magazines

"A Rough Ride." *Economist*. 9 July 2015. Web. 3 Nov. 2016.

Appel, Jeremy. "The Harper Doctrine in Red? Justin Trudeau's Foreign Policy." *Canadian Dimension*. 1 June 2015. Web. 21 Jan. 2017.

"Arctic Naval Facility at Nanisivik Completion Delayed to 2018." *CBC News*. 4 Mar. 2015. Web. 1 Apr. 2016.

"Arctic Sovereignty 'Non-Negotiable': Harper." *CBC News*. 20 Aug. 2010. Web. 3 May 2011.

Austen, Ian, and Clifford Krauss. "For Justin Trudeau, Canada's Leader, Revival of Keystone XL Upsets a Balancing Act." *New York Times*. 25 Jan. 2017. Web. 31 Jan. 2017.

Austen, Ian. "Justin Trudeau's Message to U.N.: 'We're Canadian and We're Here to Help'." *New York Times*. 20 Sep. 2016. Web. 24 Jan. 2017.

---. "Syrian Asylum Claims in Canada Slowed by Stephen Harper's Office." *New York Times*. 8 Oct. 2015. Web. 28 Jan. 2017.

Axworthy, Lloyd, and Mary Simon. "Is Canada Undermining the Arctic Council?" *Globe and Mail*. 4 Mar. 2014. Web. 3 Apr. 2015.

Bambury, Brent. "How Oil Pipelines Became One of the Most Divisive Issues in Canadian Politics." *CBC Radio*. 2 Dec. 2016. Web. 21 Jan. 2017.

Banerjee, Sidhartha. "Freeland sees silver lining for Canada in protectionist era." *Maclean's*. 5 Jan. 2017. Web. 22 Jan. 2017.

Battersby, Sarah-Joyce. "'We are very happy to be in Canada,' says newly arrived Syrian refugee." *Toronto Star*. 11 Dec. 2015. Web. 30 Jan. 2017.

Beck, Stewart. "How Does Ottawa Balance Human Rights and Trade with China?" *Globe and Mail*. 30 Aug. 2016. Web. 1 Sept. 2016.

Bendavid, Naftali. "Just Five of 28 NATO Members Meet Defense Spending Goal, Report Says." *Wall Street Journal*. 22 Jun 2015. Web. 16 June 2016.

Berthiaume, Lee. "Canada Is Not a Referee in the World, John Baird Says." *Canada.com*. 21 Dec. 2012. Web. 5 July 2015.

---. "Canada's peacekeeping plan not politically motivated, says top general." *CBC News*. 21 Sep. 2016. Web. 25 Jan. 2017.

---. "Political fight brewing over Canada's peacekeeping role." *Maclean's*. 8 Sep. 2016. Web. 24 Jan. 2017.

---. "Religious Freedom Office Faces Uncertain Future as Liberals Consider Wider Human-Rights Proposals." *Ottawa Citizen*. 17 Jan. 2016. Web. 15 Apr. 2016.

---. "Sensitivity Key for Canadian Foreign Service, Says Religious Freedom Envoy." *Ottawa Citizen*. 5 Jan. 2016. Web. 5 June 2016.

Black, Conrad. "Why Canada Is Justified in Selling Arms to the Saudis." *National Post*. 13 May 2016. Web. 5 July 2016.

Blanchfield, Mike, and Lee Berthiaume. "Canada able to join NATO mission, launch peacekeeping operation, experts say." *Toronto Star*. 14 July 2016. Web. 25 Jan. 2017.

---. "Canada axes foreign studies program despite being told of economic spinoffs." *Globe and Mail*. 16 May 2012. Web. 25 May 2012.

---. "Dalai Lama In Ottawa: Stephen Harper Risks Angering China By Meeting With Exiled Tibetan Leader." *Huffington Post Canada*. 27 Apr. 2012. Web. 4 May 2015.

---. "Dion digs at Tories with new foreign policy label: responsible conviction." *CBC News*. 29 Mar. 2016. Web. 23 Jan. 2017.

---. "Liberals grapple with a new era of UN peacekeeping." *Globe and Mail*. 25 Apr. 2016. Web. 25 Jan. 2017.

---. "Trudeau cabinet retreat to confront the reality of Trump's presidency." *CTV News*. 22 Jan 2017. Web. 27 Jan. 2017.

Blatchford, Andy. "Canada Will Sign TPP Trade Deal, But Ratification Not Certain." *Maclean's*. 25 Jan. 2016. Web. 28 Jan. 2017.

---. "Canada's Books Are Back in Black for First Time in 8 Years after Surprise $1.9 Billion Surplus." *Financial Post*. 14 Sept. 2015. Web. 5 June 2016.

Bloomberg. "Canada in 'Identity Crisis' amid Petro-State Concerns." *Calgary Herald*. 4 Jan. 2016. Web. 4 Feb. 2016.

"Bono, Geldof Slam Canada as a 'Laggard' on African Aid." *CBC News*. 8 June 2007. Web. 3 Feb. 2011.

Bonokoski, Mark. "Obama (and a Mute Trudeau) Join Gang-Swarming of Israel." *Toronto Sun*. 26 Dec. 2016. Web. 23 Jan. 2017.

Boswell, Randy. "Canada Is 'Arctic Superpower': Cannon." *Edmonton Journal*. 28 June 2009. Web. 20 Oct. 2015.

Brach, Bal. "Canada limits the number of privately sponsored Syrian refugee applicants in 2017." *CBC News*. 23 Dec. 2016. Web. 31 Jan. 2017.

Brewster, Murray. "Defence Experts Call Warm Embrace of NATO by Harper Gov't an about-Face." *CTV News*. 2 Apr. 2014. Web. 2 June 2015.

Brinded, Lianna. "Mercer 2016 Quality of Living Worldwide City Rankings – Business Insider." *Business Insider*. 2016. Web. 20 Mar. 2016.

Buckley, Chris. "China's Foreign Minister Castigates Canadian Reporter for Rights Question." *New York Times.* 2 June 2016. Web. 7 July 2016.

Burgman, Tamsyn. "Hamas and Hezbollah Reject Own Blacklisting by Canada." *Globe and Mail.* 16 Apr. 2015. Web. 27 May 2015.

Burney, Derek H., and Fen Osler Hampson. "No More Mr. Fixit at the UN." *iPolitics.* 1 Oct. 2012. Web. 24 Nov. 2014.

Burton, Charles. "CNOOC's Bid for Nexen Is a Key Move on China's Global Chess Board." *Toronto Star.* 22 Apr. 2012. Web. 23 Mar. 2013.

Campbell, Clark. "Canada Falls out of Top 10 in UN's Human Development Index." *Globe and Mail.* 14 Mar. 2013. Web. 20 Jan. 2017.

---. "Canada Rejects UN Request to Lead Congo Mission." *Globe and Mail.* 30 Apr. 2010. Web. 2 May 2013.

---. "Harper Pledges $105-Million to Help Jordan Handle Influx of Syrian Refugees." *Globe and Mail.* 23 Jan. 2013. Web. 4 May 2013.

---. "In Accepting World Statesman Award, Harper Paints Picture of Uncertain World." *Globe and Mail.* 27 Sept. 2012. Web. 1 June 2014.

---. "John Baird Crafts Canadian Foreign Policy with a Hard Edge." *Globe and Mail.* 28 Dec. 2012. Web. 1 June 2014.

---. "Stephen Harper Calls for 'Enlightened Sovereignty'." *Globe and Mail.* 28 Jan. 2010. Web. 10 Feb. 2012.

---. "Too Much Navel-Gazing and Not Enough Action in Syria, Baird Tells United Nations." *Globe and Mail.* 1 Oct. 2012. Web. 1 June 2014.

Campion-Smith, Bruce. "Canada cannot 'sit back' in a dangerous world, Justin Trudeau says." *Toronto Star.* 4 Dec. 2016. Web. 26 Jan. 2017.

---. "Justin Trudeau Defends New Strategy to Battle ISIS." *Toronto Star.* 17 Feb. 2016. Web. 18 Jan. 2017.

"Canada and the United Nations: Half a Century of Constructive Engagement." *Canada World View* 6 (1999): 18-19. Print.

"Canada under Fire over Kyoto Protocol Exit." *BBC News.* 11 Dec. 2011. Web. 2 Jan. 2012.

"Canada, Slamming Iran's Nuclear Program and Incitement against Israel, Severs Diplomatic Relations." *Times of Israel.* 7 Sept. 2012. Web. 4 May 2014.

"Canada's Climate Policy: Let the Haggling Begin." *Economist.* 22 Oct. 2016. Web. 27 Jan. 2017.

"Canada's Election: Veiled Attack." *Economist.* 8 Sep. 2015. Web. 29 Jan. 2017.

"Canada's Example to the World: Liberty Moves North." *Economist.* 29 Oct. 2016. Web. 31 Jan. 2017.

"Canada's Immigration Policy: No country for old men." *Economist.* 8 Jan. 2015. Web 27 Jan. 2017.

"Canada's Kyoto Withdrawal Draws International Response." *CBC News*. 2011. Web. 3 Feb. 2012.

"Canada's refugee policy questioned after Syrian boy's drowning." *CBC News*. 4 Sep. 2015. Web. 29 Jan. 2017.

"Canadian Foreign Policy: Trudeaumania 2." *Economist*. 3 Mar. 2016. Web. 25 Jan. 2017.

"Canadian peacekeepers on hold amidst uncertainty over Trump." *Maclean's*. 24 Jan. 2017. Web. 26. Jan 2017.

"Canadian troops, helicopters needed in war-torn Mali: top UN official." *Maclean's*. 18. Nov. 2016. Web. 26 Jan. 2017.

Canadians for Justice and Human Rights in Gaza. "The Partisan Approach to Gaza Is a Discredit to Canada." *Globe and Mail*. 24 July 2014. Web. 2 July 2015.

"Can Canada fix the UN, and should it even try?" *National Post*. 2 July 2012. Web. 3 Apr. 2015.

"Cannon Blames Ignatieff for Canada's UN Vote Loss." *CBC News*. 12 Oct. 2010. Web. 28 May 2014.

Caplan, Gerald. "On Foreign Policy, Canada Is Avoiding the Tough Human Rights Questions." *Globe and Mail*. 6 Sept. 2016. Web. 10 Nov. 2016.

---. "Trudeau Continues Harper's Policies on Israel." *Globe and Mail*. 13 Dec. 2016. Web. 23 Jan. 2017.

---. "Is Trudeau really 'just not ready'? Maybe." *Globe and Mail*. 10 Aug. 2015. Web. 20 Jan. 2017.

"CETA Impasse: How tiny Wallonia Can Hijack the EU-Canada deal." *CTV News*. 25 Oct. 2016. Web. 25 Jan. 2017.

Chase, Steven, and Robert Fife. "Cancelling Saudi Arms Deal Would Have No Effect on Human Rights: Dion." *Globe and Mail*. 29 Mar. 2016. Web. 21 Jan. 2017.

---. "Saudi Arabian officials say arms deal with Canada an act of friendship." *Globe and Mail*. 29 Sep. 2016. Web. 21 Jan. 2017.

Chase, Steven, and Richard Blackwell. "Ottawa Touts Sale of Military Vehicles to Saudi Arabia." *Globe and Mail*. 14 Feb. 2014. Web. 3 Apr. 2015.

Chase, Steven, and Shawn McCarthy. "Leaked Internal Report Warns of Canada's Declining World Influence." *Globe and Mail*. 25 Sept. 2015. Web. 7 Nov. 2016.

Chase, Steven. "Arctic Claim Will Include North Pole, Baird Pledges as Canada Delays Full Seabed Bid." *Globe and Mail*. 9 Dec. 2013. Web. 2 Apr. 2014.

---. "As Canada Faces Heat over Saudi Deal, Sweden Looks to Restrict Arms Exports." *Globe and Mail*. 20 May 2016. Web. 4 July 2016.

---. "Canada Now the Second Biggest Arms Exporter to Middle East, Data Show." *Globe and Mail.* 14 June 2016. Web. 10 Jan. 2017.

---. "Defence Minister to tour Africa on mission to learn about peacekeeping." *Globe and Mail.* 4 Aug. 2016. Web. 25 Jan. 2017.

---. "Flaherty Aims to Reduce Number of Tax Brackets." *Globe and Mail.* 10 June 2011. Web. 4 July 2011.

---. "Harper Orders New Draft of Arctic Seabed Claim to Include North Pole." *Globe and Mail.* 4 Dec. 2013. Web. 6 Feb. 2015.

---. "Harper Tells Putin to 'Get out of Ukraine' in G20 Encounter." *Globe and Mail.* 14 Nov. 2014. Web. 3 Dec. 2014.

---. "Harper Vows to Fast-Track Boost to Spy, Policing Powers after Shooting." *Globe and Mail.* 23 Oct. 2014. Web. 3 Dec. 2014.

---. "Leaks Reveal How Ottawa Cultivated Ties before $15-Billion Saudi Arms Deal." *Globe and Mail.* 25 June 2015. Web. 20 June 2016.

---. "Liberals won't hold parliamentary vote on peacekeeping deployment." *Globe and Mail.* 8 Sep. 2016. Web. 25 Jan. 2017.

---. "Myth versus Reality in Stephen Harper's Northern Strategy." *Globe and Mail.* 17 Jan. 2014. Web. 4 Mar. 2015.

---. "New Religious-Freedom Watchdog Faces Uphill Battle." *Globe and Mail.* 7 July 2013. Web. 8 Dec. 2014.

---. "Niqabs 'rooted in a culture that is anti-women,' Harper says." *Globe and Mail.* 10 Mar. 2015. Web. 29 Jan. 2017.

---. "Religious-freedom envoy to ensure that 'Canada will not be silent,' PM says." 19 Feb. 2013. Web. 8 Dec. 2014.

---. "The Big Deal." *Globe and Mail.* 5 Feb. 2016. Web. 9 Sept. 2016.

"China Condemns Dalai Lama's Planned Norway Visit." *Reuters.* 20. Dec. 2013. Web. 2 Mar. 2014.

Chivers, C.J. "Russians Plant Flag on the Arctic Seabed." *New York Times.* 3 Aug. 2007. Web. 2 Mar. 2014.

"Christian College Dean to Head Religious Freedom Office." *CBC News.* 19 Feb. 2013. Web. 8 Sept. 2014.

"Christie Freeland on CETA: 'OK, we did it'!" *Maclean's.* 30 Oct. 2016. Web. 23 Jan. 2017.

"Chronology: Canada's Involvement in the Fight against ISIS." *CBC News.* 8 Feb. 2016. Web. 4 Apr. 2016.

"Clyde River Groups Challenge Nunavut Seismic Testing in Court." *Nunatsiaq Online.* 28 July 2014. Web. 1 Sept. 2015.

Coleman, James, and Sarah Jordaan. "B.C. LNG Could Reduce Emissions Overseas – If It's Done Correctly." *Globe and Mail.* 24 Apr. 2016. Web. 3 July 2016.

Connolly, Amanda. "Dion lays out Liberal foreign policy doctrine: 'Responsible conviction'." *iPolitics*. 29 Mar. 2016. Web. 23 Jan. 2017.

---. "Liberals Would Fund Abortion Services under Maternal Health Initiative." *iPolitics*. 16 Oct. 2015. Web. 12 Dec. 2015.

"Could U.S. uncertainty mean more foreign-student cash for Canada?" *CBC News*. 2 Feb. 2017. Web. 3 Feb. 2017.

Cullen, Catherine. "Justin Trudeau Says Canada Will 'Do Its Part' in Anti-ISIS Coalition." *CBC News*. 16 Nov. 2015. Web. 2 Mar. 2016.

Curry, Bill. "'Canadians' views at odds with Liberal immigration plans, government poll shows." *Globe and Mail*. 23 Sep. 2016. Web. 30 Jan 2017.

"Dalai Lama Praises Harper's Balancing Act on Tibetan Rights, Chinese Trade." *Globe and Mail*. 28 Apr. 2012. Web. 3 Apr. 2013.

De Souza, Mike. "Canada Strengthening 'evil Forces' with Threat to Boycott Commonwealth Summit: Sri Lankan Official." *National Post*. 2 May 2013. Web. 4 June 2014.

---. "Trudeau approves Kinder Morgan pipeline, rejects one of two Enbridge projects." *National Observer*. 29 Nov. 2016. Web. 25 Jan. 2017.

Dharssi, Alia. "'We need new blood': Despite major economic downtown, Albertans want more immigration, McCallum says." *National Post*. 20 Aug. 2016. Web. 31 Jan. 2017.

Dickinson, Tim. "Crude Awakening: How the Keystone Veto Dashes Canada's 'Superpower' Dreams." *Rolling Stone*. 24 Feb. 2015. Web. 30 Jan 2017.

"Dion Introduces 'Green Shift' Carbon Tax Plan." *CTV News*. 19 June 2008. Web. 2 Apr. 2011.

Do, Trinh Theresa. "'Fragmented' Maternal Health Aid Data a Step Away from Accountability." *CBC News*. 28 May 2014. Web. 25 Apr. 2015.

"Donald Trump Backs Two Big Oil Pipelines." *Economist*. 28 Jan. 2017. Web. 31 Jan. 2017.

Donnelly, Aileen. "Alan Kurdi's father blames Canada for death of his family as PM suggests he will expedite refugee applications." *National Post*. 10 Sep. 2015. Web. 28 Jan. 2017.

"Feds send team to examine peacekeeping in Mali." *Maclean's*. 31 Aug. 2016. Web. 25 Jan. 2017.

Fekete, Jason. "Justin Trudeau says Canada 'is back' at climate-change meeting." *National Post*. 30 Nov. 2015. Web. 25 Jan. 2017.

Fife, Robert, and Mark MacKinnon. "Canada Set to Renew Ukraine Military Training Mission amid Trump Fears." *Globe and Mail*. 20 Feb. 2017. Web. 25 Feb. 2017.

Fife, Robert. "Trudeau sets sights on free-trade deal with China." *Globe and Mail*. 5 Jan. 2016. Web. 22 Jan. 2017.

Fine, Sean. "Tories move to revoke citizenship of convicted terrorist born in Canada." *Globe and Mail.* 1 Oct. 2015. Web. 29 Jan. 2017.

Fisher, Matthew. "Russia Suspended from G8 over Annexation of Crimea, Group of Seven Nations Says." *National Post.* 24 Mar. 2014. Web. 5 Apr. 2015.

Fisk, Robert. "In Canada, Harper's Conservatives seem to have forgotten a cherished tradition about refugees." *Independent.* 20 Sep. 2015. Web. 28 Jan. 2017.

---. "Niqab row: Canada's government challenges ruling Zunera Ishaq can wear veil while taking oath of citizenship." *Independent.* 30 Sep. 2015. Web. 29 Jan. 2017.

Fitzgerald, Andy. "Why Won't the West Call out Saudi Arabia for Persecution of Democratic Activists?" *Guardian.* 29 Dec. 2013. Web. 25 May 2016.

Flannery, Tim. "Why Canada Failed on Kyoto and How to Make Amends." *Toronto Star.* 22 Nov. 2009. Web. 2 Mar. 2011.

Freeman, Linda. "Nelson Mandela, the Honorary Canadian." *Globe and Mail.* 5 Dec. 2013. Web. 19 Apr. 2016.

Friesen, Joe. "Canada Is a Global Heavyweight in the Eyes of Emerging Powers: Survey." *Globe and Mail.* 20 June 2010. Web. 3 Dec. 2016.

Friscolanti, Michael. "Tories move to strip citizenship from Canadian-born terrorist." *Maclean's.* 30 Sept. 2015. Web. 29 Jan. 2017.

---. "Liberals face reality of national security in a dangerous world." *Maclean's.* 16 Oct. 2016. Web. 29 Jan. 2017.

"Frozen Promises." *Economist.* 14 May 2013. Web. 3 May 2014.

Frum, David. "The Delusions of the Canadian Mind." *The Atlantic.* 19 Aug. 2015. Web. 2 Mar. 2016.

Gajanan, Mahita. "Justin Trudeau Praises the Women's Marches in Canada as Inspirational." *Time.* 22 Jan. 2017. Web. 28 Jan. 2017.

Galloway, Gloria. "Canada Condemns UN 'Hatefest'." *Globe and Mail.* 25 Nov. 2010. Web. 2 Mar. 2011.

Gattinger, Monica. "Canada Is an Energy Superpower with a Super-Problem." *iPolitics.* 24 June 2014. Web. 6 Apr. 2015.

Geddes, John. "How the Liberals are taking on their toughest files." *Maclean's.* 16 Oct. 2016. Web. 30 Jan. 2017.

---. "How the Liberals took down the Tories." *Maclean's.* 20 Oct. 2015. Web. 15 Jan. 2017.

---. "The Trudeau Report Card: A look at the bumpy road ahead." *Maclean's.* 16 Oct. 2016. Web. 23 Jan. 2017.

George, Robert P., and Katrina Lantos Swett. "Why Canada Should Keep Its Religious Freedom Office." *Globe and Mail.* 25 Mar. 2016. Web. 4 Apr. 2016.

Gilchrist, Emma. "Trudeau just broke his promise to Canada's First Nations."
    National Observer. 30 July 2016. Web. 25 Jan. 2017.

Gilles, Rob. "Canada less welcoming to refugees under Harper." *Times of Israel*.
    6 Sep. 2015. Web. 28 Jan. 2017.

Gilmore, Scott. "Has Harper Hurt Canada's Position in the World?" *Maclean's*.
    24 Sept. 2014. Web. 2 Feb. 2015.

---. "The Sinking of the Canadian Navy." *Maclean's*. 4 Aug. 2015. Web. 2 Oct.
    2016.

Goldenberg, Suzanne. "Canada Election: How Stephen Harper's Fossil Fuel
    Gamble May Have Backfired." *Guardian*. 16 Oct. 2015. Web. 2 Mar. 2016.

---. "Oil Sands Pipeline Battle Turns Ugly." *Guardian*. 9 Jan. 2012. Web. 3 Apr.
    2013.

Goold, Douglas, and Amitendu Palit. "Why a Canada-India Trade Deal Is
    within Reach." *Globe and Mail*. 8 June 2014. Web. 5 Oct. 2016.

Gopnik, Adam. "Freedom and the Veil." *New Yorker*. 9 Oct. 2015. Web. 29 Jan.
    2017.

Gordon, Julie. "British Columbia imposes 15 percent property transfer tax on
    foreign home buyers." *Reuters*. 25 July 2016. Web. 31 Jan. 2017.

Gordon, Stephen. "Stephen Harper's economic legacy." *National Post*. 29 Apr.
    2016. Web. 29 Jan. 2017.

"Government says it never got refugee application from family of drowned
    Syrian boys." *Ottawa Citizen*. 3 Sep. 2015. Web. 28 Jan. 2017.

Greenaway, Norma. "Tories Want Armed Ships to Patrol Arctic." *Ottawa
    Citizen*. 25 Dec. 2005. Web. 4 Mar. 2011.

Greenspon, Edward; Andrew Mayeda; Rebecca Penty, and Theophilos Argitis
    "How Obama Shocked Harper as Keystone Frustrator-in-Chief." *Bloomberg*.
    26 Apr. 2014. Web. 3 May 2015.

Greenspon, Edward; Andrew Mayeda; Jeremy van Loon, and Rebecca Penty.
    "Harper's Petro-Folly: How Canada Fumbled Its Post-Keystone Energy Vision
    of a Gateway to China." *Financial Post*. 2 May 2014. Web. 4 May 2015.

Grenier, Eric. "Harper Disapproval Hits 50 Per Cent In New Poll." *Huffington
    Post Canada*. 24 Sept. 2012. Web. 12 Nov. 2012.

Gurney, Matt. "When It Comes to Climate, Canada Is Back – and It Looks
    Pretty Much the Same as before." *National Post*. 19 Sept. 2016. Web. 21 Jan.
    2017.

Gwiazda, Wojtek. "Canada Welcomes Decision of PMs of India and Mauritius
    Not to Attend Commonwealth Meeting." *Radio Canada International*.
    13 Nov. 2013. Web. 25 May 2015.

Hall, Chris. "Behind the Scenes: How Softwood Lumber Interrupted Obama and Trudeau's Bilateral Bromance." *CBC News*. 30 June 2016. Web. 21 Jan. 2017.

---. "Harper Offers Obama Climate Plan to Win Keystone Approval." *CBC News*. 6 Sept. 2013. Web. 4 Sept. 2014.

---. "Harper Wants to Keep Refugee Crisis Focus on Big Picture." *CBC News*. 4 Sep. 2015. Web. 28 Jan. 2017.

Hannay, Chris. "Trade Is Voters' Top Foreign-Policy Concern, Poll Suggests." *Globe and Mail*. 28 Sept. 2015. Web. 9 Sept. 2016.

"Harper Brushes off U.S. Criticism of Arctic Plan." *CBC News*. 26 Jan. 2006. Web. 3 Oct. 2011.

"Harper calls on La Francophonie to put an end to forced marriages." *Globe and Mail*. 29 Nov. 2014. Web. 2 Aug. 2016.

"Harper Grilled over Prorogation, Detainees." *CBC News*. 4 Mar. 2010. Web. 2 Mar. 2011.

"Harper Joins Controversy over Russia's Anti-Gay Law." *Globe and Mail*. 9 Aug. 2013. Web. 2 Aug. 2014.

"Harper Signs Business, Travel Pacts in Brazil." *CBC News*. 7 Aug. 2011. Web. 2 Mar. 2012.

Harper, Stephen, and Stockwell Day. "Canadians Stand With You." *The Washington Post*. 28 Mar. 2003. Web. 20 Oct. 2016.

Harper, Stephen. "Our Duty Is to Stand Firm in the Face of Russian Aggression." *Globe and Mail*. 25 July 2014. Web. 3 Feb. 2016.

"Harper's Letter Dismisses Kyoto as 'Socialist Scheme'." *CBC News*. 20 Jan. 2007. Web. 4 May 2011.

"Harper's Nunavut Campaign Stop Preaches to the Converted." *Nunatsiaq Online*. 17 Aug. 2015. Web. 7 Oct. 2016.

Harris, Kathleen. "'Extraordinary initiative': Canada's private refugee sponsorship system exported as model for the world." *CBC News*. 14 Dec. 2016. Web. 30 Jan. 2017.

---. "Federal Court denies bid to block Canada-Saudi Arabia arms deal." *CBC News*. 24 Jan. 2017. Web. 30 Jan 2017.

---. "Irresponsible populism: Lisa Raitt slams Kevin O'Leary, Kellie Leitch." *CBC News*. 4 Jan. 2017. Web. 31 Jan. 2017.

Hashem, Mohamed. "A haven no more: Canada's conservative refugee policy." *Al Jazeera*. 15 Sep. 2015. Web. 28 Jan. 2017.

Hong, Paul. "Canada's Special Relationship With the Dalai Lama." *Huffington Post Canada*. 13 Oct. 2014. Web. 3 June 2015.

---. "How Canada Has Maintained a Strong, Principled Voice in China." *Huffington Post Canada*. 11 Sep. 2014. Web. 3 June 2015.

"How Keystone XL soured the 'special relationship' between Stephen Harper and Barack Obama." *National Post*. 24 Apr. 2014. Web 12 Feb. 2016.

Hui, Ann. "Canadian Ambassador Rebukes China for Jailing Rights Activist." *Globe and Mail*. 26 Jan. 2014. Web. 20 Oct. 2015.

Hunter, Justine. "Christy Clark applauds Canada-U.S. move to sign softwood lumber deal." *Globe and Mail*. 10 Mar. 2016. Web. 21 Jan. 2017.

Ibbitson, John, and Joanna Slater. "Security Council Rejection a Deep Embarrassment for Harper." *Globe and Mail*. 12 Oct. 2010. Web. 17 Nov. 2016.

Ibbitson, John. "A New Era for Canada Rises in the East." *Globe and Mail*. 8 Dec. 2009. Web. 9 Oct. 2011.

---. "Harper Can't Ignore Opposition to Nexen Sale by His Political Base." *Globe and Mail*. 1 Aug. 2012. Web. 3 Apr. 2013.

---. "How Harper Transformed Canada's Foreign Policy." *Globe and Mail*. 31 Jan. 2014. Web. 2 Feb. 2014.

---. "Tories' new foreign-affairs vision shifts focus to 'economic diplomacy'." *Globe and Mail*. 27 Nov. 2013. Web. 22 Jan. 2017.

"Iraq War a Mistake, Harper Admits." *CTV News*. 3 Oct. 2008. Web. 7 July 2011.

Ivison, John. "'Through Fire and Water, Canada Will Stand with You': Harper Gives Historic First Address to Israeli Parliament." *National Post*. 20 Jan. 2014. Web. 20 May 2015.

---. "Crimea Crisis Forcing Harper to Rethink NATO, Arctic Defence." *National Post*. 17 Mar. 2014. Web. 2 May 2015.

---. "Where will Trudeau's foreign policy lead us? Even the Liberals probably don't know." *National Post*. 3 Nov. 2015. Web. 23 Jan. 2017.

Jabir, Humera, and Murtaza Hussain. "Why Is Ottawa Selling Arms to Oppressive Regimes?" *Toronto Star*. 10 Mar. 2014. Web. 25 May 2015.

Jang, Brent, and Shawn McCarthy. "Liberals approve Pacific NorthWest LNG project with environmental conditions." *Globe and Mail*. 27 Sep. 2016. Web. 29 Jan. 2017.

"John Baird Slams Nigeria over Anti-Gay Bill." *CBC News*. 30 Nov. 2011. Web. 25 Apr. 2014.

Juneau, Thomas. "Iran after a Nuclear Deal: Where Will Canada Stand?" *Globe and Mail*. 14 July 2015. Web. 3 July 2016.

Kassam, Ashifa. "Environmentalists 'Expected Better' of Trudeau as Canada Backs Gas Project." *Guardian*. 28 Sept. 2016. Web. 21. Jan. 2017.

Kennedy, Mark. "Harper to Tout Capitalism, Canadian Oil at World Economic Forum." *National Post*. 25 Jan. 2012. Web. 3 Apr. 2016.

"Keystone Flops." *Economist*. 14 Nov. 2015. Web. 3 Feb. 2016.

Kirby, Jason. "Canada's demographic gap can't be filled with immigrants." *Maclean's*. 30 Sep. 2016. Web. 29 Jan. 2017.

---. "The Perils of Being an Energy Superpower." *Maclean's*. 12 Nov. 2015. Web. 6 Apr. 2016.

Kirton, John. "Canada Shows Its Strength." *Toronto Star*. 31 Oct. 2006. Web. 3 Apr. 2011.

Kissinger, Henry A. "Realists vs. Idealists." *New York Times*. 12 May 2005. Web. 3 Apr. 2011.

Kliff, Sarah. "'Maple Leaf Miracle': How Canada and four other countries regained AAA ratings." *Washington Post*. 12 Aug. 2011. Web. 14 Nov. 2014.

Koring, Paul. "Arctic Treaty Leaves Much Undecided." *Globe and Mail*. 24 Aug. 2012. Web. 3 Apr. 2016.

---. "Keystone Pipeline Good for Canada, Not U.S., Obama Says." *Globe and Mail*. 14 Nov. 2014. Web. 3 Apr. 2016.

---. "Resources Minister Touting Keystone in U.S. Slams Climate Scientist." *Globe and Mail*. 24 Apr. 2013. Web. 3 Apr. 2016.

Krugel, Lauren. "Canada Could Replace Russia as Europe's Gas Supplier – Eventually." *Globe and Mail*. 27 Mar. 2014. Web. 3 May 2015.

---. "Trudeau says he 'misspoke' when suggesting oilsands need to be phased out." *Maclean's*. 24 Jan. 2017. Web. 30 Jan. 2017.

"Kyoto and out." *Economist*. 17 Dec. 2011. Web. 23 Dec. 2011.

Labott, Elise, and Dan Berman. "Obama rejects Keystone XL pipeline." *CNN*. 6 Nov. 2015. Web. 31 Jan. 2017.

Lawson, Guy. "Trudeau's Canada, Again." *New York Times*. 8 Dec. 2015. Web. 25 Jan. 2017.

Levi, Joshua. "Harper: I'd Never Sell out Israel." *Australian Jewish News*. 17 Feb. 2017. Web. 20 Feb. 2017.

Levitz, Stephanie. "Conservative Motion to Save Religious Freedoms Office Fails to Pass Commons." *Global News*. 21 Mar. 2016. Web. 20 Nov. 2016.

---. "John Baird: Won't Sell 'Canada's Principled Foreign Policy' for UN Security Council Seat." *National Post*. 1 May 2013. Web. 4 May 2016.

---. "Opening Syrian refugee 'floodgates' too risky for Canada: Harper." *CTV News*. 8 Sep. 2015. Web. 28 Jan. 2017.

"Liberals Applaud Donald Trump's Keystone XL Support." *Maclean's*. 24 Jan. 2017. Web. 31 Jan. 2017.

"Liberals Commit More Money to Maternal Health, Including Contraception." *CBC News*. 7 Mar. 2016. Web. 25 Apr. 2016.

Ljunggren, David. "Every G20 Nation Wants to Be Canada, Insists PM." *Reuters*. 25 Sept. 2009. Web. 20 Oct. 2011.

Lou, Ethan. "TransCanada Natgas Mainline No Substitute for Asian Markets." *Reuters*. 20 Mar. 2017. Web. 20 Mar. 2017.

Lukacs, Martin. "Harper's Canada has more than one refugee death on its hands." *Guardian*. 4 Sep. 2015. Web. 28 Jan. 2017.

Lunn, Susan. "China-Canada Trade Ties Stall over Cabinet Divisions." *CBC News*. 21 Apr. 2014. Web. 20 May 2016.

MacCharles, Tonda, and Ben Spurrs. "Harper pitting country against Muslims, some Niqab wearers say." *Toronto Star*. 7 Oct. 2015. Web. 29 Jan. 2017.

MacCharles, Tonda. "Free-Trade Agreement with India a 'high priority' for Canada." *Toronto Star*. 19 Jan. 2017. Web. 20 Jan. 2017.

Macdonell, Beth. "Trump's travel ban causes migrants to trek across Canadian border into Manitoba." *CTV News*. 31 Jan. 2017. Web. 1 Feb. 2017.

MacKinnon, Leslie. "Mark Carney Named Bank of England Governor." *CBC News*. 26 Nov. 2012. Web. 31 May 2015.

MacKinnon, Mark. "Canadian Troops Arrive in Ukraine to Train Soldiers Fighting Separatists." *Globe and Mail*. 14 Sept. 2015. Web. 25 May 2016.

---. "Harper's World: Canada's New Role on the Global Stage." *Globe and Mail*. 28 Sept. 2015. Web. 4 Nov. 2016.

Mackrael, Kim. "'Huge Opportunities' for Canadian Mining Industry to Work in Developing Countries." *Globe and Mail*. 19 June 2013. Web. 4 May 2015.

---. "Commercial Motives Driving Canada's Foreign Aid, Documents Reveal." *Globe and Mail*. 10 Jan. 2014. Web. 20 Feb. 2016.

---. "Fantino Defends CIDA's Corporate Shift." *Globe and Mail*. 3 Dec. 2012. Web. 4 May 2013.

---. "Michaëlle Jean Elected New Head of La Francophonie." *Globe and Mail*. 30 Nov. 2014. Web. 28 May 2016.

Mansbridge, Peter. "Interview with Stephen Harper (Part One)." *CBC The National*. 19 Jan. 2011. Television. 2 Dec. 2015.

Markusoff, Jason. "Canada remains on Donald Trump's nice list – for now." *Maclean's*. 23 Jan. 2017. Web. 27 Jan. 2017.

Marowits, Ross. "Renegotiation of Pacific trade deal not possible: Trade Minister." *Globe and Mail*. 14 Jan. 2016. Web. 27 Jan 2017.

Martin, Patrick. "Nearly Half Canadians Say Ottawa's Policy on Israeli-Palestinian Conflict 'Strikes Right Balance'." *Globe and Mail*. 31 Jan. 2012. Web. 20 Feb. 2013.

Mas, Susana, and Alison Crawford. "Justin Trudeau's government drops controversial niqab appeal." *CBC News*. 16 Nov. 2015. Web. 29 Jan. 2017.

Mas, Susana. "Delayed China Trade Deal Reflects Tory Dissent, NDP Says." *CBC News*. 22 Apr. 2013. Web. 20 Apr. 2015.

---. "Harper Won't Take No for an Answer on Keystone XL." *CBC News*. 26 Sept. 2013. Web. 10 Jan. 2015.

---. "Immigration changes to watch for in 2015." *CBC News*. 1 Jan. 2015. Web. 28 Jan. 2017.

McCarthy, Shawn, and Steven Chase. "Ottawa Approves Nexen, Progress Foreign Takeovers." *Globe and Mail*. 7 Dec. 2012. Web. 3 Apr. 2014.

McCarthy, Shawn. "Support for Climate Action Still Strong in Canada, Poll Finds." *Globe and Mail*. 30 Nov. 2011. Web. 1 Dec. 2011.

McKenna, Barrie. "Canada 'Deeply Skeptical' Iran Will Follow through on Nuclear Deal." *Globe and Mail*. 24 Nov. 2013. Web. 4 May 2014.

---. "The U.S. isn't out to hurt Canada. We're just too small to worry about." *Globe and Mail*. 6 July 2014. Web. 21 Jan. 2017.

McMillan, Tim. "Natural Gas Is a Key Piece of Canada's Climate Puzzle, at Home and Abroad." *Globe and Mail*. 8 June 2016. Web. 21 Jan. 2017.

Meissner, Dirk. "Softwood dispute with U.S. sees B.C. looking to sell lumber in China, India." *National Observer*. 30 Nov. 2016. Web. 22 Jan. 2017.

Milewski, Terry. "Shipbuilding Contract Holds $250M Mystery." *CBC News*. 4 May 2013. Web. 4 Apr. 2015.

"Military's Arctic Training Facility Opens in Resolute." *CBC News*. 13 Aug. 2013. Web. 2 Oct. 2014.

Momani, Bessma. "Who's really 'chasing headlines'? Domestic and foreign relations intertwine at Munk debate." *Globe and Mail*. 29 Sep. 2015. Web. 28 Jan. 2017.

"Most Canadians Disagree with Trudeau's Plan to Withdraw CF-18s, Poll Suggests." *CBC News*. 6 Feb. 2016. Web. 4 May 2016.

Mulroney, Brian. "Canada Can Lead: Remember Our Apartheid Fight." *Globe and Mail*. 8 Dec. 2015. Web. 19 Apr. 2016.

Murphy, Jessica, and Nicky Woolf. "Justin Trudeau Elected New Canadian Prime Minister as Liberals Return to Power." *Guardian*. 20 Oct. 2015. Web. 15 Jan. 2017.

Murphy, Rex. "An Institution That Accepts North Korea and Iran Has Nothing over Us." *National Post*. 16 Oct. 2010. Web. 3 Apr. 2011.

Nerenberg, Karl. "Trudeau should rescind safe country status for U.S., and all others." *Rabble.ca*. 31 Jan. 2017. Web. 31 Jan. 2017.

"New Zealand releases text of Trans-Pacific Partnership agreement." *Maclean's*. 5 Nov. 2015. Web. 22 Jan. 2017.

Nicholls, Gerry. "Why the elites hate Harper." *Toronto Sun*. 20 Sep. 2015. Web. 22 Jan. 2017.

"Nicholson Deflects Criticism over Canada's Arctic Council Chairmanship." *CTV News*. 25 Apr. 2015. Web. 30 May 2015.

Nicky, Adam. "Free-Trade Agreement with Canada to Open up New Markets in Jordan." *National Post.* 10 Oct. 2012. Web. 12 Dec. 2014.

Nicolaou, Anna. "Canada delays plan to bring in 25,000 Syrian refugees." *Financial Times.* 25 Nov. 2015. Web. 30 Jan. 2017.

Oliver, Joe. "An Open Letter from Natural Resources Minister Joe Oliver." *Globe and Mail.* 9 Jan. 2012. Web. 3 Apr. 2015.

Omar, Mohamed. "Harper Says Canada 'Most Admired' Country in the World." *Huffington Post Canada.* 13 Sep. 2015. Web. 28 Jan. 2017.

"Palestinians Summon Canadian Envoy over Foreign Minister John Baird's East Jerusalem Meeting." *Toronto Star.* 15 Apr. 2013. Web. 2 Mar. 2014.

Panetta, Alexander. "A Carbon Tax or Cap-and-trade: Liberals Suggest Every Province Must Choose." *CBC News.* 21 Sep. 2016. Web. 25 Jan. 2017.

---. "Canadian border bill passes U.S. Congress: enables long-awaited reforms." *CTV News.* 10 Dec. 2016. Web. 22 Jan. 2017.

Patriquin, Martin. "With Anti-Muslim Campaign, Canada Has Its Trump Moment." *New York Times.* 16 Oct. 2015. Web. 29 Jan. 2017.

Payton, Laura. "Baird Promotes Record on Women's Rights around World." *CBC News.* 14 Sept. 2012. Web. 25 Apr. 2015.

---. "Canada's Foreign Aid Commitment to Contraception Low despite Great Need." *CBC News.* 25 June 2015. Web. 25 July 2015.

---. "Commonwealth Countries Ignoring Hatred, Baird Says." *CBC News.* 23 June 2012. Web. 25 Apr. 2014.

---. "Federal government to appeal ruling reversing 'cruel' cuts to refugee health." *CBC News.* 4 July 2014. Web. 28 Jan. 2017.

---. "Religious Freedom Speech Offers Few Clues about New Office." *CBC News.* 24 May 2012. Web. 25 May 2015.

---. "Stephen Harper Vows Loyalty to Israel in Speech to Knesset." *CBC News.* 20 Jan. 2014. Web. 4 Apr. 2015.

"Peace and Security: Canada's Hallmark in World Affairs." *Canada World View* 6 (1999): 10-16. Print.

"Peace, Order and Rocky Government." *Economist.* 1 Dec. 2005. Web. 2 Mar. 2010.

Press, Jordan. "Canada is now an intellectual powerhouse rather than a resource-based economy, Justin Trudeau tells Davos." *National Post.* 21 Jan. 2016. Web. 28 Jan. 2017.

"Prime Minister Stephen Harper Announces He Won't Attend Russia's Winter Olympics in Sochi." *National Post.* 18 Dec. 2013. Web. 4 May 2014.

Proctor, Jason. "Northern Gateway Pipeline Approval Overturned." *CBC News.* 30 June 2016. Web. 12 Dec. 2016.

Proudfoot, Shannon. "Ottawa drops the hammer on carbon pricing. Now what?" *Maclean's.* 16 Oct. 2016. Web. 27 Jan. 2017.

Proussalidis, Daniel. "Greenpeace Slams Kyoto Withdrawal." *Toronto Sun.* 13 Dec. 2011. Web. 20 Dec. 2013.

Pugliese, David. "Canadian Army headed to mission in Africa 'very soon': top general." *National Post.* 14 July 2016. Web. 25 Jan. 2017.

Quan, Douglas. "Harper appeals court ruling that struck down ban on wearing niqab during citizenship oath." *National Post.* 9 Mar. 2015. Web. 29 Jan. 2017.

Reguly, Eric. "The world is passing Harper by on carbon tax issue." *Globe and Mail.* 5 June 2015. Web. 25 Jan. 2017.

"'Religious Freedom Is under Attack': How a Canadian Agency Teaches Respect Where It's Tough to Find." *National Post.* 20 Mar. 2016. Web. 5 June 2016.

"Religious Freedom Office Defended by Baird." *CBC News.* 2 Jan. 2012. Web. 20 Feb. 2013.

"Republicans Aim to Take Keystone XL Decision out of Obama's Hands." *Maclean's.* 22 May 2013. Web. 20 June 2014.

"Richard Gere Lauds Harper for Meeting Dalai Lama, but Criticizes Him for Not Doing It in Public." *National Post.* 27 Apr. 2012. Web. 5 July 2014.

Robillard, Alexandre. "Michaëlle Jean urges 'new relevance' for la Francophonie." *Toronto Star.* 30 Nov. 2014. Web. 20 Oct. 2016.

Robson, John. "Stephane Dion's fog-bound foreign policy doctrine." *National Post.* 31 Mar. 2016. Web. 23 Jan. 2017.

Russell, Andrew. "New poll suggests Justin Trudeau 'Just not ready' ad is effective among voters." *Global News.* 6 Sep. 2015. Web. 20 Jan. 2017.

Saunders, Doug. "On Israel, Harper Stands Alone at G8 Summit." *Globe and Mail.* 25 May 2011. Web. 8 Sept. 2012.

Savage, Luiza Ch. "Land of the freeloaders: The battle for a new cross-border bridge." *Maclean's.* 21 May 2015. Web. 21 Jan. 2017.

---. "The Untold Story of Keystone." *Maclean's.* 27 Jan. 2014. Web. 4 May 2015.

Schofield, John. "Canada: An Energy Superpower?" *20/20 Magazine.* 2011. Web. 6 Apr. 2015.

Sevunts, Levon. "How will Canada's foreign policy change under Stéphane Dion?" *Radio Canada International.* 8 Nov. 2015. Web. 23 Jan. 2017.

Shephard, Michelle. "How Canada has abandoned its role as peacekeeper." *Toronto Star.* 31 Oct. 2014. Web. 22 Jan. 2017.

Shiab, Naël. "Marchandises Militaires: La Grande Hypocrisie Canadienne." *L'actualité.* Feb. 2017. Web. 20 Mar. 2017.

Shum, David. "TPP members look to salvage Pacific Rim trade deal after U.S. withdrawal." *Global News.* 24 Jan. 2017. Web. 27 Jan. 2017.

Siddiqui, Haroon. "How Harper systematically mined anti-Muslim prejudices."
    Toronto Star. 10 Apr. 2016. Web. 27 Jan. 2017.

Siebert, John. "An Idea Whose Time Has Come." *The Ploughshares Monitor* 33.3
    (2012): 14-19. Print.

Simon, Bernard. "Canada Leaves Kyoto to Avoid Heavy Penalties." *Financial
    Times.* 13 Dec. 2011. Web. 12 May 2012.

Simon, Darran, and Eliott C. McLaughlin. "Keystone and Dakota Access
    pipelines: How did we get here?" *CNN.* 25 Jan. 2017. Web 28 Jan. 2017.

"Six Diplomats Differ on Canada's New 'Dollar Diplomacy'." *Globe and Mail.*
    27 Nov. 2013. Web. 4 May 2014.

Slater, Joanna. "Harper 'Won't Take No for an Answer' from U.S. on Keystone
    XL." *Globe and Mail.* 26 Sept. 2013. Web. 20 Apr. 2014.

---. "Harper in New York, but Won't Address UN." *Globe and Mail.* 25 Sept.
    2013. Web. 20 Oct. 2014.

Solomon, Evan. "In Defence of the Defunct Office of Religious Freedom."
    Maclean's. 30 Mar. 2016. Web. 4 May 2016.

---. "Is NAFTA a goner? Don't bet on it. We've heard this before." *Maclean's.*
    27 July 2016. Web. 23 Jan. 2017.

---. "Why Canada – and its economy – has plenty to fear from Trump."
    Maclean's. 30 Jan. 2017. Web. 2 Feb. 2017.

Sorensen, Chris. "Stephen Harper: Oil's Worst Enemy." *Maclean's.* 5 Jan. 2015.
    Web. 10 Sept. 2016.

Stastna, Kazi. "Immigrants the Proudest Canadians, Poll Suggests." *CBC News.*
    15 Feb. 2012. Web. 20 Mar. 2016.

"Staying the Course in Libya." *Toronto Star.* 15 June 2011. Web. 16 Dec. 2016.

"Stéphane Dion: On 'responsible conviction' and Liberal foreign policy."
    Maclean's. 29 Mar. 2016. Web. 23 Jan. 2017.

Stewart, Brian. "The New 'Harper Doctrine' in Foreign Relations." *CBC News.*
    11 June 2011. Web. 10 Dec. 2016.

Stiem, Tyler. "Race and real estate: how hot Chinese money is making Vancouver
    unlivable." *Guardian.* 7 July 2016. Web. 31 Jan. 2017.

"Strong, Proud and Free-Riding." *Economist.* 12 Sept. 2015. Web. 23 Dec. 2016.

Taber, Jane. "NATO Official Questioning Canada's Commitment." *Globe and
    Mail.* 24 Nov. 2013. Web. 12 Oct. 2015.

---. "PM Brands Canada an 'Energy Superpower'." *Globe and Mail.* 15 July
    2006. Web. 6 Apr. 2015.

Talwani, Manik. "Canada: The next Oil Superpower?" *National Post.* 15 Aug.
    2003. Web. 6 Apr. 2015.

Tasker, John Paul. "Iran sanctions lifted by Canada, but Justin Trudeau still faces
    'delicate dance'." *CBC News.* 13 Feb. 2016. Web. 25 Jan. 2017.

---. "Trudeau welcomes Trump's Keystone XL decision." *CBC News.* 24 Jan. 2017. Web. 31 Jan. 2017.

Tharoor, Ishaan. "How a Muslim veil is dominating Canada's election race." *Washington Post.* 5 Oct. 2015. Web. 29 Jan. 2017.

"The Foreign Account Tax Compliance Act: Border babies v the IRS." *Economist.* 3 Mar. 2016. Web. 21 Jan. 2017.

"The Last Liberals." *Economist.* 29 Oct. 2016. Web. 10 Nov. 2016.

"The Melbourne Supremacy." *Economist.* 13 Aug. 2013. Web. 20 Dec. 2016.

"The Political Predator." *Economist.* 13 Sept. 2014. Web. 3 Dec. 2016.

"The World's Most Liveable Cities." *Economist.* Aug. 2016. Web. 20 Oct. 2016.

"These Are The Names Of All The Canadians Who Died In The War In Afghanistan." *Huffington Post Canada.* 9 May 2014. Web. 20 May 2016.

"Tories Defend Withdrawal from UN Drought 'Talkfest'." *CBC News.* 28 Mar. 2013. Web. 3 July 2013.

Tran, Mark. "Canada's delegation to Nato mocks Russia with Ukraine geography lesson." *Guardian.* 28. Aug. 2014. Web. 2 Feb. 2015.

"Trudeau affirms support of NATO after Trump calls it obsolete." *Maclean's.* 17 Jan. 2017. Web. 26 Jan. 2017.

"Trudeau Tells UN Conference: Canada Not Finished Helping Syrian Refugees." *CTV News.* 19 Sep. 2016. Web. 30 Jan. 2017.

Trudeau, Justin. "The World Needs Canada to Be a Meaningful Member of the UN." *Huffington Post Canada.* 27 Sep. 2015. Web. 24 Jan. 2017.

"Trudeau's Global Debut Finds Him on Same Page as G20 on Key Issues." *Maclean's.* 13 Nov. 2015. Web. 2 Feb. 2016.

"Trump Sells Idea of U.S. Minus NAFTA, TPP." *Maclean's.* 29 June 2016. Web. 25 Jan. 2017.

"U.S. Sub May Have Toured Canadian Arctic Zone." *National Post.* 19 Dec. 2005. Web. 2 Mar. 2011.

"Vancouver and Seattle seek to come closer together." *Economist.* 13 Oct. 2016. Web. 26 Jan. 2017.

Vanderklippe, Nathan, and Laura Stone. "Canadian Ambassador Criticizes Chinese President during Trudeau Trip." *Globe and Mail.* 31 Aug. 2016. Web. 12 Dec. 2016.

"Vote Compass: Justin Trudeau perceived winner in foreign policy debate." *CBC News.* 1 Oct. 2015. Web. 20 Jan. 2017.

Waldie, Paul. "Trudeau signs CETA but final ratification still required by European Union." *Globe and Mail.* 30 Oct. 2016. Web. 23 Jan. 2017.

Weber, Bob. "Canada's Arctic Council Leadership to Be Handed over at Iqaluit Meeting." *Globe and Mail.* 19 Apr. 2015. Web. 10 May 2015.

Webster, Paul Christopher. "The Silent Partner." *Globe and Mail.* 5 Jan. 2017.
    Web. 4 Feb. 2017.

Wells, Paul. "Freeland 'visibly moved' during CETA negotiations." *Toronto Star.*
    7 Nov. 2016. Web. 19 Dec. 2016.

---. "Justin Trudeau, man of substance." *Maclean's.* 29 June 2015. Web. 29 Jan.
    2017.

"What Does Canada Trade with China?" *CBC News.* 12 July 2012. Web. 3 July
    2013.

Wherry, Aaron. "Canada Does Not Just 'Go Along' in Order to 'Get Along'."
    Maclean's. 26 Sept. 2011. Web. 2 Feb. 2013.

---. "On softwood lumber, Canada and the United States still 'far apart'." *CBC
    News.* 18 Aug. 2016. Web. 21 Jan. 2017.

Whyte, Kenneth. "In Conversation: Stephen Harper." *Maclean's.* 5 July 2011.
    Web. 17 Dec. 2012.

Wilfert, Bryon. "Canada Needs Leadership on Climate Change – not Rhetoric."
    Embassy. 2 Apr. 2013. Web. 1 Feb. 2016.

Williams, Nia. "Canada energy sector sidelined as Big Oil chases fatter profits."
    Reuters. 24 Feb. 2017. Web. 24 Feb. 2017.

Willick, Frances. "Pearson Centre Closing." *The Chronicle Herald.* 5 Oct. 2013.
    Web. 29 May 2014.

Woodley, Thomas. "Pro-Israel Government Policies Don't Speak For Most
    Canadians." *Huffington Post Canada.* 17 Feb. 2017. Web. 20 Feb. 2017.

Woods, Allan. "Justin Trudeau 'Just not ready' ad was effective: Poll." *Toronto
    Star.* 5 Sep. 2015. Web. 20 Jan. 2017.

Woolley, Frances. "Sorry, but Canada Was Never the No. 1 Place to Live." *Globe
    and Mail.* 19 Mar. 2013. Web. 20 Jan. 2017.

"WTI tops $50 a barrel for 1st time since June." *CBC News.* 6 Oct. 2016. Web.
    20. Feb. 2017.

York, Geoffrey. "Oil Thirst from China Adds Fuel to Trade Tussle." *Globe and
    Mail.* 14 Oct. 2005. Web. 12 Apr. 2014.

Zerbisias, Antonia. "Israel Need Not Worry about Justin Trudeau." *Al Jazeera.*
    11 Nov. 2015. Web. 20 Nov. 2016.

Zilio, Michelle. "Canada, Denmark Reach Tentative Deal on Decades-Long
    Arctic Waters Dispute." *iPolitics.* 28 Nov. 2012. Web. 12 May 2015.

---. "Canada's Religious Freedom Ambassador Joins Christian Think Tank."
    Globe and Mail. 16 Mar. 2016. Web. 20 May 2016.

---. "Liberals to Close Office of Religious Freedom, Dion Says." *Globe and Mail.*
    29 Mar. 2016. Web. 20 May 2016.

Others

Anderson, Bruce, and David Coletto. "Public Opinion on Stephen Harper's Approach to Foreign Affairs." *Abacus Data*. 2014. Web. 20 May 2016.

Anderson, Mary B.; Dayna Brown, and Isabella Jean. *Time to Listen: Hearing People on the Receiving End of International Aid*. Cambridge, MA: CDA Collaborative Learning Projects, 2012. Web. 20 May 2016.

Asia Pacific Foundation of Canada. "2016 National Opinion Poll: Canadian Views on Asia." *Asia Pacific Foundation of Canada*. 2016. Web. 2 Oct. 2016.

Axworthy, Lloyd, and Allan Rock. "A Victory for the Responsibility to Protect." *University of Ottawa*. 2011. Web. 20 Apr. 2016.

Bratt, Duane. "Implementing the Reform Party Agenda: The Roots of Stephen Harper's Foreign Policy." *Canadian Political Science Association*. 2016. Web. 2 Jan. 2017.

---. "Mr. Harper Goes to War: Canada, Afghanistan, and the Return of 'High Politics' in Canadian Foreign Policy." *Canadian Political Science Association*. 2007. Web. 20 Oct. 2015.

Bryant, Tyler. "Pipe dreams: What's next for Keystone XL?" *David Suzuki Foundation*. 17 Nov. 2011. Web. 25 Jan. 2017.

"Canada Crude Oil Production by Year." *Index Mundi*. 2016. Web. 1 Feb. 2017.

Canada-Asia Energy Futures Task Force. "Securing Canada's Energy Future." *Asia Pacific Foundation of Canada*. 2012. Web. 4 Oct. 2016.

Chapin, Paul, and George Petrolekas. "The Strategic Outlook for Canada." *Conference of Defence Associations Institute*. 2012. Web. 4 Mar. 2013.

Cherniak, Cyndee Todgham. "What Is 'Enlightened Sovereignty'?" *Trade Lawyers Blog*. 2010. Web. 16 Jan. 2017.

Clark, Joe. "Canada as 'Denier and Outlier': Joe Clark on Harper's Foreign Policy." *The Tyee*. 28 Aug. 2015. Web. 20 June 2016.

Coleman, Jesse. "Why Trump's Dakota Access and Keystone XL pipeline plans don't add up." *Greenpeace*. 1 Feb. 2017. Web. 2 Feb. 2017.

Cutler, Robert. "Canadian Company Strikes Deal for LNG Exports to Europe." *Oilprice.com*. 2013. Web. 5 Dec. 2016.

de Kerckchove, Ferry. "The Strategic Outlook for Canada 2014: The Search for Leadership." *Conference of Defence Associations Institute*. 2014. Web. 5 Dec. 2016.

de Kerckhove, Ferry, and George Petrolekas. "Canada as an Energy Superpower: Myths and Realities." *German Marshall Fund*. 2014. Web. 23 May 2015.

de Trenqualye, Madeleine. "Climate Change Politics in the Age of Trudeau and Trump: What's Next?" *The Tyee*. 16 Dec. 2016. Web. 28 Jan. 2017.

Ditmars, Hadani. "Why Is Canada Israel's New Best Friend?" *Middle East Eye.* 2015. Web. 2 Sept. 2016.

Engler, Yves. "Canada Strengthens Ties with Saudi Arabia." *Global Research – Centre for Research on Globalization.* 2012. Web. 25 May 2015.

Environics Institute. "Focus Canada 2012." 2012. Web. 26 July 2016.

"Federal Election Debate: The Munk Debate on Canada's Foreign Policy." *The Munk Debates.* 28 Sep. 2015. Web. 17 Jan. 2017.

"Gareth Evans and the Responsibility to Protect." 2016. Web. 20 June 2016.

Gattinger, Monica. "Is Canada an 'energy Superpower'?" *Energy Exchange.* 2015. Web. 1 Dec. 2016.

"Global Stockpiles of Antipersonnel Mines." Landmine and Cluster Munition Monitor. 2016. Web. 21 Jan. 2017.

"Harper's Northern Strategy Couched in Empty Rhetoric." *Greenpeace.* 2014. Web. 5 June 2016.

Hester, Annette. "Canada as the 'Emerging Energy Superpower': Testing the Case." *Canadian Defence and Foreign Affairs Institute.* 2007. Web. 20 Oct. 2016.

Isard, Philip. "Northern Vision: Northern Development during the Diefenbaker Era." UWSpace. 2010. Web.

Jaccard, Mark; Mikela Hein, and Tiffany Vass. "Is Win-Win Possible? Can Canada's Government Achieve Its Paris Commitment… and Get Re-Elected?" 2016. Web. 21 Jan. 2017.

Jaccard, Mark. "Canadian Climate Policy Report Card: 2015." *Energy and Materials Research Group.* 2015. Web. 20 Nov. 2016.

Jarratt, Emma, and James Thomson. "Canada Slow to Deliver on Arctic Commitments." *Barents Observer.* 2014. Web. 3 July 2016.

John Humphrey Centre for Peace and Human Rights. "The Universal Declaration of Human Rights." Web. 19 June 2016.

King, Ed. "Justin Trudeau: climate leader or charlatan?" *Climate Home News.* 25 Jan. 2017. Web. 31 Jan. 2017.

Kirton, John. "Canada as a G8 and G20 Principal Power." 2010. Web. 4 May 2015.

---. "Canada as a Principal Financial Power: G-7 and IMF Diplomacy in the Crisis of 1997-9." 2017. Web. 1 Feb. 2017.

---. "The Harper Years." 2013. Web. 3 Apr. 2015.

Lackenbauer, P. Whitney. "If It Ain't Broke, Don't Break It: Expanding and Enhancing the Canadian Rangers." 2013. Web. 3 May 2014.

---. "Mixed Messages from an 'Arctic Superpower'? Sovereignty, Security, and Canada's Northern Strategy." 2011. Web. 20 Mar. 2014.

Lemphers, Nathan. "Climate concerns are key in Keystone XL pipeline debate." *Pembina Institute*. 17 Jan. 2013. Web. 25 Jan. 2017.

Lenard, Patti Tamara. "Stephen Harper's abhorrent record on refugees and immigration." Broadbent Institute. 21 Sep. 2015. Web. 30 Jan. 2017.

Lennox, Patrick. "Canada as a Specialized Power." *Canadian Political Science Association*. 2007. Web. 1 Mar. 2009.

"Looking Back: Canada's Arctic Council Chairmanship." *Greenpeace*. 2015. Web. 20 Nov. 2016.

Loukacheva, Natalia. "Legal Challenges in the Arctic." *The Borderless North, Oulu: The Fourth Northern Research Forum*. 2008. Web. 20 Nov. 2016.

Mackay, Derek. "The Evolution of Canadian Diplomacy towards the Israeli-Palestinian Conflict." *Univeristy of Ottawa Research*. 2015. Web. 4 May 2016.

Marceau, Richard J., and Clement W. Bowman, eds. "Canada Becoming a Sustainable Energy Powerhouse." *Canadian Academy of Engineering*. 2014. Web. 20 Sept. 2016.

Marsh, James H. "Québec Conferences 1943, 1944." *Canadian Encyclopedia*. 2015. Web. 29 Sept. 2016.

"Munk Debate on Foreign Policy: The best debate of all?" *OpenCanada.org*. 28 Sep. 2015. Web. 20 Jan. 2017.

Nafzinger, Gloria. "Refugee resettlement serves to protect the most vulnerable among the refugees." *Amnesty International*. 24 Nov. 2015. Web. 31 Jan. 2017.

Naylor, Sherry. "Election Debate: Date Announced for First Ever Federal Election Debate on Foreign Policy." *The Munk Debates*. 14 Aug. 2015. Web. 16 Jan. 2017.

Nikiforuk, Andrew. "Harper's Revolutionary Foreign Policy." *The Tyee*. 2015. Web. 14 June 2016.

Nossal, Kim Richard, and Leah Sarson. "About Face: Explaining Changes in Canada's China Policy, 2006-2012." *Canadian Political Science Association*. 2013. Web. 20 Apr. 2015.

Nossal, Kim Richard. "Primat der Wahlurne: Explaining Stephen Harper's Foreign Policy." *International Studies Association*. 2014. Web. 12 Apr. 2016.

Peace Operations Training Institute. "Closure of the Pearson Centre, Canadian Peacekeeping Training Centre." 2013. Web. 22 Sept. 2016.

Petrolekas, George, and Ferry de Kerckchove. "The Strategic Outlook for Canada." *Conference of Defence Associations Institute*. 2013. Web. 6 July 2016.

Plouffe, Joël. "Stephen Harper's Arctic Paradox." *Canadian Global Affairs Institute*. 2014. Web. 3 Dec. 2014.

Riddell-Dixon, Elizabeth. "Canada's Arctic Policy." *The Canada-U.S. Institute*. 2012. Web. 20 Apr. 2014.

Saint-Cyr, Yosie. *Government of Canada v. Face Coverings: A Debate on the Limits to Freedom of Religion.* CanLII. 27 Sep. 2015. Web. 29 Jan. 2017.

Schönwälder, Gerd. "Principles and Prejudice: Foreign Policy under the Harper Government." *CIPS Policy Briefs.* 2014. Web. 3 Oct. 2015.

"Seven Foreign Policy Wishes for Canada's New Government." *OpenCanada.org.* 20 Oct. 2015. Web. 31 Jan. 2017.

Stanford, Jim. "A Cure for Dutch Disease: Active Sector Strategies for Canada's Economy." *Canadian Centre for Policy Alternatives.* 2012. Web. 20 Sept. 2016.

Swift, Anthony. "Paris Climate Agreement Explained: What's next for Canada?" *Natural Resources Defense Council.* 2015. Web. 20 Nov. 2016.

---. "Significant Obstacles Remain in Building Keystone XL." *Natural Resources Defense Council.* 25 Jan. 2017. Web. 30 Jan. 2017.

Tiagi, Raaj, and Lu Zhou. "Canada's Economic Relations with China." *The Fraser Institute.* 2009. Web. 12 Dec. 2015.

"The Changing Atmosphere Implications for Global Security." 1988. Web. 12 Dec. 2015.

"The Soft Power 30: A Global Ranking of Soft Power." 2015. Web. 20 Dec. 2016.

"Think Ahead. Act Together: Leaders' Declaration G7 Summit, 7-8 June 2015." 2015. Web. 21 Jan. 2017.

Vucetic, Srdjan. "A Nation of Feminist Arms Dealers? Canada and Military Exports." 2017. Web. 20 Feb. 2017.

Wilt, James. "Why Trudeau's Commitment to Harper's Old Emissions Target Might Not Be Such Bad News After All." *DeSmog Canada.* 2016. Web. 23 Jan. 2017.

---. "Conservatives 'Had No Intention' of Dealing with Climate Change: Mark Jaccard." *DeSmog Canada.* 2015. Web. 10 Oct. 2016.

World Wildlife Fund. "WWF Statement on the Keystone XL: Environmental Impact Statement." 3 Feb. 2014. Web. 25 Jan. 2017.

Abbreviations

AI	Amnesty International
APEC	Asia-Pacific Economic Cooperation
AWACs	Airborne Early Warning and Control
BRICS	Brazil, Russia, India, China and South Africa
CAD	Canadian dollar
CBC	Canadian Broadcasting Corporation
CCC	Canadian Commercial Corporation
CETA	Comprehensive Economy and Trade Agreement
CIDA	Canadian International Development Agency
CLCS	Commission on the Limits of the Continental Shelf
CNOOC	China National Offshore Oil Corporation
COP21	The 21st session of the Conference of the Parties of the United Nations Framework on Climate Change
CUSFTA	Canada-United States Free Trade Agreement
DART	Disaster Assistance Response Team
DEA	Department of External Affairs
DEW	Distant Early Warning (Line)
DFAIT	Department of Foreign Affairs and International Trade
DFATD	Department of Foreign Affairs, Trade and Development
DND	Department of National Defence
EFTA	European Free Trade Association
EU	European Union
FIPA	foreign investment promotion and protection agreement

FTA	free trade agreement
G20	Group of Twenty
G7/G8	Group of Seven/Eight
GATT	General Agreement on Tariffs and Trade
GDP	gross domestic product
GHG	greenhouse gases
GNI	Gross National Income
ICC	International Criminal Court
ICISS	International Commission on Intervention and State Sovereignty
IEA	International Energy Agency
IEA	International Energy Agency
ISAF	International Stabilization Assistance Force
ISDS	investor-state dispute settlement
ISIS	Islamic State of Iraq and the Levant
LAV	Light Armoured Vehicle
LGBTI	Lesbian, Gay, Bisexual, Transgeder / Transsexual, Intersexed
LGBTQ	Lesbian, Gay, Bisexual, Transgender / Transsexual, Queer / Questioning
LNG	liquified natural gas
MP	Member of Parliament
NAFTA	North American Free Trade Agreement
NATO	North Atlantic Treaty Organization
NDP	New Democratic Party
NEB	National Energy Board
NGO	non-governmental organization
NORAD	North American Aerospace Defense Command
NORDREG	Northern Canada Vessel Traffic Services
OAS	Organization of American States
ODA	official development assistance
OECD	Organisation for Economic Co-operation and Development
OPEC	Organization of the Petroleum Exporting Countries
ORF	Office of Religious Freedom
OSCE	Organization for Security and Co-operation in Europe
R&D	research and development
R2P	Responsibility to Protect

SAH   Sponsorship Agreement Holder
TPP   Trans-Pacific Partnership
TTIP   Transatlantic Trade and Investment Partnership
U.N.   United Nations
U.S.   United States
UDHR   Universal Declaration of Human Rights
UK   United Kingdom
UNCLOS   United Nations Convention on the Law of the Sea
UNEF   United Nations Emergency Force
UNFCCC   United Nations Framework Convention on Climate Change
UNSC   United Nations Security Council
USA   United States of America
USD   United States dollar
USSR   Union of Soviet Socialist Republics
WTI   West Texas Intermediate
WTO   World Trade Organization

Index of names

Abbott John 20

Abdullah, king of Saudi Arabia 188, 238

Aglukkaq Leona 120, 157

Ahmadinejad Mahmoud 185

Aitken Hugh 21

Al-Asad Bashar 155

Alexander Chris 230

Anderson Bruce 78, 204

Anderson Mary B. 170

Annan Kofi 116, 146

Appel Jeremy 298

Appel Molot Maureen 201, 290

Arbour Louise 49, 146

Argitis Theophilos 306

Audet François 177, 287

Austen Ian 221, 231, 234, 251, 254

Axworthy Lloyd 46, 85, 133, 138, 145-146, 154-155, 169, 184, 195, 270

Badawi Raif 151

Baird John 86, 110, 121, 141, 148-150, 154, 156, 162, 164, 167, 185, 187

Baker Fox Annette 45, 47

Bambury Brent 255

Banerjee Sidhartha 268, 298

Barry Donald 22

Battersby Sarah-Joyce 237

Bélanger Louis 46

Bendavid Naftali 25, 298

Bennett Andrew 150-152

Berman Dan 249

Bernard Prosper M. Jr. 71, 146, 186

Bernstein Steven 116

Berthiaume Lee 151-152, 164, 222-223, 225-226

Berzins Christopher 49-50, 60

Bhushan Aniket 86

Biello David 118

Black Conrad 167

Blackwell Richard 287

Blake Edward 29

Blanchfield Mike 69, 138-139, 216, 225-226, 259, 267

Blatchford Andy 92, 266

Blencowe Andrew 64

Boer Stephen de 17

Boessenkool Ken 123, 163, 195

Bondy Matthew 209, 213-214, 248, 257

Bono, leader of U2 189

Bonokoski Mark 165
Bosold David 8
Boswell Randy 126
Botero Giovanni 40-41, 57
Bothwell Robert 57
Bouchard Charles 203
Bouchard Lucien 35
Bowman Clement W. 102-103
Brach Bal 244, 299
Bratt Duane 34, 88, 113, 118-120,
    122-124, 139-141, 156, 160-163,
    180-182, 185, 187-188, 192, 194,
    200-201, 204
Brebner John Bartlet 33, 57
Brewster Murray 197-199, 203-205
Brimelow Peter 201
Brinded Lianna 84
Brooks Stephen 30
Brown Dayna 170
Brown Robert Craig 20
Brown Stephen 171-173, 176, 179
Bryant Tyler 251
Buckley Chris 143
Bugailiskis Alexandra 17
Burgman Tamsyn 162
Burney Derek 85, 101, 185-186, 188,
    263
Burns Eedson Louis Millard "Tommy"
    50
Burton Charles 137-139, 141-143
Bush George Walker 94, 200
Buteux Paul 26, 33
Byers Michael 129, 131, 134

Campbell Clark 72, 85, 100, 121, 147,
    162, 187, 191, 203
Campbell Kim 213

Campion-Smith Bruce 204, 227
Cao Huhua 99
Caplan Gerald 144, 165-166, 211
Carney Mark 89
Chapin Paul 54, 65-66
Chapnick Adam 35-36, 41-43, 86, 154
Chase Steven 83-84, 131, 135, 142,
    147, 151, 153, 156, 167-170, 196,
    203, 225-226, 232, 270-271
Chivers Christopher John 132
Chrétien Jean 67, 79, 82, 87, 93-94,
    116-118, 124, 136-137, 143, 145,
    159, 161, 169, 171, 175-176, 179,
    189, 191, 195, 200-201, 215, 230,
    264
Churchill Winston 34-35, 41
Clark Charles Joseph "Joe" 81-82, 164,
    186, 204, 213
Cleland Mike 106
Clinton Hillary 249, 259
Coates Ken 131, 135
Cohen Andrew 54, 201
Coleman James 112
Coleman Jesse 250
Coletto David 78, 204
Combet Greg 121
Connolly Amanda 87, 216
Cooper Andrew Fenton 45, 64
Cox Robert 45
Crawford Alison 233
Creighton Donald 29
Cullen Catherine 204
Curry Bill 244
Cutler Robert 110

Dalai Lama 137-139, 143
Dallaire Roméo 51, 169, 193

Dawson Laura 93, 99, 101, 141
Day Stockwell 200
De Souza Mike 148, 253
Dembicki Geoff 245, 247
Dewitt David 36
Dharssi Alia 238
Dickinson Tim 248
Diefenbaker John 47, 124, 135, 149, 213
Dimat Frank 165
Dion Stéphane 117, 120, 143, 153, 215-222, 226, 258, 269-271
Ditmars Hadani 164-165
Do Trinh Theresa 86
Donaldson Gordon 31
Donnelly Aileen 230
Dorn A. Walter 50-51, 225
Doxey Margaret 47
Drohan Madelaine 180, 195-196
Dyck Rand 24-25

Eayrs James 36, 57
Elliot-Meisel Elizabeth R.B. 25
Emerson David 138
Enderle Georges 216-217
Engler Yves 167
Entezam Nasrollash 49
Ewart John Skirving 31-32, 84
Exner-Pirot Heather 136, 157

Fast Ed 141, 167
Fekete Jason 245-246
Fernandez de Kirchner Cristina 155
Fife Robert 157, 168, 270, 272
Fine Sean 232
Fiřtová Magdalena 179
Fisher Matthew 156

Fisk Robert 231, 234
Fitzgerald Andy 166
Flanagan Tom 134
Flannery Tim 122
Fowler Robert 180
Fréchette Louise 49
Freeland Chrystia 260, 266, 268
Freeman Linda 47, 145
Friesen Joe 89
Friscolanti Michael 227, 232
Frum David 85

Gabryś Marcin 196
Gaddafi Muammar 155, 185, 200, 203
Gajanan Mahita 262
Galt Alexander 20
Gandhi Mahatma 217
Gattinger Monica 105-106, 108-109, 112, 114-115
Gecelovsky Paul 42, 50
Geddes John 209, 215, 234, 241
Gelber Lionel 41, 44, 57
George Robert Peter 21, 65, 94, 153
Gheciu Alexandra 55
Gilchrist Emma 252
Gilles Rob 231
Gilmore Scott 82-83, 186, 198, 204
Giscard d'Estaing Valery 24
Glazebrook George Parkin de Twenebroker 44
Goldenberg Suzanne 108, 111-112
Goold Douglas 100
Gordon Julie 243
Gordon Mace 46
Gordon Stephen 84
Gore Christopher D. 116
Gotlieb Allan 36, 115

Granatstein John 22, 290
Grant George 21-22
Greenaway Norma 126
Greenhill Robert 82, 175-176, 178,
    194, 197
Greenspon Edward 104, 107, 112
Grenier Eric 78
Griffiths Franklyn 132
Gurney Matt 253
Gwiazda Wojtek 148

Haglund David G. 8, 35, 199
Hale Geoffrey 95-96, 103
Hall Chris 96, 113, 230
Hampson Fen Osler 101, 185-186
Hannay Chris 78-79
Harper Stephen 9-10, 12-16, 60-61,
    63, 65, 67-72, 74, 77-116, 118-120,
    122-144, 146-150, 152, 154-205,
    207-215, 217-236, 240-241, 244-
    245, 247-248, 250-253, 255-259,
    261, 264-266, 268-272, 276
Harris Kathleen 237, 242, 271
Harris Mike 170
Harrison Kathryn 116-118, 256
Hart Michael 8, 53
Hashem Mohamed 231
Heap Peter C. 190-191, 193
Hein Mikela 256
Heinbecker Paul 134, 147, 156-157,
    161, 216
Hemmat Samane 152-153
Hessey Krista 162, 166
Hester Annette 106
Higgott Richard A. 45
Hilliker John 22, 32-33
Hillmer Norman 32, 36, 57, 201

Hirsch Todd 245
Holbraad Carsten 45
Holloway Steven Kendall 27, 88-89
Holmes John 44
Hong Paul 142, 153
Hui Ann 143
Humphrey John Peters 48-49, 144
Hussain Murtaza 168
Hynek Nikola "Nik" 8, 42-43

Ibbitson John 81, 83, 99, 113, 121,
    135, 139, 141, 147, 155-157, 159-
    161, 178, 180, 186-187, 200, 203,
    209, 212-214, 257
Ignatieff Michael 239
Isard Philip 124
Ishaq Zunera 233
Ivison John 159, 203, 215

Jabir Humera 168
Jaccard Mark 119, 122-123, 256
Jackson Doreen 48-49, 195
Jackson Robert J. 48-49, 195
Jang Brent 119, 252
Jarratt Emma 129
Jean Isabella 170
Jean Michaëlle 180, 182
Jockel Joseph T. 26, 55, 194-195
Jordaan Sarah 112
Juneau Thomas 162-163

Karp Aaron 170
Kassam Ashifa 254
Keating Tom 24, 26-27, 55, 72, 147,
    179, 181, 184
Kelly Brent 212, 214, 269
Kennedy Mark 92

Kenney Jason 84, 139, 141, 229-230
Kent Peter 111, 113, 121
Keohane Robert 45
Kerckchove Ferry de 71, 80-81, 163
Kikwete Jakava 86
King William Lyon Mackenzie 31-35, 41, 44, 51, 57
Kinsman Jeremy 132, 248
Kirby Jason 103, 109, 241
Kirsch Philippe 49
Kirton John 19, 27, 36-37, 63-64, 72-73, 89-91, 103-104, 106, 115, 134, 136, 148, 171, 174-175, 181-183, 189-191, 200, 202, 205
Kissinger Henry Alfred 67
Klassen Jerome 80, 87-88, 167, 196, 200, 202, 212, 214
Kliff Sarah 69
Koring Paul 114, 130
Kraska James 129
Krauss Clifford 251, 254
Krugel Lauren 110, 254
Kurdi Alan 230, 233

Labott Elise 249
Lackenbauer P. Whitney 124-125, 127, 130, 135
Laurier Wilfrid 30-31, 57
Lavrov Sergey 157
Lawson Guy 273
Laxer Gordon 21, 39
Lee Steve 144-145
Legault Albert 26
Leitch Kellie 242
Lemphers Nathan 251
Lenard Patti Tamara 229-232
Lennox Patrick 61-63

Leuprecht Christian 199, 205
Levant Ezra 113
Levi Joshua 187
Levitz Stephanie 153-154, 187, 229
Ljunggren David 91
Lou Ethan 110
Loukacheva Natalia 125
Lower Arthur R.M. 21
Lukacs Martin 231
Lunn Janet 30-31
Lunn Susan 141-142
Lyle Greg 104
Lyon Peyton 36

MacCharles Tonda 100, 232-233
Macdonald Douglas 116-117
Macdonald Laura 101
Mace Gordon 46
MacKay Peter 137, 141
Mackay Derek 159, 161, 164
Mackay R.A. 45
Mackenzie Alexander 31, 139, 161, 164
MacKenzie Lewis 51
MacKinnon Leslie 89
MacKinnon Mark 77, 147, 157, 163, 186, 188
Mackrael Kim 172, 177, 180
Macnab Ron 126
Malcolm Andrew H. 21-22, 57
Mandela Nelson 47, 145
Manley John 53
Manning Preston 170
Mansbridge Peter 84
Marceau Richard J. 102-103
Markusoff Jason 260-261
Marowits Ross 265

Marsh James Harsh 35
Marshall Katherine 24
Martell Georg 21
Martin Paul Joseph James Sr. 49
Martin Paul Edgar Philippe Jr. 67, 79,
    82, 87, 93-94, 117-118, 125, 137-
    138, 143, 159, 161, 164, 171, 174-
    176, 179, 189-190, 194-195, 200-
    202, 215
Mas Susana 111, 141-142
Massie Justin 24-25
McCallum John 142, 238, 241
McCarthy Shawn 83-84, 119, 121,
    142, 252
McCoy John 42, 193
McInnis Edgar 44
McKenna Barrie 95-96, 162
McLaughlin Eliott C. 248
McMillan Tim 255
McNamara Robert Strange 199
McQuillan Megan 82, 175-176, 178,
    194, 197
Meissner Dirk 96
Milewski Terry 129
Minifie James M. 21
Mittany David 44
Moen Michael 97
Molot Maureen 8, 201
Momani Bessma 229
Moore Christopher 30-31
Mulcair Thomas 135, 212
Mulroney Brian 47, 107, 116, 145,
    186, 189, 213
Murphy Jessica 207
Murphy Rex 183
Murray Robert W. 42, 193, 204

Nafzinger Gloria 242
Navarro-Flores Olga 177
Naylor Sherry 209
Neack Laura 45
Nenshi Naheed 234
Nerenberg Karl 241
Nicholls Gerry 213
Nicholson Rob 157
Nicky Adam 100
Nicolaou Anna 237, 242
Nikiforuk Andrew 119, 147, 157, 164
Nossal Kim Richard 19, 21-22, 24-25,
    36, 41-43, 45-46, 114, 120, 122,
    140, 160, 192
Nye Joseph Samuel 9

Obama Barack 89, 94-97, 111, 113-
    115, 120, 123, 135, 155, 188, 248-
    249, 259
Oliver Joe 108, 113-114
Omar Mohamed 231
Onea Tudor 8

Page Kevin 197
Palit Amitendu 100
Paltiel Jeremy 101
Panetta Alexander 246, 259
Paris Roland 78, 83, 183, 196
Patriquin Martin 234
Payton Laura 86-87, 148-150, 160,
    167, 229
Pearson Lester Bowles 22, 44, 48-51,
    55, 67, 155, 169, 212, 222
Perry David 227
Petrolekas George 65-66, 71, 81, 107-
    109, 163
Plouffe Joël 134-135

Polachová Barbora 179
Potter Evan H. 56
Poy Vivienne 99
Pratt David 35, 41
Proudfoot Shannon 246, 253
Proussalidis Daniel 121
Pugliese David 222
Putin Vladimir 72, 149, 155-158

Quan Douglas 233

Randall Stephen James 25, 262
Rania Al-Abdullah, queen of Jordan 238
Rau Benegal Narsing 49
Reagan Ronald 47
Reczyńska Anna 17
Reguly Eric 247
Reid Escott 54
Rhéaume Charles 50
Riddell-Dixon Elizabeth 48-49, 52, 129-131
Riendeau Roger 30
Robertson Colin 86, 93, 114-115, 128, 162, 176-177, 179, 182, 186, 200
Robson John 216, 218, 269, 271
Rock Allan 146
Roosevelt Franklin Delano 25, 34-35
Ross Douglas A. 43
Roussel Stéphane 33, 199
Rudd Kevin 187
Rudderham Melissa A. 51
Rybkowski Radosław 17

Saint-Cyr Yosie 232
Saint-Jacques Guy 143
Sajjan Harjit 222, 225

Salley Azath 151
Sarson Leah 140, 192
Sartry Roger 27
Saunders Doug 162, 187
Savage Chwialkowska Luiza 98, 113
Schabas William Anthony 45, 51, 145
Schofield John 106
Schönwälder Gerd 83, 159, 186, 212-213
Schwarzman Stephen 261
Segal Hugh 50
Sevunts Levon 216
Sharma Arvind 150
Shephard Michelle 193
Shiab Naël 169
Shum David 266
Siddiqui Haroon 230
Siebert John 154
Simon Bernard 121
Simon Darran 314
Simon Mary 133
Simpson Jeffrey 54
Sinclair Scott 95
Skelton Oskar Douglas 32-33, 57
Slater Joanna 83, 114, 185-186
Smillie Ian 52-53
Smith Gordon S. 190-191, 193
Smith Goldwin 20-21, 57
Smith Heather A. 118, 131-132
Smith Jordan M. 213
Sokolsky Joel 26, 55, 194-195, 199, 205
Solomon Evan 151, 259, 261, 263
Sorensen Chris 109, 111-112
Spurrs Ben 232-233
St-Laurent Louis Stephen 40, 44, 48, 54, 57, 129, 212

Stacey Charles Percy 22, 34-35

Stairs Denis 46, 65, 144

Stanford Jim 111

Stastna Kazi 38, 85

Stavrianakis Anna 170

Stevenson Garth 36

Stewart Brian 84, 205

Stiem Tyler 243

Stone Craig 270

Stone Laura 143

Swett Katrina Lantos 153

Swift Anthony 88, 123, 196, 250

Taber Jane 103, 203

Talwani Manik 102

Tasker John Paul 249, 271

Taylor Adam 168

Taylor Ken 163

Taylor Sarah 46

Tharoor Ishaan 234

Thatcher Margaret 47

Thompson John Herd 25, 262

Thomson James 129

Tiagi Raaj 136

Tomlin Brian 36

Tran Mark 84

Trenqualye Madeleine de 255-256

Trent John E. 89, 91, 157-158, 161

Trew Stuart 95

Trudeau Justin 13, 15-16, 61, 66-67,
    69-70, 74, 77, 81, 84, 87, 96, 100-
    101, 109-110, 112, 115, 135, 143-
    144, 153, 165-166, 169-170, 176,
    193, 204, 207-208, 210-212, 215-
    216, 218-228, 233-236, 238-240,
    244-256, 258-265, 267-270, 272-
    273, 276, 279

Trudeau Pierre Elliott 27, 50, 148,
    189, 207, 245

Trump Donald 16, 97, 226-227, 234,
    243-244, 249, 256-257, 259-263,
    266-267, 273

Turner John 136, 143

Vance Jonathan 224

Vanderklippe Nathan 143

Vass Tiffany 256

Vital David 44

Vucetic Srdjan 167, 169

Waite Peter Busby 29

Waldie Paul 268

Wallace James C. 150

Walz Audrey 22

Walz Jay 22

Wang Yi 143

Way Laura 106, 111

Weber Bob 157

Weber Max 216-217

Webster Paul Christopher 168-169

Wells Paul 168-169

Welsh Jennifer 47, 183-184

Wen Jiabao 140

Westdal Christopher 157

Wherry Aaron 97, 186

Whyte Kenneth 72, 147, 160, 179,
    191, 196, 203

Wight Martin 40, 45

Wilfert Bryon 122

Wilkins David 126

Willson Roland 251

Wilt James 123, 254

Wiseman Richelle 150

Wood Bernard 45

Woodley Thomas 166
Woods Allan 211
Woolf Nicky 207
Woolley Frances 85
Wrong Hume 44

Xu Zhiyong 143

Yanukovych Viktor 155-156
York Geoffrey 142

Zaretskaya Victoria 109
Zerbisias Antonia 165
Zhou Lu 136
Zilio Michelle 131, 153
Zyla Benjamin 27, 55-56, 194

W serii *Societas* pod redakcją Bogdana Szlachty ukazały się:

1. Grzybek Dariusz, *Nauka czy ideologia. Biografia intelektualna Adama Krzyżanowskiego*, 2005.
2. Drzonek Maciej, *Między integracją a europeizacją. Kościół katolicki w Polsce wobec Unii Europejskiej w latach 1997-2003*, 2006.
3. Chmieliński Maciej, *Max Stirner. Jednostka, społeczeństwo, państwo*, 2006.
4. Nieć Mateusz, *Rozważania o pojęciu polityki w kręgu kultury attyckiej. Studium z historii polityki i myśli politycznej*, 2006.
5. Sokołów Florian, *Nahum Sokołów. Życie i legenda*, oprac. Andrzej A. Zięba, 2006.
6. Porębski Leszek, *Między przemocą a godnością. Teoria polityczna Harolda D. Laswella*, 2007.
7. Mazur Grzegorz, *Życie polityczne polskiego Lwowa 1918-1939*, 2007.
8. Węc Janusz Józef, *Spór o kształt instytucjonalny Wspólnot Europejskich i Unii Europejskiej 1950-2005. Między ideą ponadnarodowości a współpracą międzyrządową. Analiza politologiczna*, 2006.
9. Karas Marcin, *Integryzm Bractwa Kapłańskiego św. Piusa X. Historia i doktryna rzymskokatolickiego ruchu tradycjonalistycznego*, 2008.
10. *European Ideas on Tolerance*, red. Guido Naschert, Marcin Rebes, 2009.
11. Gacek Łukasz, *Chińskie elity polityczne w XX wieku*, 2009.
12. Zemanek Bogdan S., *Tajwańska tożsamość narodowa w publicystyce politycznej*, 2009.
13. Lenczarowicz Jan, *Jałta. W kręgu mitów założycielskich polskiej emigracji politycznej 1944-1956*, 2009.
14. Grabowski Andrzej, *Prawnicze pojęcie obowiązywania prawa stanowionego. Krytyka niepozytywistycznej koncepcji prawa*, 2009.
15. Kich-Masłej Olga, *Ukraina w opinii elit Krakowa końca XIX – pierwszej połowy XX wieku*, 2009.
16. Citkowska-Kimla Anna, *Romantyzm polityczny w Niemczech. Reprezentanci, idee, model*, 2010.
17. Mikuli Piotr, *Sądy a parlament w ustrojach Australii, Kanady i Nowej Zelandii (na tle rozwiązań brytyjskich)*, 2010.
18. Kubicki Paweł, *Miasto w sieci znaczeń. Kraków i jego tożsamości*, 2010.
19. Żurawski Jakub, *Internet jako współczesny środek elektronicznej komunikacji wyborczej i jego zastosowanie w polskich kampaniach parlamentarnych*, 2010.
20. *Polscy eurodeputowani 2004-2009. Uwarunkowania działania i ocena skuteczności*, red. Krzysztof Szczerski, 2010.
21. Bojko Krzysztof, *Stosunki dyplomatyczne Moskwy z Europą Zachodnią w czasach Iwana III*, 2010.
22. *Studia nad wielokulturowością*, red. Dorota Pietrzyk-Reeves, Małgorzata Kułakowska, Elżbieta Żak, 2010.
23. Bartnik Anna, *Emigracja latynoska w USA po II wojnie światowej na przykładzie Portorykańczyków, Meksykanów i Kubańczyków*, 2010.
24. *Transformacje w Ameryce Łacińskiej*, red. Adam Walaszek, Aleksandra Giera, 2011.
25. Praszałowicz Dorota, *Polacy w Berlinie. Strumienie migracyjne i społeczności imigrantów. Przegląd badań*, 2010.
26. Głogowski Aleksander, *Pakistan. Historia i współczesność*, 2011.
27. Brążkiewicz Bartłomiej, *Choroba psychiczna w literaturze i kulturze rosyjskiej*, 2011.

28. Bojenko-Izdebska Ewa, *Przemiany w Niemczech Wschodnich 1989-2010. Polityczne aspekty transformacji*, 2011.

29. Kołodziej Jacek, *Wartości polityczne. Rozpoznanie, rozumienie, komunikowanie*, 2011.

30. *Nacjonalizmy różnych narodów. Perspektywa politologiczno-religioznawcza*, red. Bogumił Grott, Olgierd Grott, 2012.

31. Matyasik Michał, *Realizacja wolności wypowiedzi na podstawie przepisów i praktyki w USA*, 2011.

32. Grzybek Dariusz, *Polityczne konsekwencje idei ekonomicznych w myśli polskiej 1869-1939*, 2012.

33. Woźnica Rafał, *Bułgarska polityka wewnętrzna a proces integracji z Unią Europejską*, 2012.

34. Ślufińska Monika, *Radykałowie francuscy. Koncepcje i działalność polityczna w XX wieku*, 2012.

35. Fyderek Łukasz, *Pretorianie i technokraci w reżimie politycznym Syrii*, 2012.

36. Węc Janusz Józef, *Traktat lizboński. Polityczne aspekty reformy ustrojowej Unii Europejskiej w latach 2007-2009*, 2011.

37. Rudnicka-Kassem Dorota, *John Paul II, Islam and the Middle East. The Pope's Spiritual Leadership in Developing a Dialogical Path for the New History of Christian-Muslim Relations*, 2012.

38. Bujwid-Kurek Ewa, *Serbia w nowej przestrzeni ustrojowej. Dzieje, ustrój, konstytucja*, 2012.

39. Cisek Janusz, *Granice Rzeczypospolitej i konflikt polsko-bolszewicki w świetle amerykańskich raportów dyplomatycznych i wojskowych*, 2012.

40. Gacek Łukasz, *Bezpieczeństwo energetyczne Chin. Aktywność państwowych przedsiębiorstw na rynkach zagranicznych*, 2012.

41. Węc Janusz Józef, *Spór o kształt ustrojowy Wspólnot Europejskich i Unii Europejskiej w latach 1950-2010. Między ideą ponadnarodowości a współpracą międzyrządową. Analiza politologiczna*, 2012.

42. *Międzycywilizacyjny dialog w świecie słowiańskim w XX i XXI wieku. Historia – religia – kultura – polityka*, red. Irena Stawowy-Kawka, 2012.

43. *Ciekawość świata, ludzi, kultury… Księga jubileuszowa ofiarowana Profesorowi Ryszardowi Kantorowi z okazji czterdziestolecia pracy naukowej*, red. Renata Hołda, Tadeusz Paleczny, 2012.

44. Węc Janusz Józef, *Pierwsza polska prezydencja w Unii Europejskiej. Uwarunkowania – procesy decyzyjne – osiągnięcia i niepowodzenia*, 2012.

45. Zemanek Adina, *Córki Chin i obywatelki świata. Obraz kobiety w chińskich czasopismach o modzie*, 2012.

46. Kamińska Ewa, *Rezeption japanischer Kultur in Deutschland. Zeitgenössische Keramik als Fallstudie*, 2012.

47. Obeidat Hayssam, *Stabilność układu naftowego w warunkach zagrożeń konfliktami w świetle kryzysu w latach siedemdziesiątych XX i na progu XXI wieku*, 2012.

48. Ścigaj Paweł, *Tożsamość narodowa. Zarys problematyki*, 2012.

49. Głogowski Aleksander, *Af-Pak. Znaczenie zachodniego pogranicza pakistańsko-afgańskiego dla bezpieczeństwa regionalnego w latach 1947-2011*, 2012.

50. Miżejewski Maciej, *Ochrona pluralizmu w polityce medialnej Włoch*, 2012.

51. Jakubiak Łukasz, *Referendum jako narzędzie polityki. Francuskie doświadczenia ustrojowe*, 2013.

52. *Skuteczność polskiej prezydencji w Unii Europejskiej. Założone cele i ich realizacja*, red. Krzysztof Szczerski, 2013.

53. *Stosunki państwo–Kościół w Polsce 1944-2010*, red. Rafał Łatka, 2013.

54. Gacek Łukasz, Trojnar Ewa, *Pokojowe negocjacje czy twarda gra? Rozwój stosunków ponad Cieśniną Tajwańską*, 2012.

55. Sondel-Cedarmas Joanna, *Nacjonalizm włoski. Geneza i ewolucja doktryny politycznej (1896-1923)*, 2013.

56. Rudnicka-Kassem Dorota, *From the Richness of Islamic History*, 2013.

57. Fudała Piotr, Fyderek Łukasz, Kurpiewska-Korbut Renata, *Budowanie parlamentaryzmu. Doświadczenia z Afganistanu, Iraku i Kurdystanu irackiego*, 2012.

58. Dardziński Piotr, *Kapitalizm nieobjawiony. Doktryna ładu społecznego, politycznego i ekonomicznego w myśli Wilhelma Röpkego*, 2013.

59. *The Taiwan Issues*, ed. Ewa Trojnar, 2012.

60. Rebes Marcin, *Martina Heideggera i Józefa Tischnera hermeneutyka odpowiedzialności w horyzoncie ontologii, agatologii i aksjologii*, 2013.

61. Kurpiewska-Korbut Renata, *Społeczność międzynarodowa wobec Kurdów irackich*, 2013.

62. Pietrzyk-Reeves Dorota, *Ład rzeczypospolitej. Polska myśl polityczna XVI wieku a klasyczna tradycja republikańska*, 2012.

63. Matykiewicz-Włodarska Aleksandra, *Marion Gräfin Dönhoff. Idee i refleksje polityczne*, 2012.

64. Reczyńska Anna, *Braterstwo a bagaż narodowy. Relacje w Kościele katolickim na ziemiach kanadyjskich do I wojny światowej*, 2013.

65. *Współczesne transformacje. Kultura, polityka, gospodarka*, red. Monika Banaś, Joanna Dziadowiec, 2013.

66. Grott Olgierd, *Instytut Badań Spraw Narodowościowych i Komisja Naukowych Badań Ziem Wschodnich w planowaniu polityki II Rzeczypospolitej Polskiej na Kresach Wschodnich*, 2013.

67. *Teoretyczne i praktyczne problemy kultury politycznej. Studia i szkice*, red. Monika Banaś, 2013.

68. *Podejścia badawcze i metodologie w nauce o polityce*, red. Barbara Krauz-Mozer, Paweł Ścigaj, 2013.

69. *Narratives of Ethnic Identity, Migration and Politics. A Multidisciplinary Perspective*, eds. Monika Banaś, Mariusz Dzięglewski, 2013.

70. *Promoting Changes in Times of Transition and Crisis: Reflections on Human Rights Education*, eds. Krzysztof Mazur, Piotr Musiewicz, Bogdan Szlachta, 2013.

71. Bar Joanna, *Po ludobójstwie. Państwo i społeczeństwo w Rwandzie 1994-2012*, 2013.

72. *Włochy wielokulturowe. Regionalizmy, mniejszości, migracje*, red. Karolina Golemo, 2013.

73. *Stany Zjednoczone wczoraj i dziś. Wybrane zagadnienia społeczno-polityczne*, red. Agnieszka Małek, Paulina Napierała, 2013.

74. Plichta Paweł, *Estera w kulturach. Rzecz o biblijnych toposach*, 2014.

75. Czekalska Renata, *Wartości autoteliczne w kulturze symbolicznej na przykładzie indyjsko-polskich spotkań literackich*, 2014.

76. Włodarski Bartosz, *Szkoła Nauk Politycznych UJ 1920-1949*, 2014.

77. *Arabska wiosna w Afryce Północnej. Przyczyny, przebieg, skutki*, red. Szczepankiewicz-Rudzka Ewa, 2014.

78. Bajor Piotr, *Partnerstwo czy członkostwo. Polityka euroatlantycka Ukrainy po 1991 r.*, 2014.

79. Gabryś Marcin, Kijewska-Trembecka Marta, Rybkowski Radosław, Soroka Tomasz, *Kanada na przełomie XX i XXI wieku. Polityka, społeczeństwo, edukacja*, red. Marta Kijewska-Trembecka, 2014.

80. Trojnar Ewa, *Tajwan. Dylematy rozwoju*, 2015.

81. Głogowski Aleksander, *Policja Państwowa i inne instytucje bezpieczeństwa na Wileńszczyźnie w latach 1918-1939*, 2015.

82. Krzyżanowska-Skowronek Iwona, *Teorie zmiany na przykładzie włoskiej polityki wschodniej*, 2015.

83. Rysiewicz Mikołaj, *Monarchia – lud – religia. Monarchizm konserwatywnych środowisk politycznych Wielkiej Emigracji w latach 1831-1848*, 2015.

84. Szymkowska-Bartyzel Jolanta, *Nasza Ameryka wyobrażona. Polskie spotkania z amerykańską kultura popularną po roku 1918*, 2015.

85. Napierała Paulina, *In God We Trust. Religia w sferze publicznej USA*, 2015.

86. Paluszkiewicz-Misiaczek Magdalena, *Szacunek i wsparcie. Kanadyjski system opieki nad weteranami*, 2015.

87. *Детерминанты и перспективы политики европейской интеграции Республики Молдова*, под научной редакцией Петра Байора, 2015.

88. *Eastern Chessboard. Geopolitical Determinants and Challenges in Eastern Europe and the South Caucasus*, ed. Piotr Bajor, Kamila Schöll-Mazurek, 2015.

89. Mazur Wojciech, *Pod wiatr. Francja i lotnictwo wojskowe II Rzeczypospolitej (1921-1938)*, 2015.

90. Węc Janusz Józef, *Traktat lizboński. Polityczne aspekty reformy ustrojowej Unii Europejskiej w latach 2007-2015*, 2016.

91. Fyderek Łukasz, *Autorytarne systemy polityczne świata arabskiego. Adaptacja i inercja w przededniu Arabskiej Wiosny*, 2015.

92. Kwieciński Rafał, *Zjednoczenie Chin? Proces reintegracji Wielkich Chin na przełomie XX i XXI w.*, 2016.

93. Grabowski Marcin, *Rywalizacja czy integracja? Procesy i organizacje integracyjne w regionie Azji i Pacyfiku na przełomie XX i XXI wieku*, 2015.

94. Laidler Paweł, Turek Maciej, *Cena demokracji. Finansowanie federalnych kampanii wyborczych w Stanach Zjednoczonych Ameryki*, 2016.

95. Bajor Piotr, *Contemporary Azerbaijan in Social and Political Dimension*, 2016.

96. Balwierz Ida, *Czasopismo „Apollo". Jego miejsce i rola w odrodzeniu poezji i kultury arabskiej*, 2016.

97. Bajor Piotr, *Kierunek Zachód. Polityka integracji europejskiej Ukrainy po 1991 r.*, 2016.

98. *Polska i Rumunia w Europie Środkowej w XX i XXI wieku. Studia, materiały i eseje poświęcone pamięci prof. dra hab. Wojciecha Rojka. Polonia şi România în Europa Centrală în secolele XX şi XXI. Studii, materiale şi eseuri dedicate in memoriam prof. univ. dr. Wojciech Rojek*, red. Agnieszka Kastory, Henryk Walczak, 2017.

99. Mazur Wojciech, *Lot ku burzy. Polska w przygotowaniach Zachodu do wojny powietrznej marzec-sierpień 1939 roku*, 2017.